Congressional Elections

CONGRESSIONAL ELECTIONS

Campaigning at Home and in Washington

Fourth Edition

Paul S. Herrnson
UNIVERSITY OF MARYLAND

CQ PRESS

A Division of Congressional Quarterly Inc.
Washington, D.C.

CQ Press
1255 22nd Street, N.W., Suite 400
Washington, D.C. 20037

202-729-1900; toll-free: 1-866-4CQ-PRESS (1-866-427-7737)

www.cqpress.com

Copyright © 2004 by CQ Press, a division of Congressional Quarterly Inc.

Printed and bound in the United States of America

07 06 05 04 03   5 4 3 2 1

⊚ The paper used in this publication exceeds the requirements of the
American National Standard for Information Sciences—Permanence of
Paper for Printed Library Materials, ANSI Z39.48-1992.

Cover design: Auburn Associates, Inc.

Cover photo credits: Clockwise from top center: U.S. Capitol—file photo;
Chris Van Hollen—Van Hollen for Congress; Connie Morella—Associated
Press; Mike Feeley—Associated Press; Bob Beauprez—Bob Beauprez for
Congress.

Library of Congress Cataloging-in-Publication Data

Herrnson, Paul S.
    Congressional elections : campaigning at home and in
  Washington / Paul S. Herrnson. — 4th ed.
        p.   cm.
    Includes bibliographical references and index.
    ISBN 1-56802-826-1 (pbk. : alk. paper)
    1. United States. Congress—Elections.   2. Political cam-
  paigns—United States.   3. Campaign funds—United States.
  4. Political action committees—United States.   I. Title.
  JK1976.H47 2004
  324.973′0931—dc22

2003017650

In Memory of
Harry Perlman

Contents

Tables and Figures

Preface

Each congressional election cycle unveils both continuities and changes in the way congressional campaigns are conducted. Writing this new edition of *Congressional Elections* gave me the opportunity not only to analyze in depth the 2002 House and Senate campaigns and election outcomes but also to assess the far-reaching changes that have taken place in recent years. Although just a few years have gone by since publication of the third edition, congressional elections and the context in which they are waged continue to evolve in ways that are both major and minor, predictable and surprising. It has been my challenge to show how these developments affect an enduring but imperfect election system.

The significance of independent, parallel, and coordinated campaigns as important new components of competitive House and Senate elections cannot be overstated. These party- and interest group–sponsored campaigns comprise massive, broad-based efforts in election agenda setting, television and radio issue advocacy advertisements, direct mail and mass telephone calls, and grass-roots mobilization, most of which are financed with soft money. The level of planning and resources dedicated to these campaigns is unsurpassed by previous election cycles.

Another set of changes involves the increasing complexity of interest group participation. In addition to political action committees (PACs), groups have created a veritable alphabet soup of legal entities for the purpose of carrying out a variety of political functions designed to influence elections. PACs, 501(c)(3) and 501(c)(4) organizations, and 527 committees—defined by different provisions of federal law—offer different organizational advantages such as the ability to contribute directly to congressional campaigns, to collect tax-deductible donations, to claim tax-exempt status, or to raise and spend soft money.

A final development I discuss in this edition involves the Bipartisan Campaign Reform Act of 2002, which was designed to close many of the loopholes commonly exploited in the campaign system. Its ban on soft money, restrictions on issue advocacy advertising, and increased contribution limits promise to have powerful effects on the ways in which campaigns are financed and waged. The law was under challenge in the Supreme Court at the time this edition went to press. Updates on the Court's ruling and the law will be available on the book's companion web site (http://herrnson.cqpress.com).

My focus on these developments characterizes this revision, but the fourth edition of *Congressional Elections* remains a comprehensive text about congressional elections and their implications for Congress and, more generally, for American government. Most congressional elections are contests between candidates who have vastly unequal chances of victory. Incumbents generally win not only because of their own efforts but also because of the catch-22 situation in which many challengers find themselves. Without name recognition, challengers and candidates for open seats have trouble raising funds, and without funds they cannot enhance their name recognition or attract enough support to run a competitive race. This conundrum hints at a fundamental truth of congressional elections: candidates wage two campaigns—one for votes and one for money and other resources. The former takes place in the candidate's district or state. The latter is conducted primarily in the Washington, D.C., area—where many political consultants, PACs, other interest groups, and the parties' national, senatorial, and congressional campaign committees are located. The timing of the two campaigns overlaps considerably, but candidates and their organizations must conceptualize the campaigns as separate and plot a different strategy for each.

Although congressional election campaigns are the main focus of this book, voters, candidates, governance, and campaign reform receive considerable attention. I have gathered information from candidates, campaign aides, political consultants, party strategists, PAC managers, journalists, and other political insiders to describe their goals, strategies, decision-making processes, and roles in congressional campaigns. I also have assessed the influence that the efforts of these individuals and groups have on election outcomes.

I conclude that the norms and expectations associated with congressional campaigns affect who runs, the kinds of organizations the candidates assemble, how much money they raise, the kinds of party and interest group support they attract, the strategies and communications techniques they use, and ultimately whether they win or lose. Incumbents are the major beneficiaries of the congressional election system, but the system constrains their reelection campaigns, as it does the efforts of challengers and candidates for open seats.

Moreover, the need to campaign for votes and resources affects how members of Congress carry out their legislative responsibilities and the kinds of reforms they are willing to consider. These observations may seem intuitive, but they are rarely discussed in studies of voting behavior and are usually overlooked in research that focuses on the role of money in politics. Given their importance, it is unfortunate that congressional campaigns have not received more attention in the scholarly literature.

Throughout the book, I systematically analyze empirical evidence collected from candidates, consultants, parties, and interest groups that have participated in congressional elections since the early 1990s. The analysis in this edition is based primarily on interviews with and questionnaires from nearly four hundred House and Senate candidates and other political insiders who participated in the 2002 elections. It also relies on campaign finance data furnished by the Federal Election Commission, the Center for Responsive Politics, Political Money Line, and Public Citizen as well as on public opinion data collected in the American National Election Study. Memoranda and interviews provided by campaign organizations, party committees, PACs, and other interest groups further contribute to the study. Generalizations derived from the analysis are supported with concrete—and what I hope are lively—examples from case studies of individual campaigns. The analysis also draws insights from my own participation in congressional campaigns and from the questionnaires and interviews provided by the more than eight hundred candidates and campaign aides who have contributed information and data for past editions. I hope the evidence presented convinces readers that the campaigns candidates wage at home for votes, and in Washington for money and campaign assistance, significantly affect the outcomes of congressional elections. My analysis of these sources also leads to the conclusion that the activities of party committees, interest groups, campaign volunteers, and journalists also are important.

This book gives students of politics a powerful tool to help them think about campaigns, elections, and their own political involvement. Professors using the book as a classroom text might be interested in reviewing the questionnaires I used to collect information from congressional campaigns. Students in my seminars found them valuable in guiding their field research on campaigns. The questionnaires, my syllabus, class assignments and other course materials, links to Internet resources, and methodological background information are all available on the companion web site.

The publication of *Congressional Elections* would not have been possible without the cooperation of many individuals and institutions. I am indebted to the hundreds of people who consented to be interviewed, completed questionnaires, or shared election targeting lists and other campaign materials with me. Their participation in this project was essential to its success.

The Center for American Politics and Citizenship at the University of Maryland provided a stimulating and productive environment in which to work. Virtually every member of the center participated in some aspect of the project. The data collection, data entry, statistical analysis, case study research, and writing proceeded smoothly because of the efforts of Owen Abbe, Nathan Bigelow, John Blessing, David Clifford, Timothy Daly, Peter Francia, Philip Krauss, Jennifer Lucas, Randy Roberson, Atiya Stokes, Nidhi Thakar, and Samantha Yellin. Chris Bailey, William Bianco, Robert Biersack, James Gimpel, John Green, Thomas Kazee, Sandy Maisel, Kelly Patterson, Stephen Salmore, Frank Sorauf, James Thurber, Ric Uslaner, and Clyde Wilcox made helpful comments on earlier editions of the book. Anthony Corrado, John Geer, and Jeff Gulati, as well as two anonymous reviewers, made valuable suggestions for this edition. CQ Press's Michael Kerns, Charisse Kiino, and Gwenda Larsen played vital roles in preparing the manuscript, as did copy editor Amy Marks. I am delighted to have the opportunity to express my deepest appreciation to all of them.

Finally, a few words are in order about the person to whom this book is dedicated. My uncle, Harry Perlman, did not live to see the completion of this book, but his contributions to it were critical. The construction jobs he gave me were the most important form of financial aid I received while pursuing my college education. His ideas about politics and philosophy helped me to appreciate the virtues of democratically held elections and to recognize the inferiority of other means of conferring political power. His unwavering belief that people can be taught to value what is good about their political system and to recognize its shortcomings was a source of inspiration that helped me complete the first edition of this book, and it continues to inspire me today.

Congressional Elections

Introduction

Elections are the centerpiece of democracy. They are the means Americans use to choose their political leaders, and they give those who have been elected the authority to rule. Elections also furnish the American people with a vehicle for expressing their views about the directions they think this rule ought to take. In theory, elections are the principal mechanism for ensuring "government of the people, by the people, for the people." [1]

An examination of the different aspects of the electoral process provides insights into the operations of our political system. Separate balloting for congressional, state, and local candidates results in legislators who represent parochial interests, sometimes to the detriment of the formation of national policy. Private financing of congressional campaigns, which is consistent with Americans' belief in capitalism, favors incumbents and increases the political access of wealthy and well-organized segments of society. Participatory primaries and caucuses, which require congressional aspirants to assemble an organization in order to campaign for the nomination, lead candidates to rely on political consultants rather than on party committees for assistance in winning their party's nomination and the general election. These factors encourage congressional candidates and members of Congress to act more independently of party leaders than do their counterparts in other democracies.

Congressional elections are affected by perceptions of the performance of government. Americans' satisfaction with the state of the economy, the nation's foreign policy and security, as well as their own standard of living provides a backdrop for elections and a means for assessing whether presidents, individual representatives, and Congress as an institution have performed their jobs adequately. Issues related to the internal operations of Congress—such as the perquisites enjoyed by members—can affect congressional elections.

Conversely, congressional elections can greatly affect the internal operations of Congress, the performance of government, and the direction of domestic and foreign policy. Major political reforms and policy reversals generally follow elections in which substantial congressional turnover has occurred.

One of the major themes developed in this book is that campaigns matter a great deal to the outcome of congressional elections. National conditions are significant, but their impact on elections is secondary to the decisions and actions of candidates, campaign organizations, party committees, organized interests, and other individuals and groups. This comes as no surprise to those who toil in campaigns, but it is in direct contrast to what many scholars would argue.

In order to win a congressional election or even to be remotely competitive, candidates must compete in two campaigns: one for votes and one for resources. The campaign for votes is the campaign that generally comes to mind when people think about congressional elections. It requires a candidate to assemble an organization and to use that organization to target key groups of voters, select a message they will find compelling, communicate that message, and get supporters to the polls on election day.

The other campaign, which is based largely in Washington, D.C., requires candidates to convince the party operatives, interest group officials, political consultants, and journalists who play leading roles in the nation's political community that their races will be competitive and worthy of support. Gaining the backing of these various individuals is a critical step in attracting the money and campaign services that are available in the nation's capital and in other wealthy urban centers. These resources enable the candidate to run a credible campaign back home. Without them, most congressional candidates would lose their bids for election.

In this book I present a systematic assessment of congressional election campaigns that draws on information from a wide variety of sources. Background information on the more than 16,000 major-party contestants who ran between 1978 and 2002 furnished insights into the types of individuals who try to win a seat in Congress and the conditions under which they run. Personal interviews and survey data provided by almost 8,800 candidates and campaign aides who were involved in the House or Senate elections held between 1992 and 2002 permitted analysis of the organization, strategies, tactics, issues, and communications techniques used in congressional campaigns. They also provided insights into the roles that political parties, political action committees (PACs), and other groups play in those contests.

Case studies of campaigns conducted in the 2002 elections illustrate with concrete examples the generalizations drawn from the larger sample. These include some typical elections, such as Republican representative Douglas Ose's twenty-seven-point victory over Howard Beeman in California's 3rd congressional district. They also include a few unusual contests, such as that in which Democratic challenger Christopher Van Hollen survived a hotly contested primary and went on to defeat GOP eight-term representative Connie Morella of Maryland; Republican Robert Beauprez's 121-vote win over Democrat Michael Feeley in an open-seat race in Colorado's 7th congressional district; and the Senate contest in South Dakota in which Democratic incumbent Tim Johnson defeated Republican challenger representative John Thune. The latter three contests are noteworthy not only because of their competitiveness but also because both political parties and many interest groups invested huge sums of money in so-called issue advocacy ads and grassroots organizing. All three races highlight the importance of money and assembling a professional campaign organization in congressional elections.

Some races are included because they illustrate the role of scandal or negative campaigning in campaigns. Six-term incumbent Gary Condit, D-Calif., lost his 18th congressional district primary to challenger Dennis Cardoza in 2002 as a result of the scandal surrounding his involvement with intern Chandra Levy, who fell victim to foul play in Washington, D.C.'s Rock Creek Park. New York's 1st district race is included because first-term Republican representative Felix Grucci Jr. lost to Democrat Timothy Bishop largely as a result of self-inflicted wounds that resulted when the incumbent made some outrageous attacks on the challenger.

Most of the discussion focuses on House candidates and campaigns because they are easier to generalize about than Senate contests. Differences in the sizes, populations, and political traditions of the fifty states and the fact that only about one-third of all Senate seats are filled in a given election year make campaigns for the upper chamber more difficult to discuss in general terms. Larger, more diverse Senate constituencies also make Senate elections less predictable than House contests. Nevertheless, insights can be gained into campaigns for the upper chamber by contrasting them with those waged for the House.

Interviews with party officials, conducted over the course of the 1992 through 2002 elections, give insights into the strategies used by the Democratic and Republican national, congressional, and senatorial campaign committees. Similar information provided by a representative group of interest group leaders is used to learn about PAC contribution, endorsement, issue advocacy, and grassroots mobilization strategies. Campaign contribution and spending data furnished by the Federal Election Commission, the Center for Responsive Politics, and Political Money Line are used to examine the role of money in politics. Web sites, newspapers, press releases, and advertising materials distributed by candidates, parties, and interest groups furnish examples of the communications that campaigns disseminate. Public opinion surveys provide insights into voters' priorities and the roles of issues. Collectively these sources of information, along with scholarly accounts published in the political science literature and insights drawn from my own participation in congressional and campaign politics, have permitted a comprehensive portrayal of contemporary congressional election campaigns.

In the first five chapters I examine the strategic context in which congressional election campaigns are waged and the major actors that participate in those contests. Chapter 1 provides an overview of the institutions, laws, party rules, and customs that constitute the framework for congressional elections. The framework has a significant impact on who decides to run for Congress; the kinds of resources that candidates, parties, and interest groups bring to bear on the campaign; the strategies they use; and who ultimately wins a seat in Congress. It also focuses on the setting for the congressional elections held since the early 1990s, with special emphasis on 2002.

Chapter 2 contains a discussion of candidates and nominations. I examine the influence of incumbency, redistricting, national conditions, and the personal and career situations of potential candidates on the decision to run for Congress. I also assess the separate contributions that the decision to run, the nomination process, and the general election make toward producing a Congress that is overwhelmingly white, male, middle-aged, and drawn from the legal, business, and public service professions.

The organizations that congressional candidates assemble to wage their election campaigns are the subject of Chapter 3. Salaried staff and political consultants form the core of most competitive candidates' campaign teams. These professionals play a critical role in formulating strategy, gauging public opinion, fundraising, designing communications, and mobilizing voters.

Political parties and interest groups—the major organizations that help finance elections and provide candidates with important campaign resources—are the subjects of the next two chapters. Chapter 4 includes an analysis of the goals, decision-making processes, and election activities of party committees. I discuss many recent innovations, including party "independent," "parallel," and "coordinated" campaigns comprising so-called issue advocacy advertisements and voter mobilization efforts. In Chapter 5 I concentrate on the goals, strategies, and election efforts of PACs and other interest group organizations. Among the innovations covered are business- and union-sponsored issue advocacy ads and the political activity of groups that enjoy tax-exempt status.

In Chapter 6 I examine the fundraising process from the candidate's point of view. The campaign for resources requires a candidate to formulate strategies for raising money from individuals and groups in the candidate's own state, in Washington, D.C., and in the nation's other major political and economic centers. It is clear from Chapters 4, 5, and 6 that Washington-based elites have a disproportionate effect on the conduct of congressional elections.

In Chapters 7 through 9 I concentrate on the campaign for votes. A discussion of voters, campaign targeting, issues, and other elements of strategy makes up Chapter 7. Campaign communications, including television, radio, the Internet, direct mail, and field work, are the focus of Chapter 8. The subject of winners and losers is taken up in Chapter 9, in which I analyze what does and does not work in congressional campaigns.

In Chapter 10 I address the effects of elections on the activities of individual legislators and on Congress as an institution, including the collective impact that individual elections have on the policy-making process and substantive policy outcomes. Finally, Chapter 11 takes up the highly charged topic of campaign reform. In it, I recommend specific reforms and discuss the obstacles that had to be overcome in order to pass the Bipartisan Campaign Reform Act of 2002 (BCRA; also referred to as the McCain-Feingold Act, after its Senate sponsors), and the courtroom and other challenges that may undermine its implementation. Should the BCRA survive these challenges, it will force political parties and interest groups to modify their activities in congressional elections, including altering their spending in those contests.[2]

CHAPTER ONE

The Strategic Context

Congressional elections, and elections in the United States in general, are centered more on the candidates than are elections in other modern industrialized democracies. In this chapter I discuss the candidate-centered U.S. election system and explain how the Constitution, election laws, and the political parties form the system's institutional framework. I also explain how the nation's political culture and recent developments in technology have helped this system flourish.

Also covered is the influence of the political setting in a given election year on electoral competition and turnover in Congress. The political setting includes some predictable factors such as the decennial redrawing of House districts; some highly likely occurrences such as the wide-scale reelection of incumbents; and transient, less predictable phenomena such as congressional scandals and acts of terrorism. These features of the political setting affect the expectations and behavior of potential congressional candidates, the individuals who actually run for Congress, political contributors, and voters.

THE CANDIDATE-CENTERED CAMPAIGN

Candidates, not political parties, are the major focus of congressional campaigns, and candidates, not parties, bear the ultimate responsibility for election outcomes. These characteristics of congressional elections are striking when viewed from a comparative perspective. In most democracies, political parties are the principal contestants in elections, and campaigns focus on national issues, ideology, and party programs and accomplishments. In the United States, parties do not run congressional campaigns nor do they become the major focus of elections. Instead, candidates run their own campaigns, and parties contribute money or election services to some of them. Parties also may advertise or mobilize voters on behalf of candidates. A comparison of the terminology commonly used to describe elections in the United States with that used in Great Britain more than hints at the differences. In the United States, candidates are said to *run* for Congress, and they do so with or without party help. In Britain, by contrast, candidates are said to *stand* for election to Parliament, and their party runs most of the campaign. The difference in terminology only slightly oversimplifies reality.

Unlike candidates for national legislatures in most other democracies, U.S. congressional candidates are self-selected rather than recruited by party organizations.[1] They must win the right to run under their party's label through a participatory primary, caucus, or convention, or by scaring off all opposition. Only after they have secured their party's nomination are major-party candidates assured a place on the general election ballot. Until then, few candidates receive significant party assistance. Independent and minor-party candidates can get on the ballot in other ways, usually by paying a registration fee or collecting several thousand signatures from district residents.

The nomination process in most other countries, alternatively, begins with a small group of party activists pursuing the nomination through a "closed" process that allows only formal, dues-paying party members to select the candidate.[2] Whereas the American system amplifies the input of primary voters, and in a few states caucus participants, these other systems respond more to the input of local party members and place more emphasis on peer review.

The need to win a party nomination forces congressional candidates to assemble their own campaign organizations, formulate their own election strategies, and conduct their own campaigns. The images and issues they convey to voters in trying to win the nomination carry over to the general election. The efforts of individual candidates and their campaign organizations typically have a larger impact on election outcomes than do the activities of party organizations and other groups.

The candidate-centered nature of congressional elections has evolved in recent years as parties and interest groups have developed so-called issue advocacy advertisements and worked to mobilize voters in competitive races. However, the basic structure of the system remains intact. That structure has a major impact on virtually every aspect of campaigning, including who decides to run, the kinds of election strategies the candidates employ, and the resources available to them. It affects the decisions and activities of party organizations, political action committees (PACs), other interest groups, and journalists. It also has a major influence on how citizens make their voting decisions and on the activities that successful candidates carry out once they are elected to Congress. Finally, the candidate-centered nature of the congressional election system affects the election reforms that those in power are willing to consider.

THE INSTITUTIONAL FRAMEWORK

In designing a government to prevent the majority from depriving the minority of its rights, the framers of the Constitution created a system of checks and balances to prevent any one official or element of society from amassing too much power. Three key features of the framers' blueprint have profoundly influenced congressional elections: the separation of powers, bicameralism, and federalism. These aspects of the Constitution require that candidates for the House of Representatives, Senate, and presidency be chosen by different methods and constituencies. House members were and continue to be elected directly by the people. Senators were originally chosen by their state legislatures but have been selected in statewide elections since the passage of the Seventeenth Amendment in 1913. Presidents have always been selected through the electoral college. The means for filling state and local offices were omitted from the Constitution, but candidates for these positions were and continue to be elected independently of members of Congress.

Holding elections for individual offices separates the political fortunes of members of Congress from one another and from other officials. A candidate for the House can win during an election year in which his or her party suffers a landslide defeat in the race for the presidency; experiences severe losses in the House or Senate; or finds itself surrendering its hold over neighboring congressional districts, the state legislature, the governor's mansion, and various local offices. The system encourages House, Senate, state, and local candidates to communicate issues and themes that they perceive to be popular in their districts even when these messages differ from those advocated by their party's leader. The system does little to encourage teamwork in campaigning or governance. In 2002 most GOP candidates distanced themselves from President George W. Bush's proposal to privatize part of the Social Security system. Such an act would be labeled party disloyalty and considered unacceptable under a parliamentary system of government with its party-focused elections, but it is entirely consistent with the expectations of the Constitution's framers. As James Madison wrote in *Federalist* no. 46,

> A local spirit will infallibly prevail. . .in the members of Congress. . . .
> Measures will too often be decided according to their probable effect, not on

the national prosperity and happiness, but on the prejudices, interests, and pursuits of the governments and people of the individual States.

When congressional candidates differ from their party's presidential nominee or national platform on major issues, they seek political cover not only from the Constitution but also from state party platforms, local election manifestos, or fellow party members who have taken similar positions.

Of course, congressional candidates usually adopt issue positions held by other party candidates for the House, Senate, or presidency. In 1932 most Democrats embraced Franklin D. Roosevelt's call for an activist government to battle the Great Depression. In 2002 many Republican candidates followed the advice of White House senior advisor Karl Rove and made the war on terrorism and national security key components of their campaigns. Democratic candidates, many of whom had hoped to focus on the nation's ailing economy, were encouraged by their party's leadership to support the war on terrorism following the attacks of September 11. Democratic leaders also recommended that they discuss both national security and economic security and blame the president's domestic policies for the nation's economic doldrums.

Federal and state laws further contribute to the candidate-centered nature of congressional elections. Originally, federal law regulated few aspects of congressional elections, designating only the number of representatives a state was entitled to elect. States held congressional elections at different times, used different methods of election, and set different qualifications for voters. Some states used multimember at-large districts, a practice that awarded each party a share of congressional seats proportional to its share of the statewide popular vote; others elected their House members in odd years, which minimized the ability of presidential candidates to pull House candidates of their own party into office on their coattails. The financing of congressional campaigns also went virtually unregulated for most of the nation's history.

Over the years, Congress and the states passed legislation governing the election of House members that further reinforced the candidate-centered nature of congressional elections at the expense of parties. The creation of geographically defined, single-member, winner-take-all congressional districts was particularly important in this regard. These districts, which were mandated by the Apportionment Act of 1842, encouraged individual candidates to build locally based coalitions. Such districts gave no rewards to candidates who came in second, even if their party performed well throughout the state or in neighboring districts.[3] Thus, candidates of the same party had little incentive to work together or to run a party-focused campaign. Under the multimember district or general ticket systems that existed in some states prior to the act—and that continue to be used in most European nations, members of parties that finish lower than first place may receive seats in the legislature. Candidates have strong incentives to run cooperative, party-focused campaigns under these systems because their electoral fortunes are bound together.

The timing of congressional elections also helps to produce a candidate-centered system. Because the dates are fixed, with House elections scheduled biennially and roughly one-third of the Senate up for election every two years, many elections are held when there is no burning issue on the national agenda. Without a salient national issue to capture the voters' attention, House and Senate candidates base their campaigns on local issues or on their personal qualifications for holding office. Incumbents stress their experience, the services they provide to constituents, or seniority. Challengers, on the other hand, attack their opponents for casting congressional roll-call votes that are out of sync with the views of local voters, for pandering to special interests, or for "being part of the problem in Washington." Open-seat races focus mainly on local issues, the candidates' political experience, or character issues.

In contrast, systems that do not have fixed election dates, including most of those in western Europe, tend to hold elections that are more national in focus and centered on political parties. The rules regulating national elections in those systems require that elections be held within a set time frame, but the exact date is left open. Elections may be called by the party in power at a time of relative prosperity, when it is confident that it can maintain or enlarge its parliamentary majority. Elections also may be called when a burning issue divides the nation and the party in power is forced to call a snap election because its members in parliament are unable to agree on a policy for dealing with the crisis. In contrast to congressional elections, which are often referenda on the performance of individual officeholders and their abilities to meet local concerns, these elections focus on national conditions and the performance of the party in power.

Because the boundaries of congressional districts rarely match those for statewide or local offices and because terms for the House, the Senate, and many state and local offices differ from one another, a party's candidates often lack incentives to work together. House candidates consider the performance of their party's candidates statewide or in neighboring districts to be a secondary concern, just as the election of House candidates is usually not of primary importance to candidates for state or local office. Differences in election boundaries and timing also encourage a sense of parochialism in party officials similar to that of their candidates. Cooperation among party organizations can be achieved only by persuading local, state, and national party leaders that it is in their mutual best interest. Cooperation is often heightened during elections that precede or follow the decennial taking of the census, when politicians at all levels of government focus on the imminent redrawing of election districts or on preserving or wresting control of new districts or those that have been significantly altered.

Although the seeds for candidate-centered congressional election campaigns were sown by the Constitution and election laws, not until the middle of the twentieth century did the candidate-centered system firmly take root. Prior to the emergence of this system, during a period often called the "golden age" of political parties, party organizations played a major role in most election campaigns, including many campaigns for Congress. Local party organizations, often referred to as old-fashioned political machines, had control over the nomination process, possessed a near monopoly over the resources needed to organize the electorate, and provided the symbolic cues that informed the electoral decisions of most voters.[4] The key to their success was their ability to command the loyalties of large numbers of individuals, many of whom were able to persuade friends and neighbors to support their party's candidates. Not until the demise of the old-fashioned machine and the emergence of new campaign technology did the modern candidate-centered system finally blossom.

Reforms intended to weaken political machines played a major role in the development of the candidate-centered system. One such reform was the adoption of the Australian ballot by roughly three-quarters of the states between 1888 and 1896.[5] This government-printed ballot listed every candidate for each office and allowed individuals to cast their votes in secret, away from the prying eyes of party officials. The Australian ballot replaced a system of voting in which each party supplied supporters with its own easily identifiable ballot that included only the names of the party's candidates. The Australian ballot, by ensuring secrecy and simplifying split-ticket voting, made it easy for citizens to focus on candidates rather than parties when voting. This type of ballot remains in use today.

State-regulated primary nominating contests, which were widely adopted during the Progressive movement of the early 1900s, deprived party leaders of the power to handpick congressional nominees and gave that power to voters who participated in their party's nominating election.[6] The merit-based civil service system, another progressive reform, deprived the parties of patronage. No longer able to distribute government jobs or contracts, the parties had difficulty maintaining large corps of campaign workers.[7] Issues, friendships, the excitement of politics, and other noneconomic incentives could motivate small numbers of people to become active in party politics, but they could not motivate enough people to support a party-focused system of congressional elections.

Congressional candidates also lacked the patronage or government contracts needed to attract large numbers of volunteer workers or to persuade other candidates to help them with their campaigns. By the mid-twentieth century the "isolation" of congressional candidates from one another and from their own party organizations was so complete that a major report on the state of political parties characterized congressional candidates as the "orphans of the political system." The report, published by the American Political Science Association's Committee on Political Parties, went on to point out that congressional candidates "had no truly adequate party mechanism available for the conduct of their campaigns,. . .enjoy[ed] remarkably little national or local support, [and] have mostly been left to cope with the political hazards of their occupation on their own." [8]

Voter registration and get-out-the-vote drives and redistricting were about the only areas of election politics in which there was, and remains, extensive cooperation among groups of candidates and party committees. But even here the integration of different party committees and candidate organizations—and especially those involved in congressional elections—was and continues to be short of that exhibited in other democracies.

The Federal Election Campaign Act of 1974 and the amendments, regulatory rulings, and court decisions that have shaped federal campaign finance law (collectively known as the FECA) further reinforced the pattern of candidate-centered congressional elections.[9] The original 1974 law placed strict limits on the amount of money parties could contribute to or spend in coordination with their congressional candidates' campaigns. Many of these limits remained in place in 2002 (see Table 1-1). The FECA further limited the parties' involvement in congressional elections by placing ceilings on individual contributions and an outright ban on corporate, union, and trade association contributions to the accounts the parties use to contribute to or expressly advocate the election or defeat of federal candidates (see Table 1-2). Moreover, the FECA provided no subsidies for generic, party-focused campaign activity.[10]

The law's provisions for political parties stand in marked contrast to the treatment given to parties in other democracies. Most of these countries provide subsidies to parties for campaign and interelection activities.[11] The United States is the only democracy in which parties are not given free television and radio time.[12] The support that other democracies give to parties is consistent with the central role they play in elections, government, and society, just as the lack of assistance afforded to American parties is consistent with the candidate-centered system that has developed in the United States.

Lacking independent sources of revenue, local party organizations are unable to play a dominant role in the modern cash-based system of congressional campaign politics.[13] The national and state party committees that survived the reform movements and changes in federal election laws lack sufficient funds or staff to dominate campaign politics. Perhaps even more important, party leaders have little desire to do so in most cases. For the most part, they believe a party should bolster its candidates' campaigns, not replace them with a campaign of its own.[14]

Nevertheless, the evolution of campaign finance law has enabled parties to play a greater role in recent congressional elections. The 1979 amendment to the FECA exempted from federal contribution and spending limits voter registration drives, get-out-the vote efforts, and other grassroots activities sponsored by state and local party committees. It also allowed these organizations to distribute slate cards and other materials that list federal candidates without reporting these activities to the Federal Election Commission (FEC). The amendment, combined with various FEC rulings and court decisions, created a legal loophole that permits campaign spending that is technically outside of the federal campaign finance system but is used to influence the outcome of federal elections. The funds that flow through this loophole, commonly referred to as "nonfederal," "soft," or "outside" money (as opposed to the "federal," or "hard," money spent inside the system), include contributions to parties that come from sources and in amounts banned under the federal system. Some soft money contributions are collected from corporations, unions, and wealthy individuals in amounts in excess of $1 million.[15]

Most soft money is raised and spent by political parties, but other groups, some of which are closely affiliated with party committees, also collect and distribute money outside the federal system in order to influence federal elections. National party soft money expenditures surpassed $509.6 million during the 2002 contests, setting a new record for either a midterm or presidential election year.[16] The outside spending of interest groups cannot be accounted for fully because it does not have to be reported to the FEC; however, it is estimated that groups spent in excess of $20 million on television alone in the 2002 elections.[17] Groups spent millions of additional dollars on voter identification, direct mail, mass telephone calls, and other communications and voter mobilization activities.

Another change in the campaign finance system that has increased the role of interest groups and party-affiliated organizations in elections concerns the use of funds collected by tax-exempt organizations for political use. These groups, classified as 501(c)(3), 501(c)(4), and 527 committees in the federal tax code, do not pay taxes because they purportedly exist for charitable, educational, or other civic purposes rather than to earn profits. In recent years, however, some tax-exempt groups have carried out activities financed with soft money to influence congressional and other elections. Among these groups are the Club for Growth, an anti-tax group that supports Republican candidates who favor free-market

TABLE 1-1

Campaign Contribution and Spending Limits in the 2002 Congressional Elections under the FECA

| | Hard money | | | | Independent expenditures | Soft money |
| | Contributions | | Coordinated expenditures | | | Issue advocacy and other expenditures |
	To a House candidate	To a Senate candidate	On behalf of a House candidate	On behalf of a Senate candidate	To expressly help or harm a candidate	To help or harm a candidate without expressly advocating the candidate's defeat
Individuals	$1,000	$1,000	Prohibited	Prohibited	No limit	No limit
Political action committees (PACs)	$5,000	$5,000	Prohibited	Prohibited	No limit	No limit
Corporations, unions, trade associations, and other groups	Prohibited	Prohibited	Prohibited	Prohibited	Prohibited except by qualified non-profit organizations	No limit
Party congressional campaign committees	$5,000	Can make a portion of another party committee's coordinated expenditures	$10,000 (adjusted for inflation)	Can make a portion of another party committee's coordinated expenditures	No limit	Must be allocated in proportion to hard money expenditures in a given state

Party senatorial campaign committees	$5,000	$17,500	Can make a portion of another party committee's coordinated expenditures	2¢ per voter for Senate candidates (adjusted for inflation)	No limit	Must be allocated in proportion to hard money expenditures in a given state
Party national committees	$5,000	Can make a portion of another party committee's contributions	Can make a portion of another party committee's coordinated expenditures		No limit	Must be allocated in proportion to hard money expenditures in a given state
State and local party committees	$5,000	$10,000 (adjusted for inflation)		2¢ per voter for Senate candidates (adjusted for inflation)	No limit	Must be allocated in proportion to hard money expenditures in a given state

Notes: Individuals and PACs can make the maximum contribution in each stage of the election (primary, runoff, and general election). The same is true of party committees' contributions in House races, but the committees rarely contribute to primary or runoff candidates. The senatorial campaign committees can contribute a total of $17,500 per Senate candidate in all three stages of the election. PACs must have been registered for at least six months, received contributions from more than fifty contributors, and made contributions to at least five federal candidates. Otherwise, they are subject to the same limits as those imposed on individual contributors. Corporations, labor unions, and federal government contractors are prohibited from making independent expenditures, but qualified nonprofit social welfare organizations that do not engage in business activities and have no shareholders other than employees or creditors can make independent expenditures. The limits for coordinated expenditures made on behalf of House candidates in states with only one House seat are twice the normal amount. A party committee can make agency agreements allowing other party organizations to make some or all of its coordinated expenditures. National party soft money expenditures cannot exceed 35 percent of the total party expenditures in presidential election years and 40 percent of the total party expenditures in midterm election years. The limits for state and local party soft money expenditures vary according to the composition of a state's ballot. The Bipartisan Campaign Reform Act of 2002, now under judicial review, has changed some aspects of the law. See this book's accompanying web site (http://herrnson.cqpress.com) for details on how court rulings have altered contribution and spending rules.

TABLE 1-2
Annual Federal Contribution Limits for Individuals, Party Committees, PACs, and Other Interest Groups in 2002 under the FECA

	Hard money contributions				Soft money contributions			
	To national party committees	To state party committees	To political action committees	Total annual contributions	To a House or Senate candidate	To national party committees	To state party committees	Total annual contributions
Individuals	$20,000	$5,000	$5,000	$25,000	Prohibited	No limit	Subject to state law	No limit
Political action committees	$15,000	$5,000	$5,000	No limit	Prohibited	No limit	Subject to state law	No limit
Corporations, unions, trade associations, and other groups	Prohibited	Prohibited	Prohibited	Prohibited	Prohibited	No limit	Subject to state law	No limit
Party congressional campaign committees	No limit	No limit	$5,000	No limit	Prohibited	No limit	Subject to state law	No limit
Party senatorial campaign committees	No limit	No limit	$5,000	No limit	Prohibited	No limit	Subject to state law	No limit
Party national committees	No limit	No limit	$5,000	No limit	Prohibited	No limit	Subject to state law	No limit
State and local party committees	No limit	No limit	$5,000	No limit	Prohibited	No limit	Subject to state law	No limit

Notes: Total annual contributions also include contributions to all federal candidates (see Table 1-1). "National party committees" refers to the parties' national committees, congressional campaign committees, and senatorial campaign committees. Changes in the law are posted at http://herrnson.cqpress.com.

economics; the League of Conservation Voters, an environmental group that supports mainly Democrats; the United Seniors Association, which is funded largely by U.S. pharmaceutical companies; and numerous groups associated with members of Congress, political parties, and other politicians.[18]

A series of court decisions, including one handed down in the midst of the 1996 election season, increased the activities that parties, PACs, and other interest groups can use to influence federal elections.[19] These rulings allow these organizations to spend unlimited sums of hard or soft money on issue advocacy ads that closely resemble electioneering ads that in the past could be financed only with hard money.[20] Most issue advocacy ads are nearly identical to hard money ads in that they praise or criticize federal candidates by name or feature their likenesses. The major differences between the two types of ad are that issue advocacy ads *cannot expressly* call for a candidate's election or defeat, and they tend to be more negative than hard money ads.[21] The courts also asserted the parties' right to make unlimited independent expenditures on campaign communications that *expressly* advocate the election or defeat of a federal candidate—by using phrases like "vote for" or "vote against"—as long as these expenditures are made with hard money and without the candidate's knowledge or consent.

Soft money offers parties and interest groups a number of advantages. It can be raised in huge chunks from a small number of deep-pocketed sources, and it can be spent in competitive elections where it can presumably have a substantial impact on election outcomes. It furnishes political access, and presumably influence, to those who contribute it, and it enables political parties and interest groups to spend extra—and once banned—resources to influence campaigns and ultimately the composition of Congress. Soft money, issue advocacy campaigns, and independent expenditures have significantly increased the influence of political parties and interest groups in congressional elections. These new forms of party and group participation have not done away with the candidate-centered nature of congressional elections, but they have altered it significantly. Soft money was among the most controversial aspects of the election system, and its elimination was a major goal of the Bipartisan Campaign Reform Act of 2002. Should the law pass constitutional muster, it could have a major impact on the flow of money in future congressional elections.

POLITICAL CULTURE

Historically, U.S. political culture has supported a system of candidate-centered congressional elections in many ways, but its major influence stems from its lack of foundation for a party-focused alternative. Americans have traditionally held a jaundiced view of political parties. *Federalist* no. 10 and President George Washington's farewell address are evidence that the framers of the Constitution and the first president thought a multitude of overlapping, wide-ranging interests preferable to class-based divisions represented by ideological parties. The founders designed the political system to encourage pragmatism and compromise in politics and thus to mitigate the harmful effects of factions. Although neither the pluralist system championed by the framers nor the nonpartisan system advocated by Washington has been fully realized, both visions of democracy have found expression in candidate-centered campaigns.

Congressional elections test candidates' abilities to build coalitions of voters and elites from diverse individuals. The multiplicity of overlapping interests, lack of a feudal legacy, and relatively fluid social and economic structure in the United States discourage the formation of class-based parties like those that have developed in most other democracies.[22] The consensus among Americans for liberty, equality, and property rights and their near-universal support for the political system further undermine the development of parties aimed at promoting major political, social, or economic change.[23]

Americans' traditional ambivalence about political parties has found expression during reform periods. The Populist movement of the 1890s, the Progressive movement that came shortly after it, and the rise of the New Left in the 1960s all resulted in political change that weakened the parties. Turn-of-the-century reformers championed the Australian ballot, the direct primary, and civil service laws for the explicit purpose of taking power away from party bosses.[24] Similarly, the reform movement that took hold of the Democratic Party during the 1960s and 1970s opened party conventions, meetings, and leadership positions to the increased participation of previously underrepresented groups. The reforms, many of which were adopted by Republican as well as Democratic state party organizations, made both parties more permeable and responsive to pressures from grassroots activists. They weakened what little influence party leaders had over the awarding of nominations, giving candidates, their supporters, and issue activists more influence over party affairs.[25]

Post–World War II social and cultural transformations undermined the parties even further. Declining immigration and increased geographic mobility eroded the working-class ethnic neighborhoods that were an important source of party loyalists. Increased educational levels encouraged citizens to rely more on their own judgment and less on party cues in political matters. The development of the mass media gave voters less-biased sources of information than the partisan press. The rise of interest groups, PACs, and other forms of functional and ideological representation created new arenas for political participation and new sources of political cues.[26] The aging of the parties, generational replacement, and the emergence of new issues that cut across existing fault lines led to the decline of party affiliation among voters and to more issue-oriented voting.[27] These developments encouraged voters to rely less on local party officials and opinion leaders for political information.[28] Cultural transformations created a void in electoral politics that individual candidates and their organizations came to fill.

Current attitudes toward the parties reflect the nation's historical experience. Survey research shows that most citizens believe that parties "do more to confuse the issues than to provide a clear choice on the issues," and "create conflict where none exists." Half of the population believes that parties make the political system less efficient and that "it would be better if, in all elections, we put no party labels on the ballot." [29]

Negative attitudes toward the parties are often learned at an early age. Many schoolchildren are routinely instructed to "vote for the best candidate, not the party." This lesson appears to stay with some of them into adulthood. Typically less than 10 percent of all registered voters maintain that the candidate's political party is the biggest factor in their vote decision. Candidates and issues rank higher.[30]

Although American history and culture extol the virtues of political independence and candidate-oriented voting, the electoral behavior of citizens provides an element of partisanship in congressional elections. Approximately two-thirds of all voters were willing to state that they identified with either the Democratic or the Republican Party in 2002, which is typical of the preceding two decades. More than 80 percent of all self-identified independents indicate they lean toward a major party, holding attitudes and exhibiting political behaviors similar to those of self-identified partisans. Although few registered voters state that they cast their votes chiefly on a partisan basis, 81 percent of them cast their congressional ballots along party lines in 2002. Such high levels of party-line voting are common in modern American politics, and partisanship is among the best predictors of voting behavior in congressional elections, ranking second only to incumbency. The fact that roughly nine out of ten members of the voting population perceives, retains, and responds to political information in a partisan manner means that elections are not entirely candidate centered.[31] Yet the degree of partisanship that exists in the contemporary United States is still not strong enough to encourage a return to straight-ticket voting or to foster the development of a party-focused election system.

CAMPAIGN TECHNOLOGY

Political campaigns are designed to communicate ideas and images that will motivate voters to cast their ballots for particular candidates. Some voters are well informed; have strong opinions about candidates, issues, and parties; and will vote without ever coming into contact with a political campaign. Others will never bother to vote, regardless of politicians' efforts. Many voters need to be introduced to the candidates and made aware of the issues to become excited enough to vote in a congressional election. The communication of information is central to democratic elections, and those who are able to control the flow of information have tremendous power. Candidates, campaign organizations, parties, and other groups use a variety of technologies to affect the flow of campaign information and win votes.

Person-to-person contact is one of the oldest and most effective approaches to winning votes. Nothing was or is more effective than a candidate, or a candidate's supporters, directly asking citizens for their votes. During the golden age of parties, local party volunteers assessed the needs of voters in their neighborhoods and delivered the message that, if elected, their party's candidates would help voters achieve their goals.[32] Once these organizations lost their control over the flow of political information, they became less important, and candidate-assembled campaign organizations became more relevant players in elections.

The dawning of the television age and the development of modern campaign technology helped solidify the system of candidate-centered congressional elections.[33] Television and radio studios, printing presses, public opinion polls, personal computers, and sophisticated targeting techniques are well suited to candidate-centered campaign organizations because they, and the services of the political consultants who know how to use them, are readily available for hire. Congressional candidates can assemble organizations that meet their specific needs without having to turn to party organizations for assistance, although many candidates request their party's help.

New technology has encouraged a major change in the focus of most congressional election campaigns. It has enabled campaigns to communicate more information about candidates' personalities, issue positions, and qualifications for office. As a result, less campaign activity is now devoted to party-based appeals. Radio and television were especially important in bringing about this change because they are well suited to conveying images and less useful in providing information about abstract concepts, such as partisan ideologies.[34] The overall effect of the electronic mass media is to direct attention away from parties and toward candidates.

The increased focus on candidate imagery that is associated with the "new style" of campaigning encourages congressional candidates to hire professional technicians to help them convey their political personas to voters.[35] Press secretaries, pollsters, issue and opposition researchers, and media experts are commonplace in most congressional campaigns. Local party activists became less important in congressional elections as the importance of political consultants grew and the contributions of semiskilled and unskilled volunteers diminished. The emergence of a national economy of campaign finance and the rise of a cadre of fundraising specialists with the skills, contacts, and technology to raise money from individuals and PACs further increased the candidate-centered character of election campaigns because they provided candidates with the means for raising the contributions needed to purchase the services of political consultants.

Changes in technology transformed most congressional campaigns from labor-intensive grassroots undertakings, at which local party committees excelled, to money-driven, merchandised activities requiring the services of skilled experts. Most local party committees were unable to adapt to the new style of campaign politics.[36] Initially, party committees in Washington, D.C., and in many states also were unprepared to play a significant role in congressional elections. However, the parties' national, congressional, and senatorial campaign committees and several state party organizations proved more adept at making the transition to the new-style politics. They began to play meaningful roles in congressional election campaigns during the late 1970s and early 1980s and continued to do so into the start of the twenty-first century.[37]

THE POLITICAL SETTING

Candidates, campaign managers, party officials, PAC managers, and others who are active in congressional elections consider more than the institutional framework, the culturally and historically conditioned expectations of voters, and the available technology when planning and executing electoral strategies. They also assess the political setting, including the circumstances in their district, their state, or the nation as a whole. At the local level, important considerations include the party affiliation, tenure, and intentions of the incumbent or other potential candidates, and the partisan history of the seat. Relevant national-level factors include whether it is a presidential or midterm election year, the state of the economy, the president's popularity, international affairs, and the public's attitude toward the government. Hostile sentiments directed at congressional Democrats and President Bill Clinton led to the

Republican takeover of Congress in 1994. Disapproval of the two federal government shutdowns and some elements of the "Republican revolution" helped make many 1996 congressional elections competitive. In 2002, national security issues and the war on terrorism that followed the attacks of September 11 had a major impact on the national political agenda. The issue was pivotal in GOP representative Saxby Chambliss's seven-point victory over Democratic senator Max Cleland in Georgia and in a number of other House and Senate races.

Of course, one's perspective on the limits and possibilities of the political setting depends largely on one's vantage point. Although they talk about the competition and are, indeed, wary of it, congressional incumbents, particularly House members, operate in a political setting that works largely to their benefit. As explained in later chapters, incumbents enjoy significant levels of name recognition and voter support, are able to assemble superior campaign organizations, and can draw on their experience in office to speak knowledgeably about issues and claim credit for the federally financed programs and improvements in their state or district. Incumbents also tend to get favorable treatment from the media. Moreover, most can rely on loyal followers from previous campaigns for continued backing: supporters at home tend to vote repeatedly for incumbents, and supporters in Washington and the nation's other wealthy cities routinely provide incumbents with campaign money.

Things look different from the typical challenger's vantage point. Most challengers, particularly those with some political experience, recognize that most of the cards are stacked against an individual who sets out to take on an incumbent. Little in the setting in which most congressional campaigns take place favors the challenger. Most challengers lack the public visibility, money, and campaign experience to wage a strong campaign. Moreover, because those who work in and help finance campaigns recognize the strong odds against challengers, they usually see little benefit in helping them. As a result, high incumbent success rates have become a self-fulfilling prophecy. Senate reelection rates ranged from 55 percent to almost 97 percent between 1950 and 2002. Between 1982 and 2002 almost 4 percent of all Senate incumbents had no major-party opponent, and just over half of those involved in contested races won by 60 percent or more of the two-party vote. Only 16 percent of all senators seeking reelection in 2000 and 2002 were defeated. Between 1950 and 2002, House incumbents enjoyed an overall reelection rate of better than 93 percent; the 2000 and 2002 elections returned to Congress roughly 98 percent and 96 percent, respectively, of those who sought to keep their jobs. Even during the tidal wave that swept away thirty-four Democrats in the House in the 1994 elections, just over 90 percent of all House incumbents who sought to remain in office did so.[38] With some important exceptions, most experienced politicians wait until an incumbent retires, runs for another office, or dies before running for office. Thus, many House seats fail to attract meaningful competition.

Most elections for open seats are highly competitive. They attract extremely qualified candidates who put together strong campaign organizations, raise huge amounts of money, and mount lively campaigns. Even House candidates of one party campaigning for seats that have been held by the other party for decades can often attract substantial resources, media attention, and votes.

Many explanations exist for the relative lack of competition in House elections. Some districts are so dominated by one party that few individuals of the other party are willing to commit their time, energy, or money to running for office. In many cases, the tradition of one-party dominance is so strong that virtually all the talented, politically ambitious individuals living in the area join the dominant party. When an incumbent in these districts faces a strong challenge, it usually takes place in the primary, and the winner is all but guaranteed success in the general election.[39]

Uncompetitive House districts are often the product of the redistricting process. In states where one party controls both the governorship and the state legislature, partisan gerrymandering is often used to maximize the number of House seats the dominant party can win. In states where each party controls at least some portion of the state government, compromises are frequently made to design districts that protect congressional incumbents. Party officials and political consultants armed with computers, election returns, and demographic statistics can "pack" and "crack" voting blocs in order to promote either of these goals.[40] The result is that large numbers of congressional districts are designed to be uncompetitive. In 2002, for example, only three of California's fifty-three House elections were decided by a margin of less than twenty points, and one of those seats might not have been competitive if scandal-plagued Gary Condit had not lost the Democratic primary. States that use nonpartisan commissions, which often ignore incumbency, tend to produce more competitive House races. In contrast to the situation in California, four of Iowa's five House seats were decided by fewer than fifteen points.

The desire of incumbents to retain their seats has changed Congress in ways that help discourage electoral competition. Most of those who are elected to Congress quickly understand that they will probably never hold a higher office because there are too few of such offices to go around. Like most people, they do everything in their power to hold on to their jobs. Congress has adapted to the career aspirations of its members by providing them with resources that can be used to increase their odds of reelection. Free mailings, WATS lines, Internet web sites, district offices, and subsidized travel help members gain visibility among their constituents. Federal "pork-barrel" projects also help incumbents win the support of voters.[41] Congressional aides help members write speeches, respond to constituent mail, resolve problems that constituents have with executive branch agencies, and follow the comings and goings in their bosses' districts.[42] These perquisites of office give incumbents tremendous advantages over challengers. They also discourage experienced politicians who could put forth a competitive challenge from taking on an entrenched incumbent.

The dynamics of campaign finance have similar effects. Incumbents have tremendous fundraising advantages over challengers, especially among PACs and wealthy individual donors. Many incumbents build up large war chests to discourage potential challengers from running against them. With the exception of millionaires and celebrities, challengers who decide to contest a race against a member of the House or Senate typically find they are unable to raise the funds needed to mount a viable campaign.

Given that the cards tend to be stacked so heavily in favor of congressional incumbents, most electoral competition takes place in open seats. Open-seat contests draw a larger than usual number of primary contestants. They also attract significantly more money and election assistance from party committees, individuals, PACs, and other groups than do challenger campaigns.[43] Special elections, which are called when a seat becomes vacant because of an incumbent's resignation or death, are open-seat contests that tend to be particularly competitive and unpredictable. They bring out even larger numbers of primary contenders than normal open-seat elections, especially when the seat that has become vacant was formerly held by a longtime incumbent.

The concentration of competition in open-seat elections and the decennial reapportionment and redistricting of House seats have traditionally combined to produce a ten-year, five-election cycle of political competition. Redistricting leads to the creation of many new House seats and the redrawing of the boundaries of numerous others. It encourages an increase in congressional retirements, usually leads more nonincumbents than usual to run for the House, and typically increases competition in many House elections—though the 2002 elections proved to be an exception to the rule.[44]

Another cyclical element of the national political climate that can influence congressional elections is the presence or absence of a presidential election. Presidential elections have higher levels of voter turnout than midterm elections, and they have the potential for coattail effects. A presidential candidate's popularity can become infectious and lead to some increase in support for the party's congressional contestants. A party that enjoys much success in electing congressional candidates during a presidential election year is, of course, likely to lose some of those seats in the midterm election that follows.[45] An unpopular president can further drag down a party's congressional contestants.[46] Presidential election politics had a strong impact on the election of 1932, in which the Democrats gained ninety seats in the House and thirteen seats in the Senate. The Democratic congressional landslide was a sign of widespread support for the Democratic presidential candidate, Franklin D. Roosevelt, as well as a repudiation of the incumbent president, Herbert Hoover, and his policies for dealing with the Great Depression.[47] Although coattail effects have declined since the 1930s, Ronald Reagan's 1980 presidential campaign is credited with helping the Republicans gain thirty-three seats in the House and twelve seats in the Senate.[48] Bill Clinton's presidential elections were conspicuous for their lack of coattails. Democrats lost ten House seats and broke even in the Senate in 1992; they gained only ten seats in the House and lost two seats in the Senate in 1996. George W. Bush's 2000 election similarly lacked coattails, as the Republicans lost two seats in the lower chamber of Congress and four seats in the upper chamber. Coattail effects are rarely visible when a presidential candidate wins by margins as small as Clinton's 43 percent of the popular vote in 1992 and 49 percent in 1996. Of course, Bush won the historic 2000 presidential election, despite receiving 539,947 fewer popular votes than Al Gore.

Congressional candidates who belong to the same party as an unpopular president also run the risk during midterm elections of being blamed for the failures of their party's chief executive.[49] The Republicans' forty-nine-seat House and four-seat Senate losses in 1974 grew out of a sense of disgust about the Nixon administration's role in the Watergate break-in and President Gerald Ford's decision to pardon Nixon.[50] The Democrats' loss of fifty-two seats in the House and eight seats in the Senate in 1994 was caused largely by voter animosity toward Clinton, dissatisfaction with his party's failure to enact health care reform or a middle-class tax cut, and the Republicans' successful portrayal of the White House and the Democratic-controlled Congress as corrupt and out of step with the views of most voters. The Democrats' net gain of five House seats in 1998 bucked a sixty-year trend in which the president's party always suffered losses in midterm elections.[51] The Republicans net gain of six House seats in 2002 also ran against the norm, and their picking up of two seats in the upper chamber reversed sixty-eight years worth of precedent in which the president's party either lost seats or broke even in midterm Senate elections.

The economy, foreign affairs, homeland security, and other national issues can affect congressional elections. The president's party has historically lost congressional seats in midterm elections when economic trends are unfavorable, although the relationship between economic performance and congressional turnover has weakened in recent years.[52] Foreign affairs may have contributed to the Democrats' congressional losses in 1972 during the Vietnam War, and the wars on terrorism and in Afghanistan may have cost them seats in 2002. Americans, however, tend to be less concerned with "guns" than with "butter," and so international events generally have less of an effect on elections than domestic conditions.

Other national issues that can affect congressional elections are civil rights, social issues, and the attitudes of voters toward political institutions. The civil rights revolution, the women's movement, urban decay, the emergence of the hippie counterculture, and the protests they spawned influenced voting behavior during the 1960s and 1970s.[53] Political scandal, and the widespread distrust of government that usually follows, can lead to the defeat of politicians accused of committing ethical transgressions, but as the 1974 and 1994 elections demonstrate, individual members of Congress who are not directly implicated in scandal can also suffer because of it.

National issues are likely to have the greatest effect on congressional elections when candidates take unambiguous stands on them.[54] Presidential politics are likely to have the most influence on congressional elections when voters closely identify congressional candidates with a party's presidential nominee or an incumbent president. House and Senate candidates generally respond strategically to national politics in order to improve their electoral fortunes. When their party selects a popular presidential candidate or has a popular incumbent in the White House, congressional candidates ally themselves with that individual to take advantage of the party cue. When their party selects an unpopular nominee or is saddled with an unpopular president, congressional candidates seek to protect themselves from the effects of partisanship by distancing themselves from the comings and goings of the executive branch. The partisan campaigns that Democratic congressional candidates ran during the New Deal era and in 1996, and that Republicans mounted in 2000 and 2002, exemplify the former strategy. The independent, nonpartisan campaigns that many congressional Republicans conducted in 1992 and 1996, and that Democrats carried out in 1998 and 2002, are representative of the latter.

RECENT CONGRESSIONAL ELECTIONS

The political settings that have shaped the opportunities presented to politicians, parties, interest groups, and ultimately voters since the early 1990s have had some important similarities. All but the 1994 midterm elections took place during a period of divided control, which made it difficult to credit or blame only one party for the government's performance or the nation's affairs. Most of the elections also took place under the shadow of a weak economy and were haunted by the specter of huge budget deficits. The 1998 and 2000 elections were important exceptions, occurring as the two parties debated how to spend projected budget surpluses.

Civil rights and racial and gender discrimination were issues in many campaigns during this period as a result of the highly publicized studies of the unequal salaries and advancement prospects for women and African Americans and the murder of James Byrd, an African American who was dragged to death behind a truck in Texas. Women's issues also were highlighted by the Clinton-Lewinsky scandal and by an admission of adultery that led House Speaker designate Robert Livingston, R.-La., to retire from the House in 1998. Gay rights found its place on the agenda as the nation debated the military's long-standing policy against homosexuals serving in the military. The issue stayed prominent, partially as a result of the gruesome slaying of gay university student Matthew Shepard in Laramie, Wyoming.

A final arena in which civil rights issues were fought was redistricting. In 1986 the Supreme Court ruled that any gerrymandering of a congressional district that purposely diluted minority strength was illegal under the 1982 Voting Rights Act.[55] Most states interpreted the ruling cautiously, redrawing many of the districts after the 1990 census with the explicit purpose of giving one or more minority group members better-than-even chances of being elected to the House. Several opposition groups successfully sued in more than a half dozen states, including North Carolina, where redistricting battles continued to be fought well into the 1998 congressional election season. Several of the redistricting plans drawn prior to the 2002 elections also were subject to court challenges. Indeed, only twenty-nine plans went unchallenged before the election, and Mississippi's redistricting plan continued to be challenged after the election.[56]

Dissatisfaction with the political establishment in Washington also occupied a prominent position on the political agenda at the close of the twentieth century. Gridlock and the federal government's inability to solve problems associated with drug abuse, crime, the environment, rising health care costs, the unsatisfactory performance of the nation's schools, the deficit, and myriad other seemingly intractable issues resulted in voter frustration with national politicians. Much of this hostility was directed toward Congress, and many incumbents responded with a strategy that had served them well in the past— running for reelection by campaigning against Congress itself.[57]

Political scandal and the anti-Washington mood gave open-seat and challenger candidates for Congress many powerful issues to use in campaigns during the elections held in the early 1990s. Support for the national legislature plummeted to an all-time low prior to the 1994 elections, with polls estimating that roughly three-fourths of all Americans disapproved of Congress's performance.[58]

Conditions were ripe for the Republicans to pick up a significant number of congressional seats in the 1994 elections. Public hostility toward Washington, Democratic control of both the executive and legislative branches of the national government, and the Democrats' historical association with the growth of federal programs and the bureaucracy put that party in a precarious position. Moreover, Clinton's early missteps on health care reform, gays in the military, and tax cuts, and allegations of ethical misconduct by the president and his administration, energized Republican candidates and their supporters while demoralizing Democrats and their allies. Under Newt Gingrich's leadership, the Republicans capitalized on these circumstances by running a nationalized anti-Washington campaign that drew on the Contract with America.[59]

Following their takeover of Congress in 1994, House Republicans passed most of the popular elements of their contract, including congressional reform, crime control, welfare reform, and other contract provisions that would promote a smaller, less expensive government.[60] However, the public objected to elements of the GOP plan, particularly those seeking to provide tax cuts to the very rich while reducing spending on Medicare, Medicaid, and education. Political stalemate led to two federal government shutdowns, which were largely blamed on Gingrich, increasing public misgivings about the Republican Congress. Democrats sought to capitalize on the Republicans' difficulties by campaigning against what they labeled "the extremist Republican Congress" and offering policy proposals designed to appeal to middle-income and blue-collar families.

The settings for the 1998 and 2000 elections were more promising for incumbents of both parties. Most Americans benefited from a strong economy marked by rising incomes, low inflation, a high employment rate, a booming stock market, and the first federal budget surplus in three decades, leading them to favor incumbents' reelections. Moreover, most individual representatives and senators read polls taken in their districts that were even more favorable than the public's evaluations of Congress as a whole. Constituents typically have much higher opinions of their own representatives than they do of Congress as an institution and its other members.[61] The 1998 and 2000 elections took place in an environment that favored the status quo, gave neither party a strong advantage, and benefited incumbents in general, few of whom were defeated.

At their outset, the 2002 elections also were shaping up to favor incumbents. Public approval of Congress was relatively high, despite economic concerns arising from a falling stock market that was triggered in part by the collapse of many high-tech "dot.com" companies and reports of fraudulent accounting, which brought down companies such as Enron and Arthur Andersen.[62] As noted earlier, House incumbents in most states had worked with state legislative leaders and governors—and party organizations, interest groups, and political consultants with expertise in redistricting—to redraw congressional seats in ways that virtually reassured most of their reelections.

Nevertheless, the pro-incumbent bias of the 2002 elections did not prevent the parties from seeking to create a national issue agenda that would benefit their candidates. Early in the campaign season, Democrats tried to focus attention on the economy and jobs, education, prescription drug costs and health care, the environment, and Social Security. For the Republicans, tax cuts, government downsizing, family values, and other moral issues were central. Following the attacks of September 11, the issue agenda took on a life of its own. National security and the war on terrorism, which had barely registered among the public, rose to prominence in national opinion polls. The president's approval ratings skyrocketed, as has historically occurred when the United States has become involved in an international crisis. Republican congressional candidates benefited from the changed political agenda and from being able to bask in the rays of Bush's high ratings.[63]

Although incumbents generally derive tremendous advantages from the strategic environment, the political setting in a given year can pose obstacles for some of them, resulting in significant numbers losing their seats. The political settings for the congressional elections of 1992 through 1996, for instance, produced more serious challenges to national legislators, particularly House members, than had occurred in the previous decade (see Table 1-3). Nineteen House incumbents lost their primaries in 1992—a post–World War II record; and another thirty-four lost in the general election two years later— the most since the post-Watergate housecleaning of 1974. The results of the 1998 and 2000 elections deviated significantly from the moderate-to-high levels of incumbent losses recorded since 1992. Only one incumbent was defeated in the 1998 primaries, a mere six lost their general elections, and ninety-four enjoyed the luxury of running unopposed by a major-party candidate, one fewer than the record set in 1950.[64] Incumbents fared only slightly worse in 2000, when three lost their primaries and six fell during the general election.[65]

Historical patterns suggested the number of incumbents at risk should have increased substantially in 2002. Elections that immediately follow redistricting are usually marked by large numbers of incumbent defeats in both the

TABLE 1-3

Number of Unchallenged and Defeated House Incumbents, 1982–2002

	1982	1984	1986	1988	1990	1992	1994	1996	1998	2000	2002
Incumbents unchallenged by majorparty opposition in general election	49	63	71	81	76	25	54	20	94	63	78
Incumbents defeated											
In primary	10	3	3	1	1	19	4	2	1	3	8
In general election	29	16	6	6	15	24	34	20	6	6	8

Sources: Compiled from various editions of *CQ Weekly* and *Congressional Roll Call* (Washington, D.C.: CQ Press). The primary and general election results are from Norman J. Ornstein, Thomas E. Mann, and Michael J. Malbin, *Vital Statistics on Congress, 2001–2002* (Washington, D.C.: AEI Press, 2002), 69.

Note: The 1982, 1992, and 2002 figures include incumbent-versus-incumbent races.

primaries and the general election. The pitting of incumbents against each other almost always accounts for some of these losses, as does the fact that the prospect of newly-drawn seats often encourages more candidates than usual to challenge sitting House members. Nevertheless, the unique aspects of the most recent wave of redistricting significantly altered this pattern. Only eight incumbents lost their party's nominations in 2002, as opposed to nineteen in 1992 and ten a decade earlier. More remarkably, only eight incumbents lost in the general election in 2002, as opposed to twenty-four and twenty-nine in the previous two post-redistricting contests. The fact that seventy-eight incumbents faced no major-party opposition—more than three times as many as in 1992 and 50 percent more than in 1982—contributed to the high reelection rates in 2002.

The lack of competition in the 2002 House elections is even more apparent when the candidates are divided into categories based on the closeness of their elections. During the post-redistricting elections of 1982, 38 percent of the House candidates in major-party contested races ran in marginal districts. Included in this group are the 15 percent of the candidates classified as "incumbents in jeopardy," on the basis of their having lost the general election or having won by a margin of 20 percent or less of the two-party vote; the 15 percent of the candidates who opposed them—labeled "hopeful challengers"; and the 8 percent of the candidates—classified as open-seat "prospects"—who ran in contests decided by 20 percent or less of the two-party vote (see Table 1-4). The remainder of the candidates, who were involved in uncompetitive races, are referred to as "incumbent shoo-ins," "likely-loser challengers," and

TABLE 1-4

Competition in House Elections, 1982–2002

	1982	1984	1986	1988	1990	1992	1994	1996	1998	2000	2002
Incumbents											
In jeopardy	15%	13%	9%	8%	15%	14%	17%	15%	14%	11%	8%
Shoo-ins	27	34	35	39	32	25	27	29	31	35	35
Challengers											
Hopefuls	15	13	9	8	15	14	17	15	14	11	8
Likely losers	27	34	35	39	32	25	27	29	31	35	35
Open-seat candidates											
Prospects	8	5	7	5	5	13	9	8	7	6	8
Mismatched	7	1	4	3	1	9	5	4	3	3	5
(*N*)	(750)	(736)	(720)	(712)	(696)	(794)	(766)	(812)	(680)	(746)	(694)

Source: Compiled from Federal Election Commission data.

Notes: Figures are for major-party candidates in contested general elections, excluding incumbent-versus-incumbent races (which occasionally follow redistricting), runoff elections, and contests won by independents. Incumbents in jeopardy are defined as those who lost or who won by 20 percent or less of the two-party vote. Shoo-ins are incumbents who won by more than 20 percent of the two-party vote. Hopeful challengers are those who won or who lost by 20 percent or less of the two-party vote. Likely loser challengers are those who lost by more than 20 percent of the two-party vote. Open-seat prospects are those whose election was decided by 20 percent or less of the two-party vote. Mismatched open-seat candidates are those whose election was decided by more than 20 percent of the two-party vote. Some columns do not add to 100 percent because of rounding.

"mismatched" open-seat candidates.[66] Slightly more 1992 post-redistricting House elections were competitive than 1982 races because a greater number of retirements led to an increase in the number of marginal open-seat races. A mere 24 percent of the 2002 House elections were competitive by this standard, largely because bipartisan coalitions of sitting House members drew district lines to protect themselves.

The decline in competitive races was not merely the result of redistricting. The realignment of the South from Democratic-controlled, to competitive, to characterized by pockets of one-party domination also had an impact.[67] High reelection rates and the increased costs of campaigning also undoubtedly discouraged many would-be challengers from running for Congress.[68] Incumbency remained a valuable asset, especially in discouraging opposition in 2002.

The Senate elections held in 2002 were not much different from those held in the two decades that preceded them (see Table 1-5). Relatively few

TABLE 1-5

Number of Unchallenged and Defeated Senate Incumbents, 1982–2002

	1982	1984	1986	1988	1990	1992	1994	1996	1998	2000	2002
Incumbents unchallenged by major-party opposition in general election	0	1	0	0	5	1	0	0	0	1	4
Incumbents defeated											
In primary	0	0	0	0	0	1	0	1	0	0	1
In general election	2	3	7	4	1	4	2	1	3	6	3

Sources: Compiled from various issues of *CQ Weekly* and *Congressional Roll Call* (Washington, D.C.: CQ Press). The primary and general election results are from Norman J. Ornstein, Thomas E. Mann, and Michael J. Malbin, *Vital Statistics on Congress, 2001–2002* (Washington, D.C.: AEI Press, 2002), 70.

members of the upper chamber were defeated in a primary. Rep. John Sununu defeated Sen. Robert Smith, who felt the wrath of New Hampshire Republicans who were angry over his quitting the GOP in July 1999 and blasting it as "hypocritical" and "not a party that means anything"—only to rejoin it in November.[69] When the classification scheme used for House candidates is applied to the Senate it becomes clear that the number of competitive incumbent-challenger contests in 2002 was not significantly greater than in the previous two years (see Table 1-6). If anything, that four general election races went uncontested in 2002 indicates that there was less competition that year than in many preceding contests.

The competitiveness of congressional elections influences the number of new faces in Congress. As a group, those serving in the 108th Congress are more diverse than those who served a decade ago. The House opened its first session of the 108th Congress with twenty-eight more women, eleven more African Americans, and eleven more Hispanics than had served in the 102d Congress. Change generally comes more slowly to the upper chamber. The number of female senators increased to thirteen.[70] The Senate currently has no African Americans; one Native American, Ben Nighthorse Campbell, R-Colo.; and only two Asian Americans, Hawaii Democrats Daniel Inouye and Daniel Akaka.

Despite this increased diversity, the vast majority of newcomers had at least one thing in common with one another and with their more senior colleagues: they came to Congress with significant political experience under their belts. Fifty of the fifty-three new House members elected to the 108th Congress had previously held another public office, served as a party official, worked as a

TABLE 1-6

Competition in Senate Elections, 1982–2002

	1982	1984	1986	1988	1990	1992	1994	1996	1998	2000	2002
Incumbents											
In jeopardy	26%	17%	20%	17%	20%	22%	23%	21%	15%	17%	18%
Shoo-ins	20	27	20	24	25	16	14	9	28	26	20
Challengers											
Hopefuls	26	17	20	17	20	22	23	21	15	17	18
Likely losers	20	27	20	24	25	16	14	9	28	26	20
Open-seat candidates											
Prospects	10	10	12	12	3	21	14	35	9	15	24
Mismatched	0	3	6	6	7	3	11	6	6	0	0
(*N*)	(66)	(64)	(68)	(66)	(60)	(68)	(70)	(68)	(68)	(66)	(60)

Source: Compiled from Federal Election Commission data.

Notes: Figures are for major-party candidates in contested general elections. Incumbents in jeopardy are defined as those who lost or who won by 20 percent or less of the two-party vote. Shoo-ins are incumbents who won by more than 20 percent or less of the two-party vote. Hopeful challengers are those who won or who lost by 20 percent or less of the two-party vote. Likely loser challengers are those who lost by more than 20 percent of the two-party vote. Open-seat prospects are those whose election was decided by 20 percent or less of the two-party vote. Mismatched open-seat candidates are those whose election was decided by more than 20 percent or less of the two-party vote. Some columns do not add to 100 percent because of rounding.

political aide or consultant, or run for Congress at least once before getting elected.[71] Only one of the candidates elected to the Senate for the first time in 2002 had not previously held at least one elective office and she—Elizabeth Dole, R.-N.C.—was no amateur. A former cabinet official, presidential candidate, and wife of former Senate majority leader and presidential candidate Robert Dole, R-Kan., she had an abundance of political experience.

SUMMARY

The Constitution, election laws, campaign finance regulations, and participatory nominations provide the institutional foundations for the candidate-centered congressional election system. The United States's history and individualistic political culture, which inform Americans' traditional ambivalence toward political parties, shore up that system. Candidates who can afford to hire political consultants to learn about and contact voters have benefited from technological advancements, which have allowed the system to assume its contemporary pro-incumbent, professionally oriented, money-fueled form.

How campaigns are conducted in the future will be influenced by changes currently under way in the strategic environment in which congressional elections are waged. Recent changes in campaign finance law, for example, especially those concerning soft money and issue advocacy ads, will affect the abilities of political parties and interest groups to influence the tenor and outcomes of congressional elections.

CHAPTER TWO

Candidates and Nominations

Can I win? Is this the right time for me to run? Who is my competition likely to be? These are the kinds of questions that have always gone through the minds of prospective candidates. During the golden age of political parties, party bosses helped individuals decide whether to run for Congress. In many places the bosses' control over the party apparatus was so complete that, when in agreement, they could guarantee the nomination to the person they wanted to run. Moreover, receiving the nomination usually was tantamount to winning the election because strong political machines typically were located in one-party areas.[1]

After the golden age, party leaders had less control over the nomination process and less ability to ensure that the individuals they recruited would, in fact, win the nomination. Contemporary parties are no longer the primary recruiters of congressional candidates. Parties continue to play a role in encouraging some individuals to run for office and in discouraging others. But they serve more as vehicles that self-recruited candidates use to advance their careers than as organizations that can make or break those careers. Party recruitment has been largely replaced by a process referred to as candidate emergence.[2]

In this chapter I examine who decides to run for Congress, how potential candidates reach their decisions, and the influence that different individuals and groups have on these decisions. I also examine the impact of political experience on a candidate's prospects of winning the nomination and the influence of nominations and general elections on the representativeness of the national legislature.

STRATEGIC AMBITION

The Constitution, state laws, and the political parties pose few formal barriers to running for Congress, enabling virtually anyone to become a candidate.

35

Members of the House are required to be at least twenty-five years of age, to have been U.S. citizens for at least seven years, and to reside in the state they represent. The requirements for the Senate are only slightly more stringent. In addition to residing in the state they represent, senators must be at least thirty years old and have been U.S. citizens for at least nine years. Some states bar prison inmates or individuals who have been declared insane from running for office, and most states require candidates to pay a small filing fee or to collect anywhere from a few hundred to several thousand signatures prior to having their names placed on the ballot. As is typical for election to public offices in many democracies, a dearth of formal requirements allows almost anyone to run for Congress. Over sixteen hundred people declare themselves candidates in most election years.

Although the formal requirements are minimal, other factors, related to the candidate-centered nature of the electoral system, favor individuals with certain personal characteristics. Strategic ambition—which is the combination of a desire to get elected, a realistic understanding of what it takes to win, and an ability to assess the opportunities presented by a given political context—is one such characteristic that distinguishes most successful candidates for Congress from the general public. Most successful candidates also must be self-starters because the electoral system lacks a tightly controlled party-recruitment process or a well-defined career path to the national legislature. And, because the electoral system is candidate-centered, the desire, skills, and resources that candidates bring to the electoral arena are the most important criteria separating serious candidates from those who have little chance of getting elected. Ambitious candidates, sometimes referred to as "strategic," "rational," or "quality" candidates, are political entrepreneurs who make rational calculations about when to run. Rather than plunge right in, they assess the political context in which they would have to wage their campaigns, consider the effects that a bid for office could have on their professional careers and families, and carefully weigh their prospects for success.[3]

Strategic politicians examine many institutional, structural, and subjective factors when considering a bid for Congress.[4] The institutional factors include filing deadlines, campaign finance laws, nomination processes that allow or prohibit preprimary endorsements, and other election statutes and party rules. The structural factors include the social, economic, and partisan composition of the district; its geographic compactness; the media markets that serve it; the degree of overlap between the district and lower-level electoral constituencies; and the possibilities for election to some alternative office. One structural factor that greatly affects the strategic calculations of nonincumbents and is prone to fluctuate more often than others is whether an incumbent plans to run for reelection.

Potential candidates also assess the political climate in deciding whether to run. Strategic politicians focus mainly on local circumstances, particularly whether a seat will be vacant or whether the results of the previous election suggest that an incumbent is vulnerable.[5] National forces, such as a public mood that favors Democrats or Republicans or challengers or incumbents, are usually of secondary importance. The convergence of local and national forces can have a strong impact on the decisions of potential candidates. The widespread hostility the public directed at Congress and its members played a major role in influencing who ran in the 1994 and 1996 primaries and general elections.[6] These forces motivated many House incumbents to retire and encouraged many would-be House members to believe that a seat in Congress was within their reach.[7] Favorable circumstances and these candidates' positive self-assessments encouraged them to think they could win the support of local, state, and national political elites; raise the money; build the name recognition; and generate the momentum needed to propel them into office.[8] In 1998 and 2000 the nation's overall prosperity and the public's positive feelings toward incumbents had the opposite effect. The same is true of pro-incumbent redistricting and other national and local factors in 2002.

Incumbents

For House incumbents the decision to run for reelection is usually an easy one. Congress offers its members many reasons to want to stay, including the ability to affect issues they care about, a challenging work environment, political power, and public recognition. It is also an ideal platform for pursuing a governorship, cabinet post, or even a seat in the oval office. Name recognition and the advantages inherent in incumbency—such as paid staff and the franking privilege (which have an estimated worth of $1.5 million per member per year)—are two factors that discourage strong opposition from arising.[9] Furthermore, House members recognize that the "home styles" they use to present themselves to constituents create bonds of trust that have important electoral implications.[10]

Incumbents undertake a number of additional preelection activities to build support and ward off opposition. Many raise large war chests early in the election cycle in order to intimidate potential opponents.[11] Many also keep a skeletal campaign organization intact between elections and send their supporters campaign newsletters and other political communications. Some even shower their constituents with greeting cards, flowers, and other gifts.[12] Their congressional activities and preelection efforts, as well as the fact that they have been elected to Congress at least once before, make most incumbents fairly certain that they will be reelected.

In some circumstances, however, incumbents recognize that it may be more difficult than usual to hold on to their seats. Redistricting, for example, can change the partisan composition of a House member's district or it can force two incumbents to compete for one seat.[13] A highly publicized ethical transgression usually weakens an incumbent's reelection prospects. A poor economy, an unpopular president or presidential candidate, or a wave of antigovernment hostility also can undermine legislators who represent marginal districts. These factors can influence incumbents' expectations about the quality of the opposition they are likely to face, the kinds of reelection campaigns they will need to wage, the toll those campaigns could take on themselves and their families, and their desire to stay in Congress.

When the demands of campaigning outweigh the benefits of getting reelected, strategic incumbents retire. Elections that immediately follow redistricting are often preceded by a jump in the number of incumbents who retire, as was the case in 1952, 1972, 1982, and 1992 (see Figure 2-1). The

FIGURE 2-1

Number of Retirements by House Incumbents, 1950–2002

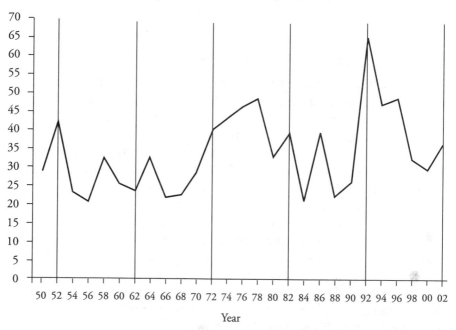

Sources: Compiled from various issues of *CQ Weekly, Congressional Roll Call* (Washington, D.C.: CQ Press), and Norman J. Ornstein, Thomas E. Mann, and Michael J. Malbin, *Vital Statistics on Congress, 2001–2002* (Washington, D.C.: AEI Press, 2002), 71.

number of retirees jumped slightly in 2002 relative to the previous two elections, but fewer House members retired that year in comparison with most previous post-redistricting elections.

Elections held during periods of voter frustration, congressional scandal, or incivility within Congress itself also are preceded by high numbers of retirements.[14] A combination of redistricting, anti-incumbent sentiments, and a decline in comity in the House led 15 percent of all House members to retire in 1992—a post–World War II record. Whereas the numerous hard-fought elections that took place in 1994 inspired many congressional retirements in 1996, retirements declined in 1998 and 2000. The relatively high appraisals of Congress that preceded those elections, and the efforts of party leaders, who wanted to minimize the number of open seats they had to defend, helped reduce the number of House retirements to thirty-three and thirty in those years, respectively, accounting for roughly 7 percent of all House members.

Elections that occur following upheaval within Congress itself also are marked by large numbers of congressional retirements. The political reforms passed during the mid-1970s, which redistributed power from conservative senior House members to more liberal junior ones, encouraged many senior members to retire from the House.[15] The Republican takeover of the House in 1994 also encouraged large numbers of Democrats, and some Republicans, to retire. For the Democrats, retirement was preferable to waging a reelection campaign that, if successful, would result in their continuing to suffer the powerlessness associated with being in the minority. For the Republicans, it was preferable to enduring the indignity of being defeated for a committee chairmanship or some other leadership post.

The retirements that took place prior to the 2002 elections showed a variety of patterns. Only a few representatives retired for reasons associated with an actual or impending loss of power. Rep. Marge Roukema, R-N.J., had been passed over for the chairmanship of the House Banking Committee in the 107th Congress. Rep. Bud Shuster, R-Pa., chairman of the House Transportation Committee, retired almost one year before the end of that Congress, stating that he had "reached the pinnacle of my congressional career" and cited personal "health scares." [16] However, other factors undoubtedly influenced his decision to step down. First, he received a reprimand from the House ethics committee for breaking House rules by allowing Ann Eppard, a transportation industry lobbyist who previously had been the congressman's chief of staff, to continue to play a major role in running his office. Second, Shuster would have lost his chairmanship in the 108th Congress as a result of the term limits that GOP House members instated for committee chairs. Third, by resigning before completing his fifteenth term, Shuster also was able to play an important role in choosing his successor.[17]

The individuals most likely to retire from Congress are senior members who decide they would rather enjoy the fruits of old age than gear up for an election campaign, members who are implicated in some kind of scandal, members who tire of their lack of influence, and members who find their districts largely obliterated by redistricting.[18] The period just before the 2002 elections was marked by several retirements motivated by these reasons. Rep. Joe Skeen, R-N.M., who has Parkinson's disease, and Rep. Eva Clayton, D-N.C., aged 68, retired for health and age-related reasons. Reps. Robert Borski, D-Pa., and Steve Horn, R-Calif., chose to retire because their districts were folded into those of other members. Scandal probably played at least some role in Shuster's retirement and was central to Democratic senator Robert Torricelli's decision to withdraw from his reelection campaign in New Jersey. Ironically, House Republican Conference chairman J. C. Watts, of Oklahoma, the fourth highest ranking GOP member of the House, stated that he retired because of his lack of influence in party policy-making circles.[19] Finally, House majority leader Dick Armey, R-Texas, and Reps. Carrie Meek, D-Fla., and Shuster, gave at least some thought to creating family dynasties in Congress. Meek succeeded in helping her son Kendrick claim her seat, and Shuster was able to help his son Bill win a special election in his district. Nevertheless, Armey's son Scott, a Denton County judge, did not fare as well, losing in the primary to physician Michael Burgess, who went on to win the general election.[20]

Nonincumbents

The conditions that affect the calculations of strategic incumbents also influence the decision making of nonincumbents who plan their political careers strategically.[21] Redistricting has a significant impact on these individuals. More state and local officeholders run for the House in election cycles that follow redistricting than in other years (see Figure 2-2).[22] Many of these candidates anticipate the opportunities that arise from the creation of new seats, the redrawing of old ones, or the retirements that often accompany elections after redistricting. The "pulling effects" of redistricting at the congressional level are sometimes accompanied by "pushing effects." The redistricting of state legislatures, county councils, and other offices may encourage current officeholders to seek a seat in the House. Term limits for state legislators, which exist in eleven states, can have the same impact.[23] The effects of redistricting encouraged almost 300 candidates who had experience holding an elective office to run in 2002.

FIGURE 2-2

Number of House Primary Candidates by Political Experience, 1978–2002

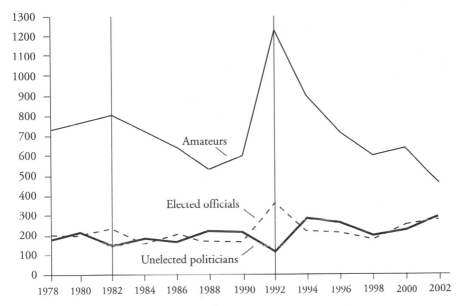

Sources: Compiled from various issues of *CQ Weekly*.

Note: Includes nonincumbent candidates for major-party nominations only.

Candidates who have significant campaign and political experience but who have never held elective office also respond to the opportunities that emerge in specific election years. These "unelected politicians" comprise legislative and executive branch aides, political appointees, state and local party officials, political consultants, and individuals who have previously lost a bid for Congress. Most of these politicians think strategically. Prior to deciding to run, they monitor voter sentiment, assess the willingness of political activists and contributors to support their campaigns, and keep close tabs on who is likely to oppose them for the nomination or in the general election.

Unelected politicians differ somewhat from elected officials and former officeholders in their perceptions of what constitutes a good time to run because elected officials weigh heavily in the strategic calculations of the unelected politicians. Unelected politicians appreciate that most elected officials possess more name recognition and fundraising advantages than they do. Unelected politicians typically balk at the opportunity to contest a primary against an elected official, even when other circumstances appear favorable. However, if a candidate with elective experience does not come forward, individuals with other significant forms of political experience will usually run. Relatively few unelected politicians viewed the 1982 and 1992 post-redistricting elections cycle as promising for their causes. The pro-incumbent political environment discouraged unelected politicians from running. However, in 2002, roughly the same number of unelected politicians ran as did politicians with office-holding experience.

Political amateurs are an extremely diverse group, and it is difficult to generalize about their political decision making. Only a small subgroup of amateurs, referred to as "ambitious amateurs," behave strategically, responding to the same opportunities and incentives that influence the decisions of more experienced politicians. Most amateurs do not spend much time assessing these factors. "Policy amateurs," comprising another subgroup, are driven by issues, whereas "experience-seeking" or "hopeless amateurs" run out of a sense of civic duty or for the thrill of running itself.[24]

The large number of amateurs who ran in the 1992 elections set a record that is likely to stand for some time. A few of these candidates were ambitious challengers, who, after weighing the costs of campaigning and the probability of winning, declared their candidacies. Many policy-oriented and experience-seeking amateurs also were compelled to run in the early and middle 1990s. These elections provided political landscapes that were ideal for running advocacy-oriented or anti-incumbency campaigns. The National Organization for Women, EMILY's List, and other pro-choice and women's groups recruited women to run for Congress and mobilized women voters and donors. Calls for change and relentless government-bashing in the media provided reform-minded candidates from both parties with ready-made platforms. Republican recruitment efforts and the Contract with America helped inspire more GOP than Democratic candidates to run in 1994 for the first time in decades. The legislation proposed and enacted by the Republican-led 104th Congress inspired many policy-oriented Democratic and GOP candidates to run in 1996. The possibilities for turnover in these elections attracted all types of amateurs.

The opportunities presented in the 1998 and 2000 elections, in contrast, did not appear to inspire as many nonincumbents as did the previous three elections. Nevertheless, many political amateurs ran for the House, demonstrating that they were less sensitive to fluctuations in the opportunities presented by the political environment than were candidates who possessed significant political experience.

The 2002 elections were somewhat of an anomaly in terms of post-redistricting elections. There was a predictable surge in the number of elected officials and unelected politicians who sensed opportunity and made a run for the House. Nevertheless, the number of amateurs who launched bids for Congress reached a low point for the preceding two decades. This trend has a few possible explanations. First, redistricting resulted in the creation of new district boundaries in most states that strongly favored incumbents, which may have disheartened ambitious and policy-oriented amateurs—the former realizing the odds of victory were virtually nil and the latter understanding they would have little ability to attract media attention either to their candidacies or to priority issues in a lopsided race. Second, and partially as a result of redistricting, only forty-nine seats were open in 2002, compared with ninety-one in 1992.[25] This, too, would have provided fewer ambitious and policy-oriented amateurs with opportunities to accomplish their respective goals. Third, the 2002 elections largely were bereft of the types of compelling national issues that motivate the candidacies of policy-oriented amateurs. Finally, the number of amateurs of all types who run for Congress appears to be declining since the 1992 elections. Some observers attribute this trend to politics having become generally less appealing to Americans, leading some potential candidates to seek fulfillment from volunteering in other civic enterprises.[26]

What appears to be a year of opportunity for strategic politicians of one party is often viewed as a bad year by their counterparts in the other party. Democrats with experience in lower office considered 1978 and 1982 to be good years to run for the House; Republicans with comparable levels of experience did not (see Figure 2-3). Republicans, in contrast, judged 1980 to be a good year, as well as 1990, when many similarly qualified Democrats were discouraged from running. The 1992 election was somewhat unusual in that strategic politicians of both parties judged the effects of redistricting, a weak economy, congressional scandal, and voter antipathy to hold tremendous possibilities. The 1994 election witnessed a significant decline in candidates with elective experience from both parties, but especially Democrats, giving unelected politicians of both parties greater opportunities to run.

The Republican takeover of Congress had a significant effect on candidate emergence in the 1996 elections. The number of Republican candidates with elective or significant unelective experience decreased slightly after 1994 because many individuals in the GOP's candidate pool undoubtedly believed that their party had captured virtually every vulnerable Democrat-held seat in the tidal wave of that year. Many Democratic elected officials also opted not to run in 1996. Demoralized by their party's low standing in the polls, the president's unpopularity, the House Republicans' initial legislative success, and the risk of political defeat, many declined to run against GOP freshmen, including some who were vulnerable to a strong challenge. Democratic unelected politicians filled the void in some of these districts; political amateurs did likewise in others.

FIGURE 2-3

House Primary Candidacies of Politicians by Party and Experience, 1978–2002

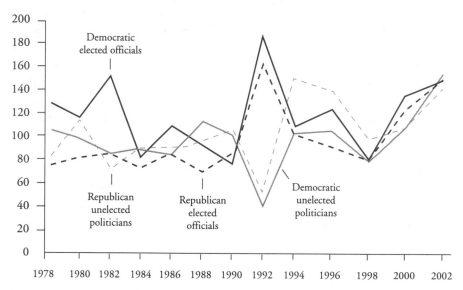

Sources: Compiled from various issues of *CQ Weekly*.

Note: Includes candidates for major-party nominations only.

Experienced politicians of both parties responded similarly to the political conditions present early in the 1998, 2000, and 2002 election cycles. Nearly identical numbers of elected officials from both parties ran for Congress. Similar numbers of unelected politicians from both parties also ran.

Typically, most of the best-qualified office seekers wait until a seat opens, through either the retirement or the death of the incumbent, before throwing their hats into the ring.[27] Once a seat becomes vacant, it acts like a magnet, drawing the attention and candidacies of many individuals. Usually several strategic politicians will express interest in an open seat. Open-seat races, defined as contests in which there is no incumbent at the beginning of the election season, accounted for roughly 10 percent of 2002 elections. Forty-seven percent of the Democratic elected officials who ran for the House in 2002, and 52 percent of their Republican counterparts, ran in open-seat races (see Table 2-1).

Incumbency discourages competition in primary elections, especially within the incumbent's party. Only 15 percent of the Democratic elected officials who ran for the House in 2002 were willing to challenge one of their party's

TABLE 2-1

Effect of Seat Status on Nonincumbent Candidates for House Nominations in 2002

	Democrats			Republicans		
	Elected officials	Unelected politicians	Political amateurs	Elected officials	Unelected politicians	Political amateurs
Open seat	47%	37%	23%	52%	26%	29%
Democratic incumbent seeking reelection	15	9	25	38	55	57
Republican incumbent seeking reelection	38	54	53	10	19	14
(*N*)	(146)	(155)	(204)	(147)	(141)	(280)

Sources: Compiled from various issues of CQ *Weekly.*

Note: Figures exclude incumbent versus-incumbent primaries. Some columns do not add to 100 percent because of rounding.

incumbents for the nomination. Their Republican counterparts were similarly gun-shy about attempting to commit political fratricide: only 10 percent were willing to challenge a GOP House member in the primary.

The candidacies of elected officials usually contrast with those of unelected politicians and amateur candidates. Unelected politicians and political amateurs are often more willing to run for a seat held by an incumbent than are elected officials. Compared with elected officials, these candidates have fewer political costs to weigh when considering whether to enter a congressional primary. Prospective candidates who do not hold an elective office do not have to give up a current office to run for Congress, as do most officeholders whose positions are coterminous with congressional elections.[28] They also do not have to be concerned about the effect a defeat could have on an established political career.

Others Involved in the Decision to Run

The drive to hold elective office may be rooted in an individual's personality and tempered by the larger political environment, but potential candidates rarely reach a decision about running for Congress without touching base with a variety of people.[29] Nearly all candidates single out their family and friends as being highly influential in their decision to enter a race.[30] More than one young, talented, experienced, and well-connected local politician who wanted a seat in Congress has remarked only half in jest that family members would probably shoot them if they decided to run. Family concerns, financial considerations, and career aspirations have kept many ambitious and highly regarded local politicians from running for Congress.

Political parties, labor unions, other organized groups, and political consultants also can affect a prospective candidate's decision, but they have much less impact than the people directly involved in an individual's daily life. Potential candidates usually discuss their plans with these groups only after mulling over the idea of running. Sometimes would-be candidates approach local party leaders; fellow party members in the House or the Senate; or officials from their party's state, national, congressional, or senatorial campaign committees to learn about the kinds of assistance that would be available should they decide to run. On other occasions the party initiates the contact, seeking to nurture the interest of good prospects.

Barred from simply handing out the nomination, party leaders can influence a prospective candidate's decision to run in a variety of ways. State and local party leaders can help size up the potential competition and try to discourage others from contesting the nomination.[31] In some states party leaders can help a candidate secure a preprimary endorsement, but this does not guarantee nomination.

Members of Congress and the staffs of the Democratic and Republican congressional and senatorial campaign committees often encourage prospective candidates to run. Armed with favorable polling figures and the promise of party assistance in the general election, they search out local talent. Party leaders crisscross the country looking to sound out the best possible candidates for competitive districts. Once they have identified these individuals, they take steps to entice them to run. Promising individuals are invited to meet with members of Congress and party leaders in Washington and to attend campaign seminars. They also are given lists of PACs and political consultants who possess some of the resources and skills needed to conduct a congressional campaign.[32] Sometimes presidents, vice presidents, cabinet officials, high-ranking White House aides, or individuals who have previously held those posts try to entice prospective candidates to enter the race.

When more than one candidate signs up to run for a nomination, the national parties usually remain neutral unless a primary challenger seriously threatens an incumbent. However, on rare occasions the parties' congressional and senatorial campaign committees will provide their preferred candidate with assistance in winning the primary and even go so far as to air issue advocacy ads in favor of one candidate, as the Democratic Congressional Campaign Committee (DCCC) did in 2002 for Ann Hutchinson, who won her party's primary in Iowa but was ultimately defeated by six-term Republican incumbent James Nussle.[33] In addition, incumbent members of Congress are free to support primary candidates of their choosing. Many do, including Hill committee chairs and members, viewing a pre-primary contribution as an opportunity to help elect a candidate who has a strong chance of winning or similar policy stances or who is likely to support their own advancement up the ranks of the congressional leadership.

Party recruitment is especially important and difficult when local or national forces favor the opposing party. Just as a strong economy or popular president can encourage members of the president's party to run, it can discourage members of the opposition party from declaring their candidacies, most notably when an incumbent of the opposing party is seeking to remain in the seat. Sometimes the promise of party support can encourage a wavering politician to run under what at the outset appear to be less than optimal conditions.

Recruiting candidates to run for traditionally uncompetitive seats is not a major priority, but party committees work to prevent those seats from going uncontested. According to staffers from both parties' congressional and senatorial campaign committees, getting candidates to run for these seats is an important part of building for the future. These candidacies can strengthen state and local party committees by giving them a campaign on which to focus and deepening the farm team from which candidates emerge. They also help prepare a party for opportunities that might arise when an incumbent retires, House districts are redrawn, or a scandal or some other event changes the partisan dynamics in the district. GOPAC, a political action committee headed by Newt Gingrich before he became Speaker of the House, played a major role in recruiting Republicans to run for office, including many who helped the GOP win its House majority in 1994.

Labor unions, PACs, and other organized groups typically play more limited roles in candidate recruitment, compared with parties. A few labor PACs and some trade association committees, such as the Committee on Political Education (COPE) of the American Federation of Labor–Congress of Industrial Organizations (AFL-CIO) and the American Medical Association's AMPAC, take polls to encourage experienced politicians to run.[34] Others, such as the National Federation of Independent Business's PAC, sponsor campaign training seminars to encourage individuals who support the group's position to run for the House. Some PACs, such as the pro-women EMILY's List,

WISH List, and Women's Campaign Fund, search out members of specific demographic groups and offer them financial and organizational support.[35] Labor unions focus most of their candidate-recruitment efforts, and campaign activities in general, on Democrats. Ideological PACs are among the most aggressive in searching out candidates, and many offer primary assistance to those who share their views. Few corporate PACs become involved in recruiting candidates because they fear offending incumbents.

Finally, political consultants can become involved in a potential candidate's decision making. In addition to taking polls and participating in candidate-training seminars, consultants can use their knowledge of a state or district to assist a would-be candidate in assessing political conditions and sizing up the potential competition. Politicians who have had long-term relationships with consultants usually seek their advice prior to running for Congress.

PASSING THE PRIMARY TEST

There are two ways to win a major-party nomination for Congress: in an uncontested nominating race or by defeating an opponent. It is not unusual for incumbents to receive their party's nomination without a challenge. Even in the 1992 elections, which were marked by a record number of nonincumbent candidacies, 52 percent of all representatives and 42 percent of all senators who sought reelection were awarded their party's nomination without having to defeat an opponent. In 2002 the numbers were even greater: 71 percent of all representatives and 69 percent of all senators seeking reelection faced no primary opponent.

Incumbent Victories in Uncontested Primaries

Victories by default occur mainly when an incumbent is perceived to be invulnerable. The same advantages of incumbency and preelection activities that make incumbents confident of reelection make them seem invincible to those contemplating a primary challenge. Good constituent relations, policy representation, and other job-related activities are sources of incumbent strength. A hefty campaign account is another.

The loyalties of political activists and organized groups also discourage party members from challenging their representatives for the nomination. While in office, members of Congress work to advance the interests of those who supported their previous election, and in return they routinely receive the support of these individuals and groups. With this support comes the promise of endorsements, campaign contributions, volunteer campaign workers, and votes. Would-be primary challengers often recognize that the groups whose support they would need to win the nomination are often among the incumbent's staunchest supporters.

Senior incumbents benefit from the clout—real and perceived—that comes with climbing the ranks of congressional leadership. Rep. Larry Combest, R-Texas, completed his ninth term in Congress in 2002 and is typical of most senior incumbents, who are routinely awarded their party's nomination without a fight. One of the major reasons that no one is willing to challenge Combest is that he is well-suited to Texas's 19th district. A fourth-generation farmer and staunch conservative, Combest shares the views of those in his rural, agricultural district. He opposes taxes and government regulation but does not let ideology keep him from advancing his district's interests, including fighting for federal price supports for his constituents' crops.[36]

Combest also enjoys widespread support because he excels at other aspects of his job: he maintains three district offices to provide constituent services, returns to the district on a regular basis, and votes in accordance with his constituents' views. As a long-time member of the Agriculture Committee, and its chairman in the 107th Congress, he wields tremendous influence over agriculture policy. Prospective GOP challengers, and the Republican activists whose support they would need to defeat Combest in a primary, recognize the district's interests would suffer should he leave Congress. Moreover, Combest is a prodigious fundraiser. Despite always having won with more than 60 percent of the vote since he was elected in 1984—he routinely polls better than 75 percent—and despite having run unopposed in two of his last four elections, Combest raised almost $572,000 for his 2002 election. His fundraising prowess helps to scare off primary opposition.[37]

Finally, Combest has the support of many interest groups and is covered like a hero in the local press. One western Texas paper, the *Andrews News,* wrote that "if we had about 50 more congressmen like Combest, we might eventually straighten out the mess in the Washington beltway." The support Combest has received from the press and local advocacy groups deprives would-be primary challengers of much of the organizational and financial support and media coverage needed to defeat him.[38] Not surprisingly, none of the Republican politicians who would normally be included on a list of Combest's rivals or potential successors has challenged him for the nomination.

Junior incumbents rarely have the same kind of clout in Washington or as broad a base of support as senior legislators, but because they tend to devote a great deal of time to expanding their bases of support they too typically discourage inside challenges.[39] Junior members also may receive special attention from national, state, and local party organizations. Both the DCCC and the National Republican Congressional Committee (NRCC) hold seminars immediately after each election to instruct junior members on how to use franked mail, town meetings, and the local press to build voter support. Prior to the start of the campaign season these party committees advise junior members on how to defend their congressional roll-call votes, raise money, and discourage opposition.[40]

State party leaders also give junior members of Congress advice and assistance. Before the 2002 elections, two-term representative Douglas Ose received what is perhaps the most important form of help state party leaders can bestow on a candidate: a supportive district. Republicans in California's capital redrew the state's congressional map with an eye toward improving Ose's reelection prospects. They added heavily Republican areas to the Sacramento-area district, which had been previously occupied by a Democrat, and let it be known that they considered this Ose's seat.[41] As a result, Ose faced little primary opposition. In most similar situations, incumbents face none.

Considerations of teamwork rarely protect House members who are vulnerable because of scandal. These incumbents face stronger challenges from within their own party than do others. Experienced politicians often are willing to take on an incumbent who is toiling under the cloud of scandal.

Contested Primaries with an Incumbent

When incumbents do face challenges for their party's nomination, they almost always win. Of the 115 House members who were challenged for their party's nomination in 2002, only 8 lost: 5 lost to other incumbents who shared their districts as a result of redistricting; and three—Gary Condit, D-Calif., Earl Hilliard, D-Ala., and Cynthia McKinney, D-Ga.—were defeated as a result of their implication in political scandals. With the exception of House members who are forced to run against each other, typically only those members of Congress who have allegedly committed an ethical transgression, lost touch with their district, or suffer from failing health run a significant risk of falling to a primary challenger.

What kinds of challengers succeed in knocking off an incumbent for the nomination? The answer is, candidates who have had significant political experience. Only 22 percent of the 2002 challengers who sought to defeat an incumbent in a primary had been elected to lower level office and 25 percent had other significant forms of political experience.[42] Yet, these elected officials and unelected politicians accounted for all of the primary challengers who wrested a party nomination away from an incumbent that year (see Table 2-2). Experienced candidates typically succeed where others fail because they are

TABLE 2-2

Political Experience and Major-Party Nominations for the House in 2002

	Primary challenges to an incumbent		Primary contests to challenge an incumbent		Primary contests for an open seat	
	Demo-crats	Repub-licans	Demo-crats	Repub-licans	Demo-crats	Repub-licans
Level of experience						
Elected officials	26%	18%	22%	19%	40%	40%
Unelected politicians	16	34	34	26	33	19
Political amateurs	58	48	43	55	27	42
(*N*)	(86)	(79)	(247)	(295)	(172)	(194)
Primary winners						
Elected officials	75%	0%	17%	20%	62%	68%
Unelected politicians	25	0	35	26	25	16
Political amateurs	0	0	48	54	13	16
(*N*)	(4)	(0)	(151)	(155)	(47)	(45)
Primary success rates						
Elected officials	14%	0%	80%	85%	42%	40%
Unelected politicians	7	0	56	42	21	19
Political amateurs	0	0	46	43	13	9

Sources: Compiled from various issues of *CQ Weekly.*

Notes: Figures are for nonincumbents only. Some columns do not add to 100 percent because of rounding.

able to take advantage of previous contacts to gain the support of the political and financial elites who contribute to or volunteer in political campaigns. Elected officials can make the case that they have represented some of the voters in the district and know what it takes to get elected. Some of these candidates consciously use a lower-level office as a steppingstone to Congress.[43]

Dennis Cardoza's victory over Rep. Gary Condit in California's 18th district Democratic primary is typical of a nomination contest in which a challenger knocks off an incumbent. Condit, who had served in Congress for six full terms, and had been on the House Agriculture and Select Intelligence Committees, would have enjoyed an easy reelection in 2002 had it not been for the Chandra Levy scandal. One of the founders of the moderate Blue Dog Democratic Coalition, the congressman had learned to use the relatively conservative views of his constituents as a vehicle to increase his influence in the House, while at the same time using his growing clout to tend to his district's needs.

Condit's hold over the district, often referred to as "Condit Country" by the congressman's supporters and the local media, should have been strengthened by California's redistricting plan, which increased the ratio of Democratic to Republican voters.

However, the congressman's ties to the missing intern rocked his constituents and the Washington establishment. The media camped out at his Washington and district congressional offices, his campaign headquarters, and his Washington, D.C., and California residences, hounding Condit to try to learn more about his affair with Levy. Journalists' focus on Condit's relationship with Levy badly tarnished the congressman's image and prevented him from focusing the election on policy issues or the services he had provided to constituents. His hold on the "old 18th district" was weakened, and it became almost impossible for him to win the support of the Democratic voters added to it. After the scandal broke, five Democrats declared their candidacies for the seat: Cardoza, a member of the California Assembly, and onetime Condit protégé and friend; Ralph White, a former member of the Stockton City Council; college professor Sukhmander Singh; gas station manager Joseph Martin; and businessman Elvis Pringle.[44]

The primary campaign was largely a two-person race between Condit and Cardoza. Although the candidates sought to focus on the issues, the campaign began and ended largely as a referendum on the incumbent. Neither Cardoza nor the other candidates needed to attack Condit for his behavior following Levy's disappearance. The media did that for them, leaving Condit unable to overcome the misgivings of Democratic primary voters. He lost to Cardoza by a margin of 38 percent to 55 percent, with the remaining four candidates dividing the balance of the votes. That the most politically experienced opponent led the pack is typical in circumstances when an incumbent loses to a primary challenger.

An editorial from the *Modesto Bee,* titled "Condit to Blame for His Political Self-Destruction," provides a fitting epilogue to the campaign:

> Voters in the 18th Congressional District buried him with a solid vote of no
> confidence for irrevocably violating the public trust. His behavior after the
> April disappearance of Chandra Levy, with whom he was having an affair, put
> his own interests ahead of the effort to find her. She remains missing. His self-
> absorption was a lapse not only of judgment, but of human decency. . . . His
> political self-destruction was sad to watch.[45]

Condit was the first congressman in the history of California's Central Valley to lose a congressional primary.[46]

Open Primaries

In opposing-incumbent primaries, contestants seek the nomination of one party when an incumbent of the opposing party has decided to seek reelection. Another type of open nomination, called an open-seat primary, occurs in districts in which no incumbent is seeking reelection. Both types of primaries attract more candidates than do contests in which a nonincumbent must defeat an incumbent to win the nomination, but opposing-incumbent primaries are usually the less hotly contested of the two.

In opposing-incumbent primaries, political experience is usually a determining factor. Elected officials do well in such primaries. In 2002, elected officials made up about one-fifth of all of the candidates and one-fifth of the winners in these races. Democratic elected officials enjoyed a nomination rate of 80 percent, and their Republican counterparts had a success rate of 85 percent. Because more unelected politicians of both parties ran in opposing-incumbent primaries in 2002, it is not surprising that they won more nominations than did primary candidates with office-holding experience. Political amateurs typically outnumber politically experienced candidates, and as a consequence they win more primaries. The 2002 contests were no exception. Nevertheless, their success rates were substantially lower than those of more experienced primary contestants.

Open-seat primaries are the most competitive of all nominating contests. They typically attract many highly qualified candidates, often pitting one elected official against another. Relatively large numbers of candidates with office-holding experience ran for open seats in 2002. Elected officials of both parties made up most of the primary winners and had the highest primary success rates. Unelected politicians also did well, achieving higher success rates than did political amateurs.

The Democratic and Republican primaries in Colorado's 7th congressional district, like most open-seat primaries, were hard-fought contests that featured many qualified candidates. The origins of the race can be traced to Colorado receiving an additional House seat as a result of reapportionment. Where to place the seat became a matter of controversy, reflecting differences between the Republican-dominated state legislature and then-governor Democrat Dick Lamm. After finding its way into the courts, the Democratic redistricting plan prevailed. The new district lies largely in the suburbs surrounding Denver but also includes some urban and rural elements. It has 115,000 registered voters of each major party, and President Bush won it with 49 percent of the vote in 2000.[47] National and state leaders of both parties considered the seat highly competitive. Leaders of each party made efforts to get their top candidate to run.

The Republicans drew some of the most qualified politicians in the district: Robert Beauprez, a former Republican state party chair, farmer, and president and CEO of Heritage Bank; Joe Rogers, Colorado's lieutenant governor; Rick O'Donnell, a former director of the Governor's Office of Policy and Initiatives; and Sam Zakhem, a former state senator, state representative, and U.S. ambassador to Bahrain in Ronald Reagan's and George H. W. Bush's administrations. State treasurer Michael Coffman and Internet entrepreneur Mark Baisley undertook bids for the seat initially but withdrew early in the campaign season.

Beauprez was identified quickly by national Republican Party leaders as their most formidable candidate, partly because he had the wherewithal to finance a significant portion of his own campaign. NRCC chair Tom Davis, R-Va., took the unusual step of traveling to Colorado to tell Beauprez that he had Davis's and the committee's backing. Senior presidential advisor Karl Rove and White House political aide Ken Mehlman followed up Davis's visit with phone calls to underscore President Bush's support.[48] The encouragement of national leaders had a number of important effects. They helped convince the candidate to run—a decision complicated by the fact that Beauprez had to move into the district, which was five miles south of his home. They also gave Beauprez tremendous fundraising advantages and helped him attract press coverage.

Nevertheless, Rogers, the highest ranking Republican in the contest, also brought significant assets to the race. Having run for Congress in 1996, losing to Democratic representative Diana DeGette by a margin of 40 percent to 57 percent, he had a high level of name recognition and the ability to raise substantial funds. The fact that he is African American is believed to have given him an advantage in drawing minority votes. Nevertheless, Rogers had some liabilities. Like Beauprez, he had to relocate in order to reside in the district. His public feuding with Republican governor Bill Owens might have cost him support among some Republican primary voters. Voters also might have felt that it was disingenuous of Rogers to feature the pictures of Owens, President Bush, and Secretary of State Colin Powell in his advertising because none of these politicians had actually endorsed him.[49]

The candidates devoted considerable effort to fundraising. Beauprez led the pack, collecting more than $667,000, including $350,000 he loaned the campaign. Rogers came in second, raising nearly $360,000, almost all of it from individuals. O'Donnell collected $158,000, followed by Zakhem, who pulled together a mere $87,000.

The contest was marked by little policy disagreement among the candidates. Most are conservative on social and fiscal questions. Beauprez stated that his "highest priority in Congress will be to strengthen and expand opportunities for all Americans to take part in the American Dream. That means improving education, creating jobs, lowering taxes, and protecting Medicare and Social Security."[50] O'Donnell's platform involved reducing federal mandates and regulations, tax relief, transportation, and educational reform.[51] Rogers took similarly conservative positions on the issues.

Early in the race, O'Donnell received a significant strategic advantage by winning more support in the district's assembly caucus than did Beauprez.[52] O'Donnell's twenty-one-vote caucus victory over Beauprez gave him the advantage of occupying the first line on the August 13 primary ballot.[53] Zakhem and Rogers opted not to participate in the caucus, qualifying for the primary by instead collecting the requisite 1,000 signatures. Nevertheless, strong campaigning by Beauprez enabled him to overcome O'Donnell's ballot placement advantage and win the primary with 38 percent to O'Donnell's 31 percent; Zakhem and Rogers won 18 percent and 13 percent of the votes, respectively.

The Democratic primary drew fewer candidates than did the GOP contest. Although several prominent politicians considered running, including state senator Ed Perlmutter, for whom the district was supposedly drawn, only three ultimately declared their candidacies.[54] Michael Feeley, a former marine and Colorado state Senate minority leader who was term limited in 2000, was recruited the most heavily. He received a telephone call from House minority leader Richard Gephardt, D-Mo., and was contacted by several labor unions.[55] David Thomas, Jefferson County district attorney and a former executive director of the Colorado Department of Public Safety, also joined the race, as did former Colorado statehouse member and political science professor Robert Hagedorn, who, like Feeley, was term limited in 2000. Hagedorn, however, dropped out of the contest before the primary because he failed to collect enough legal signatures to have his name placed on the ballot.[56]

Unlike Hagedorn, Feeley succeeded in collecting enough signatures to qualify for the primary. Thomas won his first-line position on the ballot by being the sole competitor in the Democratic caucus.[57] Although Thomas enjoyed the ballot advantage, Feeley had an edge financially. He used the more than $376,000 he raised (including $80,000 he loaned the campaign) to focus on issues he had worked on in the past, including "women's health and safety, increasing opportunities for children, building strong relationships between the business and environmental communities and 'standing up for Colorado working families.'"[58] Thomas raised almost $180,000, including $41,000 that he invested in his own race. His campaign focused on reducing violent crime and domestic violence, advocating environmental protection, and improving public education.[59] Ultimately, Feeley defeated Thomas by a margin of 56 percent to 44 percent of the vote.

NOMINATIONS, ELECTIONS, AND REPRESENTATION

The electoral process—which transforms private citizen to candidate to major-party nominee to House member—greatly influences the makeup of the national legislature. Those parts of the process leading up to the general election, especially the decision to run, play an important role in producing a Congress that is not demographically representative of the U.S. population. The willingness of women and minorities to run for Congress during the past few decades and of voters to support them has helped make the national legislature somewhat more representative in regard to gender and race. Still, in many respects Congress does not mirror U.S. society.

Occupation

Occupation has a tremendous effect on the pool of House candidates and on their prospects for success. Individuals who claim law, politics, or public service (many of whom have legal training) as their profession are a minuscule portion of the general population but make up 41 percent of all nomination candidates, 48 percent of all successful primary candidates, and 58 percent of all House members (see Table 2-3). The analytical, verbal, and organizational skills required to succeed in the legal profession or in public service help these individuals undertake a successful bid for Congress.[60] The high salaries that members of these professions earn give them the wherewithal to take a leave of absence from work so that they can campaign full time. These highly paid professionals also can afford to make the initial investment needed to get a campaign off the ground. Moreover, their professions place many attorneys and public servants in a position to rub elbows with political activists and contributors whose support can be crucial to winning a House primary or general election.

Business professionals and bankers are not as overrepresented among nomination candidates, major-party nominees, or House members as are public servants and lawyers, but persons in business tend to be successful in congressional elections. Many possess money, skills, and contacts that are useful in politics. Educators (particularly college professors) and other white-collar professionals also enjoy a modicum of success in congressional elections. Of these, educators are the most successful group of candidates. They rarely possess the wealth of lawyers and business professionals, but educators frequently have the verbal, analytical, and organizational skills needed to get elected.

Just as some professions are overrepresented in Congress, others are underrepresented. Disproportionately few persons employed in agriculture or blue-collar professions either run for Congress or are elected. Even fewer students,

TABLE 2-3

Occupational Representativeness of 2002 House Candidates and Members of the 108th Congress

Occupation	General population	Nomination candidates	General election candidates	House members
Agricultural or blue-collar workers	30%	6%	4%	3%
Business or banking	4	22	22	20
Clergy or social work	1	1	1	—
Education	4	8	10	11
Entertainer, actor, writer, or artist	1	1	1	1
Law	1	18	23	27
Medicine	3	3	4	3
Military or veteran	—	1	1	—
Politics or public service	3	23	25	31
Other white-collar professionals	20	9	7	3
Outside work force	33	3	2	—
Unidentified, not politics	—	6	—	—
(*N*)	(281,400,000)	(1,472)	(776)	(435)

Sources: General population figures are from U.S. Department of Commerce, Bureau of the Census, *Statistical Abstract of the United States* (Washington, D.C.: U.S. Government Printing Office, 2001), 380–384; candidate occupation data are from various issues of *CQ Weekly.*

Notes: Figures include all 2002 major-party House candidates and all members of the 108th Congress, including Rep. Bernard Sanders, I-Vt. The figures for the general population are from 2001. Dashes = less than 0.5 percent. Some columns do not add to 100 percent because of rounding.

homemakers, and others who are considered outside the work force attempt to win a congressional seat.

Closely related to the issue of occupation is wealth. Personal wealth is a significant advantage in an election system that places a premium on a candidate's ability to spend money. Roughly 7 percent of House members have assets worth $3.1 million or more, a far greater proportion than the less than one-half of 1 percent of the general population who enjoy similar wealth.[61]

Gender

A record fifty-nine women were elected to the House in 2002, just a fraction— less than one-sixth—of the number of men.[62] The major reason for the underrepresentation of women in the legislative branch is that fewer women than men run for Congress (see Figure 2-4). Only 14 percent of all contestants for major-party nominations in 2002 were female. Women are underrepresented among congressional candidates for many reasons. Active campaigning demands greater time and flexibility than most people, particularly women, can afford. Women continue to assume primary parenting responsibilities in most families, a role that is difficult to combine with long hours of campaigning. Only since the 1980s have significant numbers of women entered the legal and business professions, which often serve as training grounds for elected officials and political activists. Women also continue to be underrepresented in state legislatures and other elective offices, which commonly serve as steppingstones to Congress.[63]

FIGURE 2-4

Gender Representativeness of 2002 House Candidates and Members of the 108th Congress

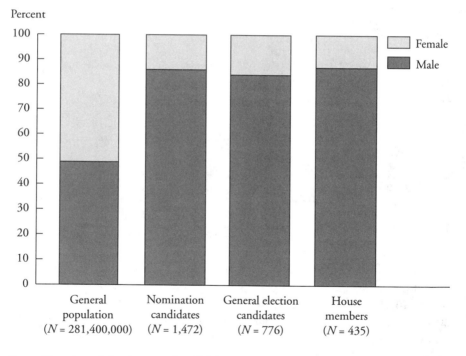

Sources: General population figures are from U.S. Department of Commerce, Bureau of the Census, *Statistical Abstract of the United States* (Washington, D.C.: U.S. Government Printing Office, 2001), 13; candidate gender data are from various issues of *CQ Weekly*.

Notes: Figures include all 2002 major-party House candidates and all members of the 108th Congress, including Rep. Bernard Sanders, I-Vt. The figures for the general population are from 2001.

Once women decide to run, gender does not affect their election prospects.[64] Women are just about as likely as men to advance from primary candidate to nominee to House member.[65] As more women come to occupy lower-level offices or to hold positions in the professions from which congressional candidates usually emerge, the proportion of women candidates and members of Congress can be expected to increase.

Age

Congressional candidates also are somewhat older than the general population, and this is due only partly to the age requirements imposed by the Constitution. The average candidate for nomination is more than three-and-a-half times as likely to be forty to fifty-four years of age as twenty-five to thirty-nine (see Figure 2-5). Moreover, successful nomination candidates tend to be older than those whom they defeat. The selection bias in favor of those who are forty to seventy-four continues into the general election; as a result, Congress is made up largely of persons who are middle-aged or older.

The underrepresentation of young people is due to an electoral process that allows older individuals to benefit from their greater life experiences. People who have reached middle age typically have greater financial resources, more political experience, and a wider network of political and professional associates to help them with their campaigns. Moreover, a formidable group of people who are forty to seventy-four years old—current representatives—also benefit from considerable incumbency advantages.

Religion

Religion has an impact on candidate emergence, sometimes providing politicians with a policy concern, such as abortion or human rights, that gives them the motivation to run. Jews and mainline Protestants are overrepresented in the candidate pool (see Figure 2-6). Evangelical Christians, those belonging to other religions, and individuals who profess to have no religious affiliation are underrepresented. Yet, once individuals enter the pool, religion has little effect on how they do.

Individuals who claim no religious identification comprise the most underrepresented "belief" group in Congress for a few reasons. People who do not participate in church activities typically have fewer political and civic skills compared with those who do, which may discourage them from running for Congress.[66] Atheists and agnostics also may believe that it would be impossible for them to get elected given the large role that organized religion plays in

FIGURE 2-5

Age Representativeness of 2002 House Candidates and Members of the 108th Congress

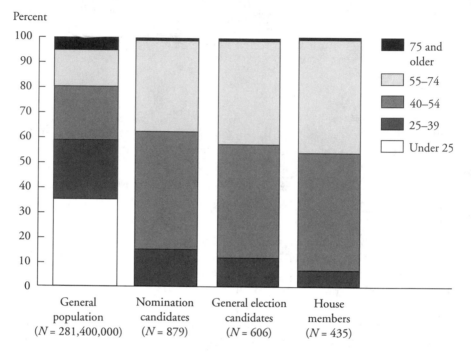

Percent

Sources: General population figures are from U.S. Department of Commerce, Bureau of the Census, *Statistical Abstract of the United States* (Washington, D.C.: U.S. Government Printing Office, 2001), 14; candidate age data are from various issues of *CQ Weekly*.

Notes: Figures include all 2002 major-party House candidates and all members of the 108th Congress, including Rep. Bernard Sanders, I-Vt. The figures for the general population are from 2001.

politics in many parts of the country. As a result, they have little presence in politics or national government.

Race and Ethnicity

Race and ethnicity, like religion and gender, have a greater effect on candidate emergence than on electoral success.[67] Whites are heavily overrepresented in the pool of nomination candidates, whereas persons of other races are underrepresented (see Figure 2-7). This situation reflects the disproportionately small numbers of minorities who have entered the legal or business professions or who occupy state or local offices.

FIGURE 2-6

Religious Representativeness of 2002 House Candidates and Members of the 108th Congress

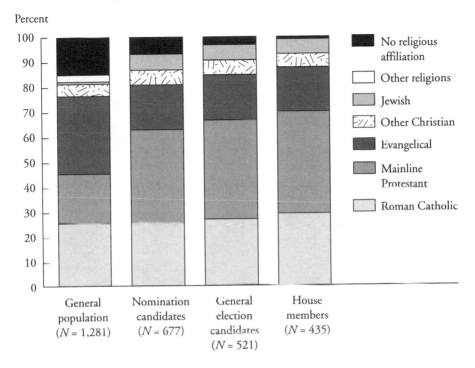

Sources: Compiled from Barry A. Kosmin and Egon Mayer, *American Religions Identification Survey.* Graduate Center, City University of New York, November 2002; candidate religion data are from various issues of *CQ Weekly.*

Notes: Figures include all 2002 major-party House candidates and all members of the 108th Congress, including Rep. Bernard Sanders, I-Vt.

Once minority politicians declare their candidacies, they have fairly good odds of winning. The recent successes of minority House candidates are largely due to redistricting processes intended to promote minority representation.[68] A few House members, such as J. C. Watts, an African American elected in 1994, won seats that were not specifically carved to promote minority representation in Congress. Still, most minority candidates are elected in districts that have large numbers of voters belonging to their racial or ethnic group, and once they win these seats they tend to hold onto them. Only two such incumbents were defeated in 2002, Hilliard and McKinney, and they lost primaries to candidates of their same race. The success of the minority members

FIGURE 2-7

Racial and Ethnic Representativeness of 2002 House Candidates and Members of the 108th Congress

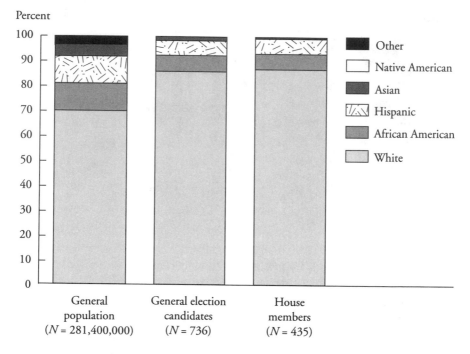

Sources: General population figures are from U.S. Department of Commerce, Bureau of the Census, *Statistical Abstract of the United States* (Washington, D.C.: U.S. Government Printing Office, 2001), 19; candidate race data are from various issues of *CQ Weekly*.

Notes: Figures include all 2002 major-party House candidates and all members of the 108th Congress, including Rep. Bernard Sanders, I-Vt. The figures for the general population are from 2001.

of Congress can be attributed to their ability to build multiracial coalitions and the advantages that incumbency confers on them.[69]

Party Differences

Public servants and members of the legal profession comprise a large portion of each party's candidate pool, but more Republican candidates come from the business world and more Democratic candidates are lawyers and public servants (see Table 2-4). The GOP's overrepresentation of business professionals continues through each stage of the election and in the House, as does the Democrats' overrepresentation of lawyers and career politicians. Attorneys and career public servants from both parties do well in elections, but they are more strongly represented in the Democratic than the Republican Party. Business executives, in contrast, have a bigger presence in the ranks of Republican legislators. Even though Republicans have historically been viewed as the defenders of the rich, members of both parties are found among Congress's wealthiest legislators.[70]

More women run for Democratic than Republican nominations for Congress. This gender gap reflects the greater number of women who identify with the Democratic Party and that party's greater acceptance of female candidates. Democratic women also are more successful in winning the nomination and getting elected to the House than are their GOP counterparts.[71]

Democratic primary candidates tend to be somewhat older than their Republican counterparts, reflecting the different orientations of the individuals in the parties' candidate pools. Democratic primary candidates are more likely to come from the ranks of politicians and to consider a congressional election as a somewhat risky opportunity to take a step up the career ladder. Members of the Republican candidate pool are more apt to have careers in the private sector. Many run for Congress before they have taken major strides in their profession, recognizing that if they wait too long they may have advanced too far professionally to want to sacrifice their career in order to run.[72] The initial age difference between Democratic and Republican candidates lays the foundation for an uneven trend toward a middle-aged Congress. The age difference between the parties gets smaller as the candidates progress through the primaries and the general election.

The parties also draw candidates from different religious, racial, and ethnic groups. Republican primary contestants are mainly Protestant and white, as are the GOP's nominees and House members. The Democratic Party attracts candidates from a wider array of groups, including significant numbers of Catholics, Jews, and African Americans. These patterns reflect the parties' electoral coalitions.

THE SENATE

The Senate historically has been less demographically representative than the House. The election of more women and minorities over the past few decades has resulted in a slow move toward more accurately mirroring the U.S. population. However, descriptions of the Senate as a bastion for white, wealthy, middle-aged, professional men are very close to the mark.

Part of the reason that the Senate has been slower to change than the House is that Senate terms are six years, and only one-third of the upper chamber is

TABLE 2-4

2002 Major-Party Nomination and General Election Candidates and House Members of the 108th Congress

	Nomination candidates		General election candidates		House members	
	Demo-crats	Repub-licans	Demo-crats	Repub-licans	Demo-crats	Repub-licans
Occupation						
Agricultural or blue-collar workers	6%	6%	3%	6%	2%	4%
Business or banking	16	27	16	28	12	27
Clergy or social work	1	1	1	1	1	—
Education	10	6	12	7	13	8
Entertainer, actor, writer, or artist	1	2	1	2	1	2
Law	24	13	29	18	33	21
Medicine	3	3	3	4	3	4
Military or veteran	1	1	1	1	—	—
Politics or public service	25	22	26	23	32	30
Other white-collar professionals	7	10	6	8	3	3
Outside work force	3	4	1	2	—	—
Unidentified, not politics	5	6	1	2	1	—
(*N*)	(703)	(769)	(383)	(393)	(205)	(230)
Gender						
Male	82%	89%	80%	88%	81%	91%
Female	18	11	20	12	19	9
(*N*)	(703)	(769)	(383)	(383)	(205)	(230)
Age						
25–39	12%	13%	12%	9%	7%	7%
40–54	46	49	44	47	42	51
55–74	40	37	42	41	48	40
75 and older	2	2	2	2	2	2
(*N*)	(444)	(435)	(306)	(300)	(205)	(230)

(Table continues)

TABLE 2-4
(continued)

	Nomination candidates		General election candidates		House members	
	Demo-crats	Repub-licans	Demo-crats	Repub-licans	Demo-crats	Repub-licans
Religion						
Roman Catholic	32%	22%	32%	22%	34%	21%
Mainline Protestant	29	45	29	50	28	53
Evangelical	17	21	17	19	18	19
Jewish	10	1	11	1	12	—
Other Christian	4	6	5	6	4	7
No religious affiliation	8	5	6	2	4	—
(N)	(324)	(353)	(249)	(272)	(205)	(230)
Race and Ethnicity						
White	80%	91%	79%	93%	72%	98%
African American	11	3	12	2	18	—
Hispanic	7	5	8	4	8	2
Other	2	1	2	1	2	—
(N)	(593)	(653)	(362)	(376)	(205)	(230)

Sources: Compiled from various issues of *CQ Weekly*.

Notes: Figures are for all major-party nomination candidates, all major-party general election candidates, and all major-party members of the 108th Congress (which excludes Rep. Bernard Sanders, I-Vt.). Dashes = less than 0.5 percent. Some columns do not add to 100 percent because of rounding. Candidates under twenty-five years of age and those affiliated with "other" religions are omitted from the table because none ran in 2002.

up for election at a time. Other reasons have to do with the heightened demands of Senate campaigns. As statewide races, Senate primary and general election campaigns require larger amounts of money, more extensive organizations, and more complex strategies than do House campaigns. Successful Senate candidates generally possess more skill, political connections, and campaign experience than do their House counterparts. The fact that so many members of the Senate had extensive political experience prior to their election suggests that the dearth of women and minorities in lower-level offices may help to explain why the upper chamber is changing more slowly than the lower. To gain seats in the Senate, members of traditionally underrepresented groups have had first to place citizens in positions that serve as steppingstones to that body. As more women, African Americans, and members of other underrepresented groups are elected or appointed to local, state, and federal offices, their numbers in the Senate will probably increase.

Nevertheless, a single election can have a great effect on the Senate's makeup. After the polls closed in 1992, four more women had secured seats in the upper chamber, including the Senate's first African American woman, Illinois Democrat Carol Moseley-Braun. In addition, the Senate prepared to swear in its first Native American, Coloradan Ben Nighthorse Campbell, who was first elected as a Democrat but later switched parties to become a Republican. Few ensuing elections had as big an impact on the demographic makeup of the Senate as that of 1992. The 1994 election added one more woman to the upper chamber; and two more were elected in 1996. The 1998 election represented a step backward in terms of racial diversity as a result of the loss of Moseley-Braun, the Senate's only African American. The next election added four more women, for a total of thirteen. The 2002 contest was a wash in terms of gender and race.

Even though traditionally underrepresented groups have increased their numbers in the Senate, this does not mean that the upper chamber has become a place of employment for individuals with a diverse array of backgrounds. Forty-four senators in the 108th Congress were drawn from the legal profession. Another thirteen came from the business and banking communities, nine from education, and thirteen from public service. An additional four had been journalists, and six had worked in agriculture. The remainder had held positions ranging from surgeon to social worker.[73] More than seventy were aged fifty-five years or older when the 108th Congress was sworn in.

Most senators had significant political experience prior to getting elected, often having held more than one office. Forty-nine of the senators in the 108th Congress had previously served in the U.S. House of Representatives, nine had been governors of their states, fourteen had held some other statewide office, seven had been state legislators, eleven had held a local office, and three came to the Senate after one or more political appointments.[74] Seven senators, including Senate majority leader Bill Frist, R-Tenn.; Robert Bennett, R-Utah; John Edwards, D-N.C.; Orrin Hatch, R-Utah; and Frank Lautenberg, D-N.J., were first elected to the Senate without having previously held elective office or some other significant political position. Of course, another senator who was elected without having been elected or appointed to a significant political post—Hillary Rodham Clinton, D-N.Y.—hardly qualifies as a political amateur.

Although senators are more likely than representatives to have to defend their nominations, Senate primaries tend to be less competitive than those for the House. Between 1982 and 2002, Alan Dixon, Sheila Frahm, and Robert

Smith were the only senators defeated in their bids for renomination. The relative ease with which members of the Senate retain their party's nomination can be attributed to a number of factors besides the tremendous demands that Senate primary contests make on challengers. For one thing, senators and Senate candidates are highly strategic. Like their counterparts in the House, members of the Senate use their office to help their state receive its share of federal projects, to garner positive coverage in the press, and to build support among voters. Senators, like representatives, also build huge campaign treasuries to discourage potential opponents. In addition, most members of the Senate are shrewd enough to recognize when it is time to step down, as demonstrated by Robert Torricelli, who originally sought reelection in 2002 but later abandoned his race after a major scandal had driven his standing in the polls so low that he chose to quit rather than face certain defeat. In 2002 four additional senators opted for voluntary retirement from politics: Strom Thurmond, R.-S.C., and Jesse Helms, R-N.C., left because of infirmities associated with old age and illness; Fred Thompson, R-Tenn., and Phil Gramm, R-Texas, retired in order to pursue more lucrative careers in acting and investment banking, respectively. Former Republican senator Frank Murkowski's decision to leave the upper chamber to wage a successful campaign for Alaska's governorship demonstrates that these politicians also are astute enough to recognize other political opportunities.

The effect of scandal, aging, infirmity, declining public support, and strategic ambition on Senate turnover tends to be felt more through retirements than primary defeats. Moreover, the most qualified opponent a senator is likely to face in a primary is a current House member or some other elected official. Because these individuals are also highly strategic, only a few are willing to risk their current positions by picking a primary fight. Most prefer to wait until a seat becomes open.

When an incumbent does announce his or her retirement, or a member of the opposite party appears vulnerable, political parties and interest groups help to shape the field of Senate candidates by encouraging potential candidates to declare their candidacies. These organizations promise the same types of support, under the same kinds of circumstances, to potential Senate candidates as they offer to House candidates. The National Republican Senatorial Committee, for example, played a major role in encouraging Rep. John Thune, R-S.D., to give up his at-large House seat in order to challenge Democratic senator Tim Johnson. The committee promised Thune that, in addition to campaign contributions and coordinated expenditures, it would provide extensive fundraising and communications assistance, including conducting an issue advocacy campaign on his behalf. President Bush personally weighed in to encourage Thune to run, recognizing that a Thune victory in South Dakota could be the key to winning GOP control of the Senate.[75] It is not surprising that Thune decided to run, given the large amount of support he was promised and that he won 73 percent of the vote in his last election from the same constituency to which he would be appealing in the Senate race.

Party organizations rarely become involved in contested Senate primaries even though they may promise a candidate from hundreds of thousands to millions of dollars in campaign support upon winning the nomination. The parties' senatorial campaign committees are singled out by candidates as the most influential organizations in the candidate-recruitment process. Nevertheless, the decision to run for the Senate, like the decision to run for the House, is a personal one. Family and friends, issues, and a desire to improve government or become a national leader are more influential in the decisions of candidates to run for the Senate than are political organizations.[76]

SUMMARY

Virtually anyone can run for Congress because there are few legal requirements for serving, and neither party committees nor interest groups have the power to simply hand out a congressional nomination. Strategic politicians, mainly individuals who have held office or have some other significant unelective experience, carefully assess political conditions before deciding to run. Most incumbents—who are the most strategic of all politicians—choose to run again, but personal considerations, a loss of political clout in Congress, redistricting, scandal, or a wave of voter hostility toward the federal government or their party can encourage incumbents to retire. These factors also have an impact on the candidacy decisions of strategic nonincumbents, but the opening of a congressional seat is even more important than other political conditions in spurring on their candidacies. Amateur politicians tend to be less discriminating and are considerably less likely to win their party's nomination.

Candidate emergence, nomination, and election processes have a major impact on who serves in Congress. Most members of the contemporary House and Senate are white, middle- or upper-class males. Most are middle-aged or older and belong to a mainstream religion. The vast majority also have had significant political experience prior to getting elected. The number of national legislators who belong to underrepresented groups has increased in recent years, but change comes slowly to Congress, especially in the Senate.

CHAPTER THREE

The Anatomy of a Campaign

Most House and Senate candidates relied on state and local party committees to wage their campaigns during the parties' golden age. An individual candidate's "organization" was often little more than a loyal following within the party. By the mid-1950s, few congressional candidates could count on party organizations to obtain their nominations and wage their campaigns. Senate campaigns became significantly more professional during the 1950s and 1960s; House campaigns followed suit during the 1970s.[1] The decline of the political machine and the legal and systemic changes that fostered it led to the development of the modern campaign organization.[2]

Most contemporary congressional campaigns are waged by highly specialized, professional organizations. Few campaign organizations are fully self-sufficient. Most campaigns employ paid staff and volunteers to carry out some of the tasks associated with running for Congress and hire political consultants to perform specialized campaign activities such as taking polls and producing campaign ads. But consultants do more than carry out isolated campaign tasks. Political consulting has become highly professional, replete with its own standards, professional associations, and trade magazines. Consultants help budding politicians learn what to expect and what will be expected of them during the campaign. Consultants' opinions of what is strategically and tactically advisable and ethical have a major impact on candidate conduct.[3] In this chapter I describe campaign organizations, focusing on the political consultants and other personnel who work in them and on how campaigns spend their money.

CAMPAIGN ORGANIZATIONS

Candidates need to achieve several interrelated objectives to compete successfully in an election, including raising money, formulating a strategy, and communicating with and mobilizing voters. Specialized skills and training are required to meet many of these objectives. Senate campaigns, which are larger and must typically reach out to more voters, employ more paid staff and consultants than do their House counterparts.

The biggest factor in House campaigns is incumbency. Assembling a campaign organization is an easy task for incumbents. Most merely reassemble the personnel who worked on their previous campaign. A substantial number of incumbents keep elements of their organizations intact between elections. Some of these organizations consist only of a part-time political aide or fundraiser. Others are quite substantial, possessing the characteristics of a permanent business. They own a building and have a large professional staff; a fundraising apparatus; an investment portfolio; a campaign car; an entertainment budget; and a team of lawyers, accountants, and consultants on retainer. House incumbents typically spend more than $200,000 on organizational maintenance during the two years leading up to an election.[4] Some congressional leaders put together "Cadillac" campaigns. In 2002, House minority leader Richard Gephardt, D-Mo., spent more than $1.1 million on staff, rent, office equipment, supplies, and other resources used solely for organizational maintenance.[5]

Few House challengers or open-seat candidates possess even a temporary organization capable of contesting a congressional election until just before their declaration of candidacy. Nonincumbents who have held an elective post usually have advantages in assembling a campaign organization over those who have not. Some have steering committees, "Friends of 'Candidate X' " clubs, or working relationships with political consultants from previous campaigns. Candidates who have never held an elective office but have been active in politics usually have advantages over political amateurs in building an organization. Previous political involvement gives party committee chairs, political aides, and individuals who have previously run for office some knowledge of how to wage a campaign and ties to others who can help them. The organizational advantages that incumbents possess over challengers are usually greater than the advantages that experienced nonincumbents have over political amateurs.[6]

Almost nine out of ten House members' campaign organizations are managed by a paid staffer or some combination of paid staffer and outside consultant (see Table 3-1). Often the campaign manager is the administrative assistant or chief of staff in the House member's congressional office. Administrative assistants and other congressional staffers routinely take leaves of absence from their jobs to work for their boss's reelection, sometimes as volunteers who consider as compensation enough the bonuses or high salaries they receive as congressional aides when they are not on leave. Shoo-in incumbents (those who won by more than 20 percent of the vote) are just about as likely as incumbents in jeopardy (those who lost or won by less than 20 percent of the vote) to hire a paid staffer to handle day-to-day management and a general consultant to assist with campaign strategy. Most hopeful challengers (those who won or lost by 20 points or less) have professionally managed campaigns, but only 37 percent of all likely-loser challengers (those who lost by more than 20 percent of the vote) have campaigns managed by a paid staffer or general consultant. Many of these campaigns rely on volunteer managers, but some have no managers at all, relying on the candidates themselves to run their own campaigns.

Open-seat campaigns are similar to those waged by incumbents. All but 12 percent of the open-seat prospects (whose races were decided by margins of 20 percent or less) rely on a paid staffer or general consultant to manage their campaigns. Many open-seat candidates who are considered mismatched (whose election was decided by more than 20 percent of the vote) also have professional managers, but a substantial portion of them rely on the candidate or volunteers for campaign management. Few campaigns are managed by personnel provided by a political party or interest group, regardless of their competitiveness.

Professional staffs carry out press relations in most campaigns. More than 85 percent of all incumbents in close races rely on a paid staffer, frequently a congressional press secretary who is on a leave of absence, to handle their relations with the media. A small number of incumbents also hire campaign consultants to issue press releases and handle calls from journalists. Challengers and open-seat candidates in close races are just as likely as incumbents to rely on paid staff to handle media relations. A somewhat larger number hire political consultants for this purpose. Slightly fewer open-seat candidates in one-sided contests rely on paid staff. Only 45 percent of all challengers in uncompetitive races are able to turn to campaign professionals to help them work the press, relying on volunteers and their own efforts instead.

Issue and opposition research is often carried out by a combination of professional staff, outside consultants, party committees, interest groups, and volunteers. Incumbents, challengers, and open-seat candidates in one-sided races are more likely to rely on volunteers or the candidate to conduct research, or not even bother with it, than are candidates in close races. Some shoo-in incumbents turn to memos that congressional staff write about the major issues facing the nation and the district. These memos are usually drafted to help House members represent their constituents, but the political payoffs from them are significant. Most likely-loser challengers, who could benefit from the research, are unable to afford it.

TABLE 3-1

Staffing Activities in House Elections

	All	Incumbents		Challengers		Open-seat candidates	
		In jeopardy	Shoo-ins	Hope-fuls	Likely losers	Pros-pects	Mis-matched
Campaign management							
Paid staff	62%	79%	82%	81%	35%	77%	65%
Consultant	6	4	6	12	2	11	12
Party/interest groups	2	—	1	—	3	—	—
Volunteer	9	3	4	3	17	3	6
Candidate	22	10	10	12	41	6	18
Not used	4	3	5	—	6	3	
Press relations							
Paid staff	66%	86%	84%	84%	37%	89%	71%
Consultant	5	—	5	12	5	3	12
Party/interest groups	1	—	—	—	1	3	—
Volunteer	10	3	4	3	20	3	—
Candidate	19	10	7	3	38	3	18
Not used	4	—	4	—	7	—	—
Issue and opposition research							
Paid staff	40%	38%	57%	62%	28%	23%	35%
Consultant	21	38	21	22	8	43	35
Party/interest groups	10	17	4	16	6	29	12
Volunteer	11	-	2	3	22	6	12
Candidate	14	3	1	3	29	3	24
Not used	10	7	17	-	12	3	—
Fundraising							
Paid staff	52%	83%	75%	59%	25%	63%	53%
Consultant	14	14	20	16	6	23	24
Party/interest groups	5	—	4	6	3	14	6
Volunteer	9	3	5	6	15	3	6
Candidate	28	7	10	25	50	11	24
Not used	4	—	—	—	10	—	—
Polling							
Paid staff	7%	3%	10%	3%	6%	14%	6%
Consultant	49	86	56	81	17	74	71
Party/interest groups	6	7	5	3	6	9	6
Volunteer	4	—	1	—	6	6	—
Candidate	4	—	3	3	6	—	—
Not used	32	3	26	12	58	—	18

(Table continues)

TABLE 3-1
(continued)

	All	Incumbents		Challengers		Open-seat candidates	
		In jeopardy	Shoo-ins	Hope-fuls	Likely losers	Pros-pects	Mis-matched
Media advertising							
Paid staff	27%	17%	40%	28%	22%	17%	41%
Consultant	46	72	51	69	20	80	53
Party/interest groups	3	3	—	6	4	3	—
Volunteer	6	—	2	3	11	3	6
Candidate	15	7	5	—	35	—	—
Not used	9	—	10	9	13	—	6
Direct mail							
Paid staff	27%	31%	41%	31%	16%	23%	24%
Consultant	34	52	42	44	10	60	65
Party/interest groups	6	—	2	12	6	11	12
Volunteer	12	7	6	12	20	6	—
Candidate	7	3	4	—	15	3	—
Not used	21	10	14	9	39	3	—
Internet web site							
Paid staff	41%	69%	41%	59%	27%	46%	41%
Consultant	17	21	21	22	7	29	35
Party/interest groups	6	3	4	12	6	6	6
Volunteer	18	—	14	6	30	20	6
Candidate	10	—	1	3	24	—	6
Not used	10	7	22	—	7	3	6
Mass phone calls							
Paid staff	15%	10%	21%	16%	13%	11%	6%
Consultant	25	31	25	34	11	46	59
Party/interest groups	12	14	7	9	11	23	18
Volunteer	24	24	21	28	23	34	18
Candidate	3	—	1	3	6	3	—
Not used	29	24	34	9	43	3	—
Get-out-the-vote							
Paid staff	30%	38%	31%	50%	14%	54%	47%
Consultant	4	—	9	6	2	6	6
Party/interest groups	33	28	30	28	34	46	29
Volunteer	31	28	29	22	37	23	35
Candidate	6	3	4	—	10	3	6
Not used	11	3	10	3	19	6	6

(Table continues)

TABLE 3-1
(continued)

	All	Incumbents		Challengers		Open-seat candidates	
		In jeopardy	Shoo-ins	Hope-fuls	Likely losers	Pros-pects	Mis-matched
Legal advice							
Paid staff	15%	10%	15%	19%	11%	23%	18%
Consultant	20	21	27	19	11	26	29
Party/interest groups	13	24	9	34	4	26	6
Volunteer	13	14	10	9	15	11	18
Candidate	9	—	3	9	17	—	6
Not used	35	35	38	19	42	14	41
Accounting							
Paid staff	51%	62%	64%	56%	31%	71%	59%
Consultant	11	14	17	12	6	14	12
Party/interest groups	3	10	1	12	—	6	—
Volunteer	19	7	12	16	30	9	18
Candidate	10	—	2	—	24	3	—
Not used	7	7	5	3	11	—	12
Average number of activities performed by paid staff or consultants	6.7	8.8	8.4	8.8	3.6	9	8.6
(*N*)	(316)	(29)	(80)	(32)	(123)	(35)	(17)

Source: The 2002 Congressional Campaign Study.

Notes: Figures are for general election candidates in major-party contested races, excluding those in incumbent-versus-incumbent races. The categories are the same as those in Table 1-4. Figures for interest groups include labor unions. Dashes = less than 0.5 percent. Some columns do not add to 100 percent because some activities were performed by more than one person or because of rounding.

Although most incumbents in jeopardy, hopeful challengers, and open-seat prospects depend on paid professionals for research, some also benefit from research packages assembled by party organizations and a few interest groups. Since at least the mid-1980s the National Republican Congressional Committee, which is the wealthier and more heavily staffed of the two congressional campaign committees, has furnished more candidates with opposition and issue research than has its Democratic counterpart.[7] Some labor unions, trade associations, advocacy groups, and other organizations also provide candidates with campaign research.

Fundraising is a campaign activity that requires skill and connections with individuals and groups that are able and willing to make political contributions. Some campaigns use a mix of a paid campaign staffer, a professional finance director, and volunteers to raise money. Incumbent campaigns rely heavily on professional paid staff and professional consultants, regardless of the competitiveness of their races. Some keep fundraising experts, including those who specialize in direct mail or in organizing fundraising events, on the payroll to collect contributions between elections. The former typically collect modest contributions, whereas the latter are known for raking in large contributions from individuals and PACs. Fewer nonincumbents, particularly those in one-sided contests, hire professional staff and consultants to help with fundraising. Their campaigns depend more heavily on the candidate, volunteers, party committees, and interest groups to raise money.

Polling, mass media advertising, and direct mail are three specialized aspects of campaigning that are handled primarily by political consultants hired on a contractual basis. Most candidates running for marginal seats hire an outside consultant to conduct polls. Substantial numbers of incumbents who were shoo-ins and mismatched open-seat candidates did not take polls in 2002. But a much greater number of challengers in lopsided races, who could have benefited from accurate public opinion information, did not take them. Most likely-loser challengers opt not to conduct surveys to save money for other campaign activities. Consultants typically consider this an ill-advised approach to campaigning. In the words of one pollster, "It's like flying without the benefit of radar."[8]

Incumbents are the most likely to have professionally produced campaign communications. The vast majority of incumbents hire a media consultant or use some combination of media consultant and campaign aide to produce television and radio commercials. Most challengers and open-seat candidates in closely contested races also hire professional media consultants. Challengers in one-sided contests, who face the biggest hurdles in developing name recognition among voters and conveying a message, are by far the least likely to employ the services of a media consultant.

Similarly, fewer likely-loser challengers hire professional staff or consultants for direct mail, one of the most effective means House campaigns can use to reach voters. Indeed, 39 percent said that they do not use direct mail at all. The vast majority of competitive challengers, open-seat candidates, and incumbents, by contrast, rely mainly on a combination of paid staff and consultants to write their direct mail copy.

Although the Internet is a fairly new weapon in campaign arsenals, it can serve a number of purposes, including providing campaigns with an inexpensive and reliable means to communicate with and organize voters, raise money, disseminate press releases, and showcase their television ads. Internet web sites also furnish voters and journalists with a place to turn for unmediated information about a candidate's professional qualifications, personal achievements, and issue positions.[9] Almost six out of ten candidates had Internet web sites in 2002 and employed professional staff or consultants to develop and maintain them. Safe incumbents were among the most likely to state they did not have a web site, reflecting the lack of electoral threat they faced and their belief that voters interested in learning about them could go to their official congressional web sites. Seven percent of the likely-loser challengers who ran against these incumbents also did not possess a web site. These challengers relied the most heavily on volunteers to develop their presence on the web, or they did it themselves.

Mass telephone calls can be made live at phone banks or can be automated and prerecorded. Although such calls are not used as routinely as mass media advertising or direct mail, roughly 70 percent of all House campaigns used telephone calls to identify and mobilize supporters. Most of the campaigns that use mass telephone calls rely on a combination of consultants and volunteers, although some candidates turn to paid campaign aides, parties, or interest groups for help with writing their scripts and making calls.

Field work involves voter identification, registration, literature drops, and get-out-the-vote (GOTV) drives. Campaign staff, parties, interest groups, and volunteers figure prominently in the GOTV activities of virtually all campaigns. Incumbents depend almost as much on these sources of help as do challenger and open-seat candidates. Where these campaigns differ is that incumbents rely somewhat less on paid staff for field work than do open-seat candidates and competitive challengers. Democratic House candidates also receive significantly more help with mobilizing voters from unions, reflecting their party's historical ties with the labor movement.

Because of the intricacies of campaign finance laws, the rules governing the use of the mass media, and requirements for getting on the ballot, almost two-thirds of all House candidates competing in 2002 needed legal expertise at some point in the campaign. House campaigns call on paid staff, volunteers, or lawyers they keep on retainer, or get help from one of the high-powered attorneys employed by a party committee or an interest group when they need legal assistance. As is the case with most other aspects of campaigning, challengers running in lopsided races are the most likely to rely on volunteers or the candidate or to forgo the use of legal counsel.

Finally, accounting has become an important aspect of contemporary cash-driven congressional election campaigns. Most candidates hire staff with accounting skills to file their Federal Election Commission reports and oversee the books. Fewer likely-loser challenger campaigns have a salaried employee or professional consultant in charge of accounting. As is the case in some other areas of electioneering, these campaigns often turn to volunteers or the candidate to perform this function.

The overall professionalism of contemporary House campaigns is reflected in the fact that the average campaign uses paid staff or political consultants to carry out roughly seven of the preceding twelve activities (see the bottom of Table 3-1). The typical incumbent in jeopardy, hopeful challenger, or open-seat prospect uses skilled professionals to carry out nine of these activities. Incumbents and open-seat candidates in uncompetitive elections also assemble very professional campaigns. Only challengers in one-sided contests are substantially less reliant on professional help. Nonincumbents who are officeholders and unelected politicians assemble more professional campaign organizations than do political amateurs.[10]

The organization Douglas Ose assembled to conduct his 2002 reelection campaign in California's 3rd congressional district is typical of those put together by most shoo-in incumbents. Following his initial victory in 1998, the congressman and his staff worked hard to raise his profile in the district, helping him get reelected by a sixteen-point margin in 2000. The Ose campaign entered the 2002 election feeling confident of victory. Redistricting added a substantial number of Republican voters to the district, and its comfort level increased further when no high-profile Democrat entered the race.

Ose drew on much of the same local talent he had used in previous years and prepared to mount a low-key campaign. Steve Rice, of McNally Temple, a Sacramento-based general consulting firm, provided strategic advice, designed the campaign's communications, hired a web site designer, and oversaw the campaign's other outreach efforts. Ann Kramer, of Kramer and Associates of Sacramento, was responsible for direct-mail fundraising and local fundraising events. Nancy Bocskor of Alexandria, Virginia, organized fundraising events in Washington, D.C. The California office of Public Opinion Strategies, a nationally renowned Republican consulting firm, conducted the campaign's one poll. Elise Brewer, of Sacramento, was responsible for the campaign's press relations and day-to-day management. Bell, McAndrews, Hiltachk and Davidian, also of Sacramento, provided accounting services. This organization was supplemented by a modest number of volunteers. Had Ose perceived the race to be more competitive, he would have put together a larger team and campaigned more aggressively.[11]

The campaign team that Howard Beeman, Ose's opponent, put together was underfunded and understaffed, as is typical of most campaigns waged by likely-loser challengers. Beeman, a retired farmer and sometime political activist had run for Congress once before, losing the Democratic nomination in 1998. In preparing for his 2002 bid, Beeman called on his family and friends to assist with the campaign. His wife and children were very involved, with his son Ezra assuming the role of campaign manager. Scott Adams, a consultant from Esparto, California, spent ten days setting up the campaign office and was on call to provide strategic advice by telephone. Tor Tarantola, a local student, handled press relations, first as a volunteer and later as a paid aide. Leading Edge, a Sacramento-based firm, provided addresses, telephone numbers, and other voter contact information at a discount rate. A couple of volunteers created the campaign's web site. Another hundred or so volunteers hand-delivered campaign literature and applications for absentee ballots in various parts of the district. The Sacramento Democratic Party provided office space and a telephone, the Democratic State Central Committee paid the candidate's filing fee, a few local Democratic and ethnic clubs provided incidental support, but little help was forthcoming from the Democratic Congressional Campaign Committee. The campaign lacked the money and staff to carry out a GOTV effort, one of the least expensive and most volunteer-dependent aspects of campaigning.[12]

The 2002 campaign waged in Maryland's 8th district by Republican incumbent Connie Morella contrasts sharply with those of Ose and Beeman, but it is typical of campaigns run by House incumbents in jeopardy. Morella was first elected in 1986, when she defeated GOP Democratic state senator Stewart Bainum in a closely-fought open-seat race in Maryland's 8th congressional district. What is unusual about Morella's initial victory and the seven that followed is that they took place in a predominantly Democratic district comprising a large number of federal government employees and workers who depend on government contracts for their livelihood. The district has consistently supported Democratic candidates for president, governor, the state legislature, and virtually all local races. Former vice president Al Gore defeated then–Texas governor George W. Bush by twenty-four points among 8th district voters in 2000.[13]

Morella, a liberal Republican, used a combination of constituent service, attention to the concerns of federal workers, and an independent voting record to help solidify her hold over the district. Her home style was characterized by graciousness, enthusiasm for the job, attention to detail, and a thorough knowledge of the major issues facing her constituents and the nation. The deep bipartisan support she developed enabled her to easily win the seat throughout the 1980s and 1990s and to gain the unflagging support of the *Washington Post.*

Nevertheless, Morella's fortunes began to change following the Republican takeover of Congress. In the three elections before the GOP captured control of the House, she was reelected with 70 percent or more of the vote. However, her shares of the vote fell to roughly 60 percent in 1996 and 1998, and then plummeted to 52 percent in 2000, when she faced Terry Lierman, a pharmaceutical industry lobbyist who might have won had his campaign not been rocked by a late-breaking scandal involving a personal loan he had made to Rep. James Moran, D-Va.[14] A major reason for Morella's weakening fortune was that Democratic voters and her opponents began to question the wisdom of reelecting a member of Congress who, though liberal, made it possible for the Republicans to preserve their slim House majority and continue to promote a conservative political agenda.

Following the 2000 census, Maryland Democrats sought to increase the competitiveness of the 8th district by replacing some Montgomery County voters with loyal Democrats from neighboring Prince George's County. In anticipation of a hotly contested election, against Kennedy scion and state delegate Mark Shriver, state senator Christopher Van Hollen, or former U.S. trade ambassador Ira Shapiro, Morella assembled a staff comprising some of the nation's leading political consultants. Linda Divall, from American Viewpoint of Alexandria, Virginia, did the polling; Bob McKernan, with Smith and Haroff, also of Alexandria, was in charge of the campaign's television and radio ads; and Brett Feinstein of Pound and Feinstein of Richmond, Virginia, handled the persuasion direct-mail.[15]

Tony Caliguiri, who had previously worked as campaign manager for Rep. Wayne Gilchrest, R-Md., and took a leave of absence from his job as the congressman's chief of staff, managed Morella's campaign. Carolyn Milkey, the campaign's treasurer, handled the accounting and filed reports with the FEC. Brandon DeFrehn, president of the University of Maryland Student Government Association and budding politician in his own right, served as field coordinator. The campaign's web site was designed and maintained by Eric Fidler, a high school student who volunteered for the job. Jarrod Agen, a former MSNBC employee, handled media relations, first as a volunteer and later as a paid aide. The campaign carried out its own direct-mail fundraising using Morella's house list; and MaryAnne Estey, a retired teacher who had worked on all of Morella's previous campaigns, organized the fundraising events. National Republican election lawyers provided legal advice, as they do for many GOP candidates. The NRCC provided opposition research, focusing first on Shriver's voting record and then turning to Van Hollen's after the latter won the Democratic primary. National and local Republicans also helped arrange for volunteers to assist the campaign. Then–House majority whip Tom DeLay's

Strategic Task Force to Organize and Mobilize People (STOMP) provided about a dozen volunteers from the Washington, D.C., area on the last few Saturdays of the election season, and the Republican National Committee's "72-Hour Task Force" provided a van and some volunteers during the last three days of the campaign. The Log Cabin Republicans and the Human Rights Campaign, two pro–gay rights advocacy groups, sent two full-time volunteers who worked for the last month and a half of the campaign. In addition, a group of between thirty and forty individuals volunteered on a regular basis beginning in the summer. Another 600 to 700 unpaid workers helped the campaign on different occasions by hosting events, distributing campaign literature, stuffing envelopes, and staffing the office. The campaign called on approximately three thousand volunteers to help turn out the vote on election day.[16]

Van Hollen's campaign was similar to many campaigns waged by hopeful challengers. Van Hollen entered the race with substantial political experience. He was elected to the Maryland state senate in 1994. Prior to that he served four years in the state house of delegates, as senior legislative advisor for federal affairs to former Maryland governor William Donald Schaefer, and worked as a legislative aide in the U.S. Senate.[17] Van Hollen's service in Annapolis and on Capitol Hill provided him with a wealth of knowledge about what it would take to run a viable congressional campaign. He assembled a very professional organization, relying heavily on the political talent available in the Washington, D.C., area. Steve Jost, a nationally known Democratic Party operative managed the campaign, assisted by Dorothy Davis, who ran the office and organized grassroots activities. Cooper and Secrest Associates, of Alexandria, Virginia, conducted the campaign's polls and focus groups. Strategic Campaign Initiatives, of Bowie, Maryland, designed the campaign's persuasion direct-mail. Doak, Carrier, O'Donnell, and Associates, of Washington, D.C., produced the campaign's television advertising. The Tyson Organization, of Fort Worth, Texas—one of the nation's premier Democratic voter turnout firms—made the persuasion telephone calls in the closing days of the primary and the general election. Mark Lewis, of Washington, D.C., headed up the campaign's fundraising; and James Buie, also of the Washington area, was responsible for the candidate's web site. Karen McMannis, a volunteer, headed the host committee that organized coffees and other local events; and Afshin Mohamadi, a graduate student at George Washington University, handled the campaign's media relations, first as a volunteer and later as a member of the paid staff.[18]

The campaign drew additional assistance from a variety of corners. The AFL-CIO and Clean Water Action, an environmental protection group, provided volunteers who worked phone banks, knocked on voters' doors, and carried out other field activities designed to get Van Hollen's message out and to get voters to the polls. Numerous other political activists, ranging from congressional aides to lobbyists based in Annapolis to members of the National Organization for Women to local party officials also volunteered, providing Van Hollen with an army of almost 40 full-time volunteers, 150 weekend volunteers, and 3,000 others who worked on a less regular basis. The DCCC helped the campaign raise money and identify Van Hollen supporters, aired television ads, and provided staff assistance.

The campaigns waged by Republican Robert Beauprez and Democrat Michael Feeley in Colorado's 7th congressional district are representative of those undertaken by most open-seat prospects. Both campaigns were professionally staffed and employed some of the nation's top political consultants. Beauprez hired Sean Murphy, who formerly worked for him as executive director of the Colorado Republican Party, to be his campaign manager. The Tarrance Group, of Alexandria, Virginia, carried out the campaign's polling. National Media, Inc., of Alexandria, produced its television and radio ads. Targeted Creative Communications, also of Alexandria, designed the campaign's persuasion direct-mail; and Direct Mail Systems, of Loveland, Ohio, carried out its direct-mail fundraising. Mass telephone calls were handled by Strategic Marketing Consultants, of Nashua, New Hampshire. Shari Williams, a Denver-based political consultant who has been active in Republican politics and the term limits movement, provided strategic advice. National Republican Party lawyers provided Beauprez with legal assistance. They were heavily involved after the polls had closed and the outcome of the race was subjected to a recount.

The Beauprez campaign received heavy support from party committees and interest groups. NRCC staff called the campaign on a near daily basis, advising it on its strategy and spending, as well as assisting with fundraising. Beauprez, like Morella, benefited from the RNC's 72-Hour Task Force, as well as from the Colorado Republican State Central Committee's "96-Hour Program." The National Federation of Independent Businesses and the Christian Coalition also carried out grassroots activities to help Beauprez and other Colorado GOP candidates.[19]

Feeley's campaign also was run by a full coterie of staff, political consultants, and volunteers. Media relations, fundraising, field operations, and campaign management were handled by paid campaign aides. Harstad Strategic Research, of Boulder, Colorado, conducted the campaign's polls; and CapAd Communications, a political telemarketing company in Falls Church, Virginia, carried out voter identification surveys and persuasion telephone calls. ArmourMedia, of Los Angeles, produced the campaign's television ads; and the Strategy Group oversaw its direct-mail efforts. The campaign's web site was created and maintained by Wade Green Consulting. Legal compliance and accounting services were provided by Rebecca and Rick Gleason. Welchert and Britz, of nearby Denver, provided general consulting advice.

Feeley's organization was less stable at the top than was Beauprez's campaign. After taking stock of campaign headquarters, the DCCC felt that the campaign had some serious shortcomings, ranging from poor message development to inadequate office equipment. Because this was one of its top targeted races, the DCCC sought to increase its presence in Feeley's campaign. In mid-August it sent Erik Greathouse to oversee the operation, effectively displacing the original campaign manager and long-time Feeley political confidante Beth Minahan. The DCCC's Midwest regional field director and Washington-based staff provided extensive strategic advice, and national Democratic Party lawyers and other operatives were on hand to participate in the election recount. The Feeley campaign also drew fundraising and volunteer support from other party organizations and interest groups. It benefited from the Colorado Democratic Party's voter mobilization program, the "96-Hour Campaign," and drew large numbers of volunteers from the ranks of party activists and union members.[20]

CAMPAIGN BUDGETS

The professionalism of contemporary congressional campaigns is reflected in how they budget their money. House candidates spend 56 percent of their campaign funds on communicating with voters and 40 percent on fundraising, staff salaries, travel, and other miscellaneous expenses (see Figure 3-1). Polling and other research account for about 4 percent of campaign costs.[21] The substantial amounts budgeted for electronic media demonstrate the important role played by modern communication techniques in most House campaigns and their rising costs. The typical 2002 House campaign spent approximately 22 percent of its budget on television and 12 percent on radio. Of course, the precise amount that a campaign spends on TV depends largely on how closely the boundaries of the district match those of the local media market. The next-largest expenses are for direct mail and campaign literature, each of which accounted for 8 percent of total costs. The remaining 5 percent was spent largely on voter registration and GOTV drives; newspaper ads; Internet web sites; and billboards, yard signs, and other campaign paraphernalia.

One of the most interesting facts about congressional elections is that the different types of candidates differ little in their approaches to budgeting. Among

FIGURE 3-1
Budget of a Typical House Campaign

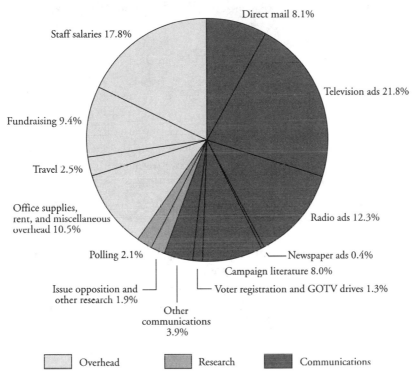

Source: Compiled from data provided by Political Money Line (http://www.tray.com).

Notes: Staff salaries include some miscellaneous consulting fees. Figures are for major-party candidates in contested general elections. $N = 694$.

the largest differences, nonincumbents commit about 65 percent of their budgets to campaign communications, whereas incumbents apportion only 48 percent. The nonincumbents compensate by scrimping on overhead, especially fundraising and the salaries and fees that incumbents incur when conducting various campaign-related activities between elections. Candidates in contests decided by 20 percent or less of the two-party vote dedicate 46 percent of their budgets to television and radio, more than twice the amount allocated by candidates in one-sided races. The amounts that Democratic and Republican House candidates budget for various campaign activities are virtually the same.

Of course, candidates tailor their campaign budgets to suit their districts. Both the Morella and Van Hollen campaigns budgeted large sums of their resources for electronic communications and direct mail, with the former spending 71 percent on television and radio ads and another 7 percent on mail and the latter budgeting 51 percent on TV and radio and 16 percent on mail. Beauprez and Feeley also each spent about half of their budgets on television and radio. Neither the Ose nor the Beeman campaigns spent money on television because of the inefficiency of advertising in their media market, which is extremely expensive and spans many congressional districts. The Beeman campaign spent $7,000 (20 percent) of its funds on direct mail, whereas the Ose campaign spent almost $2,100 (4 percent of its budget) for the same purpose.[22]

The overall similarity in campaign budgets is remarkable given the different sums that incumbent, open-seat, and challenger campaigns spend. The widespread availability of campaign technology; the tremendous growth of the political consulting industry; and the extensive dissemination of information through the American Association of Political Consultants, *Campaigns & Elections* magazine, and campaign seminars sponsored by those organizations, political parties, and interest groups have fostered a set of shared expectations about how a campaign should spend its funds. These expectations are reinforced when campaign personnel negotiate their salaries and draw up budgets, when political consulting firms set their rates, and when party officials and PAC managers scrutinize campaign budgets prior to making a contribution.

SENATE CAMPAIGNS

Senate campaigns are more expensive, are run by more professional organizations, and attract more party and interest group attention than do House campaigns. Because campaigns for the upper chamber must reach out to more voters and because members of that chamber possess more political clout than their House counterparts, candidates for the Senate typically raise and spend more money. They also rely primarily on paid staffs and nationally known political consultants to develop their strategies and carry out their campaigns. Most Senate incumbents keep a substantial organization intact between elections, often spending millions of dollars on overhead and fundraising between elections.

Senate campaigns often have combinations of individuals sharing responsibilities for various aspects of the campaign. Virtually every campaign assigns a paid aide to work with a mass media advertising firm to develop the candidate's communications. Opposition research is typically conducted by a campaign aide, often in conjunction with a private consultant or party official. Campaign staff, consultants, volunteers, party committees, and interest group representatives make substantial contributions to Senate candidates' fundraising efforts. Most Senate campaigns also hire one or more field managers to participate in coordinated voter mobilization efforts that draw on the resources of national, state, and local party committees. Democratic Senate candidates also coordinate their field work with labor unions, and most Senate candidates of both parties rely on volunteers to help with their voter registration and GOTV efforts.

The major difference in spending between Senate and House contests is in the allocation of media expenditures. The average Senate campaign spends about one-third of its money on television advertising, as opposed to the one-fifth spent by the typical House campaign. Senate campaigns also allocate far smaller portions of their budgets to radio advertising, campaign literature, newspaper ads, billboards, and yard signs than do House contestants. The differences in communications expenditures reflect both the greater practicality and the necessity of using television advertising in statewide races.

SUMMARY

Contemporary congressional elections are waged primarily by candidate-centered organizations that draw on the expertise of political consultants for polling, mass media advertising, and other specialized functions. Few candidates depend on parties and interest groups to carry out many campaign activities; the important exception is voter mobilization. Incumbents and open-seat candidates in competitive races wage the most professional campaigns; challengers in lopsided contests rely on the most amateur organizations. Despite these variations in organizations and tremendous disparities in funding, campaigns are more alike than different in how they budget their resources. The match between district boundaries and media markets and the preferences of individual candidates and their campaign aides have bigger effects on campaigns' budgetary allocations than does either incumbency or the closeness of the race.

CHAPTER FOUR

The Parties Campaign

Political parties in the United States have one overriding goal: to elect their candidates to public office. Policy goals are secondary to winning control of the government. Nevertheless, the parties' electoral influence has waxed and waned as the result of legal, demographic, and technological changes in U.S. society and reforms instituted by the parties themselves. During the golden age of political parties, local party organizations dominated elections in many parts of the country. They picked the candidates, gauged public opinion, raised money, disseminated campaign communications, and mobilized voters, most of whom had strong partisan allegiances. "The parties were, in short, the medium through which the campaign was waged." [1]

By the 1950s most state and local party organizations had been ushered to the periphery of the candidate-centered system. Party organizations at the national level had not yet developed into repositories of money and campaign services for congressional candidates. Most contenders for the House and Senate were largely self-recruited and relied on campaign organizations that they themselves had assembled to wage their bids for office. Professional consultants helped fill the void left by deteriorating party organizations, providing advice about fundraising, media, polling, and campaign management to clients willing to pay for it. [2]

During the late 1970s and early 1980s, first Republican and then Democratic national party organizations in Washington, D.C., began to adapt to the contemporary candidate-centered system. This system emphasizes campaign activities requiring technical expertise and in-depth research. Many candidates, especially nonincumbents running for the House, lack the money or professional know-how needed to run a modern congressional campaign. Candidates' needs created the opportunity for party organizations to assume a more important role in congressional elections.[3] The national parties responded to these needs, not by doing away with the candidate-centered election system but by assuming a more important role in it.[4]

The national parties also adapted to changing circumstances during the late 1990s, particularly the rise of soft money and issue advocacy advertisements that occurred as a result of the weakening of federal campaign finance laws. Both major parties, and numerous interest groups, began conducting "independent," "parallel," and "coordinated" campaigns comprising millions of dollars of spending on television, radio, direct mail, mass telephone calls, and other communications and voter mobilization efforts. By carefully tailoring these activities to meet the circumstances in a small number of competitive congressional elections, parties have greatly increased their influence in those contests, thereby assuming an even greater role in the candidate-centered system.

In this chapter I discuss the roles of party organizations in congressional elections, including their influence on the agendas around which campaigns are fought, the kinds of assistance they give to House and Senate candidates, the strategies that inform their giving, how they select candidates for support, and the effects of their assistance on candidates' campaigns. Special attention is given to four Hill committees in recognition of their impact on congressional campaigns.

NATIONAL AGENDA SETTING

Contemporary House elections are usually fought on local issues, and Senate elections typically focus on statewide concerns. That does not mean that Democratic or Republican leaders do not work to set a national agenda that favors their own party. Rather, party leaders seek to focus on issues voters associate positively with their party, or negatively with the opposition, and congressional candidates who discuss those issues typically emphasize their local implications.[5] Since the early 1980s, Democratic and Republican congressional leaders have produced lengthy issues handbooks, white papers, or "talking points" for congressional candidates that focus on national issues and include instructions on how to use party rhetoric and statistics compiled in Washington to address local concerns.[6] Many candidates found these materials useful, but the materials were not intended to produce nationalized campaigns and did not do so.

Nevertheless, congressional elections are not always dominated by local issues. In 1932 the Great Depression dominated the national political agenda and the outcomes of many House and Senate races. In 1974, Democrats nationalized the elections on Watergate, the Nixon administration's ethical lapses, and reform issues. During the 1994 elections, House Republicans focused on the ethical and policy failures of the Clinton administration and congressional Democrats, the "special interest" culture that Republicans asserted had developed in the House under forty years of Democratic control, and Newt Gingrich's Contract with America.[7]

The elections of 1996 and 1998 were less nationalized than those of 1932, 1974, and 1994. Led by President Clinton, the Democrats sought to paint congressional Republicans as "extremists" who wanted to cut appropriations for Medicare, Medicaid, and education to pay for tax breaks for the rich; who would turn corporate polluters loose on the environment; who had twice shut down the federal government; and who sought to thwart the will of the American people by impeaching a duly elected president. Congressional Democrats portrayed themselves as the champions of working Americans and focused on moderate policy proposals on health care–related issues, education, Social Security, jobs and the economy, and the environment. In 1996, Republicans had hoped to set a national campaign agenda focusing on the bills they had passed that were associated with the Contract with America. Two years later they sought to claim credit for the balanced budget, to contrast popular Republican issue stances with unpopular Democratic policy positions, and to remind voters of the president's sex scandal and impeachment. However, they were put on the defensive by public reaction to the government shutdowns, the impeachment, and Gingrich's "take no prisoners" approach to politics. Neither party was able to dominate the agenda, and the unpopularity of both Clinton and Gingrich encouraged many members of Congress and candidates to shun visits by these leaders and wage campaigns primarily on local issues.

Although they were to some extent overshadowed by the presidential campaign, the 2000 congressional elections also failed to become fully nationalized. Congressional candidates needed to address issues raised to prominence by the presidential candidates, including education, the reform of health maintenance organizations (HMOs), rising prescription drug costs, the economy, Social Security reform, and tax cuts. However, most candidates tailored these national issues to address local concerns. Moreover, the closeness of the presidential race meant that neither party was able to establish hegemony over the political agenda.

Other factors also prevented these recent elections from becoming fully nationalized. A divided government—a Democratic president and a Republican-controlled Congress—made it difficult for either party to claim full credit or to place full blame on the other party for the government's performance.

Divisions within both parties' ranks prevented partisan lines from crystallizing as clearly as they had in 1932, 1974, and 1994.

Divided government also was a factor in preventing the 2002 congressional elections from becoming fully nationalized. The attacks on the World Trade Center and the Pentagon, the war on terrorism, and the possibility of war with Iraq also had a big impact. Prior to September 11, 2001, both parties sought to focus on issues that have traditionally benefited their candidates. Democrats talked about the economy and jobs, prescription drug costs and health care reform, Social Security, the environment, and corporate corruption. Republicans discussed tax cuts, government downsizing, family values, and other moral issues. Education, which has traditionally favored Democrats, was a battleground issue to which both parties sought to lay claim. The terrorist attacks drastically changed the political agenda. Partisan considerations faded and Americans united behind the president, as usually happens when the nation is involved in an international conflict.[8] Following the advice of White House senior adviser Karl Rove, Republican leaders sought to capitalize on the international situation. President George W. Bush, Vice President Dick Cheney, New York mayor Rudolph Giuliani, and other Republican leaders used it as a rallying cry at fundraising and campaign events for GOP candidates. Many Democrats found themselves in the delicate position of needing to disagree with the president without appearing unpatriotic. Democratic leaders encouraged their candidates to support the president in the war on terrorism but to criticize him and their Republican opponents on the economy and other domestic issues.

Both parties had a substantial impact on the national political agenda in 2002. Issues raised by Democrats played a role in more individuals' congressional voting decisions than did the issues emphasized by Republicans. Nineteen percent of congressional voters considered the economy and jobs their most important voting issue, and another 12 percent ranked it their second most important voting issue (see Figure 4-1). Education was next on the list, with Social Security and Medicare, morality issues, taxes, the situation with Iraq, health care–related concerns, and the war on terrorism following closely behind. Federal spending, the environment, corporate abuse, and crime and illegal drugs were substantially less important voting issues in 2002.

Although the issues at the top of the national agenda worked to the advantage of Democratic congressional candidates, the Republicans reaped larger benefits from their partisan issue agenda than Democrats received from theirs. Of the 50 percent of all voters stating that the economy and jobs—the Democrats' top election issue—was their first or second most important voting concern, 46 percent voted for Democratic congressional candidates and 40 percent voted for Republican candidates (see Figure 4-2). This gave Democratic

FIGURE 4-1

Most Important Issues in Congressional Voting Decisions in 2002

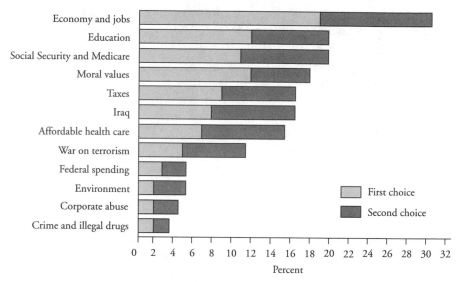

Source: Bill McInturff, *Post-Election Research 2002, Public Opinion Strategies,* at http://www.pos.org/presentations/gallery.asp?ID=20&Last=27&Pres=58, Slide 20, accessed February 10, 2002.

candidates a mere six-point voting advantage on the issue. This contrasts sharply with moral issues, the Republicans' top agenda item. Of the 31 percent of all voters who considered moral concerns one of their top two voting issues, 69 percent cast their ballots for Republican candidates and only 17 percent voted for Democrats, giving the GOP a fifty-two-point issue advantage on this issue. Similarly the Republicans' advantages on their next three partisan voting issues—federal spending, the war on terrorism, and taxes—were substantially larger than the Democrats' advantages on their next three issues.

THE NATIONAL, CONGRESSIONAL, AND
SENATORIAL CAMPAIGN COMMITTEES

Party organizations in the nation's capital have developed into major sources of campaign money, services, and advice for congressional candidates. The Democratic National Committee (DNC) and the Republican National Committee (RNC) focus most of their efforts on presidential elections but also become involved in some gubernatorial and statehouse elections and in a

FIGURE 4-2
Partisan Advantages in Congressional Voting Decisions in 2002

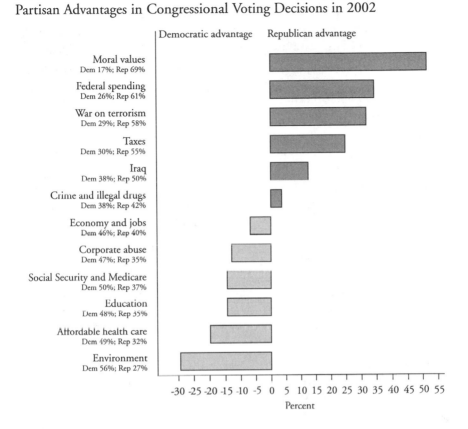

| Democratic advantage | Republican advantage

Moral values
Dem 17%; Rep 69%

Federal spending
Dem 26%; Rep 61%

War on terrorism
Dem 29%; Rep 58%

Taxes
Dem 30%; Rep 55%

Iraq
Dem 38%; Rep 50%

Crime and illegal drugs
Dem 38%; Rep 42%

Economy and jobs
Dem 46%; Rep 40%

Corporate abuse
Dem 47%; Rep 35%

Social Security and Medicare
Dem 50%; Rep 37%

Education
Dem 48%; Rep 35%

Affordable health care
Dem 49%; Rep 32%

Environment
Dem 56%; Rep 27%

-30 -25 -20 -15 -10 -5 0 5 10 15 20 25 30 35 40 45 50 55
Percent

Source: Bill McInturff, *Post-Election Research 2002*, *Public Opinion Strategies*, at http://www.pos.org/
presentations/gallery.asp?ID=21&Last=27&Pres=58, Slide 21, accessed February 10, 2002.

Note: Each bar represents the responses of individuals who considered that issue one of their top two voting issues. The partisan advantage is the percentage who voted for a Democratic House candidate minus the
percentage who voted for a Republican House candidate.

small number of mayoral elections. They also seek to set the national campaign agenda and strengthen state and local party organizations. The national
committees' involvement in House and Senate elections tends to be relatively
limited. It includes conducting candidate training seminars; furnishing candidates with party platforms, campaign manifestos, and talking points; and coordinating with congressional, senatorial, state, and local party campaign committees to mobilize partisan voters. Congressional candidates in search of
money, election services, or assistance in running their campaigns rarely turn
to their national committee for help. Any assistance the national committee

offers is usually channeled through a congressional or senatorial campaign committee or distributed at the behest of one of those organizations.[9]

The parties' congressional and senatorial campaign committees, sometimes referred to as the "Hill committees," have developed into major support centers for House and Senate candidates.[10] The congressional campaign committees focus their efforts on House races, and the two senatorial campaign committees focus on Senate contests. Three of the four Hill committees set fundraising records in 2002; only the Democratic Congressional Campaign Committee (DCCC) raised less than it had in 2000. The parties' national, state, and local organizations also set fundraising records for a midterm election. The DCCC raised $102.9 million, and its Republican rival, the National Republican Congressional Committee (NRCC) collected almost $210.8 million. The two senatorial committees—the Democratic Senatorial Campaign Committee (DSCC) and the National Republican Senatorial Committee (NRSC)—raised approximately $143.4 million and $125.6 million, respectively. Despite the DSCC's slight fundraising advantage over its Republican counterpart, GOP committees, including the RNC and Republican state and local party organizations, out-fundraised their Democratic counterparts $691.6 million to $463.3 million.[11] The Republican committees have enjoyed fundraising advantages in virtually every election in the past three decades.

Indeed, their control over the House, George W. Bush's occupancy of the White House, the close division between the parties in the Senate, and the mobilization of GOP-leaning donors helped the Republicans rake in record funds in 2002. President Bush's fundraising efforts were especially important in this regard. He raised more than $144 million at sixty-seven receptions in thirty-four states and the District of Columbia for GOP committees and candidates, including $30 million for the RNC, NRCC, and NRSC at just one event, fittingly named "The President's Dinner." In addition, Vice President Cheney raked in more than $22 million at seventy-four events.[12]

The chairs, vice chairs, and members of the Hill committees are members of Congress who are selected by their colleagues in the House or Senate. For the most part the members of each committee act like a board of directors, setting priorities and giving the committee staff the support it needs to participate in campaigns. However, one area in which members play an essential role is fundraising. Congressional and senatorial campaign committee chairs, vice chairs, and other party leaders have always raised money from individuals, political action committees, and other interest groups, but in recent years they have tapped into a new source—their colleagues in the House and Senate.

During the 2002 elections, congressional leaders of both parties established quotas for contributions by incumbents. The Senate Republicans set the highest quotas—asking their members to contribute or raise an astonishing $500,000

each in hard or soft money. Senate Democrats asked for $50,000 from commit-
tee chairmen and $20,000 from rank-and-file members.[13] The DCCC requested
anywhere from $5,000 for first-term members to $15,000 for party leaders and
committee chairs. The NRCC also established contribution and fundraising rates
for its members. House Speaker Dennis Hastert, R-Ill., incoming majority leader
Tom DeLay, R-Texas, and NRCC chair Tom Davis, R-Va., each contributed or
raised $700,000; the chairs of the powerful Ways and Means, Commerce, and
Budget Committees were asked to provide $500,000; other committee chairs
were expected to contribute $250,000; and members of Ways and Means,
Appropriations, and other prestigious committees were asked to contribute
$100,000. Rank-and-file members were expected to raise or contribute $25,000,
unless they were involved in close races. Some members tackled the chore with
relish. For example, Ways and Means Committee chairman Bill Thomas,
R-Calif., contributed $1 million from his campaign account to the NRCC and
another $5,000 to the Kern County (California) Republican Central Commit-
tee. Others grumbled about being dunned for contributions, but the competition for control over both the House and the Senate has given Hill committee
chairs persuasive arguments to employ in their fundraising efforts.

Democratic leaders coaxed members of Congress, congressional retirees,
and other politicians to donate from their election accounts and the "leadership" or "member" PACs they sponsor almost $12.1 million in hard money to
the DCCC, $2 million to the DSCC, $41,400 to the DNC, and more than
$4.3 million to state and local Democratic Party committees. Republican lead-
ers were even more successful, raising from members of the House and Senate,
congressional retirees, and leadership PACs more than $14.1 million in hard
money for the NRCC, almost $2.4 million for the NRSC, $140,800 for the
RNC, and over $1.5 million for state and local GOP organizations.[14]
Members of Congress and other party leaders also helped the parties raise millions of dollars in soft money for these organizations and other party committees during the 2002 elections.

Member contributions to party committees involve massive redistributions
of money from political leaders who can raise it to candidates who need it.
They demonstrate that Hill committee leaders can get national legislators to
look beyond their own campaigns to consider ways to help party organizations
and the candidates they assist. A sense of enlightened self-interest encourages
members to raise money for national, state, and local party organizations.
Once involving only a few party leaders and senior members, in 2002 this re-
distribution of wealth involved hundreds of lawmakers and candidates, including some first-term legislators who aspire to leadership posts.

A fairly new type of financial arrangement that sometimes involves the re-
distribution of wealth, called a "joint fundraising" or "victory" committee, is a

hybrid operation designed to raise money for participating candidates and a party organization. Joint fundraising committees typically distribute the first $2,000 in hard money raised from an individual (the legal maximum contribution in a primary and general election in 2002) to the participating candidate, the next $20,000 in hard money an individual contributes goes to the Hill committee's federal account, and any soft money raised goes to the Hill committee's nonfederal account or some other nonfederal party or candidate-related account. Most of the funds allocated to the Hill committee are used to help the participating candidate, unless, of course, that candidate is not in a close race. The idea for joint fundraising committees grew out of Federal Election Commission regulations requiring party organizations to match every soft money dollar they spend in connection with a federal election in a state with a specific amount of hard money. The exact ratio of hard money to soft money depends on whether a federal or state party committee is making the expenditure and the ratio of federal to nonfederal candidates on the ballot. Party officials motivated candidates to participate in joint fundraising committees by explaining that the candidates could increase the amount of party money that would be spent in their races.

In addition to their members, the congressional and senatorial campaign committees are composed of many highly skilled political professionals. During the 2002 elections the DCCC and DSCC employed 92 and 40 full-time staff, respectively, and their Republican counterparts had 80 and 70 full-time employees, respectively. The staffs oversee the committees' daily operations, are influential in formulating party strategies, and play a major role in the implementation of those strategies. The staffs are divided along functional lines; different divisions are responsible for administration, fundraising, research, communications, and campaign activities. Staff working in these divisions draw expertise from the constellation of consultants that service their party's candidates, including many individuals who formerly worked for a party committee. Allied pollsters, media experts, and other campaign professionals are hired by the Hill committees to provide candidates with campaign services.[15]

As major centers of political expertise and campaign support, the Hill committees are expensive to operate. They typically spend between 45 percent and 55 percent of their budgets on voter lists, computers, media studios, salaries, consulting fees, fundraising, loan repayments, and other overhead.

STRATEGY, DECISION MAKING, AND TARGETING

The Hill committees have a common overriding goal of maximizing the number of seats their parties hold in Congress.[16] They become heavily involved in some elections, giving selected candidates large contributions and making substantial expenditures on their behalf, including expenditures on issue advocacy ads and voter mobilization efforts. They also give these candidates strategic, research, technical, and transactional assistance. The latter form of help enables candidates to raise the money and other resources needed to conduct a congressional campaign. Finally, the Hill committees participate with the national committees and state and local party organizations in generic, party-focused election activities designed to help candidates for Congress and other offices get elected.

The campaign committees try to focus most of their efforts on competitive House and Senate contests. Protecting incumbents in jeopardy is a major priority. Pressures from nervous incumbents can skew the distribution of committee resources from competitive challenger and open-seat candidates toward members of Congress who hold safe seats. The funds available to a committee also can affect the way it distributes its resources. Other institutional forces that affect committee decision making are the aspirations of its chair and other members. The two individuals who had the most significant roles in modernizing the NRCC and DCCC, former representatives Guy Vander Jagt and Tony Coelho, sought to use their chairmanships as vehicles for advancement in the ranks of the House leadership. The same is true of most of their successors, including Rep. Martin Frost, D-Texas, who became chair of the House Democratic Caucus in the 106th Congress following his term as DCCC chairman, and NRCC chairman Davis, who took over as chair of the House Government Reform Committee in the 108th Congress.[17] Similarly, Tennessee senator Bill Frist's meteoric rise to Senate majority leader in 2002, after having served only eight years in Congress, can be attributed at least partially to his successful chairmanship of the NRSC during the 107th Congress.

National political and economic conditions are additional factors that influence which candidates get campaign resources. When the president is popular or the economy is strong, the campaign committees of the president's party usually invest more resources in challenger and open-seat races. Conversely, the out-party committees use more of their resources to support incumbents. When national conditions do not favor the president's party, the patterns are reversed: the in-party committees take a defensive posture that favors incumbents, and the out-party committees go on the offensive, using more of their resources to help nonincumbents.[18] The unpredictable nature of national political conditions and economic trends and of events that take place in states and congressional districts means that committee decision making and targeting are necessarily imperfect. As a result, some safe incumbents and uncompetitive nonincumbents inevitably receive committee assistance, whereas some competitive nonincumbents get little or no help.

The conditions surrounding the elections held in the early and mid-1990s made strategic decision making and targeting difficult, especially for the two House campaign committees.[19] Redistricting, always fraught with ambiguities, was complicated by racial redistricting issues that delayed many 1992 House elections while districts were being redrawn. It also introduced complications into later elections for the same reason. Court rulings over majority-minority House districts in Florida, Georgia, Illinois, New York, North Carolina, and Virginia required that the boundaries of numerous neighboring districts be moved before the 1998 elections.

Redrawn districts or newly created seats are only two of several factors that complicate the committees' tasks. The president's popularity often shifts up and down, making it difficult for the committees to decide whether to pursue an offensive or a defensive strategy. Congressional scandals and voter frustration with Congress result in some incumbents unexpectedly finding themselves in jeopardy. These circumstances give some challengers a correspondingly unexpected boost. The late retirements of some House members and the primary defeats of others further complicate the committees' efforts.

Because of the uncertainty surrounding post-redistricting elections, the NRCC and DCCC in the early 1990s drew up huge "watch" lists of so-called "opportunity," or competitive, races. During the 1992 elections, each committee's watch list initially included approximately 300 elections. The committees shortened the lists over the course of the campaign season, but going into the last week of the election each list still had more than 150 opportunity races—more than three times the number included at that point in the 1990 election. During the elections held between 1994 and 2000, the committees initially focused on about 150 seats before they pared down their lists to about 75 races midway in the campaign season, and further reduced them later.[20] As discussed in Chapter 1, 2002 was very different from previous election years. Immediately following redistricting, the parties concentrated on about 90 races each before honing in on around 45 competitive contests midway through the election season, and about 20 during the last two weeks or so.[21]

Individual candidates are selected for placement on the committees' watch lists on the basis of several criteria. The competitiveness of the district and incumbency are the first two considerations. Candidates running in districts that were decided by close margins in the last election or who are competing for open seats are likely to be placed on a committee's watch list. The strength of the candidate is another consideration in the case of nonincumbents. Those who have had political experience or have celebrity status are likely to be targeted for assistance. Challengers and open-seat contestants who demonstrate an ability to raise money and do well in the polls also are likely to receive support, as are those who field a professional campaign organization. Having an organization comprising talented campaign staff assures the committee that its resources will not go to waste. In some cases the Hill committees insist that certain personnel be hired as a precondition for receiving their assistance.

A variety of idiosyncratic factors also come into play when the committees select the candidates who will be given the most support initially. An incumbent who is accused of committing an ethical transgression, perceived to be out of touch with people in the district, in poor health, or in trouble for some other reason is a likely candidate for extra committee help. These difficulties often provoke a response by the other party's campaign committee, resulting in the incumbent's opponent also benefiting from extra party money and campaign services. Although party leaders work aggressively to recruit women and minorities to run for Congress, neither party uses gender or race as a criterion for determining who gets campaign assistance. Ideology also is not used to select candidates for support. Women, minorities, liberals, and conservatives are assisted only to the degree that their races are expected to be competitive.[22] As Davis, NRCC chair in the 106th and 107th congresses, explains,

> We don't have an ideological litmus test. We have one litmus test: Will the candidate vote for Denny Hastert [the Republican House leader for Speaker]? We try to be as cost effective as we can. We don't spend feel-good money to encourage a candidate who can't win. We make hard business decisions.[23]

The committees' lists of competitive elections are revised throughout the election season. Regional coordinators who monitor congressional races within designated parts of the country advise their colleagues in Washington about the latest developments in individual elections. As a result, some candidates drop in priority or are cut off from party help, and others gain more committee attention and support. The 2002 elections were notable for the number of unpredictable events that led the parties to change their initial resource allocations: Democratic senator Robert Torricelli quit his reelection campaign when it became apparent that his ethical transgressions would drag him down in defeat; Republican challenger Michael Taylor suspended his race for the Senate in Montana after the DSCC aired TV commercials showing him grooming a man's hair and alleging Taylor's hairstyling institute had defrauded the Department of Education's student aid program; and Sen. Paul Wellstone, D-Minn., died tragically just eleven days before the election.

Because of the tremendous uncertainty surrounding recent House elections, both the Democratic and Republican congressional campaign committees distribute their resources incrementally. Rather than drop a large quantity of money or extensive election services in a candidate's lap early in the campaign season, the committees distribute them piecemeal in response to the candidate's ability to meet a series of discrete fundraising and organizational goals. Incumbents usually meet these goals quickly, but they pose more formidable hurdles for challengers and open-seat candidates. Nonincumbents who meet their goals in a timely fashion are usually within reach of victory at the end of the election season and receive substantial party support. Of course, a party committee's ability to give them these contributions is limited by available funds.

CAMPAIGN CONTRIBUTIONS AND COORDINATED EXPENDITURES

Party contributions to candidates in the congressional elections held between 1974 and 2002 were restricted by the Federal Election Campaign Act.[24] National, congressional, and state party campaign committees could each give $5,000 to a House candidate at each stage of the election process: primary, runoff, and general election (see Table 1-1).[25] The parties' national and senatorial campaign committees could give a combined total of $17,500 in an election cycle to a candidate for the Senate. State committees could contribute an additional $5,000 to Senate candidates.

Parties also can spend larger sums to expressly help individual candidates. These outlays, referred to as "coordinated expenditures" because they can be made in direct coordination with a candidate's campaign, typically are for campaign services that a Hill committee or some other party organization gives to a candidate or purchases from a political consultant on the candidate's behalf. Coordinated expenditures often take the form of polls, TV commercials, radio ads, fundraising events, direct-mail solicitations, or issue research. They differ from campaign contributions in that both the party and the candidate share control over them, giving the party the ability to influence some aspects of how the campaign is run. Originally set in 1974 at $10,000 for all national party organizations, the limits for coordinated expenditures on behalf of House candidates are adjusted for inflation and reached $35,910 in 2002.[26] The limits for national party coordinated expenditures in Senate elections vary by state population and are indexed to inflation. In 2002 they ranged from $71,820 per committee in the smallest states to $1,092,023 in Texas. Had there been a Senate race in California, the limit for coordinated expenditures would have been set at $1,781,136.

State party committees are authorized to spend the same amounts in coordinated expenditures in House and Senate races as are the parties' national organizations, but some state party committees do not have the funds to do so. In races in which a state party lacks resources and a party's congressional or senatorial campaign committee deems it important for the party to spend as much money as possible, the state and national party organizations form "agency agreements" that transfer the state party's quota for coordinated expenditures to the national party.[27] In situations in which a state party has enough money to make the maximum legal contribution and coordinated expenditure in a targeted congressional race but has other priorities, such as a gubernatorial election or state legislative elections, national party organizations may induce the state party to spend their hard money in the congressional election by offering them a "money swap."[28] In many of these agreements, national party organizations make campaign contributions to state or local candidates or soft money transfers to state party organizations in sums that are equal to or slightly greater than the amounts of hard money they ask state parties to spend in congressional races. Other money swaps involve contributions and financial transfers across state lines. Money swaps involving soft money became more common than agency agreements in recent elections. They enable the parties to concentrate funds raised from across the nation into Senate and House races taking place in a small number of states and districts. By controlling the money flow, agency agreements and money swaps are among the methods Washington-based party organizations have used to coordinate national spending strategies in congressional elections.

From the mid-1970s through the early 1990s, most party activity in congressional elections took the form of cash contributions or coordinated expenditures on polling, fundraising, research, and other campaign services. The 1996 contests were the first in which the parties made independent expenditures with hard money and spent significant sums of hard and soft money on issue advocacy ads. During ensuing elections, the parties made an important tactical adjustment: they chose to conserve their federal dollars so that they could be concentrated, along with soft money, on issue advocacy ads in a small number of highly competitive races. To accomplish this objective the Democratic Party reduced its contributions and coordinated expenditures in congressional elections by 59 percent between 1996 and 2002. The Republican Party, which raised considerably more federal dollars than its Democratic counterpart, increased its contributions and coordinated expenditures by a mere 9 percent during this same period, a much lower rate of increase than in preceding years.

Nevertheless, the parties' total contributions and coordinated expenditures remained significant. The Democrats distributed approximately $1.6 million in contributions and $2.8 million in coordinated expenditures in the 2002 House races; the Republicans distributed roughly $2.2 million and $5.4 million in these contests (see Table 4-1). The Republican advantage in contributions and coordinated expenditures was even greater in the 2002 Senate races, with the GOP outspending the Democrats by a combined total of $12.5 million to $2.8 million.

Coordinated expenditures are an important aspect of party activity in congressional elections. Their higher limits, compared with those for cash contributions; the possibility for creating agency agreements; and the control they afford party committees in candidates' campaigns make coordinated expenditures an attractive avenue for party involvement. Coordinated spending also enables the parties to take advantage of economies of scale when purchasing and distributing campaign services. Because the parties purchase the services of political consultants in large quantities they pay below-market rates, which enables them to provide candidates with services whose true market value exceeds the FECA's coordinated expenditure limits.

The four Hill committees determine the parties' congressional campaign spending strategies and are an important source of party funds spent in

TABLE 4-1

Party Contributions and Coordinated Expenditures in the 2002 Congressional Elections

	House		Senate	
	Contributions	Coordinated expenditures	Contributions	Coordinated expenditures
Democratic				
DNC	$6,000	$0	$5,000	$0
DCCC	517,731	1,646,123	10,140	0
DSCC	0	0	362,796	93,628
State and local	1,124,715	1,122,021	182,705	2,112,163
Total Democratic	$1,648,446	$2,768,144	$560,641	$2,205,791
Republican				
RNC	$299,500	$4,859,308	$17,518	$9,137,632
NRCC	582,144	198,190	70,655	0
NRSC	65,000	0	352,458	553,206
State and local	1,237,391	387,183	2,103,386	171,594
Total Republican	$2,184,035	$5,444,681	$2,544,017	$9,962,432

Source: Compiled from Federal Election Commission data.

Note: Figures include party spending in all congressional elections, including primaries, runoffs, and uncontested races.

congressional elections (some funds are transferred to state and other party committees before they are distributed to candidates). The Hill committees also direct the contributions of many other party organizations. Indeed, the Republican committees were very successful in 2002 using money swaps and other inducements to persuade party committees in one state to contribute to congressional candidates running in other states. Finally, the Hill committees deliver most of the parties' campaign services.[29]

The campaign committees distribute most of their campaign support to candidates in close elections (see Table 4-2). The Democrats' allocation patterns for House candidates in 2002 indicate the party followed a modified

TABLE 4-2
Allocation of Party Contributions and Coordinated Expenditures in the 2002 Congressional Elections

	House		Senate	
	Democrats	Republicans	Democrats	Republicans
Incumbents				
In jeopardy	27%	19%	35%	15%
	(32)	(22)	(6)	(5)
Shoo-ins	12	6	3	2
	(119)	(127)	(5)	(7)
Challengers				
Hopefuls	17%	23%	15%	29%
	(22)	(32)	(5)	(6)
Likely losers	4	6	7	2
	(127)	(119)	(7)	(5)
Open-seat candidates				
Prospects	33%	39%	41%	52%
	(29)	(29)	(7)	(7)
Mismatched	6	7	—	—
	(18)	(18)	(0)	(0)
Total ($, thousands)	$3,324	$7,044	$2,589	$11,664
	(347)	(347)	(30)	(30)

Source: Compiled from Federal Election Commission data.

Notes: The categories of candidates are the same as those in Table 1-4. Figures include contributions and co-ordinated expenditures by all party committees to major-party general election candidates in contested races, excluding those in incumbent-versus-incumbent races. They do not include soft money expenditures. Dash = less than 0.5 percent. Some columns do not add to 100 percent because of rounding. The numbers of candidates are in parentheses.

defensive strategy. The party directed 39 percent of its money to incumbents. The remaining funds were committed to challengers and candidates for open seats. The minority party usually takes a more aggressive posture than does the majority party, especially in a midterm election year in which a member of the opposing party occupies the White House. However, 2002 was unusual in that redistricting, the war on terrorism, and President Bush's high approval ratings created a political landscape that was somewhat more hostile to Democratic House incumbents than their Republican counterparts. The DCCC's strategy in 2002 reflected these uncertainties and the worries voiced by Democratic legislators, including some who were not involved in close contests.

Democratic Party contributions and coordinated expenditures were fairly well targeted in 2002. The party delivered 27 percent of its funds to incumbents in jeopardy, 17 percent to hopeful challengers, and 33 percent to open-seat prospects. The party's ability to distribute 77 percent of its funds to candidates in elections decided by twenty or fewer percentage points was an improvement over some years, including 1992, when it distributed only 53 percent of its funds to candidates in close races, but fell short of other contests, such as 1996 and 2000, when the party distributed 82 percent of its funds to similarly classified candidates.[30] Part of the reason the Democrats' resource distribution is not better is that the party tends to be fairly indulgent of shoo-in incumbents.

In contrast to the Democrats' strategy, the plan adopted by the Republican Party in the 2002 House elections was moderately aggressive. Redistricting and the other factors that encouraged Democrats to err on the side favoring incumbents emboldened the Republicans to distribute somewhat more funds to GOP House challengers and open-seat candidates. Moreover, the Republican Party's hard money advantage enabled it to more than match the funds the Democratic Party distributed to its incumbents in jeopardy while still providing the lion's share of its funding to the party's House nonincumbents. The GOP delivered 62 percent of its funds to hopeful challengers and open-seat prospects and only 19 percent to incumbents in jeopardy. Republican party organizations, which traditionally distribute their resources more effectively than do the Democrats, distributed 81 percent of their funds to House candidates in competitive contests and only 19 percent to those in one-sided races—whose chances of victory were unlikely to change even with additional party money. According to NRCC Chairman Davis, his committee spent funds on likely-loser challengers to some extent because of a "war of attrition." Recent elections showed that spending money against nervous but safe Democratic incumbents would result in the relatively cash-strapped DCCC spending some of its scarce dollars in their races, preventing the Democratic committee from investing those resources on behalf of challengers and open-seat candidates in competitive contests.[31]

It is relatively easy for the parties to target their money in Senate elections. DSCC and NRSC officials typically have to assess their candidates' prospects in only thirty-three or thirty-four races per election season, and those races take place within borders that do not shift every ten years because of redistricting. Polling data also are available for all of the races. As a result, virtually all the parties' funds are spent in close elections. In 2002 the fact that there were only thirty two-party contested races made senatorial campaign decision-makers' jobs easier than usual. As a result, Democrats spent all but 10 percent of their money in competitive contests. They favored incumbents in jeopardy over hopeful challengers. The Republicans distributed all but 4 percent of their funds to candidates in close elections, favoring hopeful challengers over incumbents in jeopardy. Both parties perceived open-seat elections to be where many of the hardest-fought battles would take place, with the Democrats and the Republicans devoting 41 percent and 52 percent of their respective contributions and coordinated expenditures on those contests.

In addition to distributing campaign contributions and coordinated expenditures directly to candidates, the Hill committees encourage the flow of "party-connected" contributions from incumbents' leadership PACs and re-election accounts to needy candidates, such as nonincumbents and some new members. Leadership PACs have been involved in congressional elections since Rep. Henry Waxman, D-Calif., founded the first one in 1978, but they were few in number and distributed relatively little money before the late 1980s.[32] Their numbers had grown to 186 by 2002, when they distributed almost $24.3 million in contributions to congressional candidates. Although leadership PACs are technically political action committees rather than party organizations—and although contributions from one candidate to another are not the same as those from the party—the candidates who make these contributions share several of the party committees' objectives, and many rely on party cues when making them. Their ties to the congressional parties, their reliance on them for information, and the fact that, with few exceptions, all of their contributions flow to members of their party warrant the labeling of these contributions as party-connected.

During the 2002 elections, former and current members of Congress—mostly incumbents seeking reelection—and a small number of other prominent politicians contributed more than $31.9 million from their campaign accounts or leadership PACs to 692 primary and general election candidates (see Table 4-3). The biggest contributors were party leaders and policy entrepreneurs. Rep. Charles Rangel of New York, the Democrats' ranking member on

TABLE 4-3

Party-Connected Contributions in the 2002 Congressional Elections

	House		Senate	
	Democrats	Republicans	Democrats	Republicans
Leadership PAC contributions	$5,487,814	$9,061,160	$565,889	$1,420,970
Candidate contributions	3,813,465	2,327,788	250,230	337,547
Contributions from retirees and members not up for reelection	1,744,674	1,602,362	2,537,276	2,598,177
Contributions from nonfederal PACs	60,946	35,373	42,319	20,850
Total	$11,106,899	$13,026,683	$3,395,714	$4,377,544

Source: Compiled from data provided by the Center for Responsive Politics.

Note: Figures are for contributions from leadership PACs, congressional candidates, retired members, members of Congress not up for reelection in 2002, and PACs sponsored by nonfederal politicians to candidates in all congressional elections, including those in primaries, runoffs, and uncontested races.

the House Ways and Means Committee, and Republican representative Jerry Lewis of California, chairman of the Subcommittee on Defense of the House Appropriations Committee, led their respective parties in individual contributions, giving almost $115,000 and $108,000 from their own war chests. The two House whips, DeLay and Nancy Pelosi, D-Calif., led their parties in leadership PAC contributions. Pelosi's PAC to the Future and DeLay's Americans for a Republican Majority PAC each contributed more than $1 million to congressional candidates. The Majority Leader's Fund, associated with then–Republican majority leader Dick Armey contributed more than $326,000— the largest sum contributed by a former member of Congress or a member not running for reelection, followed by former House member and presidential candidate John Kasich's Pioneer PAC, which contributed in excess of $141,000. Armey and Kasich also contributed approximately $25,500 and $13,500, respectively, from their campaign accounts. Leadership '02, a PAC associated with former vice president Al Gore, came next, contributing $110,500, the next highest amount given by a former member.[33]

Party-connected contributions were distributed strategically, the vast majority of them to candidates in competitive contests (see Table 4-4). The major difference between party-connected contributions and money contributed by formal party organizations is that the distribution of party-connected funds

TABLE 4-4

Distribution of Party-Connected Contributions in the 2002 Congressional Elections

	House		Senate	
	Democrats	Republicans	Democrats	Republicans
Incumbents				
In jeopardy	30%	28%	35%	21%
Shoo-ins	15	18	11	10
Challengers				
Hopefuls	18%	14%	19%	33%
Likely losers	2	1	5	2
Open seats				
Prospects	30%	31%	31%	33%
Mismatched	5	8	—	—
Total (thousands)	$9,100	$10,869	$2,918	$3,927

Source: Compiled from data provided by the Center for Responsive Politics.

Notes: Figures are for contributions from leadership PACs, candidates, retired members, and members of Congress not up for reelection in 2002 to general election candidates in major-party contested races excluding those in incumbent-versus-incumbent races. Categories and numbers of candidates are the same as those in Table 4-2. Some columns do not add to 100 percent because of rounding.

favors incumbents, particularly shoo-ins, somewhat more. This difference reflects the fact that individuals who contribute party-connected funds, like party committees, are concerned with maximizing the number of seats under their party's control, but they also want to do favors (on which they can later collect) for congressional colleagues, including those who occupy safe seats. Party-connected contributions demonstrate that parties have become important vehicles for redistributing wealth among congressional candidates.

CAMPAIGN SERVICES

The parties' congressional and senatorial campaign committees provide selected candidates with assistance in specialized campaign activities, such as management, gauging public opinion, issue and opposition research, and communications.[34] They also provide transactional assistance, acting as brokers between candidates and the interest groups, individual contributors, political consultants, and powerful incumbents who possess some of the money, political contacts, and campaign expertise that candidates need. The DCCC and NRCC typically become closely involved in the campaigns of candidates on their watch lists and have little involvement in others. The DSCC and NRSC focus most of their attention on Senate candidates in competitive contests, but with so few elections to monitor they are better able to structure their relationships in response to the specific needs of individual candidates. As DSCC political director Andrew Grossman explains,

> We love all of our campaigns as much as they need to be loved. Some campaigns need a huge amount of help; some need little help, but help of a specific kind. Some campaigns build relationships around one party service; some campaigns build relationships around several services. Our help is customer-based.[35]

It is difficult to estimate precisely the value of Hill committee assistance. However, candidates in close races typically receive campaign services that would cost hundreds of thousands of dollars if purchased from a professional political consultant.

Campaign Management

Candidates and their campaign organizations can get help from their Hill committees with hiring and training campaign staff, making strategic and tactical decisions, and other management-related activities. The committees maintain directories of campaign managers, fundraising specialists, media experts, pollsters, voting list vendors, and other political consultants whom candidates can use for free and from whom they can purchase campaign services. Committee officials sometimes recommend that candidates, particularly nonincumbents in targeted races, hire from a list of "trusted" consultants, many of whom have worked for the party or an interest group that routinely supports the party. In some cases, hiring from a Hill committee's list of recommended consultants is a requirement for receiving other forms of party assistance.[36]

The Hill committees' field representatives and political staffs in Washington also serve as important sources of strategic advice. In most close races, specific party aides or consultants they hire are assigned to work with specific campaigns. Because they follow House and Senate elections nationwide and can draw on experiences from previous elections, the Hill committees are among the few organizations that have the knowledge and institutional memory to advise candidates and their managers on how to deal with some of the dilemmas they encounter. The congressional and senatorial campaign committees' political staffs are usually most heavily involved in the planning and tactical decision making of open-seat and challenger candidates. However, they also provide a great deal of advice to first-term members, members in close races, and House members running in heavily redrawn districts. National party strategic advice is usually appreciated, but some candidates and campaign aides have complained that Hill committee staff can be heavy-handed.

The six Washington party organizations train candidates and managers in the latest campaign techniques. The DCCC and NRCC hold training seminars at their headquarters for incumbents that cover topics such as staying in touch with constituents, getting the most political mileage out of franked mail, defending unpopular votes, and PAC fundraising. Congressional campaign committee staff also work with the national committees to host seminars for challengers and open-seat candidates around the country. These seminars focus on more basic subjects, such as giving the "stump" speech, filing campaign finance reports with the FEC, and building coalitions. Even long-term members of the House and Senate find the seminars beneficial as reminders of what they ought to be doing. Hill committee assistance is generally more important to hopeful challengers and open-seat prospects than to incumbents in jeopardy, reflecting the fact that incumbents' electoral difficulties are rarely the result of inexperience or a lack of knowledge about how to wage a campaign.

In 2002 both the DNC and the RNC hosted campaign training seminars across the nation for political candidates and activists. The DCCC held two candidate retreats in Washington and several "campaign colleges" in different regions of the nation. These featured presentations by DCCC directors and deputy directors on how to outline a campaign budget and develop finance, field, and media plans. DCCC staff also offered two-hour media training sessions at Harriman Communications Center, in its headquarters building.[37] The NRCC also held two specialized week-long training seminars in Washington to advise challengers and open-seat candidates how to discuss Social Security, education, and other national issues.[38] DSCC and NRSC staff met one-on-one with candidates when they came to Washington and sent aides to meet with candidates and their campaign staffs early in the election season to help them start writing a budget and campaign plan. The DSCC also provided up to six weeks of training for staff hired by its candidates and state party committees to conduct issue and opposition research.[39] According to political director Grossman, their philosophy was to help candidates staff their campaigns properly so that they could do the bulk of the work on their own and call on the DSCC for assistance when needed.

Gauging Public Opinion

Many candidates receive significant assistance in gauging public opinion from national party committees. The DNC and RNC disseminate the findings of nationwide polls via newsletters, memoranda, faxes, and e-mails to members of Congress, party activists, and congressional candidates. The parties' congressional and senatorial campaign committees commission hundreds of district and statewide polls and targeting studies in a given election season. Early on, they use recruitment surveys to show potential candidates the possibilities of waging competitive races and benchmark polls to inform declared candidates of their levels of support and of public opinion on the major issues. They use tracking polls to assist a small group of candidates who are running neck-and-neck with their opponents at the end of the campaign season. Some of these surveys are paid for entirely by a Hill committee and reported to the FEC as in-kind contributions or coordinated expenditures. Many are jointly financed by a committee and the candidates the polls serve.

Parties have significant advantages over individual candidates when it comes to purchasing polls. Parties are able to get polls at discount rates because they contract for so many of them. Parties also can use their extensive connections with polling firms to arrange to "piggyback" questions on polls taken for other clients. Benchmark polls, which can be useful weeks after they were taken, give party committees special opportunities to provide candidates with highly useful information at low cost. A party can purchase a poll for roughly $10,000 and give it to a candidate as an in-kind contribution or coordinated expenditure that is valued at a mere fraction of that amount if the party turns it over using a depreciation option allowed by the FEC. The party also can split the costs of a poll evenly with a candidate and claim that it is using the poll for planning purposes, thereby allowing the candidate to receive the full poll for half price.[40] All six Washington party organizations commission national polls to research issues they expect to occupy a prominent position on the national agenda.

In 2002 the NRCC spent $5 million on polling—five times more than it had spent in 1998—in order to keep its fingers on the pulse of voters in approximately sixty-five races. According to Chairman Davis, polling was critical to its decision making and planning in specific campaigns. Indeed, the committee hired more than one pollster to conduct surveys in a few elections.[41] In most cases the party shared with the candidates the gist of the poll results but did not give them the actual data or numbers so that the polls did not count as a party contribution or coordinated expenditure. The NRSC took at least one poll for every Senate race and several in close contests.[42] The DSCC took polls in the seventeen closest races, spending almost $1.1 million on gauging public opinion.[43] Officials from the six national party organizations agree on the importance of polling. Good polling combined with the right research helps produce the right message and makes for an effective campaign, especially when followed by a good voter turnout program.

Selected candidates also receive precinct-level targeting studies from the Hill committees. The DSCC and DCCC use geodemographic data provided by the National Committee for an Effective Congress (NCEC) to help their candidates develop targeting strategies. These data are matched with previous election results and current polling figures and are used to guide the candidates' direct-mail programs, media purchases, voter mobilization drives, and other campaign efforts.[44] Republican candidates receive similar targeting assistance from the NRCC's and NRSC's political divisions.

Issue and Opposition Research

During the 1980s, party organizations in Washington became major centers for political research. The DNC and RNC extended their research activities in several directions, most of which were and continue to be focused on the party rather than directed toward congressional candidates. The national committees routinely send materials on salient national issues to candidates for Congress, governorships, and state legislatures; to "allied" consultants and interest groups; and to activists at all levels. Party research typically includes statistics, tables, and charts drawn from major newspapers, the Associated Press wire service, the Internet, the LexisNexis computerized political database, national public opinion polls, and government publications. It weaves factual information with partisan themes and powerful anecdotes to underscore major campaign issues. Some individuals receive this information through the U.S. mail, but most get it by way of "blast-faxes," e-mails, and web site postings that the committees transmit daily to hundreds of thousands during the campaign season. Many journalists and political commentators also are sent issue research—albeit with a partisan spin—by the national committees.

The congressional and senatorial campaign committees also disseminate massive amounts of issue-related materials by mail, fax, and e-mail to candidates, party activists, and partisan political consultants. During the past few Congresses, both parties' House and Senate leaderships distributed talking points, memoranda, pamphlets, and issue handbooks designed to help candidates develop issue positions, write speeches, and prepare for debates. In 2002 the Hill committees furnished their candidates with information on a variety of issues. For example, the DCCC gave its candidates research and talking points stating that the Republicans' plan for Social Security privatization would result in seniors' benefits being cut. Its GOP counterpart sent out a two-page memo to its candidates elaborating the differences between Social

Security privatization and the creation of Social Security personal accounts, and urged them to correct their opponents and reporters when they conflated them because "In politics, words matter." [45]

More important than this generic research are the more detailed materials that the Hill committees distribute to individual candidates. Each committee routinely distributes information on the substance and political implications of congressional roll-call votes. Many nonincumbents, who are unable to turn to congressional aides, the Library of Congress, or Washington-based interest groups for information on important issues, use this information to develop policy positions. Challengers also use it to plan attacks on incumbents.

The two House campaign committees assemble highly detailed issue research packages for some candidates involved in competitive races. These packages present hard facts about issues that are important to local voters and talking points that help candidates discuss these issues in a thematic and interesting manner. The committees also provide information pinpointing vulnerabilities in an opponent's issue positions, previous roll-call votes, and professional and personal lives. A fairly new aspect of their research concerns the use of satellite technology to monitor campaign ads. This technology enables the committees to identify attacks their opponents use against their candidates almost immediately, greatly accelerating their ability to prepare a response.

During the 2002 elections the DCCC provided individualized research packages for roughly forty of its candidates in targeted races. The packages presented detailed information on how Republican House members' votes on legislation concerning health care, gun control, education, the environment, and other major issues would affect different groups of constituents. The NRCC invested $2 million and hired six researchers to conduct similar kinds of detailed research in forty-six campaigns. This research highlighted how Republican-supported tax cuts, anticrime legislation, and other popular GOP proposals helped people living in individual congressional districts. It also identified aspects of the opponent's candidacy that were vulnerable to attack.[46] The DSCC provided substantial research assistance in nineteen states, but most of its efforts went to training campaign and state party aides in how to conduct research.[47] The NRSC provided issue and opposition research for all of its Senate candidates.[48]

Campaign Communications

The Hill committees assist selected candidates with campaign communications. The DCCC and the NRCC own television and radio production facilities complete with satellite capabilities, and for much of the 1980s and 1990s they furnished large numbers of candidates with technical and editorial assistance in producing campaign ads. By 1998, technological developments made it possible for candidates and media consultants to gain access to high-quality, inexpensive recording and editing technology without visiting their party's Washington headquarters or renting an expensive editing suite. As a result, fewer congressional candidates used the DCCC's and NRCC's production facilities to tape or edit their ads, and only a handful received a full-service media package wherein the committee developed the campaign's advertising themes, wrote its scripts, and arranged for its advertisements to be aired on local television stations. However, some nonincumbents who had limited budgets used voiceovers, sound, and text to customize party-produced "generic" or "doughnut" ads. Many incumbents, and a few nonincumbents, used the center's satellite capabilities to appear "live" on television news shows, at fundraisers, and at events in their districts. Satellite technology is extremely popular with incumbents from western states, who are not able to get back to their districts as frequently as those living on the East Coast or in the Midwest. Finally, the committees played an active role in advising their campaigns on the quality of their television and radio ads. Using streaming video on the Internet, committee aides were able to receive campaign television ads within minutes of when they were produced, review them seconds later, and discuss their recommendations with campaign representatives right away. Campaign committee assistance was made available to candidates free of charge or at well below market rates.

The DSCC and NRSC traditionally have been less involved than their House counterparts in candidates' campaign communications. Rather than produce television, radio, or direct-mail advertisements, committee staff often comment on ads created by private consultants. They also finance some ads through in-kind contributions and coordinated expenditures.

Moreover, the Hill committees take on supporting roles in other aspects of campaign communications by doing work that candidates' campaign committees cannot. They plant stories with the *New York Times, Washington Post,* and other national media. They release negative information about the opposing party's candidates. And, as is discussed later, their issue advocacy and independent expenditures can have a major impact on the tenor of a congressional campaign. Senatorial and congressional campaign committee research and communication efforts have clearly contributed to the nationalization of American politics.

Fundraising

In addition to providing contributions, coordinated expenditures, and campaign services directly to candidates, and steering party-connected contributions to them, the Hill committees help selected candidates raise money from individuals and PACs. To this end, the committees give the candidates strategic advice and fundraising assistance, introducing their top prospects to potential donors and getting these candidates' campaign plans into the donors' hands. Committee staff also furnish PACs and other Washington insiders with other forms of information they can use when formulating their contribution strategies and selecting individual candidates for support.

All six national party organizations give candidates tips on how to organize fundraising committees and events. The Republican Hill committees and the DSCC even furnish some candidates with contributor lists, with the proviso that the candidates surrender their own lists to the committee after the election. Sometimes the parties host high-dollar events in Washington or make arrangements for party leaders to attend events held around the country either in person or via satellite television uplink. The Speaker of the House and other congressional leaders can draw lobbyists, PAC managers, and other big contributors to even the most obscure candidate's fundraising event. Of course, nothing can draw a crowd of big contributors like an appearance by the president, and President Bush set a new record in this regard, as noted earlier.

The committees also steer large contributions from wealthy individuals, PACs, or members of Congress to needy candidates. It is illegal for the parties to earmark checks they receive from individuals or PACs for specific candidates, but committee members and staff can suggest to contributors that they give to one of the candidates on the committee's watch list. Sometimes they reinforce this message by sending out fundraising letters on behalf of a candidate, sponsoring events that list congressional leaders as the event's hosts, or organizing joint fundraising events.

The Hill committees also give candidates the knowledge and tools needed to obtain money from PACs. The committees help candidates design "PAC kits" they can use to introduce themselves to members of the PAC community.[49] They also distribute lists of PACs that include the name of a contact person at each PAC and indicate how much cash the PAC has on hand, so that candidates will neither waste their time soliciting committees that have no money nor take no for an answer when a PAC manager claims poverty but still has funds. Candidates are coached on how to fill out the questionnaires that some PACs use to guide their contributions and on how to build coalitions of local PAC contributors so that they can raise money from national PACs. All four Hill committees make meeting rooms and telephones available to facilitate PAC fundraising, which cannot be conducted legally on Capitol grounds.

The committees also help candidates raise money from PACs by manipulating the informational environment in which PACs make their contribution decisions. The committees' PAC directors work to channel the flow of PAC money toward their party's most competitive congressional contenders and away from their opponents. This is an especially difficult task to perform for House challengers and open-seat candidates because they are largely unknown to the PAC community. Some junior House members also need to have attention called to their races. The PAC directors often call on party leaders, committee and subcommittee chairs, or ranking members to attend a candidate's fundraising event or to telephone a PAC manager on the candidate's behalf.

The Hill committees use several methods to circulate information about House and Senate elections to PACs and other potential contributors. The committees publicize their targeting lists and contribution activities to draw the attention of PACs and wealthy individual contributors. The committees also host receptions, often referred to as "meet and greets," at their headquarters and national conventions to give candidates, especially nonincumbents, an opportunity to ask PAC managers for contributions. Campaign updates are mailed, e-mailed, or faxed to about one thousand of the largest PACs on a weekly basis during the peak of the election season to inform them of targeted candidates' electoral prospects, financial needs, poll results, endorsements, campaign highlights, and revelations about problems experienced by their opponents. Streams of communications are also sent to the editors of the *Cook Political Report,* the *Rothenberg Political Report,* and other political newsletters that handicap congressional races. A favorable write-up in one of these can help a nonincumbent raise more PAC money.

The Hill committees also hold briefings to discuss their opportunity races and to inform PAC managers about their candidates' progress. These are important forums for networking among campaign finance elites. They give PAC managers the opportunity to ask Hill committee staffers about specific campaigns and to discuss contribution strategies among themselves.

The campaign committees' PAC directors and party leaders spend a tremendous amount of time making telephone calls on behalf of their most competitive and financially needy candidates. Some of these calls are made to PAC managers who are recognized leaders of PAC networks. The DCCC and DSCC, for example, work closely with the NCEC and the AFL-CIO's COPE; their GOP counterparts work closely with the Business-Industry Political Action Committee (BIPAC). The committees encourage these "lead" PACs to endorse the party's top contestants and to communicate their support to other PACs in their networks.

One of the more controversial ways that the Hill committees raise money for needy candidates is by "leveraging" it. Campaign committee staffs organize functions and clubs that promise PAC managers, lobbyists, and others access to congressional leaders in return for large contributions. Following the Republican takeover of Congress in the mid-1990s, Majority Whip DeLay greeted lobbyists with a list that categorized the four hundred largest PACs as "Friendly" or "Unfriendly," depending on the proportion of their contributions that went to Republicans in the 1994 elections, to hammer home the message that groups that wanted access to Republican leaders would be expected to give most of their PAC money to GOP candidates and party committees in the future.[50] He continued to deliver this message through the 2002 elections.

The Hill committees also use "buddy systems" to match financially needy but promising nonincumbents and freshmen with committee chairs and other powerful incumbents for fundraising purposes. These senior incumbents offer their partners contributions, provide advice on campaign-related topics, and use their influence to persuade PAC managers and individuals who have made large contributions to their campaigns to contribute to their "buddy." [51] The buddy system's impact on fundraising is hard to estimate, but during the 2002 elections, Republican and Democratic House and Senate party leaders, committee chairs, and ranking members raised millions of dollars for colleagues who were in jeopardy or for competitive nonincumbents. As suggested by the number of incumbents who made contributions from their campaign accounts and leadership PACs to other House candidates, even more members of Congress were involved in redistributing the wealth during the 2002 elections.

The Hill committees are important intermediaries in the fundraising process because they help needy challengers, open-seat candidates, and incumbents raise money from other PACs, other candidates, and individuals who make large contributions. The committees have created symbiotic relationships with some PACs, resulting in parties' becoming important brokers between candidates and contributors.[52] The relationships are based largely on honest and reliable exchanges of information about the prospects of individual candidates. Hill committee officials and PAC managers recognize that accurate information is the key to this relationship and to the ability of both groups to help candidates.

Party communications to PACs are somewhat controversial because they can harm some individual candidates' fundraising prospects. Candidates who receive their Hill committee's endorsement derive significant fundraising advantages from such communications, but nonincumbents who do not are usually unable to collect significant funds from PACs. Some PAC managers justify refusing a contribution request because a nonincumbent was not included on a Hill committee's watch list. Hill committee fundraising efforts can create both winners and losers in congressional elections.

Grassroots Activities

Not all of the campaign assistance that House and Senate candidates get from parties comes from Washington, and not all of it is given by the parties' congressional and senatorial campaign committees. Some state and local party committees give candidates assistance in a few of the aspects of campaigning discussed above, but these committees tend to be less influential than the Hill committees in areas requiring technical expertise, in-depth research, or connections with Washington PACs and political consultants.[53] State and local party committees do, however, provide congressional candidates with substantial help in grassroots campaigning. Most state committees help fund and organize registration and get-out-the-vote drives, set up telephone banks, and circulate campaign literature to voters.[54] Many local parties conduct these same activities as well as organize informal coffees to introduce candidates to voters, canvass door-to-door, distribute posters and lawn signs, put up billboards, and engage in other types of campaign field work.[55] Some of this activity is organized and paid for by the state and local party organizations themselves; however, a significant portion of it is funded by party committees in Washington under the guise of the coordinated campaign—a cooperative party-building and voter mobilization program discussed below.

INDEPENDENT, PARALLEL, AND COORDINATED CAMPAIGNS

As noted earlier, party campaigning extends beyond the money and campaign services party organizations provide directly to candidates. The national parties' increased roles in setting the national political agenda and their provision of campaign funds and services to candidates and state and local party organizations constitute their earliest adaptations to the campaign finance system and the enactment of the FECA. As the regulatory environment established by the FECA was weakened and the candidate-centered system continued to evolve, political parties began to extend their roles in congressional elections using soft money, issue advocacy, and new voter mobilization techniques. By 2002 the parties were using independent, parallel, and coordinated campaigns involving pollsters and other researchers, media consultants, direct-mail and mass telephone experts, and other strategists to influence congressional elections. The Hill committees were at the epicenter of these campaigns, but national, state, and local party committees also were involved in them. The same is true of numerous party-connected groups, mostly sponsored by current and former members of Congress, and allied interest groups.

The independent campaign consists primarily of what the FECA classifies as independent expenditures—advertisements that *expressly* call for the election or defeat of a federal candidate. They are conducted almost exclusively in targeted races, and they are generally more aggressive than are candidate communications. The parties were first allowed to make these in 1996 after the Supreme Court's ruling in *Colorado Republican Federal Campaign Committee v. Federal Election Commission.*[56] Independent expenditures must be made with hard money and without the candidate's knowledge or consent. They usually take the form of television, radio, direct mail, or mass telephone calls. To make these expenditures effective, parties conduct polls and other research. Unlike candidate ads, independent expenditures that appear on television or radio do not qualify for lowest unit rate charges. For this reason, and because they must be made with hard money, party committees do not usually spend large sums on them. The DCCC spent less than $1.2 million on such ads in 2002, and the NRCC spent slightly more than $1.3 million. State and local Democratic Party committees spent almost $514,000 and their Republican counterparts spent about $122,000. The DNC, DSCC, and NRSC opted not to make independent expenditures in the 2002 elections, preferring to use these funds on issue advocacy ads.

The parallel campaign features many of the same organizational efforts as do candidate campaigns and independent expenditures, including polling, issue research, and campaign communications. Among the earliest efforts at parallel campaigning were the RNC's televised ads "Vote Republican, For a Change," aired in 1980 and the Democrats' "It Isn't Fair, It's Republican," aired in 1982. Both of these ads were designed to set a broad national political agenda intended to benefit a party's candidates without running afoul of campaign finance laws that at the time prohibited political parties from financing candidate-focused campaign commercials as independent expenditures or with soft money. This element of the law was interpreted by the courts in 1996 to allow parties to make candidate-focused independent expenditures and issue advocacy ads.

Party parallel campaigns, like independent campaigns, are waged primarily in competitive contests. The congressional and senatorial campaign committees, which spearhead and finance most of these efforts, use their staffs and political consultants to gauge public opinion, identify a candidate's and his or her opponent's strengths and weaknesses, and fashion messages designed to work to their candidate's benefit. The parties then use television, radio, direct mail, and other issue advocacy communications to disseminate these messages directly to voters in order to influence the election outcome. Most of the party money used to finance the parallel campaign originates at the national level and is transferred to party committees in states hosting competitive elections. As such, this campaign requires greater coordination among a party's congressional, senatorial, national, and state party committees than does the independent campaign. Moreover, some aspects of the parallel campaign are coordinated with interest groups and congressional candidates.

Most party issue advocacy takes the form of television or radio advertisements, but in 2002 some issue advocacy was done through the mail and prerecorded mass telephone calls. Parties (and some interest groups) use issue advocacy to encourage citizens to support or oppose public policies or to praise or criticize specific federal candidates. Like independent expenditures of TV or radio ads, broadcast issue advocacy ads differ from candidate ads in that they do not qualify for lowest unit rate charges. Unlike independent expenditures, they can be made using a combination of hard and soft money and *cannot expressly* advocate the election or defeat of a candidate. Using issue advocacy ads, parties are able to concentrate huge sums of money collected from a tiny sector of society in a small number of hotly contested races. Whether issue advocacy ads can be coordinated with a candidate's campaign has been the subject of a legal debate, but coordination has occurred in the 1996 through 2002 elections. Indeed, a study of established political consultants who provided strategic, polling, research, fundraising, direct mail, mass media communications, or voter mobilization services to candidates in the 2002 elections showed that 63 percent of them participated in or observed such coordination. Media consultants reported the highest levels of coordination, reaching 82 percent.[57]

Party issue advocacy often resembles candidate-sponsored communications, and it is often difficult to distinguish between them. The major difference is that the latter are more negative or contrast-oriented, and they are more likely to focus on the opposing candidate. Negative and comparative party issue advocacy enables candidates to avoid taking responsibility for election mudslinging. Issue advocacy also enables parties and interest groups to influence the campaign agenda in individual congressional races, forcing candidates to discuss issues they might otherwise wish to avoid. As a result, some candidates find themselves campaigning on a political agenda set by a party organization rather than by themselves or their opponents.[58] When party committees, interest groups, or other candidates have purchased all of a television station's advertising time, candidates find themselves not only having to address a harmful set of issues but also unable to respond to those issues on air. Issue advocacy has become an important weapon in the arsenals that party committees use to help their candidates.

The DCCC's 2002 parallel campaign drew on the expertise of roughly twenty nationally renowned pollsters, media consultants, and direct-mail experts. The DCCC transferred $47.9 million in federal and nonfederal funds to Democratic state parties to help fund its parallel and coordinated campaigns in competitive districts. Approximately $35 million was spent to produce and broadcast 175 individual issue advocacy ads. Additional sums were used to design and distribute 200 unique pieces of direct mail and to contact minority voters via African American and Hispanic media.[59]

The NRCC's parallel campaign was substantially more extensive than the DCCC's, reflecting the GOP committee's greater wealth. The NRCC spent $70 million on 181 unique issue advocacy ads that were broadcast to help sixteen incumbents, eight challengers, and twenty-one candidates for open-seat races. The committee also spent $5.5 million to finance 319 pieces of direct mail to advance the causes of nine incumbents, four challengers, and nineteen open-seat candidates. Many of these communications were used to counter Democratic candidate and party attacks claiming that Republican candidates were planning to privatize Social Security. Others were targeted to African American and Hispanic radio stations as part of a larger Republican effort to expand the GOP tent.[60] Unlike the DCCC, the NRCC financed many of these expenditures directly, rather than transferring funds to Republican state central committees, which in turn paid for them. Even so, the NRCC transferred more than $29 million to Republican party committees in states that had competitive House seats.

Both senatorial campaign committees spent considerable funds on their parallel campaigns. The DSCC spent $56.2 million to televise issue advocacy ads to help six incumbents, four challengers, and six candidates for open seats. It invested almost $3.5 million on radio ads to assist five incumbents, two challengers, and two open-seat candidates. The committee spent an additional $7.9 million on direct mail for six incumbents, two challengers, and four open-seat candidates.[61] It also transferred more than $74.4 million to Democratic state party committees hosting competitive Senate races.

The NRSC also ran a spirited parallel campaign. It was assisted in its endeavors by a $10 million transfer from the RNC. The senatorial campaign committee televised 156 unique issue advocacy ads to help seven incumbents, twelve challengers, and seven candidates in open-seat races. Most of these were designed, videotaped, and edited by five media teams comprising top-ranked GOP consultants. The NRSC also spent about $5 million on direct mail, much of which was distributed in May and June, when there was little political competition in voters' mail boxes. Some of these expenditures were paid for directly by the committee, but others were paid for using the $56.9 million the committee transferred to Republican state party committees.[62]

The coordinated campaign entails traditional party campaigning enhanced by innovations in communications, database management, and voter mobilization.

Important elements of the coordinated campaign involve voter identification, absentee ballot programs, and other voter mobilization efforts. Beginning in the 1960s, first the RNC and then the DNC assisted state party organizations with voter registration, voter-list development, targeting, GOTV drives, and other campaign efforts designed to benefit a party's entire ticket. The Hill committees also participated in these efforts, often spearheading them in midterm elections. Contemporary coordinated campaigns often involve the Hill committees; national committees; state and local party organizations; allied interest groups; and federal, state, and local candidates.

Both parties invested heavily in coordinated campaigns during the 2002 congressional elections. The Republicans staged their most expensive and sophisticated GOTV and polling operation ever. In addition to the millions of dollars transferred by the NRCC and NRSC, the RNC also transferred $59.7 million to participate in these activities and help strengthen state and local Republican Party organizations. Prior to the elections, the RNC invested $1 million on more than fifty tests designed to discern the best way to get GOP voters to the polls, finding that personal contacts during the weekend before the election boosted turnout by two to three percentage points, having a bigger impact on turnout than did television ads and other high-tech approaches.[63] NRSC political director Chris LaCivita's tongue-in-cheek response to the findings are telling: "The research showed that Republicans [in the past] had mistakenly believed that 'GOTV' meant get on television, not get out the vote." [64] In response to its findings, the party embraced what party officials labeled a "back to the future approach." [65]

Under the guise of its "72-Hour Task Force," the Republican Party emulated voter turnout programs that had been developed by organized labor and the Democrats. The RNC spent millions of dollars to update state party committees' voter lists and create grassroots volunteer precinct organizations in states with targeted elections. Participants in the program residing in cities or suburban areas were asked to knock on the doors of forty or so of their GOP-leaning neighbors during the last three days of the election, urge these individuals to vote Republican, and offer them transportation to the polls. Those living in rural locations were asked to contact potential Republican voters by telephone in order to get them to vote. Urban, suburban, and rural participants were asked to take their message to local civic organizations. The RNC also recruited 1,500 volunteers from the Washington, D.C., area—mainly Republican congressional aides who took vacation days. Armed with Palm Pilots stocked with voter information, 72-Hour Task Force volunteers knocked on doors, recorded individuals' voting intentions, helped GOP supporters who needed them obtain absentee ballots, and personally contacted and telephoned other GOP voters in the final days of the election season.[66]

The RNC's efforts were supplemented by the NRSC; the NRCC; state and local Republican organizations; and STOMP, the voter mobilization program organized by DeLay. STOMP rented 73 buses and 245 vans to transport approximately eight thousand Republican volunteers residing in uncompetitive districts as far away as two hundred miles so that they could help mobilize GOP voters in close races. Finally, the White House made President Bush, Vice President Cheney, and other Republican leaders available for appearances in districts and states targeted by the NRCC or NRSC. These visits helped motivate Republican campaign workers and volunteers, drew media attention to GOP candidates' campaigns, knocked the candidate's opponents out of the news, and presumably helped the party capture extra votes in competitive contests.[67] It is difficult to gauge the success of the 72-Hour Task Force, STOMP, and other Republican voter mobilization programs. However, these programs succeeded in rounding up thousands of individuals to participate in grassroots efforts in states hosting close races, many of which were narrowly won by Republican candidates.

Possessing fewer financial resources and the ability to rely on labor unions and other groups to help get their supporters to the polls, the Democrats committed less money to voter mobilization activities than did the Republicans. The DNC spent about $15 million on voter mobilization. Some of these funds were used to rebuild state voter files, including fixing twenty-five million incorrect addresses, and scrubbing the names of 322,000 deceased voters. Other funds were committed to the Women's Vote Project, which identified and mobilized working women who did not have a college education. Additional resources were spent on door-to-door campaigning intended to mobilize African Americans, Hispanics, and other traditional Democratic constituencies. These efforts were supplemented by considerable outlays by the DCCC and DSCC, and by a $20 million effort by the AFL-CIO.[68]

Party-connected organizations sponsored by members of Congress, congressional candidates and retirees, and party committees also participate in independent, parallel, and coordinated campaigns. Many of these groups are classified as 527 committees, which were discussed in Chapter 1. Some of these organizations are leadership PACs that are fueled by hard money, others are fueled by soft money, and others by both hard and soft dollars. This makes it difficult to determine the exact amounts some of these committees spend to influence congressional elections. Nevertheless, estimates for the 2002 congressional elections suggest that the top 125 such organizations spent more than $73.5 million. Just over 70 percent of this amount was spent by sixty-seven committees sponsored primarily by Democrats; the remainder was used by fifty-eight groups sponsored by Republicans.[69] Much of this money was used to influence the outcomes of competitive congressional elections, but other sums were spent on candidate recruitment, training, and other election-related activities.

Party and party-connected independent, parallel, and coordinated campaign activities can be a tremendous boon to a candidate, but they often cost a campaign some of its autonomy and they also may backfire. Once the Hill committees target a race and decide to invest considerable resources in it, they often make demands on the campaigns receiving this largess. Some of these demands involve campaign staffing and budgeting. As noted in Chapter 2, the DCCC became directly involved in the Feeley campaign in Colorado's 7th district, placing one of its operatives over one of Feeley's long-time confidants as the campaign's de facto manager. The NRCC was not as directly involved in the management of the Beauprez campaign, but Sean Murphy, the campaign's manager, considered the committee's efforts extremely intrusive, complaining that NRCC staff "crawl up our ass on a daily basis." [70]

Pressure from Hill committee staff in Washington, D.C., can be frustrating and demoralizing to a campaign organization but not nearly as devastating as when a party commits a major blunder. Poor research or coordination between a party committee and a candidate campaign organization can result in a party advertisement having to be taken off the air because it makes a false accusation against an opponent, forcing its own candidate to go off message to address the error. Even worse, a party ad designed to directly help a candidate may misrepresent that candidate's position on a key issue. This occurred in the closely fought race between Democratic incumbent Chet Edwards and Republican challenger Ramsey Farley in Texas's 11th congressional district. The NRCC televised an issue advocacy ad stating that Farley supported President Bush's No Child Left Behind Act, but the candidate was previously quoted on a local radio station as stating, "I have to disagree very vehemently with. . .Bush's education bill. I do not really know what it contains. I've just seen [a] synopsis of it, but I don't think it was what I would have voted for." Edwards, who supported the president's bill, turned the blunder against Farley, airing a thirty-second TV ad accusing him of waffling on the issue and stating, "We can't trust what Ramsey Farley says." [71] The ad harmed Farley's credibility and his ability to focus on his core campaign issues. It probably contributed to his narrow defeat.

THE IMPACT OF PARTY CAMPAIGNING

How valuable do House and Senate candidates find the campaign services they receive from party organizations? When asked to rate the importance of campaign assistance from local, state, and national party organizations and union, business, and advocacy groups and PACs in aspects of campaigning requiring professional expertise or in-depth research, candidates and campaign aides involved in the 2002 House elections ranked their party's Hill committee highly. Campaigners gave top evaluations to the Hill committees for campaign management, information about voters, issue and opposition research, mass media advertising, and development of the candidate's public image. Interest groups received somewhat higher evaluations for assistance in fundraising.

Recall that congressional campaign committee assistance is generally targeted to a small number of close contests.[72] For example, about one-half of all Republican House candidates in elections decided by 20 percent or less of the vote, and 28 percent of their Democratic counterparts rated their party's congressional campaign committee as moderately, very, or extremely helpful in campaign management (see Table 4-5). More than half of each party's candidates in competitive races considered their party's congressional campaign committee assistance in fundraising and mass media communications to have been at least moderately important. Competitive Republicans gave more favorable evaluations to Hill committee assistance in campaign management, gauging public opinion, and issue and opposition research than did their Democratic counterparts. With the exception of fundraising, for which more incumbents in jeopardy reported receiving the most congressional campaign committee assistance, open-seat prospects provided the most positive evaluations of Hill committee campaign services. In sum, the evaluations of House campaigners indicate the Hill committees are important campaign service providers, and most congressional campaign committee help is given to candidates in close races, reflecting the parties' goal of winning as many seats in Congress as possible.

Local party committees received the strongest evaluations for assistance with registering voters, GOTV drives, and providing campaign volunteers. Roughly half of all campaigners assessed their local party's contributions to have been moderately, very, or extremely important. State party committees were rated next highest for voter mobilization activities. Republicans reported their party's state committee played a substantial role in providing campaign workers. Many Democrats were somewhat less impressed with their state parties' performance in this regard; most maintained that labor unions provided them with more volunteer campaign workers. These evaluations demonstrate the vibrancy of state and local parties in some parts of the country. They also show the congressional, senatorial, and national committees' limited involvement in grassroots campaigning, which frequently amounts to providing funding to help fuel these efforts rather than participating in them directly.

TABLE 4-5

House Campaigners' Appraisals of the Assistance Provided by the Congressional Campaign Committees

	DCCC						NRCC					
	Incumbents		Challengers		Open-seat candidates		Incumbents		Challengers		Open-seat candidates	
	In jeopardy	Shoo-ins	Hopefuls	Likely losers	Prospects	Mismatched	In jeopardy	Shoo-ins	Hopefuls	Likely losers	Prospects	Mismatched
Campaign management	12%	9%	33%	3%	37%	13%	42%	3%	47%	9%	60%	10%
Fundraising	53	30	46	9	53	25	67	8	47	7	57	20
Media advertising	47	16	50	2	67	13	58	19	53	15	63	20
Information about voters	31	42	53	13	74	25	64	29	47	18	75	20
Issue and opposition research	25	15	57	9	53	38	46	14	71	30	80	40
Voter mobilization	18	18	43	6	21	13	25	9	25	9	47	10
Volunteer workers	—	2	36	3	42	25	42	—	12	—	40	10
(N)	(16)	(45)	(15)	(68)	(19)	(8)	(11)	(35)	(17)	(54)	(16)	(10)

Source: The 2002 Congressional Campaign Study.

Notes: Figures represent the percentage of House campaigners who evaluated their congressional campaign committee as moderately, very, or extremely helpful in each campaign activity. Figures are for general election candidates in major-party contested races, excluding those in incumbent-versus-incumbent races. Dashes = less than 0.5 percent.

Colorado's 7th congressional district race between Beauprez and Feeley is an example of a House race in which both parties became heavily involved. In fact, the parties' involvement began well before the campaign season, as both parties tried to gain the upper hand in drawing the new district and reconfiguring old seats. Democratic and Republican national party leaders also were heavily involved in candidate recruitment, as noted in Chapter 2. Once the general election field was set, national, state, and local party assistance was forthcoming.

The Democratic Party provided the Feeley campaign with substantial direct support. In addition to providing the campaign staff mentioned in Chapter 3, the party gave Feeley $10,000 in contributions and $18,445 in coordinated expenditures. Democratic members of Congress, their leadership PACs, and congressional retirees contributed an additional $52,000, $82,116, and $1,000, respectively. The DCCC also provided the campaign with daily briefings; weekly access to its consultants; and fundraising, research, and other forms of assistance. The efforts of the DCCC's PAC director and other personnel undoubtedly had a major impact on Feeley's ability to raise money from PACs and individuals tied into congressional donor networks.[73]

The Democrats also carried out significant coordinated and parallel campaign activity. The DCCC transferred nearly $2.7 million to the Colorado Democratic Party (CDP), which served as a conduit for all of its issue advocacy and soft money spending. The DNC transferred an additional $654,000.[74] The CDP spent almost $622,000 on six televised issue advocacy ads and $180,000 on seven direct-mail pieces criticizing Beauprez and hailing Feeley. The DCCC also helped fund two voter personal contacts and one radio ad. The DNC financed an additional three direct-mail letters, which were targeted to senior citizens, Hispanics, and Republican young women. The Feeley campaign was informed of the content of most of this advertising. Using its own funds and money raised from other Democratic Party committees and candidates, the Colorado Democratic Party conducted a "96-Hour Program" involving literature drops, telephone calls, transportation, and other grassroots efforts aimed at getting its voters to the polls. Altogether, Democratic Party organizations were responsible for nineteen individual voter contacts, four more than were made by Feeley's campaign organization. The Democrats did not make any independent expenditures in the race.[75]

The Republican Party committees' greater resources enabled them to assume a larger role in the race compared to their Democratic rivals. The Republican Party provided the Beauprez campaign with substantial direct support, including $54,320 in contributions. Some of these contributions were made by the NRCC and the Colorado Republican Party; Republican state parties from neighboring

New Mexico, Utah, and Wyoming each contributed $10,000, at the NRCC's recommendation. The Republicans also spent $70,925 in coordinated expenditures in the race. Republican members, their leadership PACs, and congressional retirees contributed an additional $18,000, $122,961, and $1,500, respectively. Like the DCCC, the NRCC provided strategic advice on an almost daily basis. The NRCC also provided the campaign with substantial fundraising assistance. It arranged for President Bush to attend a luncheon that raised more than $1.5 million: $600,000 for the Beauprez campaign and a similar amount for the state GOP, which used much of its share to help Beauprez. The NRCC encouraged several members of Congress and Bush administration officials to frequently stump for Beauprez in the district, helping him garner media attention. The president attended a pep rally in Denver a week before election day, dominating the airwaves and energizing Republican volunteers and voters.[76]

The party also engaged in unprecedented independent, parallel, and coordinated campaign spending. The NRCC and the RNC transferred nearly $2.2 million and $1.8 million, respectively, to the Colorado Republican Federal Campaign Committee—an entity the state GOP created primarily to help House and Senate candidates.[77] A substantial portion of this money was used to pay for five televised issue advocacy ads and twenty-four direct-mail ads. These ads, which were shown in advance to the Beauprez campaign, praised Beauprez and lambasted Feeley without violating federal regulations prohibiting soft money ads from expressly calling for a candidate's election or defeat. The NRCC spent an additional $14,558 as an independent expenditure expressly calling for this outcome. It spent the remainder of the money it had committed to the race to finance another four televised issue advocacy ads, three more direct-mail pieces, two mass telephone calls, and one personal contact. Some of these activities were carried out in conjunction with the state GOP. The RNC and various state and local Republican committees provided an additional three pieces of direct mail and three personal contacts. Some of this activity was carried out in conjunction with the Colorado GOP's 96-Hour Program, a lengthier version of the RNC's 72-Hour Task Force, that involved the same types of campaign activities as did the Democrats' voter mobilization program. In total, the Republican Party was responsible for forty-six unique contacts with voters in Colorado's 7th district, twenty-nine more contacts than were carried out by the Beauprez campaign.[78]

Few would deny that party activity had a major impact on the election. Candidate expenditures in the contest were within reach of one another, with Beauprez spending more than $1.8 million and Feeley spending just over $1.2 million. However, Republican Party committees brought significantly more firepower to the contest, outspending Democratic Party committees by more than three to one. Although Republican efforts may appear like overkill at first blush, they were probably decisive in bringing about Beauprez's 121-vote election victory.[79]

Most Senate candidates and campaign aides give evaluations of Hill committee assistance that are as favorable as those given by House candidates. The senatorial campaign committees are rated above any other group in every area of campaigning, except providing information about voters, mobilizing voters, and recruiting volunteers. State and local party organizations and interest groups were ranked higher for these activities.[80]

Senate candidates in battleground races receive more campaign resources from their party than from any other group. The contest in South Dakota between Democratic incumbent Johnson and his Republican challenger, Representative Thune, demonstrates how important party activity can be in a Senate contest. The race turned out to be a battle royal, which featured heavy involvement by President Bush and South Dakota's senior senator, then–majority leader Tom Daschle.

The GOP contributed almost $263,000 to Thune, including $219,500 from state parties as distant from the campaign as Alaska and Hawaii. It also made $130,000 in coordinated expenditures, about $13,600 short of the FEC's limit for the race. GOP legislators contributed an additional $46,000 from their campaign committees and $253,000 from their leadership PACs, and former Republican members of Congress donated another $24,250. In addition to this direct support, the national Republican Party organizations transferred more than $7.2 million in hard and soft money to the state Republican Party in order to conduct record-breaking independent, parallel, and coordinated campaign activities on behalf of Thune; Republican House candidate South Dakota governor William Janklow, who was running for Thune's old seat; and state Senate majority leader Michael Rounds, who was running for Janklow's job.[81] The party spent most of these funds—more than $3.1 million—on television ads to help these candidates.[82] The party aired eight unique television ads and one radio ad and distributed seventy-three direct-mail pieces solely to influence Thune's race.

The GOP also carried out an impressive ground war campaign, comprising two rounds of personal voter contacts and three mass telephone calls. The voter contacts were spearheaded by the state Republican Party, which organized door-to-door campaigns and main street tours in 842 precincts and enlisted six thousand volunteers to mobilize voters on election day. The mass telephone calls featured President Bush; his mother, Barbara Bush; and Rudolph Giuliani. The president also made five trips to the state to help the candidate raise money and to energize Republican activists and voters. First lady Laura Bush, Vice President Cheney, Lynn Cheney, and Giuliani also visited the state.[83]

The Democratic Party also was very involved in the race. It gave Johnson $26,500 in contributions and $62,941 in coordinated expenditures. Johnson's colleagues in the Senate also donated $28,000 and $192,766 from their respective campaign committees and leadership PACs. Congressional retirees contributed an additional $9,500. However, no state Democratic Party committees besides South Dakota's contributed to the candidate. National Democratic Party organizations transferred more than $8.1 million to the South Dakota Democratic Party.[84] The party spent an impressive $2.9 million on television ads in the state. The party aired twelve TV spots and fourteen radio spots, and sent four e-mails and forty-three pieces of direct mail, which were targeted mainly at senior citizens and women. It financed five mass telephone calls and one in-person voter contact. Daschle, like Bush, cast a large shadow in the race, repeatedly visiting the state to help Johnson and recording a telephone message to mobilize Democratic voters.

Not to be outdone by the Republicans, the Democratic Party launched an extensive and highly targeted voter mobilization effort. Part of the Democrats' strategy was to register and mobilize Native Americans. It succeeded in increasing voter registration by almost 3,300 Democratic voters in three counties with a substantial Native American population. Those three counties delivered 5,251 more votes to Johnson than to Thune, contributing significantly to the incumbent's 524-vote victory.[85]

As was the case in the House race in Colorado's 7th district, it is impossible to determine exactly what led to the election outcome in South Dakota's 2002 Senate contest. Nevertheless, party activity was important. All totaled, the parties spent more than $35 per vote cast in the election, roughly equaling Johnson's and Thune's combined expenditures. Moreover, even though both campaign managers maintained they did not directly coordinate their efforts with their party's senatorial campaign committees, a division of labor occurred that is common in closely contested congressional races: the candidates left it to the parties to disseminate the communications that were the most decidedly negative.[86] If either party had a lesser presence in the race, the outcome might have been decided differently.

SUMMARY

Political parties, particularly party organizations in Washington, play important supporting roles in contemporary congressional elections. Their agenda-setting efforts encourage voters to focus on issues that traditionally work to the advantage of their candidates. The Hill committees distribute most of their contributions, coordinated expenditures, and campaign services to candidates in close races. They also help these candidates to attract funding and campaign assistance from other politicians, their leadership PACs, other PACs and interest groups, and individual contributors. Local parties assist candidates in mobilizing voters in some parts of the country. National party organizations have substantially increased their influence in congressional elections, particularly those with unpredictable outcomes, by carrying out independent, parallel, and coordinated campaigns.

Republican Party organizations are wealthier than their Democratic counterparts. GOP party committees, particularly at the national level, have traditionally played a greater role than Democratic Party organizations in congressional elections. The Democrats have increased their involvement in congressional campaigns, but Republican Party committees maintain an edge in House elections and an overwhelming advantage in Senate contests. The GOP's overall superiority is likely to persist in the near future.

CHAPTER FIVE

The Interests Campaign

Organized interests, pejoratively referred to as "special interests," have always been involved in American elections. During the earliest days of the Republic, leaders of agricultural and commercial groups influenced who was on the ballot, the coverage they received in the press, and the voting patterns that determined election outcomes. As the electorate grew and parties and candidates began to spend more money to reach voters, steel magnates, railroad barons, and other captains of industry increased their roles in political campaigns. Labor unions counterorganized with manpower and dollars.[1] Religious and ethnic groups also influenced elections, but their financial and organizational efforts paled next to those of business and labor.

Interest groups continue to flourish at the beginning of the twenty-first century, and several developments have significantly affected their roles in congressional elections. The growth in the number of organizations that located or hired representatives in Washington, D.C., resulted in the formation of a community of lobbyists that was, and continues to be, attuned to the rhythms of legislative and election politics. The enactment of the Federal Election Campaign Act of 1974 paved the way for the development of the modern political action committee—the form of organizational entity that most interest groups use to carry out the majority of their federal campaign activities. Court decisions and Federal Election Commission rulings handed down in recent years that weakened the FECA made the world of PACs, and interest groups in general, more complex. The determinations of the courts and the FEC led some interest groups to augment their federal PAC activities using nonfederal dollars from their treasuries or from nonprofit tax-exempt organizations connected to their group, including 501(c)(3), 501(c)(4), and 527 entities. Other groups pooled their resources to create new, mostly nonprofit, organizations for these same purposes. These for-profit and nonprofit organizations contribute to party committees or influence congressional elections through public relations campaigns, issue advocacy advertising, and voter mobilization activities financed with soft money.

This chapter covers the growth and development of the PAC community in Washington and the roles that PACs and other groups play in congressional elections. I analyze the motives that underlie PAC strategies and activities, the methods that PACs use to select candidates for support, and the distribution of PAC contributions and independent expenditures. I also examine other interest group activities, including politically motivated educational campaigns, issue advocacy ads, and voter mobilization efforts that comprise the independent, parallel, and coordinated campaigns that interest groups carry out to influence congressional elections.

THE RISE OF PACS AND
OTHER ELECTORALLY ACTIVE ORGANIZATIONS

Although interest groups have been active in campaigns throughout U.S. history, it was not until 1943 that the Committee on Political Education, the first forerunner to the modern political action committee, was founded by the Congress of Industrial Organizations.[2] A PAC can be best understood as the electoral arm of an organized interest. Interest groups form PACs to give campaign contributions or services directly to federal, or in some cases, state or local candidates in the hope of influencing election outcomes, the formation of public policy, or both. Some PACs also make independent expenditures for or against federal candidates. Most PACs have a sponsoring, or parent, organization, such as a corporation, labor union, trade association, or other group. However, for "nonconnected" PACs, the PAC itself is the organizing group.

The FECA set the scene for the PAC explosion of the mid-1970s. One of the goals of the act was to dilute the influence of moneyed interests on federal elections. The act limited individuals to a maximum contribution of $1,000 per candidate at each stage of the election—primary, general election, and runoff (if required)—for a total of $3,000 (see Table 1-1). It also imposed an aggregate annual limit of $25,000 on an individual's contributions to all federal candidates, federal party committees, and PACs (see Table 1-2). It barred corporations, labor unions, trade associations, cooperatives, and other organized groups from giving contributions directly to candidates for federal office.

By limiting the total contributions a candidate could collect from any one source, the FECA encouraged candidates to solicit smaller donations from a broader array of interests and individuals. The act also encouraged many interest groups to establish PACs. Although the FECA never mentioned the term *political action committee,* it allowed for "a multicandidate committee" that raises money from at least fifty donors and spends it on at least five candidates for federal office, to contribute a maximum of $5,000 per candidate at each stage of the election.[3] The low ceilings the law established for individual contributions to candidates and the $5,000-per-year limit it set for individual contributions to any one PAC have the combined effect of making PAC contributions a popular vehicle among wealthy individuals who wish to influence congressional elections.

In November 1975, in an advisory opinion written for Sun Oil Company, the FEC counseled the company that it could pay the overhead and solicitation costs of its PAC, thereby freeing the PAC to spend on federal elections all the funds it collected from donors.[4] The Sun PAC decision clarified a gray area in the law and in the process made PACs a much more attractive vehicle for collecting and disbursing funds. The advisory ruling contributed to an explosion in the number of PACs that lasted from the mid-1970s to the mid-1980s.

The Supreme Court's ruling in *Buckley v. Valeo* allowed PACs to make unlimited independent expenditures (made without the knowledge or consent of a candidate or his or her campaign organization) in congressional and presidential elections.[5] Both the FEC advisory opinion and the Supreme Court decision created new opportunities for organized groups to participate in politics. The advisory opinion was especially important, encouraging a wide range of political leaders, business entrepreneurs, and others to form new PACs.

Between 1974 and the 2002 elections, the PAC community grew from more than 600 to 4,594 committees (see Figure 5-1). Most of the growth occurred in the business sector, with corporate PACs growing in number from 89 in 1974 to 1,741 in 2002. Labor unions, many of which already had PACs in 1974, created the fewest new PACs, increasing the number from 201 to 337. The centralization of the labor movement into a relatively small number of unions greatly limited the growth of labor PACs. In addition, three new species of political action committee—the nonconnected PAC (mostly ideological and issue-oriented groups), and PACs whose sponsors are either cooperatives or corporations without stock, such as the Southern Minnesota Sugar Cooperative and the Aircraft Owners and Pilots Association—emerged on the scene in 1977. The nonconnected PACs are the most important of these. By 2002 their number had grown to 1,215; in contrast, the combined total for the two other types of PAC had reached only 159.[6]

Leadership PACs, covered briefly in Chapter 4, are the most recently formed type of PAC. Sponsored by politicians and closely tied to the parties, these

FIGURE 5-1

Growth in the Number of Registered PACs, 1974–2002

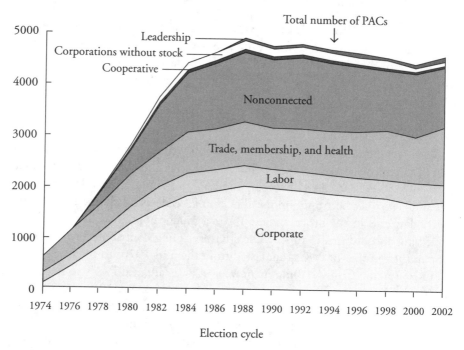

Sources: Joseph E. Cantor, *Political Action Committees: Their Evolution, Growth, and Implications for the Political System* (Washington, D.C.: Congressional Research Service of the Library of Congress, 1984), 88; various Federal Election Commission press releases.

Note: Leadership PACs are classified separately from nonconnected PACs.

PACs traditionally have been categorized as nonconnected PACs. They re- mained scarce until the late 1980s because few members of Congress could raise the money to form them. During the 1990s an increasing number of politi- cians, including some relatively junior members of the House, began to spon- sor them. Their numbers reached 58 in 1994, 86 in 1996, and 186 in 2002.

The growth in the number of PACs was accompanied by a tremendous in- crease in their activity. PAC contributions to congressional candidates grew from $12.5 million in 1974 to approximately $266.2 million in 2002. Corporate and other business-related PACs accounted for most of that growth (see Figure 5-2). In 2002, corporate PACs accounted for over 34 percent of all PAC contributions to congressional candidates, followed by trade association PACs, which accounted for almost 27 percent. Union PACs gave just under 20 percent of all contributions received by congressional candidates, leadership

FIGURE 5-2

Growth of PAC Contributions in Congressional Elections, 1974–2002

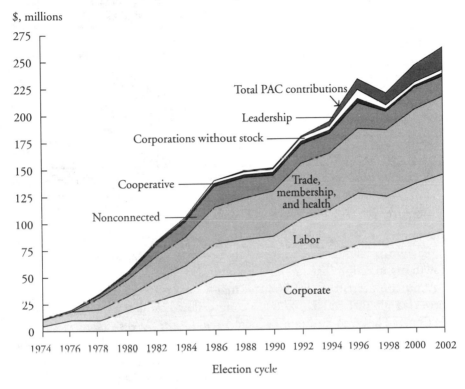

$, millions

Election cycle

Sources: Joseph E. Cantor, *Political Action Committees: Their Evolution, Growth, and Implications for the Political System* (Washington, D.C.: Congressional Research Service of the Library of Congress, 1984), 88; various Federal Election Commission press releases.

Note: Leadership PAC contributions are separated from contributions made by nonconnected PACs.

PACs contributed 9 percent, and nonconnected PACs (excluding leadership PACs) gave 8 percent. PACs sponsored by cooperatives and corporations without stock contributed the final 2 percent.

A very small group of PACs is responsible for most PAC activity. A mere 258 PACs, just under 6 percent of the entire PAC community, contributed roughly $175.4 million during the 2002 elections, representing approximately 62 percent of all PAC money given in those contests (see Table 5-1). Each of these committees, which are clearly the "all-stars" of the PAC community, gave over $250,000 to federal candidates. These include PACs sponsored by corporations, trade associations, and unions such as United Parcel Service, the National Association of Realtors, and the United Auto Workers, as well as

TABLE 5-1

Concentration of PAC Contributions in the 2002 Congressional Elections

	PACs' total contributions					
	Over $250,000	$100,001– $250,000	$50,001– $100,000	$5,001– $50,000	$1– $5,000	$0
Percentage of all PACs	6	8	7	27	19	33
(*N*)	(258)	(375)	(336)	(1,232)	(856)	(1,537)
Percentage of all PAC contributions ($, millions)	62 (175.4)	20 (57.0)	8 (23.7)	9 (24.2)	1 (1.7)	0 (0)

Source: Compiled from Federal Election Commission, "PAC Activity Increases for 2002 Elections," press release, March 27, 2003.

nonconnected PACs, such as EMILY's List, which supports pro-choice Democratic women candidates, and the Club for Growth, an anti-tax pro-economic growth organization that supports Republicans.

Another 8 percent of all PACs are "major players," each having contributed between $100,001 and $250,000 to congressional candidates during the 2002 elections. These committees, which include the Wells Fargo PAC, the American Insurance Association PAC, the National Association of Postal Supervisors' PAC, the League of Conservation Voters PAC, and Washington PAC (WASHPAC, a pro-Israel group), accounted for 20 percent of all PAC contributions. The all-stars and major players are particularly influential because their wealth allows them to contribute to virtually every candidate whose election is of importance to them.

The "players" are PACs that have the resources to give a significant contribution to many but not all of the candidates they wish to support. Comprising 7 percent of all PACs, they include PACs representing the interests of the North American subsidiary of the Guinness Brewing Company, the Airline Pilot's Association, the Brotherhood of Railroad Signalmen, and the Conservative Victory Fund, as well as the National Pro-Life Alliance PAC. Each of the players contributed between $50,001 and $100,000 during the 2002 elections, accounting for roughly 8 percent of all PAC contributions.

The contributions of the next group of PACs, which might be labeled the "junior varsity," are clearly constrained by their size. These PACs each contributed between $5,001 and $50,000. They constitute 27 percent of the PAC community and gave almost 9 percent of all PAC contributions. Their donations tend to be significantly smaller than those of the larger PACs. The managers of most junior varsity PACs routinely have to answer requests for contributions by stating that they support the candidate and would like to give a contribution but do not have the money. Such PACs include those representing the Burger King Corporation; the Bowling Proprietors' Association; and the International Association of Heat and Frost Insulators & Asbestos workers PAC; as well as WILD PAC, which seeks to protect America's wilderness and national parks.

Members of the next group, the "little league," each gave between $1 and $5,000, accounting for less than 1 percent of all PAC contributions during the 2002 elections. They include the Peter Pan Seafoods PAC, the Concerned Friends for Tobacco PAC, and the Providence (Rhode Island) Fraternal Order of Police PAC. These committees, which make up about 19 percent of the PAC community, play a marginal role in the funding of congressional elections.

Finally, 1,537 PACs gave no money in the 2002 elections. Of these, 663 are, for all practical purposes, defunct.[7] Although they registered with the FEC, they spent no money to collect contributions, pay off debts, or cover the costs of committee administration during the 2002 election cycle.

Nonprofit interest group organizations have been in existence for a long time, but their conspicuous presence in congressional elections is only a recent phenomenon, resulting primarily from the emergence of loopholes in the FECA. Some interest groups capitalized on changes in federal campaign finance regulations by using existing nonprofit entities that were part of their organizational structure or by creating new ones in order to raise and spend soft money and make issue advocacy expenditures intended to influence federal elections. Three types of legal entities became highly visible in congressional elections: 501(c)(3), 501(c)(4), and 527 committees. As defined in the U.S. Internal Revenue Service (IRS) Code, 501(c)(3) organizations are tax-exempt groups organized for charitable purposes. They are prohibited from becoming involved in federal campaigns, including endorsing or contributing to candidates or organizing a PAC, but they can conduct research and educational activities, carry out nonpartisan voter registration drives and get-out-the-vote drives, and sponsor candidate forums. Donations made to a 501(c)(3) organization are tax deductible. The IRS code defines 501(c)(4) organizations as nonprofit social welfare organizations. They are exempt from federal taxes and can engage in partisan political activities as long as these are not the group's primary purpose. Such groups are allowed to rate candidates, promote legislation, make independent expenditures, and engage in issue advocacy.[8]

Traditionally, federal candidate campaign committees and other political committees participating in federal elections were governed by section 527 of the tax code, which exempts "political organizations" from paying income taxes. This provision was originally designed to cover candidate campaigns, PACs, and party committees that disclosed their finances to the FEC, making it unnecessary for the IRS code to encompass these organizations in its contribution, expenditure, and disclosure provisions. However, some politicians and nonprofit interest groups created 527 committees solely to raise and spend soft money on voter mobilization and issue advocacy efforts intended to influence federal elections. Because these committees did not expressly advocate the election of federal candidates, they were not required to report their receipts and expenditures to the FEC and were thus able to evade contribution limits and disclosure rules. Congress reformed the tax law code to require these organizations to disclose such transactions beginning in January 2001. However, this reform did not bar them from raising and spending soft money to affect congressional elections.

The League of Conservation Voters (LCV) is an example of an interest group with a complex interconnected organizational structure that enables it to participate aggressively in the political process without violating the federal campaign finance or tax statutes. The group uses its federal PAC to make contributions to congressional candidates and independent expenditures. It employs its 501(c)(3) organization to finance its research and educational activities, including the publication of its *Green Guide,* which profiles members of Congress on environmental matters, and other publications that help candidates frame environmental issues. Its 501(c)(4) entity is the vehicle it uses to carry out activities designed to draw attention to legislators' environmental records, including publishing the "Dirty Dozen," which lists the twelve members or candidates who have the worst records on environmental issues, and the "Earth List," which lists Congress's ten most pro-environment members. The group uses soft money from a 527 account to finance issue advocacy ads. Finally, the national LCV coordinates its activities with the efforts of several state leagues of conservation voters to advance the prospects of pro-environment federal, state, and local candidates. The LCV's activities are designed to influence several audiences: the candidates who receive its contributions, other environmental groups that utilize its publications to help formulate their campaign strategies and contribution decisions, political activists who are guided by its endorsements and public relations efforts when selecting candidates for support, and ordinary voters who are influenced by its issue advocacy ads and independent expenditures.[9] The AFL-CIO, the United Seniors Association (which represents the pharmaceutical industry), and the Club for Growth are examples of other groups that use interlocking structures to make campaign contributions and conduct independent, parallel, and coordinated campaigns.

STRATEGY, DECISION MAKING, AND TARGETING

Interest group goals and strategies are more diverse than are those of the two major parties, reflecting the fact that the parties are consumed with electing candidates and the groups have other goals, such as promoting issues and influencing the policy process. Some interest groups and their PACs follow "ideological" or "electoral" strategies designed to increase the number of legislators who share their broad political perspective or positions on specific, often emotionally charged issues such as abortion. These groups are similar to political parties in that they consider congressional elections as opportunities to alter the composition of Congress and view the electoral process as their primary vehicle for changing or reinforcing the direction of public policy.[10] Nonconnected PACs have traditionally been categorized as ideological committees.

Ideological PACs make most of their contributions to candidates in close elections, in which the PACs have the biggest chance of affecting an election outcome. The same is true for the independent, parallel, and coordinated campaign activities of ideologically oriented nonprofit organizations that participate in elections. However, some groups become involved in uncompetitive contests in order to attract attention to themselves, their issues, or politicians who share their views. By gaining visibility for themselves and their causes, these organizations can more easily raise money and increase their political clout.

PACs following ideological strategies have traditionally not given much money to members of Congress for the sake of gaining access to the legislative process. The issues these PACs support are often linked to values so fundamental that legislators would not be expected to change their views in response to a contribution or visit by a lobbyist. Before giving a contribution, many of these PACs, and some others, require candidates to complete questionnaires that elicit their views on certain issues.

Other groups pursue "access" strategies designed to enable the group to gain at least an audience with members of Congress.[11] These groups, which include PACs sponsored by corporate and trade associations, view elections pragmatically. For such groups, an election is a prime opportunity to shore up relations with members of Congress who work on legislation that is of importance to their parent organization. Elections give these groups the opportunity to create goodwill with powerful legislators or at least to minimize the enmity of legislators who disagree with them. Elections thus lay the groundwork for later lobbying efforts.

A group that follows an access strategy is likely to contribute most of its money to incumbents. Members of the House and Senate who chair committees or subcommittees, occupy party leadership positions, or are policy entrepreneurs with influence over legislation are likely to receive large contributions regardless of the competitiveness of their contests.[12] In fact, many access-oriented PACs make contributions to legislators who do not even have opponents. Of course, members of Congress who have supported a group's legislation and who are involved in contests with unpredictable outcomes are singled out for extra support, including large PAC contributions, independent expenditures, or issue advocacy ads. Supporting incumbents enables PACs and other organizations to accomplish their goal of ensuring access and helping legislative allies, while meeting organizational imperatives such as backing a large number of winners and contributing to candidates who represent districts that contain many of the group's supporters.

Access-oriented groups also give significant sums to candidates for open seats. Most of these candidates have good chances of winning but need large amounts of money to run competitive campaigns. Giving an open-seat prospect a large contribution is useful to an access-oriented PAC because it can help elect an ally to Congress and create goodwill, laying the groundwork for productive relations with a future member of Congress. Independent, parallel, and coordinated campaign activities can have a similar effect.

Access-oriented groups tend to ignore challengers because most of them are likely to lose. Giving a challenger a contribution is often considered a waste of money and could lead to serious repercussions from an incumbent. Moreover, backing challengers has a high probability of reducing a group's win-loss record and could lead to criticism of the PAC's manager. The managers of access-oriented PACs that decide not to support challenger or open-seat candidates know that should these candidates win, they could make amends later by helping them retire their campaign debts.

Groups that use access strategies rarely make independent expenditures or broadcast issue advocacy ads because of the publicity these activities can generate. Such efforts could harm a corporation if they anger congressional incumbents, upset some of the group's donors, or call undue attention to the candidate or the group. Such publicity could lead to charges that a group is trying to buy influence and could hinder the achievement of its goals. The few corporations that become involved in such high-visibility campaign efforts often hide their true identity by forming one or more shell groups, such as the pharmaceutical industry's United Seniors Association, Citizens for Better Medicare, and 60 Plus Association. An innocuous name brings the added benefit of a group's advertisements being viewed more sympathetically and having a greater impact on voters. During the 2002 elections, voters viewed United Seniors much more favorably than they would have America's pharmaceutical companies, and the ads that the group broadcast undoubtedly received a more positive reception than they would have gotten had the pharmaceutical companies been listed as their sponsor.[13]

Many groups, including a large number of labor unions, practice "mixed" strategies. They support some candidates with contributions, independent expenditures, issue advocacy ads, or grassroots activities because those candidates share the group's views; they support others because they wish to improve their access to legislators who work on policies the group deems important. Campaign assistance motivated by the former reason is usually distributed to candidates in competitive contests. Assistance informed by the latter motive is given to incumbents who are in a position to influence legislation important to the group.

In some cases the ideological and access motives clash, for example, when a highly qualified challenger who represents a group's views runs a competitive race against an incumbent in a position of power. In these situations, groups usually support the incumbent, but sometimes they contribute to both candidates. Groups that follow mixed strategies and groups that follow pure access strategies are less likely than ideological groups to make independent expenditures or issue advocacy ads.

Interest Group Strategy and the Political Environment

Interest groups, like most other groups and individuals involved in politics, are strategic actors that respond to their environment in ways that enable them to pursue their goals.[14] During the 1970s most PACs used ideological strategies that followed partisan lines. They backed candidates who supported the positions to which their organizational sponsors adhered. Business-oriented PACs, including corporate and trade committees, largely supported Republican candidates. Labor organizations, which were and continue to be the most consistently partisan of all PACs, regularly gave 90 percent of their contributions to Democrats. In time, many business-oriented committees shifted from ideological to access or mixed strategies. These PACs, with the encouragement of then–Democratic Congressional Campaign Committee chair Tony Coelho, redirected their support from Republican House challengers to incumbents, many of whom were Democrats, out of recognition of the Democratic Party's decades-long control of Congress.[15]

Perhaps the clearest strategic response by PACs takes place after partisan control of one or both chambers of Congress changes hands. When control of the Senate switched from the Democrats to the Republicans in 1981 and back to the Democrats in 1987, many access-oriented PACs switched their contributions to Senate candidates, mainly incumbents, who belonged to the new majority party. Similarly, following the 1994 GOP takeover of both the House and Senate, these PACs gave most of their funds to Republicans, once again reversing their previous contribution patterns.[16]

Because of their desire to influence the composition of Congress, ideologically oriented groups are the most likely to capitalize on the conditions peculiar to a specific election. A group that uses an access strategy, such as a corporate or trade PAC, is less affected by a particular electoral setting, unless changing conditions are almost certain to influence its parent group's ability to meet with key legislators and their staffs. The strategic changes in PAC behavior that occurred in the early 1980s were the result of PACs learning how to get the most legislative influence for their dollars and the increasing aggressiveness of incumbent fundraising.[17] Those that occurred following the 1994 elections were a response to the change in partisan control of Congress. More recent changes in interest group behavior, particularly the concentration of issue advocacy ads and grassroots efforts in a small number of extremely close races, represent group responses to the slim majorities determining partisan control of the House and Senate.

Making strategic adjustments in anticipation of political change is more difficult. The manager of an access-oriented PAC who believes that a member of Congress is likely to go from having little to major influence in a policy area, for instance, may have difficulty persuading the PAC's board of directors to raise the member's contribution from a token sum to a substantial donation. The manager's prospects of convincing the board that the organization should totally revamp its strategy because partisan control of Congress might change are slim. For example, many corporate and trade groups, whose support of a pro-business agenda suggests they would want to support Republicans who have real prospects for victory, did not support Republican challengers during the 1994 elections. Some of the managers of these PACs may have been attuned to the fact that a confluence of anti-Washington sentiments, strong Republican challengers, and vulnerable Democratic incumbents enhanced the challengers' prospects, but their organization's decision-making process made it impossible for them to change its contribution patterns in anticipation of the Republicans' stunning success.

Interest Group Decision Making

The decision-making processes that an interest group uses to select candidates for support are affected by the group's overall strategy, wealth, organizational structure, and location.[18] Ideological groups spend more time searching for promising challengers to support than do groups that use access or mixed strategies. Ideological PACs also are more likely than other groups to support nonincumbents in congressional primaries. Wealthy groups tend to spend more time searching for promising nonincumbents simply because they can afford to fund more candidates.[19] Federated groups whose organizational affiliates are spread across the country typically have to respond to the wishes of these constituents when making contributions, independent expenditures, or issue advocacy ads.[20] Nonconnected PACs, leadership PACs, and groups sponsored by a single corporation or cooperative, in contrast, are less constrained by the need to please a diverse and far-flung constituency. Interest groups located in the nation's capital have more information available to them about the relative competitiveness of individual races because they can plug into more communications networks than can groups located in the hinterlands.[21]

The decision-making processes of PACs vary according to the PACs' organizational capacities. The Realtors PAC (RPAC), a large institutionalized committee with headquarters in Washington, D.C., was formed in 1969.[22] This federated PAC, which is sponsored by the National Association of Realtors (NAR), receives its money from PACs sponsored by the NAR's eighteen hundred local affiliates and state associations located in all fifty states plus the District of Columbia, Guam, Puerto Rico, and the Virgin Islands. Realtors give donations to RPAC and to these affiliated PACs, each of which passes 30 percent of its revenues to the national PAC. In 2002 RPAC distributed more than $3.6 million in contributions, more than any other political action committee.

The Realtors PAC employs a mixed strategy to advance the goals of the real estate industry. As do most other institutionalized PACs, it has explicit criteria for selecting candidates for support and uses a complex decision-making procedure. Party, incumbency, and electoral competitiveness have a major impact on RPAC contributions. Incumbents, who are typically given preference over challengers, are evaluated on a number of criteria to assess their policy proclivities, level of activism on behalf of real estate issues, and local realtor support. Members who cosponsor priority NAR legislation, give a speech on behalf of NAR legislation on the House or Senate floor, or write letters to their colleagues in support of such legislation are top priorities. The same is true of those who use their congressional authority to compel the president or independent regulatory agencies to respond to real estate industry concerns, vote for key NAR issues in committee or on the floor, or assist constituents with real estate–related matters. Leaders of both parties and members who belong to committees that deal with real estate issues are also targeted for contributions.

Nonincumbents who have previously held elective office, and thus have a record on real estate issues, are judged for contributions using similar criteria.

Most are also interviewed by RPAC representatives, usually local or state NAR members, and asked to complete an RPAC questionnaire to help the PAC further discern the candidate's political philosophy, background, and campaign skills. Nonincumbents who have not previously held office must be interviewed by RPAC representatives and complete a questionnaire to be eligible for a contribution. Finally, when considering both incumbents and nonincumbents for contributions, the PAC considers the competitiveness of the race, the amount of cash in a candidate's campaign account, and the number and partisanship of realtors who live in the district.

RPAC's contribution decisions are made in several ways. The PAC's staff and trustees and the NAR's political representatives and lobbyists deliberate using the preceding criteria to make one centralized set of contribution decisions. The PAC's In-State Reception Program constitutes a second, decentralized decision-making process. Under the program, realtors who want to attend a fundraising event held by one of their state's incumbents can make an RPAC contribution of up to $1,000, so long as the donation is approved by the chair of RPAC's state affiliate. The process for contributions to open-seat candidates is similar, except that the candidate must be personally interviewed and approved by state RPAC officials. The In-State Reception Program has a similar but more stringent process for challenger contributions because most challengers have poor prospects of success and NAR officials are concerned about angering incumbents. The state PAC's request for a contribution must be formally approved or rejected by national RPAC trustees, and the contribution is limited to a maximum of $1,000.

Other programs allow RPAC to further increase realtors' contact with legislators and to concentrate its resources in close races. The Special Recognition Fund is used to make additional contributions to party leaders, candidates who serve on committees with jurisdiction over real estate–related matters, and staunch supporters of real estate interests who are involved in competitive contests. The Washington Reception Program Fund allows NAR lobbyists to attend fundraising events held in the nation's capital and RPAC to host receptions for congressional candidates. RPAC stopped making independent expenditures after the 1992 elections.

Like many interest groups, RPAC's and the NAR's election activities extend beyond making campaign contributions. RPAC and its parent organization mobilize realtors to support their preferred candidates, distribute educational and advocacy mailings in close contests, use telephone banks to conduct voter identification and get-out-the-vote efforts, and occasionally send professional organizers to carry out grassroots activities designed to help their preferred candidates. These efforts are financed with soft money.

The decision-making process of the Realtors PAC is similar to that of other institutionalized committees, such as AT&T's PAC, the American Medical Association's PAC (AMPAC), and the LCV's PAC.[23] RPAC relies on a combination of factual information, local opinion, and national perspective to determine which candidates to support. The requirement that all recommendations receive formal approval also is typical, as is the ability to conduct research on individual elections in-house. The PAC's lack of participation as either a source or a user of the information available in Washington communications networks is unusual for a PAC located in the nation's capital, but its size, federated structure, and tremendous resources enable it to make decisions with information it has collected independently of other committees.

At the opposite end of the spectrum from the Realtors PAC are the noninstitutionalized PACs. WASHPAC is a nonconnected committee founded in 1980 by Morris J. Amitay, formerly the executive director of the American Israel Public Affairs Committee (AIPAC), to promote a secure Israel and strong American-Israeli relations.[24] WASHPAC spent $202,250 in congressional elections in 2002, contributing the vast majority of its money to incumbents.

WASHPAC and thousands of other noninstitutionalized committees are essentially one-person operations with one-person decision-making processes. Noninstitutionalized PACs rely primarily on personal contacts with candidates and other Washington insiders for the political information that guides their contribution decisions. Amitay, who started WASHPAC as a hobby, peruses candidates' speeches and press releases and incumbents' voting records and letters to constituents to gauge their support for Israel. He exchanges information about the competitiveness of different elections when meeting with other pro-Israel political activists. He is open to the suggestions of individuals who give donations to his committee but generally does not make contributions to candidates solely on the basis of donor suggestions. After all, most of WASHPAC's supporters donate to the PAC because this enables them to rely on Amitay's research and judgment rather than having to research individual candidates themselves. Moreover, those who support WASHPAC can use its list of targeted races to guide their individual candidate contributions.

Noninstitutionalized PACs and multitudes of other one-person organizations use informal decision-making processes. Their lack of formal rules and procedures allows their managers great flexibility in choosing candidates for support. Their limited staff resources force the PAC managers to turn to others for election-related information. These PACs are in a better position than more institutionalized committees to adjust their initial strategies in response to changing electoral conditions. Of course, in the case of very small committees, such as the Concerned Friends for Tobacco PAC, which contributed only $2,000 in 2002, this is true only as long as their money holds out.

Between the institutionalized PACs and the small, one-person organizations are semi-institutionalized committees that possess some of the characteristics of the PACs in the other two groups. These PACs include Powell, Goldstein, Frazer, and Murphy ("POGO") PAC, sponsored by a law firm with offices in both Washington, D.C., and Atlanta, Georgia. Semi-institutionalized PACs usually have staffs of two to four people, which are large enough to allow for a functional division of labor and to require the adoption of decision rules but small enough to render them dependent on outside research when making contribution decisions. For instance, POGO PAC, which has consistently pursued a modified access strategy, has a legal counselor, a treasurer, a PAC administrator, and a moderately active board of directors.[25] It contributed just over $119,500 during the 2002 elections, an amount sufficient to give the PAC and its law firm a presence in national and Georgia politics.

PACs with semi-institutionalized organizations typically rely on their staffs to process requests for contributions, but they look to others for political intelligence. POGO PAC gets most of its information from its parent firm's partners, associates, and clients, some of whom speak to party officials, members of other law firms and PACs, and other politically active individuals in the Washington and Atlanta metropolitan areas. The firm's members submit a short proposal for each contribution they would like the PAC to make. Then, the PAC's board, consisting of a small group of partners in Washington and Atlanta, votes on the request. Like most other semi-institutionalized committees, POGO PAC gives its board a significant role in decision making, but neither the staff nor the board becomes involved in time-consuming strategic planning sessions or searches for potential recipients of contributions.[26] These PACs do not give their officers as much flexibility as do the managers of one-person committees, but these officials have more freedom than is accorded the officers of institutionalized PACs.

Lead PACs constitute a final group of committees. These PACs, which include the National Committee for an Effective Congress, the AFL-CIO's COPE, and the Business-Industry Political Action Committee, are as complex organizationally as the institutionalized PACs.[27] Like the LCV, they are often one part of a larger interlocking interest group structure. These groups are every bit as thorough in their research and decision making as are the institutionalized committees and are motivated by ideological or policy goals. They differ from other PACs in that they carry out research and select candidates for support with an eye toward influencing the decisions of other groups. Much of the research conducted by groups that sponsor lead PACs is oriented toward assessing the electability of individual candidates. Like the Hill committees, these groups spend much time, money, and energy disseminating information about specific campaigns to other interest group organizations. They occupy central positions in the networks of PACs, lobbyists, and individual contributors in the interest group community.

PAC CONTRIBUTIONS

PACs contributed a total of $262.8 million to major-party candidates in the 2002 congressional elections (see Table 5-2). Corporate PACs accounted for the most PAC contributions, followed by trade groups, labor committees, leadership PACs, and nonconnected PACs. Corporations without stock and cooperatives contributed the least, giving less than $6.4 million.

Incumbents have laid claim to the lion's share of PAC money since the PAC boom of the 1970s. Since the mid-1980s, business-related PACs have been among the most incumbent-oriented committees, adhering more closely to an access strategy than do labor, leadership, or ideological PACs. In 2002, corporate

TABLE 5-2
PAC Contributions in the 2002 Congressional Elections (in thousands)

	House		Senate		
	Democrats	Republicans	Democrats	Republicans	Total
Corporate	$23,411	$44,263	$6,964	$16,456	$91,094
Trade, membership, and health	22,773	33,662	4,933	9,338	70,706
Cooperative	870	1,118	259	256	2,503
Corporations without stock	1,150	1,754	382	637	3,923
Labor	38,941	4,342	7,047	487	50,817
Leadership	6,831	9,955	2,728	3,672	23,186
Nonconnected	6,886	7,616	3,117	2,945	20,564
All PACs	$100,862	$102,710	$25,430	$33,791	$262,793

Source: Compiled from Federal Election Commission data.

Note: Contributions by nonconnected PACs exclude contributions made by leadership PACs. Figures are for PAC contributions to all major-party candidates, including candidates in primaries, runoffs, and uncontested races.

PACs made 87 percent of their House contributions to incumbents involved in major-party contested races (see Table 5-3), distributing 67 percent of them to shoo-ins. These committees donated virtually nothing to House challengers and made a mere 12 percent of their House contributions to open-seat candidates. Corporate PACs made only 29 percent of their House contributions to candidates in competitive races, reflecting their goal of maintaining good relations

TABLE 5-3

Allocation of PAC Contributions to House Candidates in the 2002 Elections

	Corporate	Trade, membership, and health	Labor	Leadership	Non-connected
Democrats					
Incumbents					
In jeopardy	9%	11%	18%	12%	11%
Shoo-ins	24	24	44	6	21
Challengers					
Hopefuls	—	1	8	8	4
Likely losers	—	—	4	1	2
Open-seat candidates					
Prospects	2	4	15	12	8
Mismatched	1	1	3	2	2
Republicans					
Incumbents					
In jeopardy	11%	10%	1%	16%	10%
Shoo-ins	43	36	7	10	26
Challengers					
Hopefuls	1	2	—	9	3
Likely losers	—	—	—	1	—
Open-seat candidates					
Prospects	6	7	—	19	9
Mismatched	3	4	—	5	3
Total House contributions ($, thousands)	$52,785	$44,813	$36,036	$14,621	$12,015

Source: Compiled from Federal Election Commission data.

Notes: Figures are for general election candidates in major-party contested races, excluding those in incumbent-versus-incumbent races. Dashes = less than 0.5 percent. The categories and numbers of candidates are the same as those in Table 4-2. Some columns do not add to 100 percent because of rounding.

with current members, the pressures incumbents place on them for contributions, and their lack of concern with changing the composition of Congress.

Corporate PACs also pursue access-oriented goals when they contribute to Senate candidates. In 2002 they distributed 64 percent of their Senate contributions to incumbents, 12 percent to challengers, and 24 percent to open-seat candidates (see Table 5-4). Similarly, trade association PACs were generous to

TABLE 5-4

Allocation of PAC Contributions to Senate Candidates in the 2002 Elections

	Corporate	Trade, membership, and health	Labor	Leadership	Non-connected
Democrats					
Incumbents					
In jeopardy	14%	16%	29%	15%	22%
Shoo-ins	12	13	16	5	14
Challengers					
Hopefuls	1	2	18	8	5
Likely losers	—	1	8	2	1
Open-seat candidates					
Prospects	3	4	24	13	9
Mismatched	—	—	— —	—	—
Republicans					
Incumbents					
In jeopardy	18%	19%	2%	12%	16%
Shoo-ins	20	16	4	6	11
Challengers					
Hopefuls	11	12	—	18	9
Likely losers	—	—	—	1	—
Open-seat candidates					
Prospects	21	17	—	19	12
Mismatched	—	—	— —	—	—
Total Senate contributions ($, thousands)	$20,843	$12,850	$6,802	$5,976	$5,517

Source: Compiled from Federal Election Commission data.

Notes: Figures are for general election candidates in major-party contested races. Dashes = less than 0.5 percent. The categories and numbers of candidates are the same as those in Table 4-2. Some columns do not add to 100 percent because of rounding.

House and Senate incumbents and dedicated few resources to challengers and open-seat contests.

Labor PACs have consistently pursued highly partisan, mixed strategies. They contribute the vast majority of their money to Democrats. In 2002, labor contributions to House Democrats favored incumbents with 62 percent of their contributions, including 44 percent to shoo-ins. Labor's contributions to challengers and open-seat candidates, on the other hand, were tilted toward those in competitive races. Labor committees gave 45 percent of their Senate contributions to Democratic incumbents, including 29 percent to Democratic shoo-ins. The rest of its contributions strongly favored nonincumbents in close contests. Labor contributions to candidates in both chambers appear to have been motivated by both access-oriented and election-oriented goals.

The flow of leadership PAC contributions follows roughly the same pattern as that of party-connected contributions, which include contributions by candidates, members of Congress not up for reelection, and congressional retirees. Most 2002 leadership PAC money flowed to candidates in close races. Incumbents raised more from leadership PACs than did any other group of candidates, largely because they are the most likely to be in a position to help the donor with some political or legislative business in the future. Nevertheless, leadership PACs were more supportive of challengers and open-seat candidates than any other group of PACs.

Nonconnected PACs, which have traditionally followed the ideological strategy of spending most of their money in close races, deviated somewhat from that approach in 2002. They made 73 percent of their Senate contributions and a mere 45 percent of their House donations to candidates in close races, as compared with 84 percent and 68 percent in 1996.[28] Nonconnected PAC contributions to House incumbents were the most abnormal. They accounted for 68 percent of the total, and favored incumbent shoo-ins over incumbents in jeopardy by more than two to one. Nonconnected PAC contributions to Senate candidates also favored incumbents, but in keeping with previous years these contributions benefited primarily senators in tight contests. These PACs' contributions to challengers and open-seat contestants followed the familiar pattern of favoring candidates in close races.

Several factors contributed to the change in these PACs' giving patterns. The instability of the political environment in 2002—driven by the possibility of a change in partisan control of both chambers of Congress—affected most incumbents, particularly members of the House, whose seats had just undergone redistricting. As a result, some safe but nervous representatives and senators pressured nonconnected PACs for contributions to bolster their own political survival. Other safe lawmakers took advantage of the political climate to pressure ideologically sympathetic PACs to contribute to their campaigns and later donated the money to their party's congressional campaign committee, their colleagues, or nonincumbents.

Some nonconnected PACs responded to lawmakers' requests for contributions for both policy and ideological reasons. They contributed to some safe incumbents because they were not as confident as usual of their ability to judge the political environment and discern whether these incumbents were indeed safe, and they recognized that a great deal was at stake in terms of controlling Congress. Some nonconnected PACs also contributed to safe incumbents for access. They wanted to ensure that their priority issues would remain visible on these members' and Congress's legislative agendas. The Conservative Victory Fund, for example, made 44 percent of its contributions to safe incumbents, including 16 percent who faced no Democratic opposition in the general election.

CAMPAIGN SERVICES

Although most of the journalistic reporting on interest groups and PACs has focused on contributions, independent expenditures, and issue advocacy ads, many groups also carry out activities that have traditionally been conducted by political parties.[29] Some interest groups, mainly ideological organizations, including various groups on both sides of the abortion rights issue, recruit candidates to run for Congress.[30] Others provide candidates with in-kind contributions of polls, issue research, fundraising assistance, campaign ads, or strategic advice. AMPAC, RPAC, and COPE, for example, contribute polls to some candidates.[31] The National Federation of Independent Business's SAFE Trust PAC, whose name stands for Save American Free Enterprise, hosts campaign training schools and produces media advertisements for many of the candidates it supports.[32] The NCEC provides Democratic House and Senate candidates and party committees with precinct-level demographic profiles, targeting assistance, and technical advice.[33] As noted earlier, the LCV provides research, endorsements, and communications and other forms of assistance to help pro-environment candidates. These and other groups furnish campaign assistance in lieu of, or in addition to, cash contributions because they want to influence how candidates' campaigns are run or leave a more enduring impression than one can get from simply handing over a check.

One of the most important forms of assistance that a PAC can give to a candidate, particularly a nonincumbent, is help with fundraising. Lead PACs, such as BIPAC, COPE, and the NCEC, brief other PACs about the campaigns on their watch lists, using techniques similar to those used by the Hill committees. Even some smaller PACs help congressional candidates raise money by cosponsoring fundraising events or serving on candidates' fundraising committees. Most PACs and some other groups also help candidates raise money from individuals. When groups solicit donors, they usually provide them with a list of the candidates they are backing and information about the candidates' issue positions and backgrounds. Some groups include contact information for their preferred candidates and urge their supporters to contribute to them directly. Others get their members to buy tables at candidates' fundraising events or "bundle" checks from individual donors and deliver them to the candidate. The maturation of the Washington PAC community has led to the development of several networks of PACs, individual donors, and other groups, which often assist each other in selecting candidates for support and in raising money.[34]

EMILY's List, whose name stands for "Early Money Is Like Yeast" and whose motto is "It makes the dough rise," is an example of a PAC that gives candidates fundraising assistance. This nonconnected committee supports pro-choice Democratic women candidates, helping them raise money in the early, critical stages of the election, including in contested congressional primaries where campaign contributions typically have several times the impact they have in general elections.[35] EMILY's List requires its members to donate $100 to the PAC and to make minimum contributions of $100 to each of two candidates whom the PAC has designated for support. Members are instructed to write these checks to the candidates and then send them to the PAC, which in turn forwards the checks to the candidates with a letter explaining the PAC's role in collecting the money. Through bundling, the PAC acts as a clearinghouse for individual campaign contributions and is able to direct more money to candidates than it is legally allowed to contribute. Bundling works well with individuals who wish to have a candidate acknowledge both their and the group's political support. Groups that bundle, and EMILY's List in particular, have played a major role in persuading individuals who have not previously made congressional contributions to become regular donors.[36]

EMILY's list made almost $203,000 in contributions to thirty-four candidates in the 2002 congressional elections, including $58,000 in in-kind donations. This activity was important, but it pales next to the $9.4 million in contributions it bundled from its almost seventy-three thousand members to women Democratic candidates. The group spent roughly $10.8 million on television and radio issue ads and direct mail. Under the guise of its "Women Vote!" project, EMILY's List conducted polling, message testing, and precinct-by-precinct field work.[37]

The Club for Growth is another PAC that bundles contributions, gets involved in congressional primaries, and makes issue advocacy ads.[38] Founded in 1999 the Club claims nine thousand members who raised or donated over $10 million to the organization and or its endorsed candidates during the 2002 election season. The Club directly contributed almost $297,400 to 103 Republican congressional candidates competing in contested primaries and general elections in 2002, including 6 candidates in contested primaries. As is the case with EMILY's List, the Club's endorsements, bundling activities, and televised issue ads far outweigh its contributions in importance.

Although many interest groups are not known for bundling, a significant number of them influence the contributions of individuals associated with their group. Individual donors who make significant contributions to congressional candidates—at least one contribution of $200 per election cycle—comprise a group that has many similarities to the interest group community. It is a small, fairly elite, and relatively stable group. Many donors are motivated by reasons of political access, ideology, or both, although some contribute because they enjoy the social aspects of giving, including attending fundraising events. Moreover, individuals who make significant contributions also tend be active in political networks, including those associated with a variety of interest groups. Many of these individuals rely on business, industry, trade, single-issue, or ideological groups for the information they use to make contribution decisions. This magnifies the impact of the groups with which these donors associate.[39]

The financial, insurance, and real estate industries comprise a sector of the economy that makes its influence in congressional elections felt through PAC contributions, soft money contributions to parties, and the contributions of individuals associated with it. Organizations and individuals connected to these industries coalesce to influence policies ranging from mortgage regulations to building safety codes to federal appropriations for specific construction projects, as well as to try to affect the outcomes of elections. They have been extremely active in recent elections. PACs associated with these interests contributed almost $47.2 million in hard money to congressional candidates and donated an additional $89.7 million in soft money to party committees during the 2002 election cycle. Individuals linked to these interests, including corporate executives and their families, donated another $88.1 million in contributions of $200 or more to congressional candidates and party committees. These contributions accounted for 39 percent of the industries' total contributions in 2002. Republicans received 58 percent of this economic sector's largess, and Democrats collected the remainder.

Lawyers and lobbyists comprise an economic sector even more partisan in its giving and more dependent on significant individual contributions for its influence on the financing of elections. Firms identified with these trades contributed almost $21.1 million in soft money and $10.8 million to candidates during the 2002 elections. Contributions of $200 or more from individuals linked to them reached nearly $75.5 million, accounting for 69 percent of the total. More than seven out of ten dollars contributed by individuals or groups connected to the legal and lobbying trades went to Democratic candidates and party committees, with Republicans receiving the rest.[40]

Other organized interests provide a range of assistance to candidates in congressional elections. Think tanks, such as the Heritage Foundation, provide issue research. Labor unions and church-based organizations in African American and ethnic communities have long histories of political activism and have made decisive contributions to Democratic candidates' field activities; they have also conducted their own voter registration and GOTV campaigns. Business leaders have traditionally assisted Republicans. AIPAC provides information about candidates to PACs that support Israel. Even though it carries out activities similar to those of lead PACs and the Hill committees, AIPAC gives no cash contributions to congressional candidates and so does not qualify as a federally registered PAC. Environmental groups and the Christian Coalition are relative newcomers to electoral politics, but their voter guides and voter mobilization efforts have played important roles in recent congressional elections.

INDEPENDENT, PARALLEL, AND COORDINATED CAMPAIGNS

Interest groups, like political parties, carry out campaigns to help or harm individual candidates. They also provide candidates with campaign contributions and services. Independent, parallel, and coordinated interest group campaigns developed as a result of changes in the rules governing campaign finance. Another similarity between these and party campaigns is that both use polling, television, radio, direct mail, mass telephone calls, and grassroots activities to influence congressional elections. Interest group independent expenditures, like those made by parties, must be made with hard money and without the candidate's knowledge or consent. Moreover, interest group–sponsored broadcast television and radio ads, like those sponsored by political parties, do not qualify for lowest unit rate charges.

A major difference between interest group and political party issue advocacy in 2002—whether made over the airwaves, via telephone, or through the mail—is that interest group issue advocacy could be made using funds raised in amounts and from sources prohibited by the FECA, whereas party issue advocacy had to be made using a combination of federally regulated and unregulated dollars. Moreover, interest group issue advocacy spending, unlike national party advocacy spending, is not subject to the FECA's disclosure provisions. This makes it impossible to learn precisely how much money interest groups spend on issue advocacy in a given election year or the source of that money. Nevertheless, most estimates suggest that the amounts spent on issue advocacy are impressive.

Interest group independent campaigns, like party independent campaigns, consist mainly of independent expenditures financed with federal funds. Virtually all—98 percent—of the $13.5 million in interest group independent expenditures made in the 2002 congressional elections were undertaken by nonconnected, trade, and labor PACs. Independent expenditures are consistent with the ideological or mixed strategies these PACs follow. Moreover, because nonconnected PACs do not have organizational sponsors, and because labor and trade PACs are established to advance the political views of organizations that frequently have tens of thousands of members, these committees rarely worry about the retribution of an angry member of Congress or the negative publicity that might result from an independent expenditure. Unlike corporate PACs, these PACs are relatively safe from either outcome because they lack a single sponsor whose interests can be harmed directly.

In the 2002 primaries and general elections, PACs allocated almost $4.6 million in independent expenditures advocating the election of individual House candidates and nearly $452,000 calling for their defeat. They spent an additional $7.7 million advocating the election of Senate candidates and $794,500 calling for their defeat. The vast majority of independent expenditures are made in connection with closely contested elections.[41]

The majority of interest groups finance most, if not all, of their parallel and coordinated campaign efforts using nonfederal dollars collected mainly by 527 committees. During the 2002 elections, sixty-three of the wealthiest 527 committees connected with interest groups ranging from the AFL-CIO to the Sierra Club to the National Association of Realtors to Citizens for Better Medicare (representing the pharmaceutical industry) raised almost $85.2 million.[42] Labor unions and other Democratic-leaning groups raised the most, a total of $63.5 million, as compared to $12.5 million raised by conservative and Republican-leaning organizations and $9.2 million collected by groups not clearly aligned with either set of groups. Leading for labor and liberal organizations were the American Federation of State, County, and Municipal Employees, which raised $23.8 million, and EMILY's List, which raised $6.7 million. The Club for Growth was the leading conservative organization, collecting almost $4.5 million, followed by the Republican Leadership Coalition, which collected $1.7 million. Much of this money was spent to influence congressional elections; however, some was used for other political activities.

Some of the parallel and coordinated campaign activities carried out by 527 committees and other interest groups in the 2002 congressional elections were highly visible, whereas others flew largely below the radar. Interest groups are believed to have spent an estimated $12 million in soft money on televised issue advocacy ads to influence House races and $8 million on ads to influence Senate contests. These ads considerably overshadowed PAC independent expenditures on TV ads. Leading the field in the realm of televised issue advocacy was the United Seniors Association, which spent an estimated $8.7 million; followed by the AFL-CIO, spending $3.6 million; and Americans for Job Security, a conservative, business-backed pro-Republican organization that spent $1.5 million. EMILY's List ranked fourth, spending $1.3 million on televised issue advocacy ads, and the Club for Growth ranked ninth, spending $560,000.[43]

Interest groups also spent tens of millions in nonfederal dollars to communicate with their members and other voters via direct mail, e-mail, and mass telephone calls. They also committed millions of dollars to voter registration, mobilization, and other grassroots activities. Indeed, during the 2002 elections most of these groups increased their spending on grassroots campaign activities over 2000 levels, while decreasing their expenditures on television.[44] As is usually the case, labor unions devoted more resources in 2002 to these efforts than did business-oriented groups, but the business sector took significant steps in narrowing the gap. As was the case with interest group independent campaigns, groups' parallel and coordinated campaign activities were targeted primarily to very competitive races.

THE IMPACT OF INTEREST GROUP ACTIVITY

Congressional candidates and their campaign aides generally evaluate the help their campaigns get directly from labor, business, and advocacy groups and PACs less favorably than the assistance they get from party committees. The exception to this rule is fundraising, where as a function of their sheer numbers and the FECA's contribution limits, political action committees as a group are in a position to contribute more money to a House campaign than can party organizations. The assessments of House campaigners indicate that interest groups play larger roles in the campaigns of Democrats than in those of Republicans. This is especially true for labor unions and labor PACs, which for decades have made large contributions in money and manpower to Democratic campaigns. The Republican candidates' relative lack of dependence on interest groups is also partially a result of their greater reliance on party committees for campaign services, as was noted in Chapter 4.[45] Senate candidates and campaign aides of both parties find PACs and other groups to be helpful in virtually every aspect of campaigning but not as helpful as the DSCC or NRSC.

Of course, interest group election efforts, like party efforts, are targeted to selected races. The information provided by both House and Senate campaigners indicates that interest group campaign assistance tends to be focused more heavily on competitive contests and to be more important to the election efforts of hopeful challengers and open-seat prospects than to those of incumbents. This is largely the result of incumbents beginning the election with high levels of name recognition and huge war chests, both of which nonincumbents lack.

Interest groups were active in many competitive 2002 House races, including the open-seat contest in Colorado's 7th district. Feeley benefited from substantial direct support from interest groups, including the $463,400 he raised from PACs and the additional sums he raised from donors who are part of one or more interest group networks. Labor unions, lawyers, and liberal ideological groups were among Feeley's top backers. He raised $233,200 from labor PACs and another $1,400 in contributions of $200 or more from donors connected with the labor unions. Lawyers and their PACs accounted for another $203,700; and pro-choice, pro-human rights, and Democratic-leaning and liberal PACs and their networks of supporters accounted for another $42,000.[46]

Some of these groups also conducted independent, parallel, and coordinated campaign activities on behalf of Feeley. For example, as part of its campaign to mobilize union workers and their families, the Colorado AFL-CIO distributed one direct-mail piece and two e-mails to its members and contacted them by telephone and in person during the closing days of the election. The Colorado Education Association sought to mobilize its members by using direct mail to make the case that Feeley, not Beauprez, was a friend of education, and the Rocky Mountain Chapter of the Sierra Club mailed an environmental scorecard to its members. The Sierra Club's national office paid for a mass telephone call to mobilize environmentally concerned voters. The American Association of Retired Persons, Planned Parenthood, and a few other groups also sent direct-mail pieces and took other efforts to boost Feeley's prospects.[47] All of these activities took the form of issue advocacy advertising, as Feeley benefited from no independent expenditures.

Beauprez also was the beneficiary of significant interest group support. PACs contributed roughly $443,400 to his campaign, and PACs and other interest groups played a role in stimulating the contributions he raised from congressional donors. In contrast to Feeley, Beauprez raised no money from labor PACs but did very well with the business community. He raised $242,350 from corporate, cooperative, and trade association PACs.[48] The finance, insurance, and real estate industries were particularly supportive, viewing the professional banker as a natural ally. Political action committees and individuals associated with these groups contributed $252,000 to the Beauprez campaign. Republican-leaning and conservative interests also were obliging, contributing another almost $32,000.[49]

The Beauprez campaign benefited from substantially more independent, parallel, and coordinated activity than did its opponent. The Council for Better Government televised twenty-four issue advocacy ads encouraging African American and Hispanic voters to support the GOP. The National Rifle Association (NRA) sent four direct-mail pieces to its members praising Beauprez for his support of the Second Amendment and giving Feeley an "F" for his "anti-gun" voting record. The group also organized a rally in late October, at which NRA president Charlton Heston worked to mobilize gun owners to turn out for Beauprez and other Republican candidates. The Seniors Coalition, the 60 Plus Association, National Right to Life, and America 21 sent older Republicans direct mail designed to counter Feeley's attacks on Beauprez's plans for cutting prescription drug costs and supporting the privatization of Social Security. The NFIB and several other conservative groups also used mail, radio, mass telephone calls, and direct personal contact to aid Beauprez's cause.[50]

Interest group efforts in South Dakota showed that groups can play a significant role in Senate elections. Thune raised more than $1.3 million from PACs, including $494,700, $471,600, and $4,000 from corporations, trade associations, and cooperatives, respectively.[51] His best source of revenue came from PACs and individual donors associated with the finance, real estate, and insurance industries, which furnished him with more than $617,400 in contributions. Agricultural, energy, and health care–related industries each furnished the campaign with contributions well in excess of $200,000. Conservative and Republican-leaning PACs and individuals donated about $178,000.[52]

In addition to this direct support, interest groups carried out a number of outside campaign activities on Thune's behalf. Gun owners' groups were among the most active, inundating voters with direct mail, radio and newspaper ads, and telephone contacts. The NRA alone aired five television ads and one radio ad, and paid for one wave of mass telephone calls. Heston came to the state to campaign for Thune, as he had for Beauprez and many other pro-gun candidates. The Hunting and Shooting Sports Heritage Foundation ran an ad attacking Johnson in *Field and Stream.* The National Shooting Sports Foundation, the South Dakota Sportsman's Alliance, and a group called Gun Owners for Thune purchased direct-mail and newspaper ads attacking Johnson or praising Thune. National Right to Life and the Christian pro-family values group South Dakota Family Policy Council used direct mail and newspaper ads to mobilize social conservatives. Finally, business groups including the U.S. Chamber of Commerce, Americans for Job Security, and the Club for Growth used direct mail, television, radio, and telephone calls to help Thune.[53]

Interest groups provided Johnson with more direct and less indirect campaign support than they did Thune. The incumbent collected almost $2.8 million in PAC contributions from a wide range of interests. Labor gave $406,600 in PAC contributions and another $86,600 from individual donors. PACs and individuals tied to the business community contributed nearly $1.8 million, 70 percent of which came from financial, insurance, and real estate interests.[54]

Interest groups also campaigned on Johnson's behalf but not as heavily as they did for Thune. Labor was particularly active for Johnson, with the AFL-CIO purchasing four direct mail pieces and the South Dakota Education Association providing another three, plus one mass telephone contact. The LCV made Thune one of their "Dirty Dozen" and ran an ad against him in June and July. Planned Parenthood, the Save Our Environment Coalition, and AARP used targeted e-mails and telephone calls to mobilize their supporters in favor of Johnson. The Johnson campaign was not that happy with the parallel and independent campaigning that some groups did on its behalf, believing that their well-intentioned efforts constituted overkill and took the campaign somewhat off message. As such, it requested that these groups withdraw from the race.[55]

It is impossible to tell whether interest group activities—or party efforts or the candidates' own campaigns—determined the outcomes of the Beauprez-Feeley race, the Johnson-Thune match-up, or any other hotly contested congressional election. Nevertheless, these elections demonstrate that interest group–sponsored issue advocacy can be important in setting the political agenda, touting the strengths and weaknesses of candidates, and mobilizing voters in recent competitive elections. The efforts of parties and groups neither resulted in more nationalized elections nor did away with candidate-centered congressional elections, but the efforts of these organizations prevented some candidates in very close races from dominating the campaign messages received by voters. This was particularly true in elections where Washington-based interest groups and party committees outspent the candidates themselves. The efforts of these groups contributed significantly to the demand for campaign finance reform and to the passage of the Bipartisan Campaign Reform Act of 2002, discussed in Chapter 11.

SUMMARY

Interest groups, like parties, play important supporting roles in congressional elections. Most interest group activity takes the form of PAC contributions to candidates, but some PACs also distribute campaign services and make independent expenditures. In addition, some labor unions, business organizations, and issue-oriented and ideological groups provide congressional campaigns with volunteers, carry out voter mobilization drives, and use issue ads to influence the political agenda or affect individual candidates' election prospects. Because some interest groups view elections as opportunities to lay the groundwork for lobbying members of Congress, and as vehicles for changing the membership of the legislative branch, they distribute some resources to House and Senate members in safe seats and others to incumbents, challengers, and open-seat candidates in close elections. More businesses than labor unions participate in congressional elections, and business groups typically spend more money in them than do their labor counterparts.

CHAPTER SIX

The Campaign for Resources

Vice President Hubert Humphrey described fundraising as a "disgusting, degrading, demeaning experience."[1] Few politicians would disagree with this sentiment. Yet spending money on political campaigns predates the Constitution. In 1757 George Washington purchased twenty-eight gallons of rum, fifty gallons of spiked punch, forty-six gallons of beer, thirty-four gallons of wine, and a couple of gallons of hard cider to help shore up his political base and pry loose the support of enough uncommitted voters to get elected to the Virginia House of Burgesses.[2] Population growth, technological advancements, suburbanization, and other changes associated with the emergence of a modern mass democracy in the United States have driven up the costs of campaigning since Washington launched his political career. Candidates, parties, and interest groups spent well in excess of $2 billion on the 2002 elections.

Raising the funds needed to run for Congress has evolved into a campaign in and of itself. Part of this campaign takes place in the candidate's state or district, but many candidates are dependent on resources that come from party committees and PACs located in and around Washington, D.C., and from wealthy individuals who typically reside in major metropolitan areas.

The campaign for resources begins earlier than the campaign for votes. It requires a candidate to attract the support of sophisticated, goal-oriented groups and individuals who have strong preconceptions about what it takes to win a congressional election. Theoretically, all congressional candidates can turn to the same sources and use the same techniques to gather campaign funds and services. In fact, however, candidates begin and end on uneven playing fields. The level of success that candidates achieve with different kinds of contributors or fundraising techniques depends largely on whether they are incumbents, challengers, or candidates for open House seats. It also depends on the candidates' party affiliation and on whether they are running for the House or the Senate, among other factors. In this chapter I analyze the fundraising strategies and successes of different kinds of candidates.

Candidates in the 2002 House elections set a spending record of $608.5 million. One hundred and eighty-five candidates each spent more than $1 million, and thirteen spent in excess of $3 million. Democratic challenger James Humphreys spent the most of any House candidate—almost $8.2 million—nearly 96 percent his own money—in an unsuccessful rematch to defeat Rep. Shelley Moore Capito in West Virginia.

The Senate elections fell short of record setting, but candidates spent a total of $324.7 million in those races. Fifty-five of the sixty-four major-party candidates each spent more than $1 million, including thirty-seven who spent more than $3 million, twenty-seven who spent over $5 million, and five who spent in excess of $10 million. The biggest spender was Republican Elizabeth Dole, who spent $13.7 million to defeat Democrat Erskine Bowles, who spent $13.3 million, 51 percent of which was his own money, in their open-seat contest in North Carolina.[3] These candidates fell well short of the record set by Sen. Jon Corzine, D-N.J., who spent $63.2 million—$60.2 million of it his own money—to win an open seat in the Senate in 2000.

INEQUALITIES IN RESOURCES

Significant inequalities exist in the resources, including money and party coordinated expenditures, that different types of candidates are able to raise. The typical House incumbent involved in a two-party contested race raised just under $977,900 in cash and party coordinated expenditures in 2002, which is 3.75 times more than the sum raised by the typical House challenger.[4] Open-seat candidates also gathered significant resources, raising an average of almost $1.2 million.

The resource discrepancies in competitive House races are great. Incumbents in jeopardy raised almost 68 percent more in cash and party coordinated expenditures than did hopeful challengers during the 2002 elections (see Figure 6-1). Competitive open-seat contests were much more equal in regard to the amount raised. The resource discrepancies in uncompetitive House contests are even greater than are those in competitive ones. Incumbents, who begin raising funds early (often before they know whom they will face in the general election), raise much more money than do their opponents (see Figure 6-2). Incumbent shoo-ins raised almost ten times more than likely-loser challengers in 2002. The spread among Democratic and Republican open-seat

FIGURE 6-1

Average Campaign Resources Raised in Competitive House Elections in 2002

$, thousands

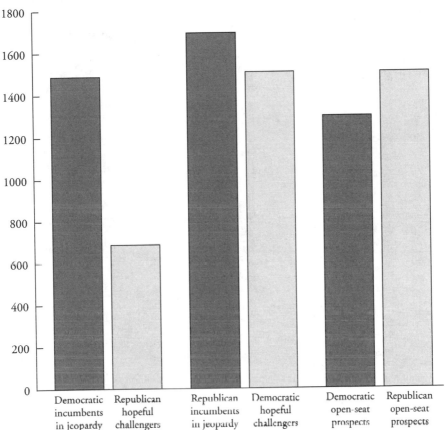

Source: Compiled from Federal Election Commission data.

Notes: Figures include receipts and party-coordinated expenditures for all two-party contests that were decided by margins of 20 percent of the vote or less, excluding incumbent-versus-incumbent races. The categories and numbers of candidates are the same as in Table 4-2.

candidates in uncompetitive races is usually much smaller, averaging about $126,000.

The typical Senate incumbent raised almost $2 million more than the typical challenger during the 2002 election (see Figure 6-3). Open-seat Senate

FIGURE 6-2

Average Campaign Resources Raised in Uncompetitive House Elections in 2002

$, thousands

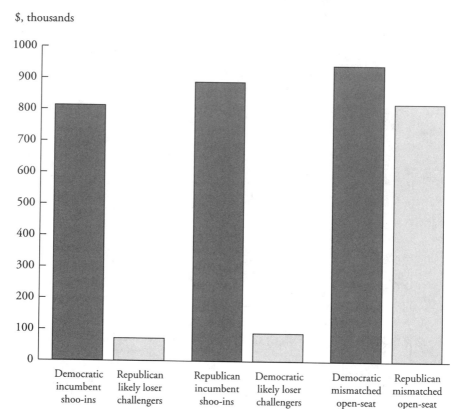

| Democratic incumbent shoo-ins | Republican likely loser challengers | Republican incumbent shoo-ins | Democratic likely loser challengers | Democratic mismatched open-seat candidates | Republican mismatched open-seat candidates |

Source: Compiled from Federal Election Commission data.

Notes: Figures include receipts and party-coordinated expenditures for all two-party contests that were decided by margins over 20 percent of the vote, excluding incumbent-versus-incumbent races. The categories and numbers of candidates are the same as in Table 4-2.

contests were fairly well funded, with contestants spending an average of almost $7.8 million. The differences in the amounts raised by Democratic and Republican candidates were fairly significant, favoring GOP contenders by about $714,100 or 16 percent. Finally, electoral competitiveness was important in attracting campaign resources. Senate candidates who defeated their opponents by 20 percent or less of the two-party vote raised almost three times more than did candidates involved in one-sided races.

FIGURE 6-3

Average Campaign Resources Raised in the 2002 Senate Elections

$, millions

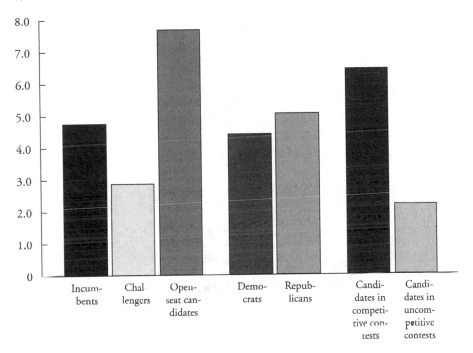

Source: Compiled from Federal Election Commission data.

Notes: Figures include receipts and party-coordinated expenditures for all two party contested races. $N = 60$.

HOUSE INCUMBENTS

Incumbents raise more money than do challengers because they tend to be visible, popular, and willing to exploit the advantages of holding office. This is reflected both in how incumbents solicit contributions and in whom they turn to for cash. Incumbents rarely hesitate to remind a potential donor that they are in a position to influence public policy and will more than likely still be in that position when the next Congress convenes.

Sources of Funds

Individuals who make contributions of less than $200, many of whom reside in a candidate's state or district, are an important source of funds for House incumbents (see Figure 6-4). In 2002 they accounted for $112,200, or 12 percent, of the typical incumbent's campaign war chest.[5] They are often viewed symbolically as an indicator of grassroots support.

Individuals who contributed $200 or more accounted for more than $380,600, or 39 percent, of the typical incumbent's funds. Many made contributions across district or state lines. Individuals living in New York City alone donated more than $19.2 million to 2002 House and Senate candidates across the United States. These contributions, along with the millions distributed by Washington-based parties and PACs, have helped to form a na-

FIGURE 6-4

Sources of House Incumbents' Campaign Receipts in the 2002 Elections

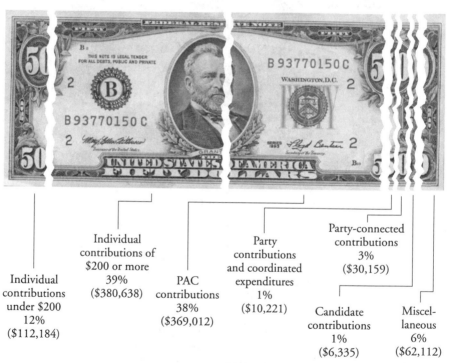

Individual contributions under $200 12% ($112,184)

Individual contributions of $200 or more 39% ($380,638)

PAC contributions 38% ($369,012)

Party contributions and coordinated expenditures 1% ($10,221)

Party-connected contributions 3% ($30,159)

Candidate contributions 1% ($6,335)

Miscellaneous 6% ($62,112)

Source: Compiled from Federal Election Commission data.

Notes: The dollar values in parentheses are averages. Candidate contributions include loans candidates made to their own campaigns. PAC contributions exclude contributions by leadership PACs. Party-connected contributions are made up of contributions from leadership PACs, candidates, retired members, and members of Congress not up for reelection in 2002. Miscellaneous sources include interest from savings accounts and revenues from investments. Figures are for general election candidates in major-party contested races, excluding those in incumbent-versus-incumbent races. Percentages do not add to 100 percent because of rounding. $N = 300$.

tional market for campaign contributions.[6] Typical House incumbents in two-party contested races relied heavily on this market, raising the vast majority of their PAC money and almost 26 percent of their individual contributions of $200 or more from outside their states' borders.[7]

PACs provided approximately $369,000, or 38 percent, of a typical incumbent's bankroll in 2002. Parties delivered much less, accounting for a mere 1 percent of the typical incumbent's total resources. Party-connected contributions from other members, leadership PACs, and congressional retirees accounted for an additional 3 percent. House members contributed even less of their own money to their campaigns. Finally, they raised about $62,100 from miscellaneous sources, including interest and revenues from investments.

Prior to the Republican takeover of Congress in 1994, Democratic House members collected a greater portion of their funds from PACs than did Republicans, who relied more heavily on individual contributors. The Democrats' procedural control of the House gave them greater influence over the substance and scheduling of legislation, which provided them with an overwhelming advantage in raising money from PACs. The 1996 elections represented a considerable change in this regard. Republican incumbents increased substantially the money they raised from PACs, although they continued to rely more on individuals than did their Democratic counterparts. Republican fundraising followed a similar pattern in the 2002 elections (see Table 6-1).

Fundraising Activities

Incumbents routinely complain about the time, effort, and indignities associated with raising funds. Their lack of enthusiasm for asking people for money figures prominently in how they raise campaign contributions. A fear of defeat and a disdain for fundraising have two principal effects: they encourage incumbents to raise large amounts of money and to place the bulk of their fundraising in the hands of others, mainly professional consultants. Forty-six percent of all major-party House incumbents spend at least one-fourth of their personal campaign schedule raising funds. Seventeen percent spend more than half of their schedule asking others for money.[8]

Most incumbents develop permanent fundraising operations. They hire direct-mail specialists and PAC finance directors to write direct-mail appeals, update contributor lists, identify and solicit potentially supportive PACs, script telephone solicitations, and organize fundraising events. These operations enable incumbents to limit their involvement to showing up at events and telephoning potential contributors who insist on having a direct conversation with them prior to making a large contribution.

TABLE 6-1

Sources of Support for House Incumbents in the 2002 Elections

	Democrats		Republicans	
	In jeopardy	Shoo-ins	In jeopardy	Shoo-ins
Individual contributions under $200	$194,150 (13%)	$81,785 (11%)	$167,981 (9%)	$110,349 (12%)
Individual contributions of $200 or more	$497,383 (33%)	$311,768 (42%)	$698,142 (38%)	$360,752 (40%)
PAC contributions	$561,932 (37%)	$356,310 (40%)	$573,433 (31%)	$367,472 (39%)
Party contributions and coordinated expenditures	$27,826 (2%)	$3,370 (—)	$61,100 (3%)	$3,299 (—)
Party-connected contributions	$84,861 (6%)	$11,306 (2%)	$136,879 (7%)	$15,554 (2%)
Candidate contributions	$3,518 (—)	$2,471 (—)	$59,455 (3%)	$1,464 (—)
Miscellaneous	$132,788 (9%)	$42,295 (5%)	$158,958 (9%)	$54,920 (6%)
(*N*)	(32)	(119)	(22)	(127)

Source: Compiled from Federal Election Commission data.

Notes: Figures are averages for general election candidates in major-party contested races, excluding incumbent-versus-incumbent races. Dashes = less than 0.5 percent. Candidate contributions include loans candidates made to their own campaigns. PAC contributions exclude contributions by leadership PACs. Party-connected contributions are made up of contributions from leadership PACs, candidates, retired members, and members of Congress not up for reelection in 2002. Miscellaneous sources include interest from savings accounts and revenues from investments. Some columns do not add to 100 percent because of rounding.

Incumbents raise small contributions by making appeals through the mail, over the telephone, at fundraising events, and via the Internet. Direct mail can be a relatively reliable method of fundraising for an incumbent because solicitations are usually made from lists of previous donors that indicate which appeals garnered earlier contributions.[9] Most direct mail and telephone solicitations generate contributions of less than $100 and are targeted at the candidate's constituents. However, many prominent House members, including Speaker Dennis Hastert and then–minority leader Richard Gephardt have huge direct-mail lists that include hundreds of thousands of individuals who reside across the United States and even a few from abroad. A significant portion of these individuals contribute large sums. In 2002 Hastert raised $266,000 and Gephardt raised more than $2.6 million in individual contributions of $200 or more from outside their respective states (representing 20 percent and 78 percent, respectively, of these candidates' large individual contributions).[10]

The Internet emerged as an important fundraising tool during the 1998 congressional elections. By 2002, 57 percent of all House candidates in major-party contested races and virtually every Senate candidate used web sites or e-mail to solicit funds.[11] Some sites directed supporters where to send their checks, and others instructed donors how to make contributions online using a credit card.

Candidates who relied on e-mail solicited contributions using e-mail addresses purchased from Internet providers, other organizations, and individuals who visited their web sites. E-mail lists of individuals who share a candidate's issue concerns are a potential source of monetary and volunteer support, especially among computer-literate youth. The greatest advantage of e-mail and Internet fundraising is that the solicitation is delivered for free, compared with the $3 to $4 it costs to send out one first-class direct-mail solicitation. The trade-off for e-mails is that they are not always appreciated. Mass-distributed e-mails, often referred to as "spam," are frequently deleted without having been read, the electronic equivalent of tossing an unopened piece of direct mail into the trash or hanging up on a telemarketer. It is doubtful that most congressional candidates will be able to emulate the e-fundraising success of some presidential candidates, most notably 2004 Democratic nomination candidate Howard Dean, but many high-profile House and Senate contestants are positioned to capitalize on the Internet for some of their fundraising needs.

Traditional fundraising events are another popular means for raising small contributions. Cocktail parties, barbecues, and picnics with admission costs ranging from $10 to $50 that are held in the candidate's district are useful ways to raise money. They are also helpful in generating favorable press coverage, energizing political activists, and building goodwill among voters.

Incumbents can ensure the success of local fundraising events by establishing finance committees that include business executives, labor officials, civic leaders, or political activists who live in their districts. These committees often begin with a dozen or so supporters who host "low-dollar" receptions (where individuals usually contribute from $20 to $100) in their homes and make telephone solicitations on the candidate's behalf. Guests at one event are encouraged to become the sponsors of others. In time, small finance committees can grow into large pyramid-like fundraising networks, consisting of dozens of finance committees, each of which makes a substantial contribution to the candidate's reelection efforts. Most House and Senate incumbents have fundraising networks that extend from their district or state to the nation's capital.

Large individual contributions and PAC money also are raised by finance committees, at fundraising events, and through networks of supporters. Events that feature the president, congressional leaders, sports heroes, or other celebrities help attract individuals and groups who are willing to contribute anywhere from a few hundred dollars to the legal maximum of $1,000 (in 2002) per each stage of the race. Some of these events are held in the candidate's state, but most are held in political, financial, and entertainment centers such as Washington, New York City, and Hollywood. In 2002 those few Republican incumbents who were the beneficiaries of a visit by President Bush raised 144 percent more than did other GOP incumbents.

Traditional fundraising events can satisfy the goals of a variety of contributors. They give individuals who desire the social side of giving, including the proximity to power, the chance to speak with members of Congress and other celebrity politicians. Persons and groups that contribute for ideological reasons are able to voice their specific issue concerns. Individuals and organizations that are motivated by material gain, such as a tax break or federal funding for a project, often perceive these events as opportunities to build a relationship with members of Congress.[12]

In raising large individual contributions, House members have advantages over challengers that extend beyond the prestige and political clout that come with incumbency and an ability to rely on an existing group of supporters. Incumbents also benefit from the fact that many wealthy individuals have motives that favor them over challengers. About 25 percent of all individuals who contribute $200 or more to a congressional candidate do so mainly because they wish to gain access to individuals who will be in a position to influence legislation once the election is over—mainly incumbents. Roughly 36 percent give contributions mainly for broad ideological reasons or because of their positions on specific, highly charged issues. These donors tend to rally around incumbents who champion their causes. Another 24 percent are motivated to contribute primarily because they enjoy attending fundraising events and mixing with incumbents and other elites who attend these functions. The final

15 percent are not strongly motivated by access, ideology, or the social side of contributing. Though they contribute for idiosyncratic reasons, they, like other donors, primarily support incumbents.[13]

Moreover, information that parties and PACs mail to their big donors often focuses on incumbents' campaigns, further leading some wealthy individuals to contribute to incumbents in jeopardy rather than to hopeful challengers. The rise of national party organizations, PACs, and other organizations and individuals that provide potential donors with decision-making cues and the Federal Election Campaign Act's ceilings on campaign contributions have led to the replacement of one type of fat cat with another. Individuals and groups that gave candidates tens or hundreds of thousands of dollars directly have been replaced by new sets of elites who help candidates raise these sums rather than contribute them directly.[14]

Incumbents consciously use the influence that comes with holding office to raise money from PACs and wealthy individuals who seek political access. Legislators' campaigns first identify potential donors who are most likely to respond favorably to their solicitations. These include PACs that supported the incumbent in a previous race, lobbyists who agree with an incumbent's positions on specific issues, and others who are affected by legislation the incumbent is in a position to influence. Members of Congress who hold party leadership positions, serve on powerful committees, or are recognized entrepreneurs in certain policy areas can easily raise large amounts of money from many wealthy interest group–based financial constituencies. It is no coincidence that the eight House incumbents who raised more than $1 million in interest group PAC contributions in 2002 each enjoyed at least one of these assets.[15]

Once an incumbent has identified his or her financial constituency, the next step is to ask for a contribution. The most effective solicitations describe the member's background, legislative goals, accomplishments, sources of influence (including committee assignments, chairmanships, or party leadership positions), the nature of the competition faced, and the amount of money needed. Incumbents frequently assemble this information in the PAC kits they mail to PACs. They also take into account the potential donors' motives for contributing.[16]

Some PACs require a candidate to meet with one of their representatives, who personally delivers a check. A few require incumbents to complete questionnaires on specific issues, but most PACs rely on members' prior roll-call votes or interest group ratings as measures of their policy proclivities. Some PACs, particularly ideological committees, want evidence that a representative or senator is facing serious opposition before giving a contribution. Party leaders and Hill committee staff are sometimes called to bear witness to the competitiveness of an incumbent's race.

Parties are another source of money and campaign services. The most important thing incumbents can do to win party support is demonstrate that they are vulnerable. The Hill committees have most of the information they need to make such a determination, but incumbents can give details on the nature of the threat they face that might not be apparent to a party operative who is unfamiliar with the nuances of a member's seat. The National Republican Congressional Committee gives incumbents who request extra party support the opportunity to make their case before a special Incumbent Review Board composed of GOP members. Once a Hill committee has made an incumbent a priority, it will go to great efforts to supply the candidate with money, campaign services, and assistance in collecting resources from others.

The financing of Rep. Douglas Ose's 2002 reelection effort is typical of that of most reelection bids involving safe incumbents. Ose raised $882,000 during the 2002 election season and received $122 in contributions from the NRCC and no party coordinated expenditures, a substantially smaller party supplement than the $3,300 received by the typical shoo-in incumbent. He collected nearly $80,400 (9 percent of his total resources) in small contributions using campaign newsletters, direct-mail solicitations, and low-dollar fundraising events held in the district. He collected another $385,200 (roughly 43 percent) in individual contributions of $200 or more at high-dollar events. Just over $21,500 (6 percent) of these funds were raised from individuals who reside outside California.[17]

Ose raised $399,700 (43 percent) from PACs (excluding leadership PACs). Corporate, trade, and other business-related committees contributed about 88 percent of these funds. Nonconnected committees accounted for 8 percent of Ose's PAC dollars. The candidate collected no contributions from other members' campaign committees but received about $5,600 from their leadership PACs. He raised $12,000 from labor PACs, which is a healthy sum for a Republican. Most of his PAC money and large individual donations were raised at events held in the district or in Washington and through solicitations coordinated by the candidate's campaign staff. Finally, the campaign raised $32,800 from interest on loans and investments (4 percent of its total campaign receipts). Like most congressional incumbents, Ose contributed no money to his own reelection effort.

Ose was successful at capitalizing on his membership on the House Financial Services Committee. The individuals and groups that are affected by the committee's business make up one of the nation's wealthiest interest group constituencies. Ose's campaign collected about $126,600 (32 percent of its PAC funds) from PACs associated with the finance, real estate, and insurance industries, and it raised another $59,100 in contributions of $200 or more from individuals who work in this economic sector (16 percent of his total large individual contributions).[18]

With only two-year terms, House incumbents usually begin raising money almost immediately after they are sworn into office. Sometimes they have debts to retire, but often they use money left over from previous campaigns as seed money for the next election. More than 23 percent of all House incumbents began the 2002 election cycle with more than $400,000 left over from their previous campaigns. In turn, over 28 percent of all successful 2002 House candidates completed their campaigns with more than $400,000 in the bank, including thirty-two incumbents who had amassed more than $1 million. These funds will provide useful seed money for their reelection campaigns in 2004 or bids for some other office.

Early fundraising is carried out for strategic reasons. Incumbents build substantial war chests early in the election cycle to try to deter potential challengers.[19] An incumbent who had to spend several hundreds of thousands or even millions of dollars to win by a narrow margin in the last election will have a greater compulsion to raise money earlier than someone whose previous election was a landslide victory. Once they have raised enough money to reach an initial comfort level, however, incumbents appear to be driven largely by the threat posed by an actual challenger.[20] Incumbents under duress seek to amass huge sums of money regardless of the source, whereas those who face weak opponents may weigh other considerations, such as developing a "diversified portfolio of contributors."[21]

A typical incumbent's campaign—one waged by a candidate who faces stiff competition in neither the primary nor the general election—will generally engage in heavy fundraising early and then allow this activity to taper off as it becomes clear that the candidate is not in jeopardy. The 2002 Ose campaign exemplifies this pattern. The campaign began the election cycle with more than $276,400 left over from the candidate's last race. Between January 1 and December 31, 2001, it raised $429,700 (about 57 percent of its total receipts). All of this money was raised before Beeman, Ose's general election opponent, had filed his candidacy with the state of California or began raising money. During the next six months, which included California's March 5 primary, the Ose campaign began to cut back on its fundraising efforts, collecting a mere $88,300 (12 percent), perhaps in response to the paltry $1,851 collected by the Beeman campaign. During the next six months the Ose campaign collected an additional $146,200 (20 percent). Between October 1 and November 25 it raised a total of 83,600 (11 percent). The campaign closed out the election year by collecting an additional $3,700 (less than 1 percent).

Ose's campaign finances demonstrate that a good deal of incumbent fundraising is challenger driven. Early money is raised to deter a strong opponent from entering the race. If a strong challenger materializes, then an incumbent's fundraising activities will usually increase. If none emerges, they will remain steady or slow down.

The 2002 Morella campaign also supports the generalization that incumbent fundraising is challenger driven: it shows how an incumbent responds to a strong challenger. The campaign collected almost $2.9 million in contributions and $81,000 in coordinated expenditures, making it the sixth most-expensive House general election campaign waged by an incumbent that year. It raised almost $935,200 (32 percent of its total resources) from PACs, excluding leadership PACs, and another $1.3 million (45 percent) in individual contributions of $200 or more, about two-thirds of which was collected from individuals living in Maryland.[22] The campaign collected $318,100 (11 percent) in individual contributions of less than $200. The Republican Party provided $96,800 in contributions and coordinated expenditures (about 3 percent). Republican members of Congress and retirees contributed $51,100, and leadership PACs gave another $185,700 (for a total of 8 percent).[23]

Morella began to solicit contributions early and aggressively because she recognized that her less-than-seven-point victory over a largely unknown Terry Lierman in 2000 and redistricting made her a prime target for a strong Democratic challenge. She began the campaign cycle with almost $166,000 left over from her previous campaign. Between January 1 and June 30, 2001, Morella's campaign raised about $212,000 (roughly 7 percent of its receipts). Between July 1 and December 31 it collected another $332,900 (12 percent). This money was raised partly in response to the tremendous sums being raised by the leading candidates for the Democratic nomination candidates—Van Hollen, Shriver, and Shapiro, each of whom had raised hundreds of thousands of dollars by this point.

The Democratic primary candidates' impressive fundraising encouraged the Morella campaign to continue collecting cash at a frenetic pace. By June 30, 2002, the campaign had raised more than an additional $1.1 million (40 percent). Between July 1 and September 30 the Morella campaign raised another $511,100 (18 percent). The campaign raised about another $631,000 (23 percent) between October 1 and November 25. Because the campaign ended with a positive balance, Morella did not need to hold any end-of-the-year fundraising events to close out debts.

The Morella campaign's fundraising was driven by the threat the candidate had anticipated, which eventually arose. Just as a lack of competition had caused Ose to raise less money than the typical incumbent, stiff competition encouraged Morella to set a personal fundraising record.

HOUSE CHALLENGERS

Challengers have the greatest need for money, but they encounter the most difficulties raising it. The same factors that make it difficult for challengers to win votes also harm their ability to collect campaign contributions. A lack of name recognition, limited campaign experience, a relatively untested organization, and a high probability of defeat discourage most contributors, especially those who give large amounts in pursuit of access, from supporting challengers. The fact that their opponents are established Washington operators who possess political clout does not make challengers' quests for support any easier.

Sources of Funds

Challengers raise less money than do incumbents, and their mix of funding sources differs from that of incumbents. House challengers collect a greater portion of their funds from individuals. Challengers competing in the 2002 elections raised an average of about $39,000, or 15 percent of their campaign budgets, in individual contributions of less than $200 (see Figure 6-5). Challengers collected more than twice as much of their funds in the form of individual contributions of $200 or more. Both challengers and incumbents raised about half of their funds from individuals, but incumbents raised, on average, four times more in individual contributions than did challengers. Moreover, challengers raised only 23 percent of these funds from out of state, a significantly smaller proportion than that collected by incumbents.

Challengers garnered a mere 9 percent of their money from PACs, trailing incumbents by a ratio of almost one to six in terms of the amounts of PAC dollars these individuals typically raised. Challengers also raised substantially less party-connected money, about $11,700, as opposed to the nearly $30,200 raised by the typical incumbent. Party contributions and coordinated expenditures, by contrast, were delivered more evenly, with challengers averaging only $1,000 less than incumbents. Finally, challengers dug far deeper into their own pockets than did incumbents. The typical challenger contributed or loaned the campaign almost $88,000—more than fourteen times the amount contributed or loaned by the typical incumbent.

Democratic challengers, especially Democratic hopefuls, raised substantially more money from PACs than did their Republican counterparts (see Table 6-2).

FIGURE 6-5

Sources of House Challengers' Campaign Receipts in the 2002 Elections

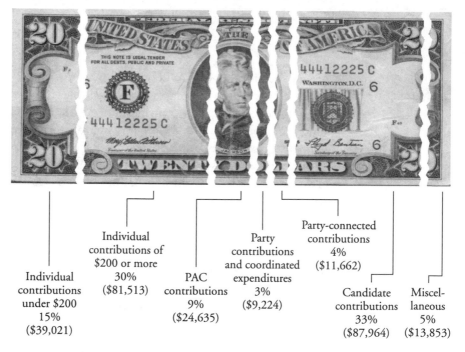

Individual
contributions of
$200 or more
30%
($81,513)

Party
contributions
and coordinated
expenditures
3%
($9,224)

Party-connected
contributions
4%
($11,662)

Individual
contributions
under $200
15%
($39,021)

PAC
contributions
9%
($24,635)

Candidate
contributions
33%
($87,964)

Miscel-
laneous
5%
($13,853)

Source: Compiled from Federal Election Commission data.

Notes: See notes in Figure 6-4. $N = 300$.

Democratic challengers also collected more money from individuals, especially those who made large contributions, than did their Republican challengers. Republican hopefuls received almost twice as much party support as did Democrats. Democrats, however, invested substantially more in their own campaigns, reflecting the greater career orientation that many Democratic politicians have toward politics.

Fundraising Activities

Incumbents may find fundraising a disagreeable chore, but at least their efforts are usually met with success. Challengers put in just as many long, hard hours on the money chase as do incumbents.[24] Yet, as noted above, they clearly have less to show for their efforts. Most challengers start raising early money at home. They begin by donating or loaning their campaigns the initial funds

TABLE 6-2

Sources of Support for House Challengers in the 2002 Elections

	Democrats		Republicans	
	Hopefuls	Likely losers	Hopefuls	Likely losers
Individual contributions under $200	$152,813 (9%)	$15,540 (16%)	$105,527 (14%)	$25,160 (35%)
Individual contributions of $200 or more	$420,966 (26%)	$27,523 (29%)	$280,959 (38%)	$22,745 (31%)
PAC contributions	$190,098 (11%)	$36,910 (10%)	$67,764 (8%)	$7,424 (2%)
Party contributions and coordinated expenditures	$26,207 (2%)	$1,128 (1%)	$51,193 (7%)	$3,440 (5%)
Party-connected contributions	$73,798 (4%)	$1,763 (2%)	$47,516 (6%)	$1,098 (2%)
Candidate contributions	$706,425 (43%)	$34,807 (37%)	$135,816 (18%)	$17,490 (24%)
Miscellaneous	$82,201 (5%)	$13,400 (4%)	$62,102 (8%)	$7,208 (2%)
(N)	(22)	(127)	(32)	(119)

Source: Compiled from Federal Election Commission data.

Notes: See notes in Table 6-1.

needed to solicit contributions from others. They then turn to relatives, friends, professional colleagues, local political activists, and virtually every individual whose name is in their personal organizer or, better, on their holiday card list. Some of these people are asked to chair fundraising committees and host fundraising events. Candidates who have previously run for office are able to turn to past contributors for support. Competitive challengers frequently obtain lists of contributors from members of their party who have previously run for office or from private vendors. In some cases these challengers receive lists from party committees or PACs; however, most of these organizations mail fundraising letters on behalf of selected candidates rather than physically turn over their contributor lists.

Only after enjoying some local fundraising success do most nonincumbents set their sights on Washington. Seed money raised from individuals is especially helpful in attracting funds from PACs, particularly for candidates who have not held elective office.[25] The endorsements of local business, labor, party, or civic leaders have a similar effect, especially if they can be persuaded to serve on a fundraising committee. If it can be obtained, the assistance of congressional leaders or members of a candidate's state delegation can be helpful to challengers who hope to raise money from their party's congressional campaign committee, PACs, or large individual contributors.[26] When powerful incumbents organize luncheons, attend "meet-and-greets," and appear at fundraising events for nonincumbents, contributors usually respond favorably. Contributors also look favorably on events attended by high-ranking executive branch officials, particularly the president. For example, Republican challenger John Kline of Minnesota, who faced off against Democratic incumbent William Luther for the third time in 2002, raised almost $1.6 million, including $500,000 at an event attended by President Bush.[27] These funds undoubtedly helped Kline to finally defeat Luther.

Unfortunately for most challengers, their long odds of success make it difficult for them to enlist the help of incumbents. House members prefer to focus their efforts on candidates who have strong electoral prospects and may someday be in a position to return the favor by supporting the member's leadership aspirations or legislative goals in Congress.

A knowledge of how party leaders and PAC managers make contribution decisions can improve challengers' fundraising prospects. Political experience and a professional campaign staff are often helpful in this regard.[28] Candidates who put together feasible campaign plans, hire reputable consultants, and can present polling figures indicating that they enjoy a reasonable level of name recognition can usually attract the attention of party officials, PAC managers, individuals who make large contributions, and the inside-the-beltway journalists who handicap elections. Political amateurs who wage largely volunteer efforts, in contrast, usually cannot.

During the 2002 congressional elections, House challengers in major-party contested races who had previously held elective office raised, on average, $24,000 from party committees and $25,700 in party-connected contributions from other candidates, retired members of Congress, and leadership PACs. Unelected politicians raised an average of $9,100 from party committees and $11,500 in party-connected dollars, whereas political amateurs raised, on average, only $4,000 and $6,700, respectively, from these sources. Challengers who relied on a professional fundraiser collected an average of $20,400 in party contributions and coordinated expenditures and $27,100 in party-connected contributions, amounting to almost four times more than was raised from these sources by challengers who relied on volunteers.

One way in which challengers can increase their chances of success in raising money from PACs is for them to identify the few committees likely to give them support. For Democrats, these committees include labor groups. Challengers can improve their prospects of attracting labor PAC money by showing they have strong ties to the labor community, have previously supported labor issues in the state legislature, or support labor's current goals.[29] Competitive Democratic challengers who were able to make this case in 2002 did quite well with the labor community, raising an average of $134,700 from labor PACs.

Challengers of both parties may be able to attract support from PACs, particularly ideological committees, by convincing PAC managers that they are committed to the group's cause. A history of personal support for that cause is useful. Challengers, and in fact most nonincumbents, typically demonstrate this support by pointing to roll-call votes they cast in the state legislature, to the backing of PAC donors or affiliated PACs located in their state or district, or to the support of Washington-based organizations that share some of the PAC's views. Nonincumbents who make a PAC's issues among the central elements of their campaign message and communicate this information in their PAC kits enhance their odds of winning a committee's backing. Properly completing a PAC's questionnaire or having a successful interview with a PAC manager also is extremely important. Taking these steps can help a challenger obtain a contribution and endorsement from a PAC, as well as gain assistance in raising money from individuals and other PACs with shared policy concerns.

Political experience and professional expertise also can help a nonincumbent raise PAC money. In 2002, challengers who had previously held office raised an average of $46,800 from PACs, roughly $13,700 more than did the typical unelected politician and $34,900 more than did the typical amateur. Challengers who hired a professional fundraiser raised, on average, approximately $53,500 more than did those who relied on volunteers.

Ideological causes have been at the forefront of many candidates' PAC fundraising strategies during the past few decades. Women challengers were able to capitalize on their gender and attract large amounts of money and campaign assistance from EMILY's List, the WISH List (the Republican counterpart of EMILY's List), and other pro-women's groups.[30] Challengers who take a stand on either side of the abortion issue are frequently able to raise money from PACs and individual donors that share their positions. By taking a side on emotionally laden issues, such as handgun control or support for Israel, some challengers are able to attract the contributions of ideological PACs and individuals that identify with those causes.

A perception of competitiveness is critical to challenger fundraising, and a scandal involving an incumbent can help a challenger become competitive. Scandal was critical in helping several Democratic primary challengers raise the funds needed to defeat Democratic incumbents. It helped Dennis Cardoza raise the $1.7 million he used to knock off Gary Condit in the primary and defeat Dick Monteith in the general election in California's 18th district. It played a key role in helping Denise Majette raise $1.9 million, which she used to defeat Cynthia McKinney in Georgia's 4th district Democratic primary and to win the general election. His hammering away at Robert Torricelli's ethical lapses was critical to Republican challenger Douglas Forrester's ability to raise the almost $10.1 million he spent in the New Jersey Senate race.

Beeman's and Van Hollen's experiences demonstrate the effect that perceptions of competitiveness have on challenger fundraising. Almost from the beginning, Beeman's campaign to unseat Ose was in trouble. Despite the fact that Beeman began his 2002 bid for Congress with $35,869 left over from a previous campaign, he encountered the fundraising doldrums that plague most House challengers, particularly those who would be classified as likely losers. Beeman's campaign began collecting money more than a year after his opponent's, which is typical in most incumbent-challenger races, and it got off to a very slow start. By March 31, 2002, the campaign had collected a mere $1,851 (less than 3 percent of its receipts). It raised another $30,000 (41 percent) between April 1 and September 30. Although it collected another $41,200 (56 percent) between October 1 and November 25, the candidate provided almost one-fifth of those funds through a loan he made to the campaign. Between November 26 and the year's end the campaign raised an additional $443 (less than 1 percent).

Besides getting a late start fundraising, the Beeman campaign suffered from having no professional operation to solicit contributions. The campaign had difficulty raising PAC money—collecting only $10,500 from PACs. Its largest PAC contribution was $2,500, which came from the National Committee for an Effective Congress in the form of precinct-level targeting data it had used in trying to influence California's redistricting process. The Democratic Party made about $4,000 in contributions and coordinated expenditures: the DCCC provided some (mostly dated) precinct-level data from its redistricting research as an in-kind contribution, and the Democratic state party contributed some money toward the candidate's filing fees.[31] Lacking encouragement by party and interest group leaders, few individuals provided large contributions; in the end these totaled only $9,500.

The Van Hollen campaign exemplifies the fundraising dynamics of a challenger who is capable of waging a competitive campaign. As a result of his service in the state legislature, Van Hollen had established the basis for a fundraising network in Maryland. His campaign fundraising is typical of that of most hopeful challengers in that he used a variety of techniques to solicit money from a broad array of individuals and groups. Experience, a professional organization, an effective strategy, and personal wealth enabled Van Hollen to raise $3 million in contributions, plus $34,200 in party coordinated expenditures, in his race against Morella. Van Hollen raised almost $299,400 from PACs (excluding leadership PACs), more than $1.6 million in individual contributions of $200 or more, $635,800 in small contributions, and $147,500 in party-connected contributions. Van Hollen raised $477,100 (29 percent) of his large individual contributions in Maryland.[32] He loaned his campaign $175,000 and contributed another $2,100.

The Van Hollen campaign, unlike the Beeman organization, began collecting money for the 2002 contest shortly after the 2000 contest was over. Beginning without any leftover funds from a previous race, Van Hollen loaned his campaign $125,000 in seed money during the first quarter of the election cycle. His investment was sound, and the campaign's initial solicitations were successful. By June 30, 2001, it had a total of $431,000 in its coffers (accounting for about 14 percent of its total funds). The campaign raised another $234,600 (8 percent) by the close of the calendar year. During the next six months it collected another $405,700 (14 percent). Over the next three months, a period that included Maryland's September 10 primary, it raised an additional $619,700 (25 percent). Boosted by its primary victory and the increasing closeness of the race, the campaign added roughly $1.1 million (almost 37 percent of its funds) to its coffers between October 1 and November 25. The campaign raised about another $61,200 (2 percent) to help retire its campaign debt before the close of the year.

Redistricting and the initial competitiveness of the race helped Van Hollen attract the support of party committees, PACs, and individuals who were drawn by the opportunity to finally wrest a Democratic-leaning seat from the Republicans. Morella's supporters also responded to the competitiveness of the race, making for a race with financial parity. The dynamics of the race were somewhat unusual for even close incumbent-challenger contests in that a hopeful challenger virtually matched an incumbent dollar for dollar and was able to win the seat.

CANDIDATES FOR OPEN HOUSE SEATS

Candidates for open seats possess few of the fundraising advantages of incumbents but also lack the liabilities of challengers. Open-seat candidates rely on many of the same fundraising strategies as challengers but usually have considerably more success. Because most open-seat contests are competitive, they receive a great deal of attention from parties, PACs, and other informed contributors, particularly individuals who make large contributions. This attention places open-seat candidates in a position to convince Washington insiders that their campaigns are worthy of support.

Sources of Funds

The campaign receipts of open-seat candidates resemble those of both incumbents and challengers. Open-seat candidates typically raise slightly more than do incumbents. Like challengers, however, they usually collect fewer large individual contributions from out of state (approximately 21 percent in 2002) and more of their funds from parties and party-connected sources (see Figure 6-6). The typical open-seat candidate's PAC receipts lie between those collected by incumbents and those amassed by challengers. Open-seat candidates contribute more of their own personal funds to their campaigns than do either incumbents or challengers.

Republican open-seat candidates collected a greater share of PAC money in 2002 than they had in elections held before the 1994 Republican takeover of Congress. Republican candidates received significantly more party and party-connected money than did their Democratic counterparts (see Table 6-3). GOP and Democratic open-seat candidates in close races bankrolled considerable portions of their own campaigns, as did Democrats in mismatched contests.

Fundraising Activities

Candidates for open seats put in the longest fundraising hours of all House contestants and, as noted above, with considerable success. Just over 60 percent devote more than one-fourth of their personal campaign schedule to attending fundraising events, meeting in person with potential donors, and dialing for dollars.[33] These candidates help their cause by informing potential contributors of the experience and organizational assets they bring to the race, but these factors have less effect than do others, such as the partisan makeup of the district, on the fundraising abilities of open-seat candidates. Elected politicians raised the most party money in 2002, averaging about $53,900,

FIGURE 6-6

Sources of House Open-Seat Candidates' Campaign Receipts in the 2002 Elections

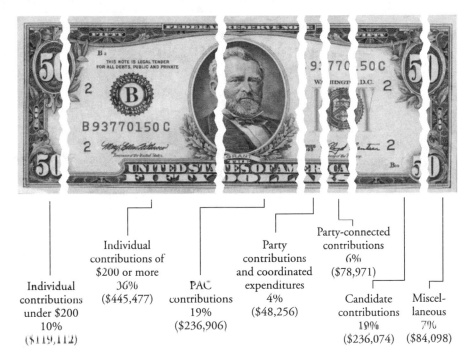

| Individual contributions under $200 10% ($119,112) | Individual contributions of $200 or more 36% ($445,477) | PAC contributions 19% ($236,906) | Party contributions and coordinated expenditures 4% ($48,256) | Party-connected contributions 6% ($78,971) | Candidate contributions 19% ($236,074) | Miscel-laneous 7% ($84,098) |

Source: Compiled from Federal Election Commission data.

Notes: See notes in Figure 6-4. *N* = 94.

about $5,000 more than that collected by the typical unelected official and approximately $31,500 more than that raised by the typical amateur. Elected politicians also raised the most party-connected contributions, averaging $90,000, roughly $16,900 more than that raised by the typical unelected official and $52,500 more than that garnered by the typical amateur. Mounting a professional campaign also helps open-seat candidates attract more party support. In 2002, open-seat candidates who hired professional fundraisers collected an average of $44,300 in party money and $78,200 in party-connected contributions, as contrasted with the $35,400 and $50,600, respectively, raised by candidates who relied mainly on campaign volunteers. Open-seat contestants who have political experience and have assembled professional campaign organizations are better able to meet the campaign objectives that Hill committee staffers set. As a result, they are among the top recipients of party

TABLE 6-3

Sources of Support for House Open-Seat Candidates in the 2002 Elections

	Democrats		Republicans	
	Prospects	Mismatched	Prospects	Mismatched
Individual contributions under $200	$135,901 (10%)	$60,381 (6%)	$154,080 (10%)	$94,459 (11%)
Individual contributions of $200 or more	$437,056 (33%)	$377,296 (40%)	$546,548 (34%)	$364,388 (43%)
PAC contributions	$304,489 (23%)	$174,665 (13%)	$264,845 (16%)	$230,147 (23%)
Party contributions and coordinated expenditures	$38,373 (3%)	$11,158 (1%)	$94,082 (6%)	$27,448 (3%)
Party-connected contributions	$95,178 (7%)	$23,951 (3%)	$114,883 (7%)	$50,021 (6%)
Candidate contributions	$225,721 (17%)	$327,122 (34%)	$294,788 (18%)	$67,112 (8%)
Miscellaneous	$91,169 (7%)	$33,634 (3%)	$136,738 (9%)	$59,293 (6%)
(*N*)	(29)	(18)	(29)	(18)

Source: Compiled from Federal Election Commission data.

Notes: See notes in Table 6-1.

money, campaign services, and fundraising assistance. Getting the endorsement of their state's congressional delegation and other incumbents can also help an open-seat contestant attract party funds.

Winning support from PACs can be a little more challenging. Although open-seat candidates use the same techniques as challengers to identify interest group constituencies and to campaign for PAC support, they usually have greater success. Because their odds of victory are better, open-seat candidates have an easier time gaining an audience with PAC managers and are able to raise more PAC money. Similarly, open-seat candidates point to the same kinds of information as do challengers to make the case that their campaigns will be competitive. Experienced open-seat contestants and those who wage professional campaigns collect more PAC money than do amateurs. In 2002, open-seat candidates who had previously held elective office raised, on average, almost $273,300, about $27,100 more than did the typical unelected politician and almost $179,600 more than did the typical amateur. Open-seat candidates who hired professional fundraisers collected $79,400 more in PAC money than did those who relied largely on volunteers.

The fundraising experiences of the candidates in Colorado's 7th district mirror those of most open-seat candidates in competitive races. Both candidates had contested primaries and both built up considerable war chests. Feeley raised about $1.2 million and received an additional $18,400 in Democratic Party coordinated expenditures. He collected roughly $367,300 (29 percent of his resources) from PACs (excluding leadership PACs), using his positions as a former state senate minority leader and lobbyist to leverage significant PAC dollars.[34] Labor committees gave Feeley about $231,200. PACs sponsored by trade associations, corporations, and cooperatives gave him an additional $74,100, $18,500, and $500, respectively.[35] Liberal nonconnected committees gave Feeley an additional $83,100.[36]

Beauprez had not served in the state legislature, but his position as Republican state party chairman and the Republicans' control of Congress made him an appealing candidate to many contributors. He raised almost $1.9 million in cash and an additional $70,900 in party coordinated expenditures. Beauprez collected $304,600 (almost 15 percent of his total resources) from PACs, receiving $252,500 from business-related committees and $123,500 from conservative nonconnected PACs.[37] Not surprisingly, Beauprez got no support from PACs affiliated with organized labor.

Both candidates raised significant sums through the mail and the Internet and at low-dollar receptions. Feeley collected about $178,500 (14 percent of his campaign's funds) and Beauprez about $137,600 (9 percent) in contributions of less than $200. Feeley raised $411,800 (33 percent) in individual contributions of $200 or more, including $291,200 from out-of-state contributors.[38] Beauprez raised nearly $762,300 (37 percent) in large individual contributions, of which approximately $56,800 came from outside Colorado.[39]

Beauprez raised more party money than did Feeley. In addition to the $70,900 he received in coordinated expenditures, he collected $54,300 in Republican Party contributions. Feeley's $18,400 in coordinated expenditures were supplemented by another $10,000 in Democratic Party contributions.

Beauprez raised an additional $19,000 from Republican members of Congress and retirees and $123,500 from GOP-sponsored leadership PACs. Feeley collected $51,500 from Democratic legislators and retirees and $83,100 from leadership PACs. Contributions from formal party organizations and party politicians and their PACs accounted for about 14 percent of each candidate's total resources.[40] Leaders of both parties clearly viewed this race as important and succeeded in rallying their colleagues to donate funds.

The candidates assumed very different roles in the financing of their campaigns. Feeley directly contributed $56,000 to his campaign but loaned it no money, whereas Beauprez loaned his campaign $455,000 but made no direct contributions. These funds accounted for about 5 percent and 32 percent of the candidate's respective resources.

The fact that the district was drawn relatively late delayed some candidate fundraising. Nevertheless, the newly drawn competitive seat attracted a great deal of attention from prospective candidates, party committees, PACs, and other contributors. This attention enabled both Feeley and Beauprez to raise large amounts of money once they began fundraising in earnest. Between January 1 and June 30, 2002, Feeley and Beauprez collected $255,300 and $417,900, respectively, accounting for roughly 22 percent of each of their campaign receipts. Feeley amassed an additional $512,700 (44 percent) between July 1 and September 30, the period that included Colorado's August 16 primary. Beauprez raised $974,600 (53 percent) during this period. The candidates continued to raise money at a feverish pitch between October 1 and November 25, with Feeley collecting another $390,500 (33 percent) and Beauprez another $376,300 (20 percent). Both campaigns continued to collect money to close out bills they had accumulated. Feeley—the loser—was able to raise $2,100 (less than 1 percent) and Beauprez—the winner—collected $84,100 (5 percent) by the year's end.

SENATE CAMPAIGNS

The differences in the campaigns that Senate and House candidates wage for resources reflect the broader differences that exist between House and Senate elections. Candidates for the Senate need more money and start requesting support earlier. They also devote more time to doing it. About 57 percent of all candidates spend more than one-fourth of their campaign schedule asking potential donors for funds.[41] They often meet with party officials, PAC managers, wealthy individuals, and other sources of money or fundraising assistance three years before they plan to run. Most Senate candidates also attempt to raise money on a more national scale than do House contestants. The monumental size of the task requires Senate candidates to rely more on others for fundraising assistance. Nonincumbent Senate candidates are more likely than their House counterparts to hire professional consultants to manage their direct-mail and event-based individual and PAC solicitation programs.

Senate candidates raised on average more than $2.2 million in large individual contributions in 2002—about 45 percent of their campaign resources (see Figure 6-7). More than 41 percent of these donations came from out of state. Small individual contributions and donations from PACs each accounted for about 15 percent, and party contributions and coordinated expenditures for 5 percent. Party-connected contributions accounted for a mere 2 percent, reflecting the fact that there are fewer senators than House members to contribute to one another. The candidates themselves provided roughly 8 percent of the money spent directly in Senate campaigns. Compared with

FIGURE 6-7

Sources of Senate Candidates' Campaign Receipts in the 2002 Elections

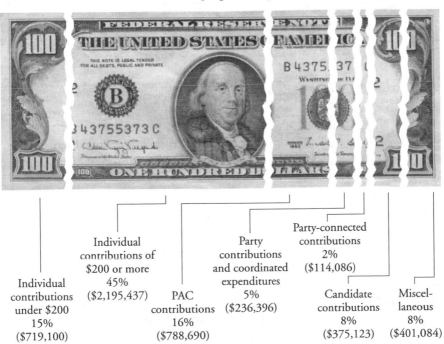

Individual contributions under $200 15% ($719,100)

Individual contributions of $200 or more 45% ($2,195,437)

PAC contributions 16% ($788,690)

Party contributions and coordinated expenditures 5% ($236,396)

Party-connected contributions 2% ($114,086)

Candidate contributions 8% ($375,123)

Miscellaneous 8% ($401,084)

Source: Compiled from Federal Election Commission data.

Notes: See notes in Figure 6-4. $N = 60$.

candidates for the House, candidates for the upper chamber rely more heavily on individuals and formal party organizations and less on PACs and their colleagues to build up their war chests.

Party affiliation affects fundraising for the upper chamber of Congress less than it does for the lower chamber. However, Republican Senate candidates raised more PAC money in the 2002 elections than did the Democrats (see Table 6-4). The GOP's success in this regard was a result of their controlling the majority from the 104th Congress through the early part of the 107th Congress and their strong odds of retaking control in the 108th Congress. Republicans also raised more party money and party-connected contributions than did their Democratic opponents, reflecting the GOP's greater wealth.

Important similarities and differences exist among incumbent, challenger, and open-seat candidates. Senate open-seat candidates typically raise more money from every source than do challengers, and, compared to incumbents, they raise more from every source but PACs. However, the proportion of funds collected from each source by all three sets of candidates is similar, with the exception of PAC contributions and contributions the candidates make to their own campaigns. Challengers and open-seat candidates rely substantially less on PAC dollars and depend more on their own resources than do incumbents, reflecting the fact that many access-oriented PACs prefer to support incumbents.

Incumbency provides members of the Senate with fundraising advantages. Senators, like House members, often begin their quest for reelection with significant sums left over from their previous campaigns and start raising funds early. Nine senators each had more than $600,000 left over after their 2002 campaigns, and four had in excess of $1 million. Sixteen senators scheduled to be up for reelection in 2004 had raised over $1 million by December 31, 2002. Sen. Charles Schumer, D-N.Y., led the pack, having raised almost $13.6 million.

Senators, like House members, are able to raise these large sums early because they have a great deal of political clout, which few challengers possess. For example, Johnson of South Dakota, was able to use his membership on the Senate Banking, Housing, and Urban Affairs, and Energy and Natural Resources Committees to raise $357,500 from finance, insurance, and real estate PACs, $58,500 from PACs representing transportation, and $19,500 from PACs representing the construction industry. His membership on the Energy and Natural Resources Committee helped him collect another $91,700 in PAC dollars. Combined, these sums accounted for roughly 19 percent of his total PAC dollars. Johnson collected more than an additional $1 million in contributions from individuals associated with these industries, which represented about 43 percent of the large individual contributions he

TABLE 6-4

Sources of Support for Senate Candidates in the 2002 Elections

	Party		Status			Competitiveness	
	Democrats	Republicans	Incumbents	Challengers	Open-seat candidates	Competitive	Uncompetitive
Individual contributions under $200	$688,867 (15%)	$749,332 (14%)	$749,277 (15%)	$516,927 (18%)	$1,001,663 (13%)	$991,961 (15%)	$309,808 (14%)
Individual contributions of $200 or more	$2,182,877 (49%)	$2,207,998 (42%)	$2,254,685 (46%)	$1,338,021 (46%)	$3,506,713 (44%)	$3,004,480 (46%)	$981,872 (44%)
PAC contributions	$686,169 (15%)	$891,211 (17%)	$1,274,045 (26%)	$310,792 (11%)	$776,441 (10%)	$921,148 (14%)	$590,004 (26%)
Party contributions and coordinated expenditures	$83,964 (2%)	$338,827 (7%)	$126,840 (3%)	$180,487 (6%)	$508,229 (6%)	$376,503 (6%)	$26,235 (1%)
Party-connected contributions	$97,267 (2%)	$130,905 (3%)	$110,822 (2%)	$90,742 (3%)	$157,801 (2%)	$163,374 (3%)	$40,154 (2%)
Candidate contributions	$376,706 (8%)	$373,540 (7%)	$913 (—)	$193,427 (7%)	$1,288,398 (16%)	$526,924 (8%)	$147,422 (7%)
Miscellaneous	$342,766 (8%)	$459,402 (9%)	$376,583 (8%)	$255,067 (9%)	$681,218 (9%)	$566,130 (9%)	$153,515 (7%)
(N)	(30)	(30)	(23)	(23)	(14)	(36)	(24)

Source: Compiled from Federal Election Commission data.

Notes: See notes in Table 6-1.

raised.[42] The senator's membership on the Senate Appropriations and Budget Committees also probably contributed to his raising these funds and hundreds of thousands of dollars more from PACs and individuals whose business interests are affected by Johnson's and his fellow committee members' actions.

SUMMARY

The campaign for resources is an important aspect of contemporary congressional elections. It requires candidates and campaign strategists to identify groups of sympathetic potential donors and fashion a pitch that will appeal to them. The campaign for resources is usually a campaign among unequals. Incumbent campaigns typically begin the election season with more money in the bank than do challengers, who usually start fundraising much later. The levels of skill and resources that incumbents and challengers bring to bear on the fundraising process, including their prospects for success and political clout, also differ markedly. As a result, incumbents raise more money than do challengers, and incumbents raise proportionately more funds from PACs and individuals interested in directly influencing the legislative process. Candidates for open seats typically raise about the same amount as do incumbents, and open-seat candidates are more likely to wage campaigns that are financially competitive with that of their opponent. Nonincumbents who have significant political experience or who have assembled professional campaign organizations typically raise more money, especially from parties, members of Congress, other party leaders, and PACs than do amateur candidates who assemble unprofessional campaign organizations.

CHAPTER SEVEN

Campaign Strategy

The campaign for votes involves voter targeting, communications, and mobilization. During the heyday of the parties, party organizations formulated and executed campaign strategies. Party leaders, candidates, and activists talked with neighbors to learn about their concerns, disseminated campaign communications to address those concerns, and turned out the vote on election day. The predisposition of voters to support their party's candidates was strong and frequently rewarded with government jobs, contracts, and other forms of patronage. Contemporary campaigns also involve targeting, communicating with, and mobilizing voters. Successful candidates craft a message with broad appeal, set the agenda that defines voters' choices, and get their supporters to the polls on election day. In the years in which a presidential election is held, that contest dominates the news and greatly influences most people's thinking about politics. Candidates who stake out positions that correspond to the national political agenda have an advantage over those who do not.

In this chapter I focus on how voters decide to cast their ballots in congressional elections and on the strategies and tactics that campaigns use to affect those decisions. The primary topics are voting behavior, strategy, public opinion research, voter targeting, and the message.

VOTING BEHAVIOR

Traditional democratic theory holds that citizens should make informed choices when voting in elections. It contends that they should be knowledgeable about the candidates, be aware of the major issues, and take the time to discern which candidate is more likely to represent their views and govern in the nation's best interests. The weight of the evidence, however, suggests that the vast majority of voters in congressional elections fall short of these expectations.[1]

Most voters make their congressional voting decisions on the basis of relatively little information. In a typical House contest between an incumbent and a challenger, for example, only about 12 percent of all voters can recall the names of the two major-party candidates. In open-seat House contests, about 37 percent of all voters can remember both candidates' names.[2] Voters tend to possess more information about contestants in Senate elections: roughly 35 percent can recall the names of both candidates in contests involving an incumbent and a challenger, and about two-thirds can identify both candidates in open-seat races.[3]

When put to the less-stringent test of merely recognizing House candidates' names, 62 percent of all voters recognize the names of both major-party contestants in incumbent-challenger races, and 82 percent recognize the names of both candidates in open-seat contests. The levels of name recognition are higher in Senate contests: roughly 83 percent recognize the names of the incumbent and the challenger, and more than 94 percent recognize the names of candidates in open-seat races.[4] Thus, the name recognition test, which demands roughly the same, minimal amount of knowledge from voters as does actually casting a ballot, shows that a substantial portion of the electorate lacks the information needed to make what might be referred to as "an informed vote choice."[5]

The inability to recall or recognize the candidates' names is indicative of the overall lack of substantive information in congressional elections. Most House election campaigns are low-key affairs that do not convey much information about the candidates' ideological orientations or policy positions.[6] Information on House challengers, most of whom wage underfunded campaigns, is usually scarce. Campaign communications, voters' assessments of the issues, and candidates' qualifications become important only in hard-fought contests.[7]

Incumbency and Voter Information

By and large, the candidates who suffer most from voter disinterest are House challengers. Whereas nine out of ten voters recognize their House member's name, fewer than 60 percent usually recognize the name of the challenger. Incumbents tend to be viewed favorably.[8] Typically more than half of those voters who recognize their representative's name indicate they like something about that person; roughly one-third mention something they dislike. The corresponding figures for House challengers are 35 percent and 32 percent.[9] As the high reelection rates for House members indicate, the name recognition and voter approval ratings of most incumbents are difficult for opponents to overcome. Only those challengers who can overcome their "invisibility prob- lem" and create a favorable image stand a chance of winning.

Senate challengers tend to be less handicapped by voter inattentiveness. They enjoy better name recognition because of their political experience, skill, superior campaign organizations, and higher levels of campaign spending. The newsworthiness of their campaigns also attracts media attention and voter in- terest. Voters learn more about the ideological orientations and issue positions of Senate challengers than of their House counterparts.[10] Even though the name recognition of Senate challengers is lower than the near-universal recog- nition enjoyed by Senate incumbents, it is high enough to make the typical in- cumbent-challenger race competitive. This helps explain why more electoral turnover occurs in the upper than in the lower chamber of Congress.

The inequalities in candidate information that characterize most incum- bent-challenger races generally do not exist in open-seat contests. The major- party candidates in an open-seat race for a marginal seat begin the campaign with similar opportunities to increase their name recognition and convey their messages to voters. The greater competitiveness of these contests results in more extensive press coverage, which helps both candidates become better known to voters. Thus more voters make informed choices in open-seat races than in incumbent-challenger contests.

Voting Decisions

Given their lack of knowledge of the candidates and issues, how do most voters make a decision on election day? Only those voters who know some- thing about the background, political qualifications, party affiliation, and issue stances of both candidates are in a position to sift through the information, weigh the benefits of voting for one candidate over another, and cast their bal- lots in accordance with classical democratic theory.[11]

Nevertheless, voters who fall short of that ideal level of awareness may re- spond to the campaign information that candidates and the media dissemi- nate. Competitive, high-intensity elections that fill the airwaves, newspapers, and voters' mailboxes with campaign information provide some voters, espe- cially those with an interest in politics, with enough information to form sum- mary judgments about the candidates. These voters often tend to rely on those judgments when deciding which candidate to support.[12]

In the absence of spirited, high-intensity elections, most voters use "voting cues"—shortcuts that enable them to cast a ballot without engaging in a lengthy decision-making process. The most frequently used voting cue is incumbency.

Knowing only an incumbent's name is sufficient for an individual to cast an adequately informed vote, some scholars argue.[13] Reasoning that the incumbent should be held accountable for the government's performance, the state of the economy, the nation's foreign involvements, or other issues, these voters quickly determine whether to support the status quo and vote for the incumbent or to advocate change and cast their ballot for the challenger.

Other voters pin the responsibility for the state of the nation on the president. When these voters are satisfied with how things are being run in Washington, they support the congressional candidate who belongs to the president's party. When they are dissatisfied with the state of the nation's affairs, as in 1994, they vote for the candidate whose party does not occupy the White House. The connection between presidential and congressional voting can help a congressional candidate when a popular president is running for reelection, but belonging to the president's party usually has more harmful than beneficial effects in midterm elections.[14] The 1998 and 2002 elections were important exceptions to this rule. The party cue, like the incumbency cue, enables voters to make retrospective voting choices without having much knowledge about the candidates or their positions on the issues. Under conditions of unified government, party cues are stronger because voters can more readily assign credit or blame for the state of the nation to the party that controls both the executive and legislative branches.[15] The power-sharing arrangements of divided government, in contrast, obscure political responsibility because they enable politicians to blame others in power.

The party cue also enables voters to speculate about a candidate's ideological orientation and issue positions. Republicans are generally identified as more conservative than Democrats and are associated with free-market economics, deregulation, lower taxes, family values, hawkish foreign policy, and the wealthier elements of society. Most Republicans profess to be for limited government, and some campaign as though they are antigovernment. Democrats are often viewed as the party of government. They are associated with greater economic intervention; the social safety net; environmental protection; public education; a more dovish foreign policy; and protecting the interests of senior citizens, minorities, the poor, and working people. Some voters project the parties' images onto candidates and use these projections to guide their congressional voting decisions.[16] Others habitually support a party's nominees regardless of their credentials, issue positions, or opponents.

Partisanship and incumbency can affect the voting decisions of individuals who possess even less political information than do those individuals described above. The voting behavior of individuals who go to the polls out of a sense of civic responsibility or habit and who lack much interest in or knowledge about politics can in many ways be equated with the behavior of shoppers at a supermarket. Individuals in both situations select a product—either a consumer good or a congressional candidate—with little relevant information. Except for first-time shoppers and newly enfranchised voters, these individuals have made similar selections before. Previous decisions and established preferences often strongly influence their current decisions. Shoppers, lacking a good reason to try a new product, such as a sale or a two-for-one giveaway, are likely to purchase the same brand-name product that they previously purchased. Voters are likely to cast a ballot for the candidates or party that they supported in previous elections.[17] If a voter recognizes one candidate's name, which is almost always the incumbent's, that candidate usually gets the individual's vote. If the voter recognizes neither candidate but tends to be favorably predisposed toward one party, then most often the person votes for that party's candidate. Situations in which voters have little information, then, usually work to the advantage of incumbents and of candidates who belong to the district's or state's dominant party.

However, if the recognized candidate or favored party is associated with scandal or a domestic or foreign policy failure, many relatively uninformed voters, as well as some who are informed, break old habits and cast their ballots against that candidate or party. During the elections held in the 1990s, for example, many challengers, with the support of Washington-based party committees and interest groups, sought to make control of Congress itself a major campaign issue. This strategy is credited with enabling the Republicans to take over Congress and end forty uninterrupted years of Democratic control of the House. Attacking Congress contributed to the electoral success of challengers of both parties throughout most of the 1990s.

VOTERS AND CAMPAIGN STRATEGY

Candidates and political consultants generally do not plan election campaigns on the basis of abstract political theories, but they do draw on a body of knowledge about how people make their voting decisions. Politicians' notions about voting behavior have some ideas in common with the findings of scholarly research. Among these are the following: (1) most voters have only limited information about the candidates, their ideologies, and the issues; (2) voters are generally more familiar with and favorably predisposed toward incumbents than they are toward challengers; and (3) voters tend to cast their ballots in ways that reflect their party identification or previous voting behavior. Candidates and consultants also believe that a campaign sharply focused on issues can be used to motivate supporters to show up at the polls and to win the support of undecided voters. They try to set the campaign agenda so that the issues that politically informed voters use as a basis for casting their ballots are the most attractive issues for their candidate.

Politicians' beliefs account for some of the differences that exist among the campaigns waged by incumbents, challengers, and open-seat candidates as well as many of the differences that exist between House and Senate campaigns. Generally, members of Congress use strategies that capitalize on the advantages of incumbency. They discuss the services and the federal projects they have delivered to their constituencies.[18] They focus on elements of their public persona that have helped make them popular with constituents and draw on strategies they have used successfully in previous campaigns.[19]

Some incumbents capitalize on their advantages in name recognition and voter approval by virtually ignoring their opponents. They deluge the district with direct mail, radio advertisements, television commercials, yard signs, or other communications that make no mention of their opponent in order to minimize the attention the challenger gets from the local media and voters. An alternative strategy is to take advantage of a challenger's relative invisibility by attacking his or her experience, qualifications, or positions on the issues early in the campaign. Incumbents who succeed in defining their opponents leave them in the unenviable position of being invisible to most voters and negatively perceived by others. The Ose campaign pursued the former strategy, treating Democratic challenger Beeman as if his candidacy would have no impact on the outcome of their 2002 California House race.[20] The Morella campaign used the latter strategy, going as far as airing a TV ad that reviewed some of challenger Van Hollen's more controversial activities in the Maryland General Assembly and ended with the statement "To hear him talk, you'd think this guy was the Republican."

House challengers are in the least enviable position of any candidates. Not only are they less well known and less experienced, but they are also without the campaign resources of their opponents. In order to win, challengers need to force their way into voters' consciousness and to project a message that will give voters a reason to cast a ballot for a little-known commodity.

Many challengers make the election a referendum on some negative aspect of the incumbent's performance. They portray the incumbent as incompetent, corrupt, an extreme ideologue, or out of touch with the district. They magnify the impact of any unpopular policy or scandal with which the incumbent can be associated. Challengers often try to link the current officeholder to unpopular policies or trends and to tout themselves as agents of change, often using negative or comparative ads to do so.

Lacking the advantages of an incumbent or the disadvantages of a challenger, both candidates in an open-seat race face the challenge of making themselves familiar to voters and becoming associated with themes and issues that will attract electoral support. They also both have the opportunity to define their opponents. Some open-seat candidates seek to define themselves and their opponents on the basis of issues. Others, particularly those running in districts that favor their party, emphasize partisan or ideological cues.

GAUGING PUBLIC OPINION

Campaigns use many different instruments to take the public's pulse. Election returns from previous contests are analyzed to locate pockets of potential strength or weakness. Geodemographic analysis enables campaigns to identify individuals who voted in previous elections and to classify them according to their gender, age, ethnicity, race, religion, occupation, and economic background. By combining geodemographic information with polling data and election returns, candidates are able to identify potential supporters and to formulate messages that will appeal to them.

Polls are among the most commonly used means of gauging public opinion. Virtually every Senate campaign and roughly seven out of ten House campaigns take at least one poll to learn about voters. Benchmark polls, which are taken early in the election season, inform candidates about the issue positions, partisanship, and initial voting preferences of people living in their state or district. House campaigns commonly commission benchmarks a year prior to the election, and Senate candidates have been known to commission them as early as three years before election day.[21] Benchmark polls also measure the levels of name recognition and support that the candidates and their opponents or prospective opponents enjoy. They help campaigns learn about the kinds of candidates voters prefer, the types of messages likely to attract support, and to whom specific campaign advertisements should be directed.

Campaigns also use benchmark polls to generate support. Challenger and open-seat candidates disseminate favorable benchmarks to attract press coverage and the support of campaign volunteers and contributors. Incumbents typically publicize benchmarks to discourage potential challengers. When poll results show a member of Congress to be in trouble, however, the incumbent quietly uses them to convince parties, PACs, and other potential contributors that he or she needs extra help to win.

Trend polls are taken intermittently throughout the campaign season to discover changes in voters' attitudes. Some senators use them to chart their public approval throughout their six-year terms. These polls are more narrowly focused than are benchmarks. They feature detailed questions designed to reveal whether a campaign has been successful in getting voters to associate their candidate with a specific issue or theme. Trend polls help campaigns determine whether they have been gaining or losing ground with different segments of the electorate. They can reassure a campaign that its strategy is working or indicate that a change in message is needed.

Just as trend and benchmark polls present "snapshots" of public opinion, tracking polls provide campaigns with a "motion picture" overview. Tracking polls typically take samples of 150 to 200 voters to discuss their reactions to a few key advertisements, issue statements, or campaign events. Each night a different group of voters is interviewed. The interviews are pooled and used to calculate rolling averages based on the responses from the three most recent nights. Changes in rolling averages can be used to reformulate a campaign's final appeals. Because tracking polls are expensive, most House campaigns wait until the last three weeks of the campaign to use them.

Candidates may supplement their polling with focus groups. Focus groups usually consist of one to two dozen participants and a professional facilitator, who meet for two to three hours. The participants are selected not to be a scientifically representative sample but to represent segments of the population whose support the campaign needs to reinforce or attract. Campaigns use focus groups to learn how voters can be expected to respond to different messages or to pretest actual campaign advertisements. Some high-priced consultants, such as Wirthlin Worldwide, a prominent Republican firm, employ computerized audience response techniques to obtain a precise record of how focus group participants react to specific portions of campaign advertisements.[22] These techniques enable an analyst to plot a line that represents the participants' reactions onto the ad itself, pinpointing exactly which portions participants liked or disliked. Focus group research is useful in fine-tuning the visuals and narratives in television communications.

Finally, candidates learn about public opinion through a variety of approaches that do not require the services of public opinion experts. Newspaper, magazine, radio, and television news stories provide information about voters' positions on major issues. Exchanges with local party leaders, journalists, political activists, and voters can also help candidates get a sense of the public mood.

When asked about the significance of different forms of information, House candidates and campaign aides typically rank direct contact with voters first, indicating that they consider it to be very important to extremely important (see Table 7-1). Voter contact is followed by public opinion polls,

TABLE 7-1

Campaigners' Perceptions of the Importance of Different Sources
of Information for Gauging Public Opinion in House Campaigns

		Incumbents		Challengers		Open-seat candidates	
	All	In jeopardy	Shoo-ins	Hope-fuls	Likely losers	Pros-pects	Mis-matched
Candidate contact with voters	4.37	4.23	4.41	4.44	4.44	4.16	4.59
Public opinion surveys	3.53	4.23	3.54	3.68	2.88	3.96	3.09
Newspaper, radio, TV	3.05	2.69	3.13	3.08	3.27	2.86	3.17
Local party activists	2.63	2.78	2.74	2.69	2.41	2.45	2.80
Mail from voters	2.45	2.65	3.43	2.19	1.99	2.00	2.29
National party publications	2.28	1.83	1.96	2.39	2.75	2.12	2.65
National party leaders	2.14	1.80	1.94	2.31	2.32	2.20	2.30
(*N*)	(325)	(48)	(70)	(52)	(82)	(49)	(24)

Source: The 1992 Congressional Campaign Study.

Notes: Candidates and campaign aides were asked to assess the importance of each source on the following
scale: 1 = not important or not used; 2 = slightly important; 3 = moderately important; 4 = very important;
5 = extremely important. The values listed are the arithmetic means of the scores. Figures are for major-party
candidates in contested general elections, excluding a small number of atypical races.

which are generally considered to be moderately helpful to very helpful in
learning about voters' opinions. News stories come next, followed by discussions with local party activists and mail from voters. Although they play a bigger role than PACs and other interest groups, national party officials and the
materials they publish are less important than local information sources.

Incumbents and candidates for open seats make greater use of surveys than
do challengers. Candidates in competitive contests of all types make greater
use of them than do those in lopsided races. Challengers and open-seat candidates in one-sided contests often cannot afford to buy polls and must rely
heavily on news reports, party publications, and the advice of national party
leaders. Incumbents, who are often sensitized to issues by the constituent mail
that floods their offices, consider letters to be a more significant indicator of

public sentiment than does any other group of candidates. Incumbents in safe seats show a greater preference than others for learning about public opinion through the mail and other forms of unmediated voter contact.

VOTER TARGETING

Campaigns are not designed to reach everyone. Targeting involves categorizing different groups of voters, identifying their political preferences, and designing appeals to which they are likely to respond. It is the foundation of virtually every aspect of campaign strategy. Candidates and campaign managers consider many factors when devising targeting strategies, including the underlying partisan and candidate loyalties of the groups that reside in the district, the size and turnout levels of those groups, and the kinds of issues and appeals that will attract their support.[23] Using this information, they formulate a strategy designed to build a winning coalition.

Partisanship is the number one consideration in the voter targeting of most campaigns. It subsumes all other factors. Almost one-half of all campaigns focus on individuals who identify with their party, independent voters, or both (see Table 7-2). About 2 percent of all campaigns primarily target voters who identify with the opposing party. Morella, who faced a tough challenge in Maryland's strongly Democratic-leaning 8th district, by contrast, undertook wide-ranging efforts to build bipartisan support over the years. Like many incumbents, she routinely sent letters to congratulate constituents who recently registered to vote in her district. Unlike most other incumbents, however, she often sent letters of congratulation to voters who had registered in the opposing party, in this case as Democrats.[24]

Challenger races are the most likely to target voters who identify with the opposing party. Many of these candidates recognize that the one-sidedness of their districts makes it impossible for them to compete without winning the support of some of the opposing party's supporters. Some challengers do not have the resources needed to carry out even a basic party-oriented targeting strategy. Lacking a poll or a precinct-by-precinct breakdown of where Republican, Democratic, and independent voters reside, some amateurs resort to unorthodox strategies, such as focusing on precincts that had the highest turnout levels in the previous election.

Other factors that campaigns consider when designing targeting strategies include demography and issues. Sixty-two percent of all House campaigns target demographic, geographic, or occupational groups: 53 percent concentrate on specific ethnic, racial, religious, gender, or age groups; 4 percent focus on

TABLE 7-2

Partisan Component of Targeting Strategies in House Campaigns in 2002

	All	Incumbents		Challengers		Open-seat candidates	
		In jeopardy	Shoo-ins	Hope-fuls	Likely losers	Pros-pects	Mis-matched
Own party	9%	17%	9%	9%	7%	9%	17%
Opposing party	2	—	1	6	2	—	—
Independents	3	3	1	3	5	—	6
Both parties	2	—	—	—	2	3	6
Own party and independents	36	35	43	38	30	40	39
Opposing party and independents	2	7	—	3	2	3	5
All voters	45	38	46	41	50	43	28
Did not target	1	—	—	—	2	3	—
(*N*)	(320)	(29)	(81)	(32)	(126)	(35)	(18)

Source: The 2002 Congressional Campaign Study.

Notes: Figures are for general election candidates in major-party contested races, excluding those in incumbent-versus-incumbent races. Dashes = less than 0.5 percent. Some columns do not add to 100 percent because of rounding.

counties, suburbs, cities, or other geographic locations; and 5 percent target union members, blue-collar workers, small-business owners, or voters involved in particular industries.[25] Issues and political attitudes, including voting intentions and partisanship, play a central role in the targeting strategies of roughly 36 percent of all campaigns.

Group-oriented and issue/attitudinal-oriented targeting strategies each offer campaigns some distinct advantages. The group-oriented, or geodemographic, approach is based on the idea that there are identifiable segments of the population whose support the campaign needs to attract and that specific communications can be tailored to win that support. Just as soliciting money from a readily identifiable fundraising constituency is important in the campaign for resources, communicating a message to identifiable groups of supporters and undecided voters is important in the campaign for votes. Campaigns that use group-based targeting strategies emphasize different aspects of their message, depending on the intended audience for a particular campaign advertisement. By tailoring their messages to attract the votes of specific population groups, these campaigns hope to build a winning coalition. During the 1990s many campaigns stressed the effect of the economy on children and families in literature mailed to women, whereas they emphasized tax cuts and economic growth issues in literature sent to business executives and upper-class and upper-middle-class voters.

Candidates focus on many groups, reflecting the diverse segments of the population represented by the two major parties, especially the Democrats.[26] More Democrats than Republicans target women, racial and ethnic minorities, and senior citizens; and Democratic candidates target senior citizens more than any other segment of the population.[27] The 2002 contest between Morella and Van Hollen gives some insights into the dynamics of geodemographic targeting. Morella anticipated winning support from her Republican base and independents and focused much of her efforts on working Democratic women, senior citizens, and Democrats in precincts she had represented prior to redistricting.[28] Van Hollen also aggressively courted Democrats, environmentalists, and voters in the new part of the district, largely Democratic Prince George's County. An overlap in targets is typical of a close election because both campaigns go after the same swing voters.

The issue/attitudinal-oriented strategy is based on the premise that issues and ideas should drive the campaign. Campaigns that target on the basis of specific policies or a broad ideology, such as conservatism or progressivism, hope to win the support of single-issue or ideological voters who favor these positions. In many cases, one or two specific issues are emphasized in order to attract the support of swing voters whose ballots a candidate believes will be a deciding factor in the election outcome. Some candidates target pro-life or pro-choice voters, believing their ballots would be decisive. Others target pro-environment or anti–gun control voters. Republicans who employ these strategies focus primarily on voters who are concerned about the deficit, taxes, the size of government, government regulation, and crime. Democrats who use them focus on voters who care about public education, jobs, the environment, health care, and the protections and services that government provides for the elderly, children, and underprivileged groups. In 2002 in California's 3rd congressional district, Beeman focused on jobs and the economy, prescription drugs, and nuclear weapons.[29] Ose concentrated on cutting federal taxes and attacking government fraud and mismanagement.[30]

Targeting strategies that are based on issues or voter attitudes more readily lend themselves to the communication of a coherent campaign message than do group-oriented strategies. They are especially effective at mobilizing single-issue voters and political activists who have strong ideological predispositions. Yet they run the risk of alienating moderate voters who agree with the candidate on most policy matters but disagree on the issues the campaign has chosen to emphasize. Campaigns waged by policy amateurs and ideologues are the most likely to suffer from this problem. Often these candidates become boxed in by their own message, are labeled "ultra-liberals" or "right wingers" by their opponents, and ultimately lose.

Incumbents target demographic, geographic, and occupational groups more than do challengers and open-seat candidates. Most incumbents have a detailed knowledge of the voting blocs that supported them in the past and target constituents who belong to these groups. Many challengers, especially those unable to mount competitive campaigns, do not have this information. Lacking good voter files, and recognizing they need to peel away some of their opponents' supporters, they target on the basis of issues.[31]

THE MESSAGE

A candidate's message gives substance to a campaign and helps to shape the political agenda, mobilize backers, and win votes. In a well-run campaign, the same coherent message pervades every aspect of the candidate's communications—from paid television advertisements to impromptu remarks. Campaign messages can be an essential ingredient for victory in close elections because they activate supporters and strongly influence the decisions of persuadable voters.

Campaign messages rely heavily on imagery. The most successful campaigns weave the candidate's persona and policy stances into thematic messages.[32] These form the core of the image the candidate seeks to project. According to Joel Bradshaw, president of the Democratic consulting firm Campaign Design Group, good campaign messages are clear and easy to communicate, are short, convey a sense of emotional urgency, reflect voters' perceptions of political reality, establish clear differences between the candidate and the opponent, and are credible.[33]

The precise mix of personal characteristics, issues, and broad themes that candidates project depends on their political views, the groups they target, and the messages they anticipate their opponents will communicate. Good strategic positioning results in the transmission of a message that most voters will find appealing; when both candidates achieve this result an election becomes what strategists refer to as a "battle for the middle ground." [34] In designing a message, campaign decision makers consider a variety of factors, which Fred Hartwig of Peter Hart and Associates refers to as "the Seven P's of Strategy": performance, professional experience, positioning, partisanship, populism, progressivism, and positivity.[35] Ladonna Lee, a leading Republican political strategist, emphasizes the importance of consistency. The different components of the message must add up to a coherent public image.[36]

Campaigns endeavor to create a favorable image for their candidates by identifying them with decency, loyalty, honesty, hard work, and other cherished values.[37] Campaign communications interweave anecdotes about a candidate's personal accomplishments, professional success, family, or ability to overcome humble origins to portray him or her as the living embodiment of the American dream—someone whom voters should be proud to have represent them in Washington. Campaigns frequently emphasize elements of their candidate's persona that point to an opponent's weakness. Veterans who run against draft dodgers, for example, commonly emphasize their war records.

Incumbents frequently convey image-oriented messages. They seek to reinforce or expand their base of support by concentrating on those aspects of their persona that make them popular with constituents.[38] Their messages convey images of competent, caring individuals who work tirelessly in Washington to improve the lives of the folks they represent back home. Incumbents' campaign communications often describe how they have helped constituents resolve problems, brought federal programs and projects to the district, and introduced or cosponsored popular legislation. Some discuss their efforts to prevent a military base or factory from closing. Those whose districts have experienced the ravages of floods, earthquakes, riots, or other disasters almost always highlight their roles in bringing federal relief to victims.

Many challengers and open-seat contestants also seek to portray themselves as caring, hard working, and experienced. Nonincumbents who have held elective office frequently contrast their accomplishments with those of their opponent. During the elections held in the early and mid-1990s, many challengers who were state legislators blamed their opponents for contributing to the federal deficit while pointing to their own budget-cutting efforts.

Political amateurs usually discuss their successes in the private sector, seeking to make a virtue of their lack of political experience. Many blame the "mess in Washington" on the "career politicians" and discuss how someone who has succeeded in the private sector is needed to make government work for the people again. Still, a challenger who focuses on experience rarely wins. As one consultant explained, "By virtue of their being the current officeholder, an incumbent can 'out-experience' a challenger to death."[39]

Issues

Most House candidates and campaign aides maintain that the bulk of their messages focus on policy concerns rather than the candidate's personality—a claim borne out by examinations of their campaign materials.[40] More than half of all House campaigns make issues—either their issue positions or their opponents'—the primary focus of their message; 44 percent, mostly incumbent campaigns, emphasize candidate imagery (see Table 7-3). Challengers and open-seat candidates run the most issue-oriented campaigns, reflecting their belief that taking policy stances is a useful way to draw support away from their opponents. Challengers run the most opposition-oriented campaigns. They point to incumbents' ethical lapses, congressional roll-call votes that are out of sync with constituents' views, or federal policies that have harmed local voters or the national interest. About 24 percent of all challengers try to make their opponent or their opponent's actions in office a defining campaign issue. A few incumbents holding marginal seats respond in kind by pointing to unpopular aspects of their challenger's background or policy stances. Twelve percent of open-seat candidates in close contests also make their opponent the central focus of their message.

Almost all candidates take policy stands that identify them with "valence" issues, such as a strong economy, job creation, domestic tranquility, and international security, which are universally viewed in a favorable light. Some make these the centerpiece of their campaign. They either ignore or soft-pedal "positional" issues (sometimes referred to as "wedge" issues), which have two or more sides.[41] When both candidates campaign mainly on valence issues, the

TABLE 7-3

Major Focus of Advertising in House Campaigns in 2002

		Incumbents		Challengers		Open-seat candidates	
	All	In jeopardy	Shoo-ins	Hope-fuls	Likely losers	Pros-pects	Mis-matched
Candidate's image	39%	54%	58%	31%	22%	44%	50%
Candidate's issue positions	47	42	39	31	59	44	44
Opponent's image	5	—	1	6	9	6	6
Opponent's issue positions	9	4	1	31	11	6	—
(*N*)	(308)	(26)	(79)	(32)	(121)	(32)	(18)

Source: The 2002 Congressional Campaign Study.

Notes: Figures are for general election candidates in major-party contested races, excluding those in incumbent-versus-incumbent races. Dashes = less than 0.5 percent. Some columns do not add to 100 percent because of rounding.

dialogue can be likened to a debate between the nearly identical Tweedledee and Tweedledum.

When candidates communicate dissimilar stands on positional issues, however, political debate becomes more meaningful. Issues such as the economy, taxes, gun control, crime, abortion, and civil rights have for several years had the potential to draw the attention of voters and affect elections. Scandals, health care, environmental issues, and social entitlement programs also have the ability to influence elections.

Challengers are especially likely to benefit from emphasizing positional issues. By stressing points of disagreement between themselves and the incumbent, challengers can help their images crystallize, attract media attention, and strip away some of their opponent's support.[42] Incumbents may not derive the same electoral benefits from running on positional issues because they are usually evaluated in personal terms.[43] Candidates who campaign on positional issues hope to attract the support of ideological voters or to overcome some weakness in their image. Some liberal Democrats emphasize crime to project "tougher" images. Some conservative Republicans discuss health care to show their compassionate side. Both groups of candidates seek to convince centrist voters that they share their concerns.

Candidates try to anticipate the issues their opponents will emphasize before taking a strong policy stance. Candidates who run against police officers rarely mount "law-and-order" campaigns because of the obvious disparities in credibility that they and their opponents have on crime-related issues.[44] For example, Feeley would have been at a disadvantage had he sought to concentrate on Colorado's agricultural interests because of Beauprez's background as a third-generation dairy farmer; instead, he made scant mention of the subject.

Van Hollen focused his media on a variety of issues that traditionally favor Democratic candidates, including education, the environment, gun control, and women's issues. Unlike most congressional candidates, he also publicly embraced his partisanship while campaigning. During virtually all of her elections, Morella emphasized issues of concern to federal employees, who comprise one of the district's largest constituencies, and women. She also stressed her constituent service and political independence. In emphasizing these issues and themes, she sought to offset the disadvantages she faced as a Republican in a Democratic-leaning district.

Johnson made his service to South Dakota the central issue of his campaign. He produced a series of ads demonstrating how he had used his seat in the Senate and position on the Appropriations Committee to help individual constituents, particular communities, or the state as a whole obtain medical care, water projects, or high-tech research centers, among other things. Although the examples used in each ad were targeted to the communities served in the media market in which the ad ran, each spot developed the theme of service. Thune structured his campaign around issues emphasizing "prairie values," including cutting taxes, reducing government waste, strengthening national defense, and protecting Social Security. He also called attention to his close ties to President Bush by developing the theme, "Elect me and we can pass the president's agenda."[45]

Candidates who learn that their opponent is vulnerable on a salient issue generally try to make it a major focus of the campaign in order to win the support of independents or pry voters from their opponent's camp. Democrats and some moderate Republicans lure women's votes by making abortion rights a major part of their campaign platforms. In 1992, 1996, and 2000, Democrats who adopted this position got the added benefit of being able to coordinate their message with their party's presidential campaigns. Divisions within the Republican Party made abortion an issue to avoid for many GOP candidates. Women who run against men are the most likely to campaign as prochoice and discuss women's concerns, and those who campaign on these issues and target women voters enjoy greater electoral success.[46] Nevertheless, some male candidates, like Van Hollen, also stake out pro–abortion rights positions to attract the support of women and liberal voters.

Economic issues—whether they be inflation, unemployment, taxes, jobs, the federal budget, or the national deficit—have been the number one concern of voters in most elections since the Great Depression. Virtually every candidate makes some aspect of the economy part of their campaign message. Democratic candidates often discuss the economy as a fairness issue. In 2002 many pointed to the increased tax burdens that Bush administration policies placed on the middle class and the tax breaks they gave to wealthy Americans. They also chastised Republicans for proposing to cut popular social safety net programs in order to give a tax break to the rich.

Republican candidates usually focus on economic growth and the deficit. Throughout the 1980s and early 1990s they sought to blame the economic woes of the country on wasteful government subsidies, excessive regulation, and profligate pork-barrel spending approved by the Democratic-controlled Congress. Their message gained supporters in 1994, as Republican candidates proclaimed that tax cuts were the crown jewel of their vaunted Contract with America.[47] Later in the decade the Republican argument for tax cuts and a balanced budget amendment lost much of its persuasiveness as a result of the improved economy, only to be revived by Bush in the 2000 and 2002 elections.

Political reform also has been an important issue for both Republicans and Democrats, reflecting the anti–Washington mood of the country. Many House challengers often raise term limits, campaign finance reform, and "reinventing government" as campaign issues, frequently contrasting their reform positions with their opponent's vote for a congressional pay raise and dependence on PAC contributions. Incumbents address political reform differently. Some seek to defend Congress, whereas others try to impress upon voters that they are part of the solution and not the problem. One House member said he "neutralized" the reform issue by arguing that he "was constructively working to improve government from the inside, while [his opponent] was content to merely lob stones from a distance."[48] Another popular incumbent strategy is to campaign for re-election to Congress by attacking the institution itself.[49] Some politicians anticipated that the passage of the Bipartisan Campaign Reform Act of 2002 would squelch the voices of reformers, but challenges to the law in the courts and a controversial rule-making process only served to reenergize Common Cause, the Center for Responsive Politics, and other critics of the political system.

Most candidates prefer themselves, not their opponents, to be the ones whom voters associate with valence issues, but candidates can also find it profitable to take strong stands on positional issues. This is especially true when their policy stances on these issues are welcomed by voters in their district or occupy a prominent place on the national agenda. The 2002 national campaign agenda was not dominated by any great domestic policy debate, as were the 1994 contests. Indeed, there was little debate on homeland security, the one domestic issue that was on the agenda in virtually every election, although Republicans were in a better position to capitalize on the war on terrorism because of Bush's occupancy of the White House. Beyond that issue, Democratic and Republican candidates took opposing positions on other domestic issues, including education, health care, and tax cuts, with members of both parties promoting a campaign agenda that worked to their advantage.[50]

House campaigners report the economy and jobs were the most important issue in their campaigns, followed by the war on terrorism and the impending hostilities with Iraq, and health care and prescription drugs (see Table 7-4). Education, local and candidate-related issues, and Social Security were mentioned significantly less often, followed by the environment, moral issues, and a potpourri of other concerns. The biggest partisan differences in campaign platforms involved health care–related issues and war-related concerns. Approximately two out of ten Democratic candidates emphasized health care and prescription drugs, as opposed to fewer than one in ten Republicans. However, GOP candidates were more likely to focus on the war on terrorism and Iraq. More Democrats than Republicans emphasized education or Social Security, whereas more Republicans than Democrats focused on taxes.

Other differences in campaign issues depended on whether the candidate had served in the 107th Congress. More incumbents of both parties, but

TABLE 7-4

Most Important Issues in House Campaigns in 2002

		Democrats			Republicans		
Issue	All	Incum-bents	Chal-lengers	Open-seat candi-dates	Incum-bents	Chal-lengers	Open-seat candi-dates
Economy and jobs	38%	33%	42%	33%	44%	35%	42%
War on terrorism and situation in Iraq	16	16	11	7	28	17	15
Health care and prescription drugs	14	23	13	26	11	11	—
Education	6	7	10	7	2	6	—
Local and candidate-related issues	6	7	6	11	4	7	4
Social Security	6	5	10	7	2	4	12
Environment	1	3	—	—	2	—	4
Morals and ethics	3	2	2	—	—	10	—
Taxes	3	2	—	7	4	3	8
Defense (other than war on terrorism)	2	2	—	—	—	1	15
Corporate fraud	—	2	—	—	—	—	—
Miscellaneous	3	—	6	—	2	6	—
(N)	(313)	(61)	(82)	(27)	(46)	(71)	(26)

Source: The 2002 Congressional Campaign Study.

Notes: Figures are for general election candidates in major-party contested races, excluding those in incumbent-versus-incumbent races. Dashes = less than 0.5 percent.

especially Republicans, focused on the war on terrorism and the situation in Iraq. Elected officials are notorious for capitalizing on the stature that comes with holding office and "wrapping themselves in the flag" during times of crisis.

Local political culture also was important. Candidates from the Midwest, home of the automobile industry and other heavy manufacturing industries that have declined in recent decades, were somewhat more likely to focus on the economy. They were likely hoping to tap into the job insecurities of Rust Belt voters. Regional differences on these issues show that geography still matters in congressional campaign politics. Locally reinforced ideological divisions pose considerable obstacles to the nationalization of congressional elections.[51]

Partisanship, Populism, and Progressivism

Candidates who run in districts made up overwhelmingly of people who identify with their party normally emphasize partisan themes and messages. They frequently mention their party in speeches and campaign literature. They also run "authorization lines" at the end of their television or radio advertisements stating, "This ad was paid for by 'Candidate X,' Democrat [or Republican] for Congress." Campaigns that are run in "hostile" or divided districts typically use nonpartisan strategies, avoiding any mention of party affiliation.

Progressive strategies have become increasingly popular with Democrats who run as agents of change. These candidates avoid the term *liberal* because voters associate it with government regulations and high taxes, which are unpopular.[52] They instead choose to call themselves progressives or "new" Democrats.

Many candidates of both parties use populist strategies. Republican populists, like Republican majority whip Tom DeLay of Texas, rail against the government, taxes, and special interests in Washington. Democratic populists also champion the cause of ordinary Americans. Rather than oppose big government, however, these candidates run against big business. For example, Democrat Byron Dorgan, who was elected North Dakota's at-large representative in 1980 and its junior senator in 1992, earned his populist credentials when, as state tax commissioner, he sued out-of-state corporations doing business in North Dakota to force them to pay taxes there.[53] Running campaigns based on populism has served Dorgan well, as he has served in Congress for more than two decades.

Negative Campaigning

Negative campaigning has always been and will probably always be a part of U.S. elections. Just as positive campaigning attempts to build up a candidate, negative campaigning endeavors to tear down an opponent. Negative campaigning can be a legitimate form of campaign communication that has the potential to enhance the electoral process. Campaign ads that question a candidate's qualifications or point to unpopular, wasteful, or unethical practices bring a measure of accountability to the political system.[54] Still, much negative campaigning amounts to little more than character assassination and mudslinging. Whether negative campaigning turns off voters and discourages them from participating in elections, thereby demobilizing a portion of the electorate, or it captures voters' attention and stimulates voter turnout, and thus serves to mobilize the electorate, is of secondary concern to candidates.[55] What matters is that more of their supporters than their opponent's show up at the polls.

Negative campaigning is used by one or both candidates in almost three-quarters of all House contests and virtually every Senate election. As elections get closer, the probability that they feature negative ads goes up.[56] The sense of urgency that pervades a close contest encourages the contestants to figuratively tar and feather each other because it is easier to discredit an opponent than to build loyalty.[57]

Attack ads can be an important component of challenger campaigns because they can help break voters of the habit of casting their ballots for the incumbent.[58] However, some incumbents have made negative advertising a central element of their strategies in recent years, using early attacks to define their challengers for voters before the challengers can define themselves.[59] Because of their competitiveness, open-seat campaigns tend to be the most negative of all.

The most effective negative ads are grounded in fact, document their sources, focus on some aspect of the opponent's policy views rather than personality, use ridicule, are delivered by a surrogate, and avoid discussing the plight of unfortunate citizens.[60] Many negative ads feature actors depicting incumbents voting themselves pay raises or attending lavish parties with lobbyists. Some show opponents flip-flopping on the issues. Ridicule is a powerful weapon in politics because it is difficult for people to vote for a candidate at whom they have just laughed. Campaign attacks that do not adhere to the preceding guidelines tend to be less effective and can backfire, making the candidate who levies the charges look dishonest or mean-spirited.

The hazards of crossing the line when using negative campaigning are something first-term congressman Felix Grucci of New York learned the hard way. Grucci was expected to defeat Democratic challenger Timothy Bishop, a college administrator who had no significant previous political experience. The incumbent was running in a district where Republicans outnumber Democrats by three to two; and he had raised $1.4 million, compared to the $990,000 raised by Bishop. Grucci began with a comfortable lead in the race, but lost it when he released a series of television, radio, and newspaper advertisements that, among other things, accused Bishop of undermining attempts to prevent future terrorist attacks and covering up rape statistics while working as provost of a local college.[61] Most politicians, both Republicans and Democrats, and journalists in the district were highly critical of the ads. As a reporter for *Newsday*, the major local newspaper in the area, wrote in response to the rape statistics ad, "The widespread revulsion to the ad gives Bishop a better chance to pull an upset." [62] Most voters apparently agreed, as Bishop defeated Grucci by 2,421 votes.

Opposition research provides the foundation for negative campaigning. Campaigns begin with a thorough examination of an opponent's personal and professional background. Current members of Congress are qualified to serve in the House or Senate by virtue of their incumbency, although the 1994 elections, which saw thirty-four Democratic House members defeated, poignantly demonstrated that incumbency can be used as a weapon against them. The backgrounds of challengers and open-seat candidates are often more open to question, especially if the candidates have no political experience or have pursued a career that most constituents would view with skepticism. Junk bond traders and dog catchers, for example, are at risk of being attacked as unqualified because of their professions.

The candidate's public record is the next thing that is usually explored. Challengers often study their opponent's attendance records, roll-call votes, and floor speeches. Incumbents and open-seat candidates usually study their opponent's political record. If an opponent has never held office, then a campaign will usually turn to newspaper or trade magazine accounts of speeches made to civic organizations, trade associations, or other groups.

Virtually all campaigns search for activities that can be construed as illegal or unethical. New Jersey senator Torricelli's acceptance of a Rolex wristwatch, a big-screen TV, and other gifts from David Chang, a friend who was convicted of funneling money to the senator's campaign, and the senator's subsequent admonition from the Senate ethics committee, provided the grist for Republican challenger Forrester's 2002 campaign.[63] Forrester's relentless attacks, and voters tiring of Torricelli's repeated ethical lapses, ultimately led the senator to abandon his bid for reelection and his subsequent replacement by retired senator Frank Lautenberg, who was easily elected.

Similarly, most contestants routinely search for unethical business transactions, evidence of tax dodging, and other questionable activities that could be used to discredit their opponents. Sometimes ex-spouses, estranged children, former friends, colleagues, and neighbors are interviewed to find examples of improper behavior or character flaws. Other times, investigations of military records, drivers' licenses, and campaign finance reports reveal that an opponent has lied about his or her service in the armed forces, is vulnerable to charges of having lived in the state or district for only a few years, or can be charged with being a tool of some wealthy special interest.

Most opposition research is tedious. Researchers scour the *Congressional Record,* search records of the floor proceedings of state legislatures, look through newspapers, surf the web, and turn to other public sources to show that a candidate is out of touch with the district, has flip-flopped on an issue, has taken an inordinate number of government-financed trips, or has committed some other questionable act. Opposition researchers often pore over campaign finance reports so that a candidate can claim that an opponent is too beholden to PACs and wealthy individuals from out of state to represent the views of constituents.

The widespread use of negative advertising has encouraged most campaigns to search for their own candidate's weaknesses. As one campaign manager involved in a close race explained, "We need to be prepared for the worst. We have to spend a lot of time looking at the things our opponent may try to pin on us." [64] Campaigns investigate their own candidates in anticipation of attacks they expect to be levied against them.

Some campaigns discuss a potential liability with members of the press before an opponent has had a chance to raise it. Preemption is an effective tactic for "inoculating" a candidate against an attack. Another approach is to hire one of the consulting firms that stakes its reputation on its ability to prepare a televised response to an attack in less than one day. Many well-financed Senate and House contenders in tight races go so far as to record television commercials that present responses to particular charges before their opponent actually makes them.

Not many incumbents were defeated in the 2002 congressional elections, but negative advertising played a role in the defeat of most of those who were, including Reps. Grucci, Bill Luther, D-Minn., and Karen Thurman, D-Fla., and Sens. Max Cleland, D-Ga., and Tim Hutchinson, R-Ark. One of the lessons to be drawn from the congressional elections of the past two decades is that, if used properly, negative campaigning can be a potent weapon.

SUMMARY

The campaign for votes, like the campaign for resources, requires candidates and strategists to identify groups of supporters and potential supporters and communicate to them a message they will find appealing. Campaign strategists recognize that most voters have little interest in politics, possess little information about congressional candidates, are more familiar with incumbents than with challengers, know more about candidates for the Senate than about those for the House, and tend to cast their ballots for candidates whom they have previously supported or who share their party identification.

Candidates and their advisers consider these factors when plotting strategies. Most campaigns use voting histories, census data, polls, and geodemographic analysis to target voters. They consider the partisan advantages associated with specific policy stances, the positions likely to be staked out by the opponent, the opinions of the blocs of supporters they need to mobilize, and the views of undecided voters they need to win. Most candidates make issues a major component of their message, but incumbents have a greater tendency to focus on imagery and their performance in office. Most candidates also seek to hold their opponent accountable for what they perceive to be weaknesses in their record. However, competitive elections usually feature the most negative campaigns.

CHAPTER EIGHT

Campaign Communications

Campaign communications range from sophisticated television advertisements and Internet web sites to old-fashioned knocking on doors. The resources at a candidate's disposal, the types of media available, and the competitiveness of the election are the factors that most strongly influence how campaigns reach voters. In this chapter I examine the techniques that campaigns use to disseminate their messages and get their supporters to the polls.

Campaign communications are meant to accomplish six objectives: to improve a candidate's name recognition, project a favorable image, set the campaign agenda, exploit the issues, undermine an opponent's credibility or support, and defend the candidate against attacks. These objectives, of course, are designed to advance the campaign's broader goals of shoring up and expanding its bases of support and getting its supporters sufficiently interested in the election to vote.

Campaign communications usually proceed through four short phases that begin in late summer and continue until election day. In the first, often called the biography phase, candidates introduce themselves to voters by highlighting their experience and personal backgrounds. Next, in the issue phase, candidates use issues to attract the support of uncommitted voters, energize their supporters, and further define themselves to the public.

The attack phase often begins after one candidate learns that he or she is slipping in the polls or failing to advance on an opponent. At this time, candidates contrast themselves with their opponent, point to inconsistencies between an opponent's rhetoric and actions, try to exploit unpopular positions the opponent has taken, or just plain sling mud at one another. In the final weeks of the campaign, most successful candidates pull their message together by reminding voters who they are, why they are running, and why they are

more worthy of being elected than their opponent. At this final, or summation, phase they commonly emphasize phrases and symbols presented earlier
in the campaign.

TELEVISION ADVERTISING

Virtually every household in the United States possesses at least one television
set, and the average adult watches three and one-half to four hours of television per day.[1] About three-fourths of all voters maintain that television is their
most important source of information about elections.[2] These factors make
television an important vehicle for campaign communications and have encouraged congressional campaigners whose races are located within cheap,
moderate-priced, and in some cases extremely expensive media markets to utilize the medium.

Television was used so heavily during the 2002 congressional elections that
registered voters reported seeing an average of almost eight ads per day during
the last week of the election.[3] Television is the best medium for conveying
image-related information to a mass audience. It is also extremely useful in setting the campaign agenda and associating a candidate with popular issues.[4]
Television ads enable candidates to transmit action-oriented visuals that demonstrate desirable qualities such as leadership. Images of candidates meeting
with voters or attending groundbreaking ceremonies convey more powerfully
than do written or verbal statements the message that these individuals are
actively involved in community affairs and have close ties to voters. Images also
have a stronger emotional impact than do words. As Republican strategist
Robert Teeter explains, "80 or 90 percent of what people retain from a TV ad
is visual. . . . If you have the visual right, you have the commercial right. If you
don't, it almost doesn't matter what you're saying."[5] Television advertisements
have the extra advantage of enabling the campaign to control its message.
Unlike interactive modes of communication, such as debates and speeches, paid
advertisements do not allow an opponent or disgruntled voter to interrupt.
Message control makes TV a potent weapon for increasing name recognition.[6]

Roughly nine out of ten Senate campaigns and 65 percent of all House campaigns use either broadcast or cable television, and these numbers would be
larger if the costs were not so high.[7] Campaigns must pay the same rates as
commercial advertisers for nonpreemptible advertising slots. These rates are
most often prohibitively expensive, especially during prime time. In
November 2002, Democratic representative José Serrano or his Republican
opponent, Frank Dellavalle, would have had to spend $58,000 to broadcast

one thirty-second advertisement during the airing of the popular TV show "The West Wing" to reach voters living in New York's 16th congressional district. The cost of broadcasting an ad to this South Bronx district is exorbitant because the district is in a media market that spans the entire New York metropolitan area. By contrast, candidates in Texas's 11th congressional seat, which includes Waco, would have paid only $1,200 to air an ad that would have blanketed virtually the entire district during this same time slot.

Some campaigns save money by forgoing the certainty that their ads will be broadcast during prime time. Those who purchase preemptible broadcast time pay considerably less for TV but run the risk of their ads being aired at some less desirable time. That is a gamble few campaigns take as election day approaches. Some campaigns, including many in major metropolitan areas, save money and improve targeting by substituting cable TV for broadcast stations.

High costs and the mismatch between media markets and the boundaries of congressional districts discourage House candidates in the highly urbanized areas of the Mid-Atlantic, West Coast, and southern New England from using television advertising. The distribution of media markets and relatively low advertising rates in most southwestern states and many rural areas, by contrast, enable many House candidates to use television extensively.[8] Senate candidates tend to make greater use of television than do candidates for the House because the configuration of state borders and media markets make television a relatively cost-efficient communications medium in statewide contests. The greater funding levels of Senate campaigns and the expectation that Senate candidates will rely on television also contribute to its greater use in contests for the upper chamber.

Televised campaign advertisements have come a long way since the days when candidates appeared as talking heads that spouted their political experiences and issue positions. Six trends define the evolution of the modern television campaign commercial: a movement toward greater emphasis on imagery, the use of action-oriented themes and pictures, the employment of emotionally laden messages, a decrease in the length of ads, an increase in negative advertising, and a reduction in the amount of time required to create an ad.[9] Gimmicky, ten- and fifteen-second spots punctuated by twenty or so words have recently become popular with congressional candidates and other political groups. An ability to counterattack in less than half a day has become a selling point for the nation's top media firms. The broadcasting of campaign advertisements under the guise of issue ads by parties and interest groups is the latest development in the use of television in elections.

During the biography phase of the campaign, incumbents' ads typically depict them as experienced leaders who know and care about their constituents.

Challengers and candidates for open seats also try to present themselves as capable and honorable by pointing to their accomplishments in politics, family life, or the private sector. All candidates broadcast advertisements that repeatedly mention and display their names, and frequently end their commercials with the line "Vote for [candidate's name] for Congress" and the required disclaimer indicating who paid for the ad.

Candidates who have led remarkable lives, come from humble origins, or compiled impressive records of public service often broadcast what are called "mini-docudramas" to showcase their war record, community activism, or road to professional success. The ad that a campaign selects to introduce its candidate is influenced both by the candidate's life and by the structure of the competition in the race.

The Van Hollen campaign's overriding objective in introducing its candidate was to find a way to make him stand out in a hotly contested four-way congressional primary. The primary field included state delegate Mark Shriver, who brought to the race the considerable notoriety and backing that a member of the Kennedy clan typically brings to the electoral arena, and Ira Shapiro, who was well known for his work on international trade as a congressional staffer and in the Clinton administration. The final candidate, Deborah Vollmer, was not given much consideration by the other candidates or the media. To demonstrate Van Hollen's achievements in the political arena, the campaign ran a thirty-second TV spot called "Best," which focused on favorable news coverage and endorsements he received while working in the state legislature. The ad opens with an announcer stating, "The *Washington Post* called Chris Van Hollen one of Maryland's best legislators." The visual is of the *Post* masthead and the words "one of the best legislators in the General Assembly, 10/29/96" (the numbers are the date of publication). The announcer then states, "The *Baltimore Sun* called him a rising star," and the *Baltimore Sun* masthead and the words "a rising legislative star, 6/13/00" appear on the screen. Next, the announcer proclaims, "One of the Senate's most effective advocates," which is accompanied by the *Sun* masthead, that phrase, and the publication date as the visual. This is followed by the pronouncement "*Time* magazine called him a hero to environmentalists, education groups and gun control advocates." The visual, once again, is the spoken text and the publication date. The ad closes with the announcer stating, "He wrote the plan that will bring an additional $130 million per year to our schools, authored laws that protect the Chesapeake Bay and took on the NRA and passed the nation's first trigger lock law. Chris Van Hollen, a congressman for people who care about issues." The final visual is the disclaimer "Paid for by Van Hollen for Congress." [10]

Not only did Van Hollen's ad establish in the minds of most Democratic voters that the candidate had a significant record of political accomplishment on which to run, it also established that he was largely responsible for Maryland's tough gun control law, not Shriver, who also sought to claim credit for it. Finally, the ad sought to appeal to the district's highly educated issue-oriented voters, who would later have to decide between the issue-oriented Democrat Van Hollen and popular incumbent representative Morella.

Morella faced a different type of challenge in the early stages of her reelection campaign. She already was popular among the largely Democratic and liberal constituents who dominated her old district—most of whom referred to her as "Connie," but her support began to erode as a result of the unpopularity of legislation passed in the Republican-led House and voters' recognition that her reelection helped make possible the razor-thin margin that kept the GOP in control. She also needed to minimize the impact of voters in the largely Democratic and minority areas that had been added to the district following redistricting. Morella's strategy focused mainly on solidifying her hold on voters in the old district and attracting new support by reminding voters of the personal characteristics and performance that had made her so popular in the past.

Morella aired the sixty-second biographical ad titled "Connie," from July 30 to August 14. The ad opens with the disclaimer "Paid for by Friends of Connie Morella for Congress" and begins with the congresswoman saying, "I serve in the people's house, and I feel that my job, my responsibility, is to stand up for the needs and the values of the people I represent." The statement "Congresswoman Connie Morella is very special" appears on the screen. Then a narrator states, "The daughter of immigrant parents, she became an educator, and with her husband, Tony, raised nine children, including six of her late sister's." Morella reappears on the screen, saying, "It got a little hectic at breakfast time, dinner time, all the time. But it was the most rewarding and defining experience of my life." The narrator's voice-over responds, "Congresswoman Connie Morella, she's put principles above partisan ties, says the *Washington Post*, and has proved pivotal in enacting major legislation." At that point the *Post* masthead and "principles above partisan ties," "pivotal in enacting major legislation," and "10/28/00" (the date of publication) come into view on the screen. Then Morella reappears and says, "People here want someone who will think independently and who is not afraid to make tough decisions." The announcer then proclaims, "A leader for the rights of women, for prescription drugs for seniors, fighting for federal workers, and common-sense gun control that's earned her Sarah Brady's endorsement." The congresswoman's web site address appears on the screen, and the announcer continues, "Connie Morella is the most independent voice in Congress." The ad closes with Morella saying, "You judge each issue on its merits, you listen to your constituency, you put partisanship aside, and you do what you think is right." The final visual is of the signature "Connie" appearing on the screen.[11]

Morella's ad mixes information about her impressive biography, legislative style, and the issues she has championed in the past to portray the congresswoman as caring, personable, and independent. It raises her nonpartisanship and leadership on liberal causes to reduce the impact of her party affiliation. Similarly, the mention of Sarah Brady's endorsement was meant to reinforce Morella's independence and to neutralize the impact of the gun control issue in the general election.

Some incumbents, and a few nonincumbents with political experience, use "community action" spots to show the impact of their efforts on behalf of constituents. As noted in Chapter 7, Senator Johnson used this approach extensively, employing ads tailored to different localities to develop this theme early in the race, followed in the closing days of the campaign by an ad combining clips from many of the earlier spots. Just as the former ads showed the candidate's efforts to meet the varied needs of South Dakota voters, the final spot displayed the breadth of his understanding and efforts and the scope of his influence.[12]

"Feel good" ads are virtually devoid of issues and are designed to appeal to the electorate's sense of community pride or nationalism. They feature visuals of a candidate marching in parades, on horseback in the countryside, or involved in some other popular local activity. "Passing the torch" ads manipulate symbols rousing the concept of succession to make the case that a candidate is the right person for the job. In 2002, Democratic Senate candidate Mark Pryor, son of popular former Arkansas governor and two-term senator David Pryor, used a passing the torch ad to help him defeat Republican incumbent Tim Hutchinson. The ad Pryor uses to introduce himself opens with the candidate saying,

> I'm Mark Pryor. You know me as Arkansas's attorney general, but I'm also my father's son. He taught me to speak my mind and to think for myself, to remember that people matter more than political parties. And just because something's a Democratic idea doesn't mean it's a good idea, and not all Republican ideas are bad ones. As your senator, I'll always listen. And like this sign that was on my father's desk says, I'll always put Arkansas first.

The ad, one of several campaign communications featuring Pryor's father, firmed up the link between the popular father and the son, and made it difficult for Hutchinson to link Pryor with national liberal Democrats. Most important from the viewpoint of both Pryors, it helped the son claim the father's old Senate seat.

During the issue phase, campaign ads communicate candidates' policy stances on valence or positional issues.[13] In Colorado's 7th district open-seat race, Beauprez aired a television commercial with a backdrop of a dairy farm to emphasize his conventionally Republican positions on freedom and economic stimulus through lower taxes. Feeley's ads, not surprisingly, focused on traditional Democratic issues. Several of his ads showed him with children in a classroom, with senior citizens, and with groups of working Americans as backdrops while an announcer discussed the candidate's commitment to cutting the costs of prescription drugs, enacting health care reform, and protecting Social Security and pensions from being threatened by tax cuts for the rich. These ads were designed to shore-up support among senior citizens and middle-class and blue-collar workers, particularly women. Although most voters have only a limited interest in any single issue, ads that focus on positional issues, such as taxes and health care reform, can help candidates pick up crucial support among single-issue voters or emphasize certain elements of their image.[14]

In the attack phase of the campaign, candidates use televised advertisements that often feature fancy graphics to point to their opponent's shortcomings. Television is ideally suited to comparative ads because it enables candidates and parties to present pictures of themselves and their opponent side-by-side and to roll down the screen lists of issues showing themselves to be on the popular side of salient policies while their opponent is on the unpopular side. That less than flattering pictures of the opponent are used is an understatement. Sometimes the opponent's head is reduced in size, "phased out," or distorted to keep voters' attention and to subtly imply that faulty issue positions are only one of an opponent's weaknesses. Television is also an effective medium for attacking an opponent for inconsistencies in issue positions. Advertisements that feature images of the opponent somersaulting back and forth across the screen or debating himself or herself are useful in highlighting inconsistencies among an opponent's speeches, campaign positions, or congressional roll-call votes.

Of course, not all comparative and negative advertising is conducted by candidates. Indeed, much of it takes the form of issue advocacy advertising by party committees and interest groups. Both candidates and parties broadcast attack ads in the Beauprez-Feeley contest. The National Republican Congressional Committee, operating through the Colorado Republican Federal Campaign Committee and on its own, ran TV ads blasting Feeley for becoming a lobbyist after leaving the Colorado Senate, and called him "a lobbyist whose services are available to the highest bidder." The ads criticized Feeley for working "for a group that wants to force people to pay rent in a nursing home up to 90 days after they die," and accused him of wanting "to deny seniors the prescription drugs they need." They also claimed he voted to "kill a plan that would have given $637 million in tax relief to working families. . .that could have gone to your children's education, better health care, or a family vacation."

The Democratic Congressional Campaign Committee, which operated through the Colorado Democratic Party, and Feeley attacked Beauprez on just as many fronts. One Feeley ad sought to connect Beauprez with corporate fraud by characterizing him as a multimillionaire developer who had to pay $700,000 in connection with a fraud suit and claiming that he was "against any new laws to stop corporate fraud and protect our pensions [and] supports $100 billion in tax cuts for the richest 1 percent of America, even though it would force major cuts in Social Security." Other Feeley and Democratic ads accused Beauprez of opposing "any new federal gun safety laws,. . .being against the federal law banning cop-killer bullets," and for "vow[ing] to take away a woman's right to choose even for victims of rape and incest." The Democrats' response to the Republicans' negative ads included putting up a commercial stating that "Even fellow Republicans have accused Bob Beauprez of playing loose with the truth and with ethics," which then goes on to rebut the GOP's charges and lay out Feeley's record. Beauprez had a more humorous response to the Democrats' assaults on him, airing an ad in which he states, "There's been a lot of nasty stuff out there said about me. As an old dairy farmer I recognize the smell." He then goes on to lay out his vision for America.

In the summation phase of the campaign, eleventh-hour television blitzes are used to solidify a candidate's message in the minds of voters. Key phrases and visuals from earlier commercials are repeated as candidates who are ahead shore-up support and those running behind appeal to undecided voters.

RADIO ADVERTISING

Radio is an extremely popular medium for congressional campaign communications. Almost two-thirds of all House candidates and virtually every Senate contestant purchase radio ads.[15] During the last week of the 2002 congressional elections, registered voters typically reported hearing four to five radio ads per day.[16] Inexpensive to record and broadcast, radio commercials are ideal for building a candidate's name identification. Another advantage is that some candidates—whether they are intimidated by the television camera, not telegenic, novices to the spotlight, or products of the pretelevision era—perform better on radio. For many incumbents, taping radio commercials is an easy extension of the radio shows they regularly send back to stations in their district. Like television, radio is an excellent vehicle for emotion-laden messages.[17]

Radio allows candidates to target voters with great precision. Radio stations broadcast to smaller, more homogeneous audiences than does television, enabling campaigns to tailor their messages to different segments of the population. Campaigns can reach Hispanic voters in the Southwest, Florida, or the inner cities of the Northeast by advertising on Spanish-language stations. "Golden oldies" stations, which feature music from the 1960s and 1970s, are ideal for reaching middle-aged voters. Radio talk programs, such as the *Rush Limbaugh Show,* are excellent vehicles for reaching voters who are committed to particular ideologies. Commuting hours furnish near-captive audiences of suburbanites who travel to work.

NEWSPAPER ADVERTISING

Newspaper advertisements dominated campaign communications for much of American history but fell in importance with the decline of the partisan press in the late 1800s.[18] Congressional campaigns still purchase newspaper ads, but they are not as widely used as radio and many other media. Sixty-three percent of all House and 80 percent of all Senate campaigns purchase ads in local or statewide newspapers.[19]

Newspapers as a campaign medium have some advantages but many shortcomings. Their major advantages are that they provide plenty of opportunities to deliver a detailed message, and because readers are educated voters they are likely to vote. Newspapers' major downsides are that they do not communicate images or convey emotion as well as does television. They also cannot be used to deliver a personalized message. Moreover, only a few congressional districts and states have large enough minority communities to sustain independent newspapers that can be used to target communications to these groups. The effectiveness of campaign advertisements that appear in newspapers is also somewhat limited.[20]

If such shortcomings exist, why do most campaigns place ads in newspapers? One reason is that they are inexpensive. Newspaper advertisements cost less than ads transmitted via television, radio, mail, or virtually any other medium. Newspaper ads can also be useful in announcing the times and locations of campaign events, which can help attract coverage by other media. Finally, some candidates and campaign aides believe that purchasing advertising space from a local newspaper can help them secure the paper's endorsement.

DIRECT MAIL AND NEWSLETTERS

Newsletters and direct mail can be used to raise money, convey a message, or encourage people to vote, but the key to success in all three areas is a good mailing list. A good fundraising list is made up of previous donors or persons who have a history of contributing to like-minded candidates; a good advertising list includes supporters and persuadable voters; and a good voter mobilization list includes only the candidate's supporters.

Direct-mail pieces and newsletters (sometimes referred to as "persuasion mail") are among the most widely used methods of campaign advertising in congressional elections. Roughly 80 percent of all House candidates and nearly all Senate candidates use them.[21] During the last week of the 2002 election season, registered voters typically received between two and three pieces of mail per day.[22] Mail is a one-way communications tool that offers significant advantages in message control and delivery. Precise targeting is its main advantage. Campaigns can purchase lists that include information such as a voter's name, address, gender, age, race or ethnicity, employment status, party registration, voting history, and estimated income.[23] This information enables campaigns to tailor the candidate profiles, issue positions, and photographs they include in their mailings to appeal to specific segments of the population. This ability makes mail an excellent medium for staking out positional issues and for campaigning in heterogeneous states or districts. Campaigns waged in highly diverse areas, such as New York's 12th district, which is 49 percent Hispanic and includes most of Chinatown, often use the mail to campaign in more than one language.

Another advantage of mail is that it is relatively inexpensive. Letters produced using personal computers and laser printers can be mailed to voters for little more than the price of a first-class stamp. Campaigns can also take advantage of post office discounts for presorted mailings. Finally, mail campaigns often fly under the radar for a while. As long as an adversary does not detect them, his or her campaign will not respond.

Nevertheless, direct mail has some disadvantages, including the fact that it is often tossed out as junk mail. Another disadvantage is that it rests principally on the power of the printed word. Whereas television and radio enable campaigns to embellish their messages with visual images or sound effects, mail depends primarily on written copy to hold voters' attention and get a message across. This makes it a less effective medium for communicating image-related information.

Direct-mail experts rely on many different techniques to combat the weaknesses of their medium. Personalized salutations, graphs, and pictures are often used to capture and hold voters' attention. Other gimmicks include the use of postscripts designed to look as though they were handwritten.

Direct mail is an especially powerful medium for challengers and candidates who have strong ideological positions because it is ideal for negative advertising or for making appeals that stir voters' emotions. Yet mail also offers some advantages to incumbents. Many members of Congress send out letters early in the election cycle to reinforce voter support without mounting a highly visible campaign.[24] These mailings often include messages reinforcing those that incumbents communicate in congressionally franked mass mailings to constituents, which are prohibited ninety days before a primary or general election for House members and sixty days before an election for senators.[25]

Direct mail plays a prominent role in many congressional elections. In Maryland's 8th district race in 2002, the Van Hollen campaign sent fourteen unique pieces of direct mail, the Maryland Democratic Party mailed another two pieces, and various interest groups mailed another three. Meanwhile, the Morella campaign mailed seven letters, the NRCC and the Republican National Committee sent out another seven, and the seniors' group 60 Plus Association mailed one.[26] In Colorado's 7th district the Beauprez campaign did three mailings; Republican Party organizations, mainly the NRCC, were responsible for another twenty; and various interest groups mailed out another ten pieces of mail. The Feeley campaign, which lacked the money to do a mailing of its own, relied on the DCCC and the Democratic National Committee for ten direct mail pieces, and interest groups sent another six letters.[27]

Not surprisingly, the direct mail distributed in conjunction with the South Dakota Senate race far outpaced that connected with the above and most other House elections. The Johnson campaign was responsible for thirteen mail pieces; various Democratic Party committees sent out another forty-three pieces; and several unions, environmental groups, women's organizations, and other interests distributed an additional twenty pieces. The Thune campaign distributed only six pieces of direct mail, but the seventy-three pieces of mail sent by Republican Party organizations, and twenty pieces mailed by various pro-life, business, gunowners, and other conservative groups, more than made up for it.[28]

MASS TELEPHONE CALLS

Mass telephone calls are a popular communications medium, used by just over 70 percent of all House campaigns and most Senate campaigns.[29] Campaigns make these calls for a variety of reasons, including identifying voters' political predispositions and candidate preferences. This information is often added to a database so that supporters and swing voters can be contacted later. Sometimes these contacts take place through the same medium. Campaigns may telephone undecided voters to try to win their support or contact supporters to ask them to volunteer, make a contribution, or attend an event. One of the major purposes of mass telephone calls is voter mobilization. Some campaigns rely on volunteers for mass telephone calls. During the closing days of the 2002 campaign the Service Employees International Union filled a mobile call center—a tractor-trailer packed with telephones—with volunteers so that they could mobilize union voters in support of Van Hollen. When it was not filled with union members, the Van Hollen campaign rented the center so that its volunteers could contact supporters for this same purpose.[30]

Although personal calls are much more effective than recorded ones, recorded messages also can mobilize voters. Some candidates, particularly challengers, ask prominent local politicians for assistance. For example, Rep. Steny Hoyer, a popular Democratic congressional leader from a neighboring district, taped a telephone message on behalf of Van Hollen. Many Republican candidates in close races benefited from prerecorded mobilization messages featuring President Bush, former first lady Barbara Bush, and other prominent Republicans; most of these candidates' opponents called on the services of former president Bill Clinton, Sen. Hillary Rodham Clinton, and Jesse Jackson to turn out Democratic voters. In some cases these efforts were financed by party committees.

Live and prerecorded telephone calls also have been used for less noble purposes. Campaigns have been known to leave prerecorded messages implicating an opponent in an alleged scandal. They also have been known to hire telephone firms to conduct so-called "push polls," which seem to be normal telephone surveys used for collecting information at the onset but soon degenerate into allegations and attacks phrased as questions. Both sets of activities are intended to demobilize voters rather than learn about or mobilize them.

THE INTERNET

The Internet has become an extremely popular communications medium in congressional elections. Almost nine out of ten 2002 House campaigns and virtually every Senate campaign had a web site (see Table 8-1). Web sites are relatively inexpensive to create, are easy to maintain, can convey a great deal of information quickly and with little effort, and because of their interactive nature are useful for getting voters involved in the election. Congressional

TABLE 8-1

Internet Use in House Campaigns in 2002

		Incumbents		Challengers		Open-seat candidates	
	All	In jeopardy	Shoo-ins	Hope-fuls	Likely losers	Pros-pects	Mis-matched
Sponsored its own web site	88%	93%	74%	94%	90%	97%	100%
Communicated with supporters	72	59	59	81	77	89	72
Recruited or organized volunteers	69	76	54	81	67	80	89
Issued press releases	65	90	49	81	55	91	83
Fundraising (including credit card contributions)	57	68	51	59	50	74	67
Reached out to undecided voters	38	28	18	47	50	37	39
Showcased TV ads (streaming video)	21	14	12	47	12	40	39
(N)	(312)	(76)	(29)	(32)	(122)	(35)	(18)

Source: The 2002 Congressional Campaign Study.

Notes: Figures are for general election candidates in major-party contested races, excluding those in incumbent-versus-incumbent races. Percentages reflect the campaigns that participated in these activities. These numbers do not add to 100 percent because campaigns could pick as many of these activities as applied.

campaign web sites usually include the candidate's biography and issue positions, favorable breaking news, a calendar of events, a directory that provides headquarters and staffing information, an area to facilitate voter involvement in the campaign, and negative information on the opposition. Roughly seven out of ten House campaigns used their site and e-mail to communicate with supporters or to recruit or organize volunteers; 65 percent used the web to issue press releases; and 57 percent used it to raise funds (see Table 8-1). Substantially smaller numbers used the web to reach out to undecided voters or to showcase their television ads. The former effort runs the risk of alienating voters who object to being "spammed," and the latter requires substantial technical skills. Perhaps streaming video ads and e-mail will be used more frequently in the future, but registered voters report having little contact with them in the 2002 congressional elections. Indeed, more than three-fourths of these individuals report receiving no e-mail communications at all during that election season.[31]

Not surprisingly, candidates in close races tend to make greater use of the Internet and e-mail than do those in lopsided contests. However, fewer incumbents, particularly shoo-ins, make use of it than do nonincumbents. Lacking a strong challenger, these members of Congress probably believe that their formal congressional web sites give them enough of a presence on the web.

The best web sites complement the candidate's campaign. They provide a place for voters to collect information that is usually available elsewhere, but to do so in a more convenient and reliable way than telephoning campaign headquarters, scouring newspapers, or contacting local political activists. Campaigns save money and effort, and avoid mistakes, when they direct voter, donor, and press inquiries to their web site. Good campaign web sites have attractive home pages that immediately tell voters about the candidate, are updated regularly, and display icons that direct them to other areas of the site. They provide on-line areas that permit individuals to volunteer for campaign activities; make a contribution; or sign up on the campaign's e-mail list, which in itself is a valuable communications tool. These data are usually integrated into the campaign's computerized volunteer and finance databases. Some web sites encourage activists to write op-ed articles, send letters to the editor, or call radio talk shows by providing the names, addresses, and telephone numbers of local media outlets. Some also provide voters with directions to their polling place.

FREE MEDIA

One of the major goals of any campaign is to generate free, or "earned," media—radio, television, newspaper, or magazine coverage that candidates receive when news editors consider their activities newsworthy. Earned media has other advantages besides free advertising. Because it is delivered by a neutral observer, it has greater credibility than do campaign-generated communications.[32] The major disadvantage of free media is that campaigns cannot control what news correspondents report. Misstatements and blunders are more likely to appear in the news than are issues raised in major policy speeches.

News coverage of congressional elections consists of stories based on press releases issued by campaigns; stories about events, issues, campaign ads, or time that a reporter has spent with a candidate; and analytical or editorial stories about a candidate or campaign.[33] Most analysis focuses on the "horse-race" aspect of the election. Those stories that get beyond handicapping the race usually discuss candidates' political qualifications, personal characteristics, or campaign organizations. Fewer stories focus on the issues.[34] Coverage by television and radio tends to be shorter, more action oriented, and less detailed and features less editorializing than does print journalism.

Most journalists strive to cover politics objectively, but this does not mean that all candidates are treated the same. Reporters follow certain norms when pursuing leads and researching and writing their stories—norms that usually work to the advantage of incumbents.[35] Moreover, editorials are largely exempt from the norms of objectivity that apply to news stories. Newspaper owners and their editorial boards do not hesitate to voice their opinions on editorial pages. Radio and television stations also air programs that feature pundits discussing the virtues and foibles of specific candidates. Most consumers of news have come to expect newspaper editors and political talk show hosts to endorse specific candidates shortly before the election. Media endorsements and campaign coverage can have a significant impact on elections.

Attracting Coverage

Attracting media coverage requires planning and aggressiveness. Besides issuing streams of press releases, campaign offices distribute copies of the candidate's schedule to correspondents, invite them to campaign events, and make special efforts to grant interviews. Candidates also submit themselves to interrogations by panels of newspaper editors with the goal of generating good press coverage or winning an endorsement.

Successful campaigns carefully play to the needs of different news media. Press releases that feature strong leads, have news value, provide relevant facts, and contain enough background information for an entire story are faxed to print reporters. Advance notice of major campaign events, including information about predicted crowd size, acoustics, and visual backdrops, is given to television and radio correspondents with the hope that the event will be one of the few they cover.[36] Interpretive information is provided to all journalists, regardless of the media in which they work, to try to generate campaign stories with a favorable news spin. News organizations routinely report stories based on materials distributed by campaigns; because few news organizations have adequate resources to research or even verify this information, most free press is uncritical.

Newspapers and radio stations are more likely than television stations to give candidates free media coverage. Television stations devote little time to covering congressional elections, particularly House races. Television news shows occasionally discuss the horse-race aspect of campaigns, cover small portions of campaign debates, or analyze controversial campaign ads, but few are willing to give candidates air time to discuss issues. Radio stations are more generous with air time. Many invite candidates to participate in call-in talk shows and public forums. Newspapers usually give the most detailed campaign coverage. Small, understaffed newspapers frequently print portions of candidates' press releases and debate transcripts verbatim.

Senate candidates attract more free media than do House candidates. Incumbents and open-seat contestants usually get more—and more favorable— press coverage than do challengers, regardless of whether they are running for the House or the Senate. Inequities in campaign coverage are due to the professional norms that guide news journalists and to the inequalities that exist among candidates and campaign organizations. The preoccupation of journalists with candidates' personalities, qualifications, campaign organizations, and probable success are to the advantage of incumbents because they are almost always better known, more qualified, in possession of more professional organizations, and more likely to win than their opponents.[37]

Press coverage in House contests between an incumbent and a challenger is so unequal that veteran Democratic political adviser Anita Dunn believes "the local press is the unindicted co-conspirator in the alleged 'permanent incumbency.' " As Dunn explains, "A vicious circle develops for challengers— if early on, they don't have money, standing in the polls, endorsements, and the backing of political insiders, they—and the race—are written off, not covered, which means the likelihood of a competitive race developing is almost nonexistent." [38]

The coverage that Morella's challengers received in the *Washington Post* (the major newspaper covering her seat) prior to the 2002 elections demonstrates this point. Morella's 1996 opponent, Don Mooers, was mentioned in a total of twenty-one election stories, and all of them implied he had little chance of winning. Typical was an article titled "Lots of Foes, Little Hope," in which the *Post* quoted one of Mooers's opponents in the Democratic primary as saying, "Heaven help whoever gets the nomination. They're going to need it." [39] An editorial cartoon published in the *Post* a week before the election, under the caption "Caught under the Morella steamroller," featured a likeness of Morella flattening six previous Democratic opponents and about to flatten Mooers.[40] Morella's 1998 and 2000 opponents, Ralph Neas, former director of the Legislative Conference on Civil Rights, and Terry Lierman, a prominent lobbyist, received about the same amount and quality of coverage in the *Post* as did the previous Democratic nominees, despite the fact that the former raised almost $812,000 and the latter raised more than $1.9 million and came within seven points of winning. By contrast, Van Hollen, who was involved in a contested primary prior to his 2002 general election battle with Morella, received favorable coverage in the main and local sections of the *Post* both before and after the primary. The *Post* published eighty-five stories about the primary contest, giving Van Hollen its primary endorsement. It published forty-two articles about the general election contest and gave a weak general election endorsement to Morella in an article that praised both candidates heavily. Campaign aides involved in the race describe the *Post*'s coverage of the race as evenhanded.

The *Post*'s policy of not reporting on challengers in uncontested primaries until they are nominated resulted in the paper ignoring all of Morella's previous opponents until after the state's September primary. That delay allowed for a total of just six weeks of press coverage, not enough for a challenger to gain the visibility needed to become a viable candidate. Although the *Post* is a nonpartisan newspaper, its policy for covering challengers functions as an incumbent-retention program when combined with primaries that take place late in the election season. Many congressional challengers are greatly disadvantaged because their local newspaper has the same policy as the *Post*.

Although many challengers can usually count on getting only four stories—the announcement of their candidacy, coverage of their primary victory, a candidate profile, and the announcement of their defeat—it is still worth pursuing free media coverage. Those few challengers who are able to make the case to journalists that they have the capacity to mount a strong campaign are able to attract significant media coverage, often enough to become known among local voters. Challengers who have held elective office or had significant unelective political experience, assembled professional campaign organizations, and raised substantial funds are in a better position to make this case than are those who have not. They typically receive extra press coverage, which helps them raise more money, hire additional help, become more competitive, and attract even greater attention from the media.[41] A similar set of relationships exists for open-seat candidates, except that it is usually easier for them to make the case that they are involved in a close contest.

Scandal can help candidates attract more media coverage. Even underdogs are taken more seriously when their opponents have been accused of breaking the law or of ethical misconduct. Forrester, the 2002 Republican Senate challenger in New Jersey, is an example of an experienced challenger who took advantage of the heightened media exposure that resulted from scandal. His repeatedly pillorying Torricelli "as an embarrassment to all of New Jersey" and asking voters, "Why do we have to have a United States senator whose reputation is as bad as Bob Torricelli's?" brought him tremendous amounts of free media, drove the incumbent's standing among voters into the ground, and ultimately resulted in Torricelli quitting the race.[42]

The 2002 Senate election in Minnesota furnishes another, somewhat unusual example of how free media coverage can unexpectedly influence an election negatively. Following Sen. Paul Wellstone's death in an airplane accident, the Minnesota Democratic-Farmer Labor Party organized a memorial service at the University of Minnesota's Williams Arena. The service, which had the potential to generate sympathy votes for former vice president Walter Mondale, Wellstone's replacement on the ballot, degenerated into an unseemly pep rally at which Republican dignitaries in attendance were booed by the audience. Footage of the event was covered heavily on television, the radio, and newspapers. It outraged many voters, including independents whose ballots were up for grabs, and discouraged them from voting for Mondale, contributing to Republican Norman Coleman's two-point victory.[43]

Campaign Debates

Debates are among the few campaign activities that receive extensive press coverage and can place a challenger on equal footing with an incumbent. The decision to participate in a debate is a strategic one. Front-runners, who are usually incumbents, generally prefer to avoid debating because they understand that debates have the potential to do them more harm than good. Nevertheless, incumbents recognize that the public expects them to debate; most do so to avoid being blasted for shirking their civic responsibility. Candidates who are running behind, usually challengers, have the most to gain from debating. They prefer to engage in as many debates as possible and to hold them when they will attract the most media coverage.

Before debates are scheduled, the candidates or their representatives negotiate certain matters in regard to them. In addition to the number and timing of debates, candidates must agree on whether independent or minor-party candidates will participate, on the format that will be used, and on where the debate or debates will be held. All these factors can influence who, if anyone, is considered the winner.[44] Negotiations about debates can become heated but are almost always successfully resolved. Roughly nine out of ten House and Senate contestants debate their opponents.[45] The few who refuse usually enjoy insurmountable leads, lack verbal agility, or both. In 2002 Ose opted not to debate Beeman for the former reason. Six years earlier, ninety-three-year-old Sen. Strom Thurmond, R-S.C., chose not to debate Elliot Close, a quick-witted Democrat, for both reasons. Whether candidates debate is one of the few questions in congressional elections that are usually decided in favor of challengers and candidates who are running behind. The Ose-Beeman and Thurmond-Close races are exceptions to the rule.

Media Bias

House challengers and incumbents disagree over the nature of the coverage the media give to House campaigns (see Table 8-2).[46] Challengers, particularly those in uncompetitive contests, are the most likely to perceive an incumbent bias, reflecting the one-sided nature of press coverage in elections for safe seats. To some extent these perceptions are a product of the norms that guide the distribution of media endorsements—which favor incumbents by almost nine to one.[47]

Partisan differences also exist in the perception of media coverage. More Republican campaigners than Democrats maintain that the press gives more coverage and endorsements to their opponent's campaign, reflecting a widely shared opinion among Republican politicians and voters that the media corps is made up of members of a liberal establishment. Nevertheless, equal numbers of campaigners from each party believe the media covered their campaign fairly. The fact that almost four out of ten campaigners from both parties believe that the media are biased against them highlights the adversarial relationship that exists between politicians and the press.[48]

FIELD WORK

Field work involves voter registration and get-out-the-vote drives, literature drops, the distribution of yard signs and bumper stickers, and other grassroots

TABLE 8-2

Campaigners' Perceptions of Media Coverage in House Campaigns in 2002

		Incumbents		Challengers		Open-seat candidates	
	All	In jeopardy	Shoo-ins	Hope-fuls	Likely losers	Pros-pects	Mis-matched
Favored your campaign	9%	—	11%	10%	9%	12%	12%
Favored your opponent's campaign	37	18	5	48	62	24	47
Equally fair	54	82	84	42	29	65	41
(*N*)	(312)	(27)	(79)	(31)	(122)	(34)	(17)

Source: The 2002 Congressional Campaign Study.

Notes: Figures are for general election candidates in major-party contested races, excluding those in incumbent-versus-incumbent races. Dash = less than 0.5 percent. Some columns do not add to 100 percent because of rounding.

activities. It also includes candidate appearances at town meetings and in parades, speeches to Rotary Clubs and other civic groups, door-to-door campaigning, and other forms of direct voter contact. Grassroots politics were the major means of campaigning during the golden age of parties, and they remain important in modern congressional elections. Sophisticated targeting plans, similar to those used in direct mail and mass telephone calling, guide many grassroots activities. Field work is the most labor-intensive and volunteer-dependent aspect of congressional elections. Candidates, their supporters, and local party workers knock on doors and make telephone calls to learn whether citizens intend to vote, whom they support, and if they have any specific concerns they would like the candidate to address. Supporters and potential supporters who express an interest in an issue, need to register to vote, desire help in getting to the polls, state a preference for casting an absentee ballot, or are willing to work in the campaign typically receive follow-up calls.

Person-to-person communication is probably the most effective means of political persuasion, especially when it takes place directly between the candidate and a voter. It also provides a campaign with useful feedback. Candidates routinely draw on conversations with individuals they meet along the campaign trail to develop anecdotes that humanize issues.

Field work is relatively inexpensive because volunteers can be used to carry out much of the actual labor. Local party activists, union members, and other volunteers are often called on to deliver campaign literature, register voters, or drive them to the polls. In 2002, campaign volunteers and other political activists personally contacted millions of people, resulting in registered voters reporting that they were contacted, on average, 0.7 times per day during the last week of the election.[49]

The development of coordinated campaigns, including the RNC's 72-Hour Task Force, STOMP, and both the Colorado Republicans' and Democrats' 96-Hour Programs, has allowed many congressional candidates to rely in part on party organizations to carry out their field work when those organizations believe the candidate has at least a fighting chance.[50] Whereas the Beeman campaign in California's 3rd district could not rally the support or money to conduct GOTV drives, the Beauprez campaign received assistance from the Colorado Republicans' 96-Hour Program, which paid "volunteers" $200 to participate in its GOTV efforts. The Morella, Van Hollen, Johnson, and Thune campaigns also conducted extensive voter mobilization and benefited from the efforts of party committees and interest groups. Sixty percent of all House campaigns report that local party committees played a moderately important to extremely important role in their registration and GOTV drives, and almost three-quarters of the campaigns maintain that local parties were a moderately important to extremely important source of campaign volunteers.[51]

THE IMPORTANCE OF DIFFERENT COMMUNICATIONS TECHNIQUES

Congressional campaigns disseminate their messages through a variety of media, each having its advantages and disadvantages. Door-to-door campaigning is inexpensive but time consuming. Television advertising requires little commitment of the candidate's time, but it is rarely cheap. Radio advertising, direct mail, and mass telephone calls require accurate targeting to be effective.

Most campaigners believe that direct contact with voters is the best means for winning votes, a recognition of the fact that unmediated personal communication is the best way to connect with voters (see Table 8-3). A firm handshake and a warm smile accompanied by an explanation as to why one wants to serve in Congress, perhaps followed by a direct response to a voter's question, are the best way to convey politically relevant information and build trust—two key ingredients to winning votes. Indeed, other campaign communications intended to win undecided voters or mobilize supporters—whether television, radio, or direct mail, or biography or issue-focused ads—aim to fulfill these objectives.[52] However, with the typical district containing approximately 646,000 constituents, candidates who wish to run competitive races cannot rely solely on communications that involve direct voter contact, to say nothing of the difficulties faced by Senate candidates and an entire state's voting population.

The next most popular communications techniques among candidates in close races are broadcast television, newsletters and direct mail, and free media. Incumbents find television, whether broadcast or cable, more important than do challengers, reflecting the fact that more incumbents can afford to broadcast TV commercials. But open-seat candidates most consistently evaluate television as very important, if not essential, to their campaigns. As shown in Chapter 6, the overwhelming majority of open-seat candidates can afford the high cost of broadcast time, and their races are usually competitive enough to warrant purchasing it.

Incumbents, regardless of the closeness of their elections, and competitive challenger and open-seat candidates also rely heavily on direct mail, newsletters, mass telephone calls, and free media to get out their message. Door-to-door campaigning, newspaper ads, candidate debates and forums, and web sites and e-mail are favored more by challengers and open-seat campaigns than

TABLE 8-3

Campaigners' Perceptions of the Importance of Different Communications Techniques in House Campaigns in 2002

		Incumbents		Challengers		Open-seat candidates	
	All	In jeopardy	Shoo-ins	Hope-fuls	Likely losers	Pros-pects	Mis-matched
Direct contact with voters	91%	86%	92%	91%	91%	94%	94%
Broadcast TV ads	50	72	47	84	23	91	72
Cable TV ads	36	55	32	52	23	58	47
Newsletters or direct mail	70	83	83	84	51	77	83
Radio ads	50	69	51	66	38	57	65
Newspaper ads	33	17	30	38	35	34	53
Free media	77	83	83	81	71	76	76
Door-to-door campaigning	68	72	54	81	69	77	78
Mass telephone calls	54	79	54	62	39	77	56
Billboards or yard signs	65	59	67	72	62	60	88
Debates and forums	52	48	36	72	54	63	56
Internet web sites or e-mail	62	38	48	62	77	54	67
(*Approximate N*)	(318)	(29)	(79)	(32)	(125)	(35)	(18)

Source: The 2002 Congressional Campaign Study.

Notes: Figures are for general election candidates in major-party contested races, excluding those in incumbent-versus-incumbent races responding that a technique was moderately, very, or extremely important. The number of cases varies slightly because some respondents did not answer every question.

by incumbents. Presumably nonincumbents depend more on door-to-door campaigning and newspaper ads because they are inexpensive. Similarly, they look to debates and forums because they are free and allow voters to make side-by-side comparisons between them and their opponent. The patterns for Internet use may be explained by the fact that most incumbents, but not other candidates, possess official congressional web sites that provide excellent introductions to the member's background, issues stances, service to the district, and other information. Unlike challengers and open-seat candidates, members of Congress, particularly those holding safe seats, may not feel the need to invest in an additional web presence.

District characteristics and campaign strategy also affect media usage patterns. Television is a more important communications medium for House campaigns in rural districts than it is for those conducted in urban and suburban settings, due to cost considerations and the mismatch between media markets and House seats in metropolitan areas. Greater population density allows campaigns waged in urban and suburban districts to make greater use of field activities, including distributing campaign literature and canvassing door-to-door, than can campaigns waged in rural areas. Campaigns that target individuals who live in particular neighborhoods, work in certain occupations, or belong to specific segments of the population (such as women, the elderly, or members of an ethnic group) make greater use of direct mail than do campaigns that focus their efforts on less easily identifiable groups, such as single-issue voters.[53]

INDEPENDENT, PARALLEL, AND COORDINATED CAMPAIGN COMMUNICATIONS

Not all of the communications that influence congressional elections are under a candidate's control. The independent, parallel, and coordinated campaigns waged by party and interest groups also can influence the messages voters receive in House and Senate campaigns. Indeed, parties and other groups are believed to have a greater impact on the campaign agenda in some elections than do the candidates, largely because these organizations spend more money than do the candidates' campaign committees. As one would expect, parties and groups are active only in a selected set of races. Indeed, 54 percent of all House campaigners reported that no outside groups tried to set the agenda in their 2002 elections, and another 16 percent stated these organizations' efforts were too unsubstantial to have any impact on their elections (see Table 8-4). Roughly eight out of ten of those who ran in one-sided contests maintained that outside groups were inconsequential in setting the agenda.

Candidates in close races, by contrast, held a different point of view. Two-thirds stated that parties and interest groups sought to set the campaign agenda, and 53 percent reported these organizations' efforts either helped or harmed their candidate.[54] Open-seat prospects were significantly more likely than incumbents and challengers to describe party and interest group communications as having had an impact on the campaign agenda in their races. Parties and interest groups are more uniformly active in open-seat contests, in which outcomes are typically less predictable. They limit their agenda-setting activities in incumbent-challenger contests largely to competitive contests,

TABLE 8-4

Impact of Political Parties and Interest Groups on the Campaign Agenda in 2002

	All	Incumbents		Challengers		Open-seat candidates	
		In jeopardy	Shoo-ins	Hope-fuls	Likely losers	Pros-pects	Mis-matched
Helped candidate	18%	32%	12%	31%	10%	34%	29%
Helped candidate's opponent	12	8	4	16	11	34	24
No impact	16	20	15	19	20	3	12
No outside group activity	54	40	69	34	60	28	35
(*N*)	(311)	(25)	(81)	(32)	(122)	(32)	(17)

Source: The 2002 Congressional Campaign Study.

Notes: Figures are for major-party candidates in contested general elections, excluding candidates in incumbent-versus-incumbent contests. Some columns do not add to 100 percent because of rounding.

viewing the results of the other races as virtually predetermined. Party affiliation had no impact on the campaigners' assessment of the roles that party and interest groups had in setting the agenda in their elections.

SUMMARY

Campaign communications are the centerpiece of any bid for elective office. Congressional candidates disseminate their messages using a variety of media. Television and radio allow candidates to powerfully convey emotional messages. Direct mail and the Internet are less expensive and enable campaigns to disseminate highly targeted, customized messages. Free media coverage is highly sought after, but it can be difficult for some candidates to attract, and it affords campaigns less control over their message than do other forms of communications. Old-fashioned person-to-person contacts between candidates, campaign and local party activists, other volunteers, and voters are among the most effective means of communications.

Of course, the specific media mix that a campaign uses depends on the size of its war chest, the match between the district's boundaries and local media markets, and the talents and preferences of the individual candidate and the campaign's consultants. Another factor that influences candidates' campaign communications is the role that political parties and interest groups choose to play in their elections. Candidates whose elections are characterized by significant party or interest group agenda-setting activity have to compete not only with their opponent for control over the election agenda but also with these organizations. Party and group agenda-setting efforts in close races often require candidates to respond by adjusting their messages and the media they use to convey them. Nevertheless, as is the case in most aspects of congressional elections, incumbents enjoy tremendous advantages when it comes to communicating with voters.

CHAPTER NINE

Candidates, Campaigns, and Electoral Success

During the golden age of parties, party loyalties dominated the voting decisions of the vast majority of citizens and were the chief determinants of the
outcomes of most congressional elections. The decline of voter partisanship in
the 1960s and 1970s paved the way for incumbency to have a greater effect on
election outcomes.[1] Reelection rates routinely exceeded 90 percent for members of the House, as legislators began to make better use of the resources that
the institution put at their disposal. Senators, capitalizing on the perks of their
offices, also enjoyed impressive reelection rates.[2] Although challenger victories
were rare, the types of campaigns that individual candidates mounted, especially in open-seat contests, could make the difference between victory and
defeat.

Incumbency, money, district partisanship, and other factors pertaining to
individual candidates and their campaigns are usually the major determinants
of modern congressional election outcomes. National forces have occasionally
been important. But not since 1994 have congressional elections been nationalized in favor of one party over the other.

What separates winners from losers in contemporary congressional elections? How great an impact do candidate characteristics, political conditions,
campaign strategy, campaign effort, media coverage, and party and interest
group activities have on the percentage of the votes that candidates receive?
Do these factors affect incumbents, challengers, and open-seat contestants
equally? Or do different candidates need to do different things to win elections? This chapter addresses these questions. It also contains a discussion
of the differences between what winners and losers think determines the
outcomes of elections.

HOUSE INCUMBENT CAMPAIGNS

Incumbency is highly important in regard to the kinds of campaigns that candidates mount, and it is the most important determinant of congressional election outcomes.[3] Virtually all House incumbents begin the general election campaign with higher name recognition and voter approval levels, greater political experience, more money, and better campaign organizations than their opponents. Incumbents also benefit from the fact that most constituents and political elites in Washington expect them to win and act accordingly. For the most part, voters cast ballots, volunteers donate time, contributors give money, and news correspondents provide coverage in ways that favor incumbents. Most strategic politicians also behave in ways that contribute to high incumbent success rates. They usually wait until a seat becomes open rather than take on a sitting incumbent and risk a loss that could harm their political careers.

The big leads that most incumbents enjoy at the beginning of the election season make defending those leads the major objective of their campaigns. Incumbent campaigns usually focus more on reinforcing and mobilizing existing bases of support than on winning new ones. The overwhelming advantages that most members of Congress possess make incumbency an accurate predictor of election outcomes in more than nine out of ten House races and three-quarters of all Senate races in which incumbents seek reelection.

However, in post-redistricting elections some House members are forced to compete against one another, in new seats, or in districts that have been heavily redrawn—sometimes in ways that work to their disadvantage. These incumbents must introduce themselves to large numbers of voters who are unfamiliar with their records. New realities often call for new tactics. This was evident in the change of tactics that incumbent Connie Morella employed in 2002. During her previous reelection campaigns, the Maryland congresswoman's strategy revolved around getting her supporters to the polls. As her 1998 campaign manager explained,

> Our candidate has a great personal story and a strong record. . . . Our goals were to remind voters of her commitment to the district and how she has served as an independent voice that represents them in Congress. We targeted federal employees and retirees, women's groups, teachers, the high-tech sector, Republicans, and independents . . . the same groups that supported us before.[4]

The new district put in place prior to the 2002 congressional elections led the Morella campaign to switch tactics. Although its message was largely the same as in previous elections, the campaign used that message for a new purpose—to introduce the candidate to large numbers of Prince George's County voters who were new to Maryland's 8th congressional district, identified with the Democratic Party, and had little knowledge of the congresswoman and her legendary constituency service. Instead of enjoying an advantage with these voters at the beginning of the campaign, Morella's Republican Party affiliation and the voters' relative unfamiliarity with her created a significant disadvantage. The Morella campaign adapted to the new environment by doing something it had not done since she was first elected—attack her opponent.[5]

Even in elections that do not follow redistricting, some incumbents find themselves in jeopardy, and a few challengers have realistic chances of winning. Incumbents who are implicated in a scandal, have cast roll-call votes that are not in accord with constituent opinions, or possess other liabilities need to mount more aggressive campaigns. They must begin campaigning early to maintain their popularity among supporters, to remind voters of their accomplishments in office, and to set the campaign agenda. They also must be prepared to counter the campaigns of the strong challengers who are nominated to run against them and the independent, parallel, and coordinated campaigns that party committees and interest groups wage in suppport of these challengers. Many incumbents in jeopardy face experienced challengers, some of whom amass sufficient financial and organizational resources to mount a serious campaign. A few of the challengers capitalize on their opponent's weaknesses and win.

Because most incumbents have established firm holds on their districts, there is little they can do to increase their victory margins. Incumbents as a group, whether Democrat or Republican; Caucasian, Hispanic, or African American; old or young; male or female, have tremendously favorable odds of being reelected. Few variables—indeed only those identified as such in Table 9-1—have a significant direct effect on the percentages of the vote that incumbents win. Such characteristics as gender, age, race, and occupation, which Chapter 2 showed to be so influential in separating House candidates from the general population, typically have no impact on the votes incumbents receive.[6] Primary challenges from within their own party rarely harm the reelection prospects of incumbents who defeat primary opponents. Moreover, incumbents' targeting strategies, issue stances, and spending on campaign communications do not significantly increase their shares of the vote in the general election.[7] Party and interest group outside communications efforts also rarely spell the difference between success and defeat in incumbent-challenger races.

The first figure in Table 9-1, labeled the base vote, represents the percentage of the vote that a House incumbent in a typical two-party contested race would have received if all the other factors were set to zero.[8] That is, a

TABLE 9-1

Significant Predictors of House Incumbents' Vote Shares

	Percentage of vote
Base vote	57.28
District is very different or completely new	−1.96
Partisan bias (per one-point advantage in party registration)	+0.15
Incumbent's ideological strength	+0.92
Incumbent implicated in scandal	−3.71
Challenger spending on campaign communications (per $100,000)	−0.84
Incumbent received most endorsements from local media	+5.22
Republican national partisan tide	+2.02

(*N* = 97)

Sources: The 2002 Congressional Campaign Study, Federal Election Commission, and Political Money Line.

Notes: The figures were generated using ordinary least squares regression to analyze data for general election candidates in major-party contested races, excluding those in incumbent-versus-incumbent races. Complete regression statistics are presented in note 8.

hypothetical incumbent who ran for reelection in 2002 in a district that was largely unchanged by redistricting and comprised roughly equal numbers of registered Democratic and Republican voters; who had developed a reputation as a moderate member of Congress; and who spent no money, faced a challenger who spent no money, was not endorsed by most local editorial boards, and was in a race that was not affected by the pro-Republican national partisan tide in 2002, would have won about 57 percent of the vote.

Certain districts and states lend themselves to the election of particular kinds of candidates. Districts that are heavily affected by redistricting, including the one in which Morella and Van Hollen competed, are usually less favorable to incumbents than are others. Incumbents who ran in 2002 in newly drawn seats or in seats that were very different from those in which they previously competed, typically suffered a net loss of about 2 percent of the vote that was not experienced by incumbents who ran in seats that were largely unchanged by redistricting.

Partisanship also is important. Districts populated mainly by Democratic voters (often urban districts that are home to many lower-middle-class, poor, or minority voters) typically elect Democrats; those populated by Republican voters (frequently suburban and more affluent districts) usually elect

Republicans. The partisan bias of the district (the difference between the percentage of registered voters who belong to a candidate's party and the percentage who belong to the opponent's party) has a positive impact on incumbents' electoral prospects.[9] As the third figure in the table indicates, for every 1 percent increase in the partisan advantage that incumbents enjoy among registered voters, they receive a 0.15 percent boost at the polls (controlling for the other factors in the table). A Democratic incumbent who represents a one-sided district with seventy-five registered Democratic voters for every twenty-five registered Republicans typically starts out the election with a 7.5 percentage point (a fifty-point advantage in party registration multiplied by 0.15) vote advantage over a Democratic incumbent in a district that is evenly split between Democratic and Republican voters. Partisan bias is an important source of incumbency advantage because most House members represent districts that are populated primarily by members of their party.

Those few House members who represent districts in which the balance of voter registration does not favor their party may be in danger of losing reelection. That was the case in the Morella–Van Hollen race. Following redistricting the partisan composition of Maryland's 8th district—which had always favored Democrats—switched from roughly 50 percent Democratic, 38 percent Republican, and 12 percent who were affiliated with no party or a minor party, to approximately 55 percent Democratic, 25 percent Republican, and 10 percent unaffiliated. The vote share of a Republican incumbent competing in a constituency similar to Maryland's old 8th district would have been 2 points lower than that of an incumbent in a district where Democratic and Republican voters were equal in number. Although a relatively large deficit for an incumbent—most incumbents benefit from substantial surpluses—this partisan bias compares favorably with the one that materialized in 2002, which typically would produce a 4.5 percent smaller vote share for the incumbent than would occur in a district with no partisan bias.

Most incumbents begin the general election campaign relatively well known and liked by their constituents. Many voters have a general sense of where their House member falls on the ideological spectrum. Like Douglas Ose, the shoo-in incumbent in California's 3rd district, most House members come from districts made up primarily of individuals who in general share their party and ideological preferences. As a result, these House members rarely face a strong general election challenge from the opposing party, though some Republican members need to be concerned with facing a stiff primary test from the right, and their Democratic counterparts must be wary of a similar challenge from the left.[10] It is moderate members of Congress, who usually represent less ideologically consistent, more middle-of-the-road voters, who are at greater political risk in the general election. They need to build broader electoral coalitions, and they often face centrist challengers who are able to position themselves to compete aggressively for the same swing voters. These representational dynamics work to the advantage of staunch conservatives, such as Ose and Republican House leaders, and unabashed liberal Democrats, including most Democratic congressional leaders. They collect about 3 points more than do moderate House incumbents of either party, such as Morella.[11]

Of course, not all incumbents begin their reelection campaigns with clean slates. Members of Congress who are caught up in a scandal run the risk of angering or disappointing constituents, attracting strong opposition, or both. Some scandals involve many members of Congress. In a 1992 House banking scandal, for example, revelations that more than 325 House members had made 8,331 overdrafts at the House bank undermined the reelection campaigns of many of them. Other scandals involve only one or a few legislators, such as those involving vacations, meals, and other gifts accepted from lobbyists; outrageous off-the-cuff (or not so-off-the-cuff) statements; or extramarital affairs. Incumbents typically pay a price at the polls for being implicated in a scandal. In 2002 it cost them almost 4 percent of the vote.

Scandal, ideology, and district conditions, usually in place before the start of the campaign season, can be important in determining an incumbent's vote share. But most of the aspects of incumbent campaigning that voters normally associate with elections do not have much influence in incumbent-challenger races. The targeting approaches that incumbents use and the themes and issues they stress do not significantly affect their vote margins.[12] Nor do the dollars incumbents spend on direct mail, television, radio, and newspaper advertising, field work, or other communications make a significant contribution to the percentage of the vote that they win.[13]

Following the usual pattern, incumbent spending in 2002 increased in direct response to the closeness of the race.[14] Shoo-ins, such as Ose, who ran against underfunded challengers undertook fairly modest reelection efforts by incumbents' standards, assembling relatively small organizations and spending moderate sums of money. Those who were pitted against well-funded challengers, however, followed Morella's example and mounted big campaigns.

Although the communications expenditures and other campaign activities of incumbents are not significantly related to higher vote margins, they are not inconsequential. A more accurate interpretation is that incumbent campaigning generally works to reinforce rather than to expand a candidate's existing base of support. Incumbents who are in the most trouble—because they represent marginal districts, have been redistricted in ways that do not favor them, have been implicated in a scandal, have failed to keep in touch with voters, or are ideologically out of step with their constituents—usually spend the most. Most either succeed in reinforcing their electoral bases or watch their shares of the vote dip slightly from those of previous years. Others watch their victory margins become perilously low. The high-powered campaigns these incumbents wage might make the difference between winning and losing. In a few cases, probably no amount of spending would make a difference. Scandal, poor performance, and other factors simply put reelection beyond the reach of a few House members. Whether an incumbent in a close race wins or loses, however, that individual would undoubtedly have done worse absent an extensive campaign effort.

House challengers' expenditures do reduce incumbents' vote shares somewhat. The typical challenger spent roughly $150,000 on voter contact in 2002, shaving about 1.3 percent more off the typical incumbent's vote share than a challenger who spent no money or just a few thousand dollars. Strong challengers who ran against weak incumbents were able to raise and spend substantially more. Hopeful challengers committed an average of $660,000 to campaign communications, which drove down the portion of the vote won by the typical incumbent in jeopardy by between 5 and 6 percentage points. Individual challengers who spent even more generally drew greater numbers of votes away from incumbents, although the impact of campaign spending may diminish in the most expensive races.[15]

Attracting favorable media coverage can help an incumbent's reelection efforts. Editorial endorsements in local newspapers can be extremely influential because many voters read them and some take them into the voting booth. Incumbents who receive the lion's share of the endorsements from local media outlets are likely to benefit at the polls.[16] In 2002 roughly 85 percent of all incumbents in major-party contested races benefited from this advantage. It improved their electoral performance by roughly 5 points over incumbents who did not enjoy such positive relations with the fourth estate. The efforts that House candidates and their press secretaries make to cultivate relationships with news correspondents are clearly worthwhile.

National partisan tides, which are beyond any one candidate's control, can affect how an incumbent fares in an election. The terrorist attacks of September 11, 2001, the war in Afghanistan, and the possibility of war with Iraq encouraged voters to focus on foreign policy and national defense, which usually works to the advantage of a sitting president and his party. These also are the issues that traditionally have been favorably associated with the GOP. President Bush sought to capitalize on this advantage by asking voters to elect GOP candidates, with whom he claimed he could better work to protect the security of the United States. Foreign policy, as well as some less salient national issues, gave the typical Republican incumbent a 2 percent boost in the vote that the typical Democratic incumbent did not receive. The pro-Republican atmosphere in 2002 helped the GOP buck the trend in which the president's party usually loses seats in midterm elections.

These generalizations hold for the vast majority of incumbent campaigns waged in 2002, as well as for most of those held throughout the 1990s and in 2000. However, a relatively small but important group of incumbent-challenger races illustrate the power of outside campaigning. As described in Chapters 4 and 5, the independent, parallel, and coordinated campaigns that political parties and interest groups mount are by and large outside a candidate's control. These campaigns often involve significant sums, including money candidates help raise by participating in joint fundraising committees and other party and interest group fundraising efforts. Outside compaigning has the potential to change the dynamics of campaigns because it forces candidates to compete with other organizations, as well as with each other, when trying to set the election agenda and influence the political debate. Party and interest group communications often result in contests becoming more competitive and contentious.

Approximately 42 percent of all candidates in two-party contested incumbent-challenger races report that at least one group mounted a significant effort to influence the campaign agenda.[17] The vast majority of them were in competitive contests. Their districts had more equal numbers of registered Democrats and Republicans than those in which parties or interest groups chose not to communicate directly with voters.[18] The incumbents holding these seats also held more moderate views.[19]

The outside campaigns of political parties and interest groups had a variety of effects on these contests.[20] Much of their political advertising was negative or comparative, with the result that scandal had a more detrimental effect on these incumbents' reelection bids than it did on incumbent contests in general. Challenger spending on campaign communications took on heightened importance, whereas the effects of incumbent spending were the same as in other incumbent contests. Newspaper endorsements brought incumbents somewhat fewer benefits, presumably because the plethora of political advertising to which voters were exposed weakened the endorsements' effects, as well as the influence of the candidates' own communications. Even independent expenditures and issue advocacy ads intended to help a candidate can cloud voters' perceptions of the race if they are "off message," presenting information that is inconsistent with the imagery and issue stances a campaign is struggling to project. The sheer volume of the candidate, party, and interest group communications in these elections washed out the pro-Republican national trend that was visible in other 2002 House contests, producing no effect on the percentage of the votes that incumbents won in these races.

Outside communications are more likely to harm than help incumbents who generally win when their elections are low-key affairs that are ignored by national party committees and interest groups.

The House race in Maryland's 8th district illustrates this generalization. Party committees and interest groups conducted more television, radio, direct-mail, and get-out-the-vote efforts intended to help Van Hollen than to aid Morella.[21] The ads inundated the airwaves, found their way into voters' mailboxes, and received extensive free media coverage. They influenced the dynamics of the race and probably contributed to the challenger's victory.

HOUSE CHALLENGER CAMPAIGNS

Most challengers begin the general election at a disadvantage. Lacking a broad base of support, these candidates must build one. Challengers need to mount aggressive campaigns to become visible, build name recognition, give voters reasons to support them, and overcome the initial advantages of their opponents. Most challenger campaigns also must communicate messages that not only will attract uncommitted voters but also persuade some voters to abandon their pro-incumbent loyalties in favor of the challenger. The typical House challenger is in a position similar to that of a novice athlete pitted against a world-class sprinter. The incumbent has experience, talent, professional handlers, funding, equipment, and crowd support. The challenger has few, if any, of these assets and has a monumental task to accomplish in a limited amount of time. Predictably, most challengers end up eating their opponents' dust. Still, not every novice athlete or every congressional challenger is destined to suffer the agony of defeat. A strong challenger who is able to assemble the money and organization to devise and carry out a good game plan may be able to win if the incumbent stumbles.

Even though the vast majority of challengers ultimately lose, the experience and resources that they bring to their races have an impact on their ability to win votes. In short, challenger campaigning matters. The figures in Table 9-2 reveal that challengers' nomination contests, election expenditures, targeting, strategies, campaign messages, and media relations affect their vote shares in meaningful ways.[22] The same is true of national forces that occasionally work to favor the candidates of one party over the candidates of the other.

The table shows that a hypothetical House challenger will finish with about 25 percent of the vote—far from victory—under the following circumstances: the candidate runs in a district that is evenly split between registered Republicans and Democrats and is handed a major-party nomination without a

TABLE 9-2

Significant Predictors of House Challengers' Vote Shares

	Percentage of vote
Base vote	25.29
Partisan bias (per one-point advantage in party registration)	+0.13
Contested primary	+2.46
Targeted own party members, independents, or both	+2.50
Advertising focused on challenger or incumbent's issue positions	+1.84
Challenger spending on campaign communications (per $100,000)	+0.31
Incumbent spending on campaign communications (per $100,000)	+0.56
Challenger received most endorsements from local media	+5.50
Republican national partisan tide	+2.50
(*N = 138*)	

Sources: The 2002 Congressional Campaign Study, Federal Election Commission, and Political Money Line.

Notes: The figures were generated using ordinary least squares regression to analyze data for general election candidates in major-party contested races, excluding those in incumbent-versus-incumbent races. Complete regression statistics are presented in note 22.

primary fight; the candidate uses an unorthodox targeting strategy, fails to offer voters a clear choice on the issues, runs a race bereft of all candidate campaign spending, and receives few endorsements from the local news media; and the contest is unaffected by national partisan forces.

Challengers who run under more favorable circumstances fare better. In most cases the partisan composition of the district works to the advantage of the incumbent, but a few challengers are fortunate enough to run in districts that include more members of their party. Challengers in districts in which the balance of registered voters favors their party by 10 percent begin the general election with a 1.3 percent advantage over those who run in neutral districts. Those few challengers who run in districts that favor their party by 20 percent possess an advantage of between 2 and 3 percent of the vote.

Political experience and campaign professionalism have indirect effects on a challenger's ability to win votes. As explained in Chapters 2 and 3, challengers with office-holding or significant nonelective political experience are more likely than are political amateurs to run when their odds of winning are greatest, to capture their parties' nomination, and to assemble organizations that draw on the expertise of salaried professionals and political consultants. Moreover, political experience and campaign professionalism help challengers to raise money, as Chapter 6 demonstrated. They also help challengers attract free media coverage and endorsements, as well as favorable outside communications by party committees and interest groups, as shown in Chapters 4 and 5. Challenger campaigns that are staffed with experienced political operatives also are presumably better at targeting, message development, communications, and grassroots activities than those run by amateurs.[23]

Contested primaries, which only rarely have negative general election consequences for the incumbents who survive them, have a positive impact on the prospects of House challengers who emerge from them victorious. It should be recalled from Chapter 2 that opposing-incumbent primaries are often hotly contested when an incumbent is perceived to be vulnerable and are usually won by strategic candidates who know how to wage strong campaigns. The organizational effort, campaign activities, and media coverage associated with contested primaries provide the winners with larger bases of support and more name recognition than they would have received had the primary not been contested. The momentum that House challengers get from contested primaries, and the incumbent weaknesses that give rise to those primaries in the first place, lead to stronger performances in general elections. In 2002 those challengers who had to defeat one or more opponents in a primary wound up winning between 2 and 3 points more than challengers who were merely handed their party's nomination.

General election campaign strategy is very important. Challengers who target members of their own party, independents, or both win more votes than those who use less conventional strategies, such as targeting all registered voters, or no strategy at all. Challengers who run issue-oriented campaigns that focus on their or their opponent's policy stances win more votes than those who focus on character and experience or who fail to deliver a clear campaign message. Van Hollen, for example, aggressively courted Democrats and swing voters. He campaigned on a variety of issues, including education, the environment, gun control, and women's issues. However, he drew the sharpest line between himself and Morella when he focused on partisanship and explained that the most important thing 8th district voters could do to get rid of Republican control in Congress was to vote for him—a Democrat—instead of the Republican incumbent. Challengers who used partisan targeting strategies in 2002 received, on average, a 2 to 3 percent boost in their vote share. Those who drew issue-oriented distinctions between themselves and their opponents received a 2 percent boost.

Not surprisingly, campaign spending is another factor that has a significant impact on the vote shares challengers receive. For every $100,000 that 2002 House challengers spent on television, radio, campaign literature, direct mail, mass telephone calls, the Internet, campaign field work, or some other form of campaign communication, they won an additional 0.31 percent of the vote. Challengers in 2002 spent an average of $150,000 on campaign communications, garnering the typical challenger an additional 0.46 percent of the ballot. Incumbent spending on campaign communications, largely a reaction to the closeness of the race and the efforts of strong challengers and their supporters, is not significantly related to challengers' vote shares. Large communications expenditures by both candidates are strongly associated with closely decided incumbent-challenger races. Van Hollen and Morella spent approximately $2.3 million each on campaign communications in a race that the challenger won by 4 percent of the vote. Howard Beeman spent only about $13,000 to communicate with voters in his twenty-eight-point loss to Douglas Ose, who spent about $95,000 in their California House race. That the typical 2002 House challenger spent less than $200,000 on campaign communications helps to explain why so few of them won and why challengers generally fare poorly.

Media relations, which involve a courtship of sorts between candidates and local media outlets, also can have significant consequences for an election. The 5 percent or so of all House challengers who are endorsed by the local press typically watch their vote shares increase between 5 and 6 percent. National partisan tides, over which challengers have no control, can be important. The pro-Republican trend of 2002 provided GOP challengers with an extra 2 to 3 percentage points.

How best to allocate scarce financial resources is a constant concern for strategists in challenger campaigns. Are radio or television commercials more effective than campaign literature? How effective is direct mail at influencing voters compared with less-precisely tailored and less well-targeted forms of advertising? Is it worthwhile to invest money in newspaper ads or grassroots activities commonly referred to as campaign field work?

Direct mail and campaign literature, which can be directed to specific voting blocs, are among the most cost-effective campaign activities.[24] For every $10,000 a challenger campaign spends on direct mail, it gains an average of about 0.24 percent of the vote. The typical challenger campaign spent about $15,000 on direct mail in 2002, helping to increase its share of the vote by 0.36 percent. Campaign literature provides a somewhat lower return, yielding 0.14 points per $10,000. Challengers spent an average of $21,000 on literature, which is associated with a net pickup of 0.28 points at the polls. Hopeful challengers spent considerably more on these activities, roughly $50,000 on direct mail and $78,000 on literature, which yielded them an extra 1.2 percent and 1.1 percent of the vote, respectively.

Television commercials are less targeted, are considerably more expensive, and bring somewhat lower returns per dollar than do the activities already mentioned. The typical House challenger campaign spent about $60,000 on television ads in 2002, which was associated with an increase of about 0.42 percent of the vote. Hopeful challengers spent almost $280,000 on TV ads, bringing them roughly 2 points more at the polls. Van Hollen and the few other challengers who had the wherewithal to spend about $775,000 on television advertising saw their vote shares increase by 5 points. Radio ads, which fall between direct mail and newspaper ads in terms of targeting, can have a positive impact on some challenger races, but they do not significantly increase challengers' vote shares overall.

Newspaper advertisements, purchased by little more than half of all 2002 challenger campaigns, are typically a low-priority, low-budget item. The typical challenger spent about $740 on newspaper ads, for no net increase in vote returns.

Field work is the most labor-intensive form of electioneering. It differs from direct mail and television advertising in that, if done properly, it requires both skillful targeting and a corps of committed campaign workers. Thus, the money that the typical challenger spends on field work does not perfectly describe the candidate's field operations. As such, contact between candidates and voters, and other field activities, which are often coordinated by specialized consultants and carried out by volunteer workers, do not have a statistically measurable impact on challengers' vote shares even though they are believed to be effective forms of campaigning.

Finally, the independent, parallel, and coordinated campaign efforts of party committees and interest groups work to the advantage of the challengers they are intended to help. Challengers in elections where parties or advocacy groups try to set the campaign agenda do 5 points better at the polls than challengers in general, even absent any candidate spending or other activities.[25] Despite the benefit challengers gain from these party and group efforts, many are ambivalent about them, and with good reason. Outside spending neutralizes the effects of some important elements of challenger strategy, including those associated with voter targeting and campaign advertising. It takes control away from the campaign and puts it in the hands of others, blurring the message the campaign intends to convey.

In sum, most House challengers lose because the odds are so heavily stacked against them. Those few who run in favorable or competitive districts, compete against a vulnerable incumbent, assemble the resources needed to communicate with voters, develop and implement a sound campaign strategy that blends partisan targeting with an issue-oriented message, and spend their money wisely win more votes than those who do not. The same is true of those who curry favor with the media and benefit from party and interest group outside spending. Despite doing all of these things correctly, these challengers rarely win enough votes to defeat an incumbent. The partisan composition of most House districts, the preelection activities that incumbents undertake to cultivate the support of constituents, and their success in warding off talented and well-funded challengers are critical in determining the outcome of most incumbent-challenger races.

Nevertheless, politics is a game that is often played at the margins. Not all House incumbents begin the general election as shoo-ins and go on to win. The few who hold competitive seats, are implicated in scandal, are out of step with their constituents, draw a strong major-party opponent, or are targeted for defeat by the opposing party and independent-spending interest groups often find themselves in a precarious position. Many of these incumbents spend huge sums of money, sometimes to no avail. If the challengers who run against them are able to apply the lessons they learned while working in politics and assemble the money and organizational resources to wage a strong campaign, they can put their opponents on the defensive. Challengers have some chance of winning if they set the campaign agenda, carefully target their base and groups of potential supporters, tailor their messages to appeal to those voters, and communicate their messages through paid ads, free media, and strong field operations. Challengers who can attract newspaper endorsements and considerable outside spending by parties and interest groups have even better odds. A win by a challenger is typically the result of both incumbent failure and a strong challenger campaign. Numerous House members were anxious about their reelection prospects before the 2002 campaign. Some of them retired. Of those who sought reelection, fifty-four House incumbents were considered somewhat at risk at some point during the general election season. Challengers succeeded in defeating only four of them in the general election.

HOUSE OPEN-SEAT CAMPAIGNS

Elections for open House seats are usually won by much smaller margins than incumbent-challenger races. Once a seat becomes open, several factors come into play. The partisanship of the district and the skills and resources that candidates and their organizations bring to bear have a greater influence on elections when there is no incumbent who can draw on voters' personal loyalties. Because voters usually lack strong personal loyalties to either candidate, campaigning becomes more important. The same is true of local media endorsements and national partisan trends. The factors that significantly affect the outcome of open-seat House races are listed in Table 9-3.[26]

TABLE 9-3

Significant Predictors of House Open-Seat Candidates' Vote Shares

	Percentage of vote
Base vote	24.15
Partisan bias (per one-point advantage in party registration)	+0.17
Targeted own party members, independents, or both	+4.68
Republican ran on Republican issues	+7.42
Open-seat candidate spending on campaign communications:	
$400,000	+25.44
$600,000	+26.98
$800,000	+28.08
$1,000,000	+28.93
$2,000,000	+31.57
$3,000,000	+33.11
Opponent spending on campaign communications:	
$400,000	−20.46
$600,000	−21.70
$800,000	−22.58
$1,000,000	−23.27
$2,000,000	−25.39
$3,000,000	−26.63
Candidate received most endorsements from local media	+6.70
Republican national partisan tide	+8.52

(*N* = 50)

Sources: The 2002 Congressional Campaign Study, Federal Election Commission, and Political Money Line.

Notes: The figures were generated using ordinary least squares regression to analyze data for general election candidates in major-party contested races, excluding those in incumbent-versus-incumbent races. Complete regression statistics are presented in note 26.

The partisan bias of open seats is important. Candidates who run for open seats in districts where the balance of voter registration favors their party do much better than others. Those who run for open seats in districts where the registration balance favors their party by 10 percent have, on average, a 1.7 percent vote advantage over those who compete in districts with the same number of Democrats and Republicans.

Campaign strategy is critical to the outcome of an open-seat contest. Campaigns that targeted party members, independents, or both in 2002 increased their votes by 5 percent over those that did not consider partisanship when formulating their targeting plans. Candidates' issue positions also had a large impact. Unlike incumbents, open-seat candidates do not have to defend a congressional voting record, nor are they in a position to emphasize their performance in office. Unlike challengers, they are not in a situation where they can attack a sitting House member for failing to tend adequately to constituents' needs, nor can they use a member's congressional roll-call votes to contrast the incumbent's issue positions with their own. Open-seat candidates are usually best served when they put together an issue-based message that is powerful enough to inspire a strong turnout by voters who identify with their party and to attract the support of swing voters. The 42 percent of the Republicans who campaigned on the war on terrorism, the pending hostilities with Iraq, other defense-related issues, or taxes—issues that are favorably associated with the GOP—performed better in 2002 than did Republicans who focused on other issues. This was to be expected given the salience of those issues and the impact they had on individuals' congressional voting decisions, which were discussed in Chapter 4. Democratic open-seat candidates did not experience a corresponding lift at the polls when they focused on issues favorably associated with either their party or with the GOP. Again, this reflects the limited impact that the traditional Democratic issues had on individuals' voting decisions in 2002.

Candidates in open-seat elections stand to make large gains in name recognition and voter support through their campaign communications. In contrast to candidates in incumbent-challenger races, both candidates in open-seat elections clearly benefit from spending on campaign advertising and voter contact. A campaign's initial expenditures are particularly influential because they help voters become aware of a candidate and his or her message. Further expenditures, although still important, have a lower rate of return; as more voters learn about the candidates and their issue positions the effects of campaign spending diminish. An open-seat candidate facing an opponent who spends virtually no money gains, on average, an additional 25 percent above the base vote of 24 percent for the first $400,000 spent to communicate with voters. That same candidate gains an additional 1.5 percent of the vote (a total increase of almost 27 percent) when he or she increases spending by $200,000. An expenditure of $3 million would increase a candidate's vote share by about 1.5 percent over the amount gained for the first $2 million in communications expenditures—the same increase a candidate wins when moving from $400,000 to $600,000.

Lopsided spending is unusual in open-seat contests; rarely does a candidate spend $3 million, $2 million, $600,000, or even $100,000 against an opponent who spends virtually nothing. More often, these elections feature two well-funded opponents. When the campaigns spend nearly the same amount on communications, their expenditures come close to offsetting each other. Once the campaigns have completely saturated the airwaves, overstuffed the mailboxes, and left about half a dozen or so voice mail messages, the quality and timing of their communications may have a bigger influence on the election outcome than the dollars each ultimately spends to reach out to voters. In the 2002 race in Colorado's 7th district, for example, Beauprez spent about $1.2 million on campaign communications to Feeley's approximately $680,000, but Beauprez won by only 121 votes.

The amounts that open-seat campaigns spend on most forms of campaign communication are positively related to the number of votes they receive, but the precise effects of the communications are difficult to evaluate because relatively few open-seat contests take place in any given election year. It is possible, however, to make some generalizations about the relative importance of the techniques open-seat candidates use to get out their message. Open-seat candidates spend substantial portions of their campaign budgets on campaign literature, direct mail, TV, and radio. Of these communications devices, literature, direct mail, and radio—which can be directed to specific individuals or voting blocs—have the greatest electoral impact.[27]

The mass media also play an important role in open-seat House races. Experienced politicians who have strong campaign organizations and run for open seats in districts that are made up mostly of voters who belong to their party usually receive better treatment from the media than do their opponents. Open-seat candidates who win the endorsements of the local press typically pick up an additional 7 percent of the vote.

The partisan tide that lifted Republican House candidates in incumbent-challenger races in 2002 had an even greater influence on campaigns for open seats. Republican candidates in the latter contests, on average, benefited from an 8 to 9 point boost in their vote shares, giving them a considerable edge over their Democratic opponents.

Competitive open-seat contests usually attract substantial independent, parallel, and coordinated campaign activity by parties and interest groups. Voters in Colorado's 7th congressional district, for example, were exposed to appreciably more campaign activities than were voters nationally in 2002. They reported seeing between twelve and thirteen television ads during the last week of the election, in contrast with the national average of 7.6 ads. They also received an average of 4.2 pieces of direct mail, as opposed to the 2.5 pieces that were the national average. The number of personal contacts these voters had with the Beauprez and Feeley campaigns was 23 percent greater than the number of contacts voters nationwide reported receiving from their House candidates. Saturation advertising has significant effects: 92 percent of the voters in Colorado's 7th district reported seeing or hearing something about the congressional election in which they were able to vote, as opposed to 68 percent of all voters nationally.[28]

Just as outside advertising can change the dynamics of incumbent-challenger races, it can influence the conduct of open-seat elections.[29] It rewards candidates whose campaigns use party affiliation to guide their tactics. Both Democratic and Republican campaigns competing in districts that were inundated by significant outside advertising received a greater boost from their use of voter partisanship to guide their targeting than did campaigns where parties and groups did not seek to influence the campaign agenda. Similarly, Republicans campaigning in contests featuring a high volume of party and interest group activity reaped greater electoral benefits from emphasizing pro-Republican issues, including the war on terrorism, national defense, and tax cuts, than GOP candidates who did so in elections free of party and interest group agenda-setting activities.

Party and advocacy group independent, parallel, and coordinated campaign efforts conducted to influence individual open-seat contests also reduce the impact of broader, less-focused national partisan forces. Such forces appear to be drowned out by the volume of communications that concentrate voters' attention on the candidates and issues involved in a particular race. Local newspaper endorsements also have little effect under such circumstances, presumably because they lose their potency when voters are saturated with political information.

SENATE CAMPAIGNS

The small number of Senate elections that occur in a given election year and the differences in the size and politics of the states in which they take place make it difficult to generalize about Senate campaigns. Nevertheless, a few broad statements are possible. Chief among them is that incumbents possess substantial advantages over challengers. The advantages that incumbency conveys in Senate elections are similar to those it bestows in House elections. Most Senate incumbents enjoy fundraising advantages, higher levels of name recognition, and more political experience—particularly in running a statewide campaign—than their opponents.

Yet the advantages that senators enjoy are not as great as those that House members have over their opponents. Most Senate challengers and open-seat candidates have previously served in the House, as governor, or in some other public capacity and are more formidable opponents than their House counterparts. Their previous political experience helps Senate challengers assemble the financial and organizational resources and attract the media coverage needed to run a competitive campaign.[30]

One of the most important differences between Senate and House contests is the effect of incumbent expenditures on election outcomes. Although increased challenger spending has a negative effect on incumbents' margins in both Senate and House elections, it is only in Senate races that spending by incumbents is positively related to the number of votes they receive. Incumbent expenditures on campaign communications are not as important as challenger expenditures, but the amounts both sides spend are influential in determining the victor in Senate elections.[31]

This difference between House and Senate contests is due to three major factors. First, because Senate challengers are usually better qualified, Senate elections tend to be closer than House contests. Second, senators tend to have weaker bonds with their constituents than do representatives. Senators' six-year terms and greater responsibilities in Washington discourage them from meeting as frequently with voters as House members do. Senators' larger constituencies also prevent them from establishing the kinds of personal ties that House members have with voters.[32] Senators from rural states are something of an exception to this norm; voters' expectations encourage them to invest considerable effort in forming personal relationships with their constituents. Third, the greater diversity of their constituencies also means that senators are more likely to offend some voters when carrying out their legislative activities. Because of these differences, campaign spending and campaigning in general are more likely to affect the electoral prospects of Senate than House incumbents.

Senate elections bear further comparison with House contests. Scandal and the partisan bias of the constituency influence the results of elections for both the upper and lower chambers. Senate campaigns' targeting strategies and issue selection also are believed to be important.[33] Whereas primary challenges have no detrimental effects on the election prospects of House incumbents, they harm those of incumbents in Senate campaigns.[34]

The 2002 Senate election in South Dakota illustrates many of the preceding generalizations. In particular, it highlights the importance of incumbency, an experienced challenger, issues, voter targeting, message, and field work.[35] In that campaign the Republican representative, Thune, sought to defeat the sitting Democratic senator, Johnson. Johnson was considered highly vulnerable, having first won the seat in 1996 by fewer than 8,600 votes—a margin of 2.6 percent. Thune, a three-term House incumbent, who was recruited to the race by President Bush, enjoyed a landslide in his previous race for the state's at-large House seat, garnering 73.4 percent of the vote. The third candidate, Libertarian Kurt Evans, spent virtually no money; he withdrew from the race prior to election day and endorsed Thune. However, his name remained on the ballot, and this would prove consequential.[36]

South Dakota is a rural, Republican-leaning state. Forty-eight percent of its registered voters are Republicans, 39 percent are Democrats, and 13 percent are unaffiliated or registered to a minor party. George W. Bush won just over three-fifths of the state's popular vote in 2000, and former Republican Senate leader Robert Dole won 47 percent, to Clinton's 43 percent and Perot's 10 percent, in 1996. The state has an inexpensive media market, making it possible for candidates, parties, and interest groups to saturate the airwaves with television ads. In 2002 the state was host to a competitive House race and a hotly contested and negative gubernatorial contest.

Both Johnson and Thune had easy routes to their respective parties' nominations. Johnson won unopposed, and Thune largely ignored and easily dispatched Paul Werner, a political amateur who spent virtually no money, in the Republican primary.[37] The incumbent had a modest financial advantage in the general election, outspending the challenger by $7 million to $6 million. Each campaign spent about $1.5 million on television ads and considerable sums on direct mail, mass telephone calls, voter mobilization drives, and other campaign communications. Both candidates held an unusually large number of dinners and ice cream socials because South Dakotans, like Iowans and New Hampshirites, expect their candidates to court them personally.

The Thune campaign's strategy consisted primarily of mobilizing the Republican base. Given the state's pro-Republican bias, the Johnson campaign sought to turn out Democrats and win the support of independent voters and "crossover Republicans"—GOP voters who occasionally will support a moderate Democrat. The Johnson campaign also worked with the state Democratic committee to mobilize Native Americans. As indicated in Chapters 7 and 8, Johnson emphasized his use of his position on the Senate Appropriations Committee and collaborations with Senate Democratic leader and fellow South Dakotan Tom Daschle to deliver federal projects to the state. Thune campaigned on so-called prairie values and his close association with President Bush.

Political parties and interest groups were very active in the race. As discussed in Chapter 4, the parties invested hundreds of thousands of dollars in contributions and coordinated expenditures, and national party organizations transferred millions of dollars to the state to help finance independent, parallel, and coordinated campaigns. Much of the money was spent on television, radio, direct mail, and voter identification, registration, and get-out-the-vote efforts. Interest groups also made millions of dollars in contributions and committed huge amounts of money to finance similar campaign activities. Indeed, parties and interest groups spent roughly twice as much on television advertising as the candidates did.

One result of all of this outside spending, which was mainly fueled by soft money, was that South Dakota voters were deluged with campaign communications. Television expenditures alone reached a state record of $11 million— the equivalent of roughly $33 per voter. Candidates, parties, and interest groups also mailed 174 unique pieces of direct mail focused on the Senate contest, with some voters reporting that they received up to ten pieces of mail a day.[38] Party and interest group electronic media ads and direct mail added considerably to the negativity of the race. As indicated in Chapter 5, the fact that Johnson asked the League of Conservation Voters to take its television ad off the air suggests that some of this outside spending was considered harmful by the candidate it was intended to help.

National party leaders assumed prominent roles in the race, and the national media billed it as a showdown between President Bush and Democratic leader Daschle. GOP leaders, including the president, made numerous visits to the state, as did their Democratic counterparts. The Republicans were able to attract more free air time for their candidates; President Bush's visits were covered by news media from touchdown to takeoff. Nevertheless, Thune's ties to Bush may not have been as helpful as were Johnson's links to Daschle. Logistical snafus were one source of harm to the Thune campaign. Bush's visits to South Dakota excited Republican activists and helped energize the party's get-out-the-vote efforts, but some of the president's visits resulted in negative press, as when several elementary school students who had been waiting outside in the cold were turned away from an event for which they had tickets. A more serious source of damage had to do with local issues. South Dakota had been suffering from severe drought during most of 2002, and many in the state were expecting the president to announce a large relief package during one of his campaign stops. When he instead announced that he opposed providing the state with relief, he hit a sour note with South Dakotans. It caused some voters to question both Thune's close ties to the president and his commitment to the state. The president's visits also may have encouraged voters to focus more on Thune's "I can work with the president" message than on his "prairie values" theme. This helped Johnson further establish himself as the candidate who had delivered for South Dakota and would continue to do so.

Two other factors worked to Johnson's advantage. First, he and the Democratic Party had a better targeting strategy and voter turnout operation than did the Republicans. By reaching beyond his base, Johnson was able to build a larger coalition than Thune. The Democrats' mobilization of Native Americans helped Johnson win the three South Dakota counties with significant Native American populations by more than 5,000 votes. Second, Kurt Evans's candidacy came back to haunt Thune. The Libertarian won 3,070 votes, which presumably would have gone to the Republican.

It is impossible to tell exactly what factors led to the outcome of a race decided by a mere 524 votes. The candidates' experience and political records, their campaign communications, as well as those of the political parties and interest groups, all were probably important. The same can be said of the stumping by Democratic and Republican national leaders, the Democrats' mobilization of Native Americans, and the continued presence of a minor-party candidate on the ballot. Regardless of whether the Democrat won because of superior targeting, message, or the activities of other politicians or outside groups, the South Dakota Senate race clearly demonstrates that campaigning matters. As Johnson campaign manager Steve Hildebrand explained, "Given the national trend, South Dakota's Republican majority, five presidential visits, and an opponent who won his last election with 70 percent of the vote, Johnson should have lost by 10 percentage points."[39]

CLAIMING CREDIT AND PLACING BLAME

Once the election is over, candidates and their campaign staffs have a chance to reflect on their contests. Their main interest, naturally, is what caused the election to turn out as it did. Winners and losers have very different ideas about what factors influence congressional election outcomes. Some differences are obvious. Losing candidates almost always obsess about money, particularly the funds that they and their opponents spent on campaigning. Unsuccessful candidates for the House generally considered the funds that they and their opponents spent to have been very important in determining the outcome of their elections, whereas the winners believed money was only moderately important (see Table 9-4).[40] Defeated candidates also placed greater emphasis on the impact of party and interest group spending on their elections than did winners. Some obviously had strong beliefs about the influence of the parties' and groups' independent, parallel, and coordinated campaigns.

Unsuccessful candidates frequently assert that if they had had more money—or if their party or interest group allies had spent more money on their behalf—they would have reached more voters and won more votes. The almost four-to-one spending advantage that victorious House incumbents had

TABLE 9-4

Winners' and Losers' Opinions of the Determinants of House Elections

	Winners	Losers
Money spent by campaigns	2.95	3.90
Money spent by political parties	2.11	2.97
Money spent by advocacy groups	1.79	2.60
Candidate's image and personality	4.53	3.53
Incumbent's record	4.10	2.79
Incumbency advantages	3.51	4.51
Local issues	3.53	2.74
National domestic issues	3.69	3.05
Foreign affairs and defense	3.36	2.96
Party loyalty	3.11	3.65
Newspaper endorsements	2.23	2.25
U.S. Senate election	1.96	2.58
State or local elections	1.96	2.55
Negative campaigning	1.86	2.04
Debates	1.72	1.85
Political scandal in own race	1.36	1.47

Source: The 2002 and 1998 Congressional Campaign Studies.

Notes: Candidates and campaign aides were asked to assess the importance of each factor on the following scale: 1 = not important; 2 = slightly important; 3 = moderately important; 4 = very important; 5 = extremely important. The values listed are arithmetic means. Figures for the impact of incumbent's record and incumbency advantages exclude responses from candidates and campaign aides from open seats. Figures are for general election candidates in major-party contested races, excluding those in incumbent-versus-incumbent races. See note 40 for more details.

over losing challengers in 2002 supports their point (see Figure 9-1). The 26 percent spending advantage that successful open-seat candidates had over their opponents is not as large, but it also lends credence to the view that money matters. The fact that the winning House challenger with the lowest total campaign expenditure in 2002, Rep. Virginia Brown-Waite, R-Fl., spent almost $923,000 further suggests that challengers must cross a high spending threshold to be competitive. Successful House challengers in normal two-party races spent an average of $1.6 million on the 2002 elections. The patterns of spending in Senate elections further reinforce the importance of money (see Figure 9-2).

Once one gets beyond the obvious factor of money, there are differences of opinion about the extent to which other factors influence election outcomes. Successful House candidates have a strong tendency to credit their victories to

FIGURE 9-1

Average Campaign Expenditures of House Winners and Losers in 2002

$, thousands

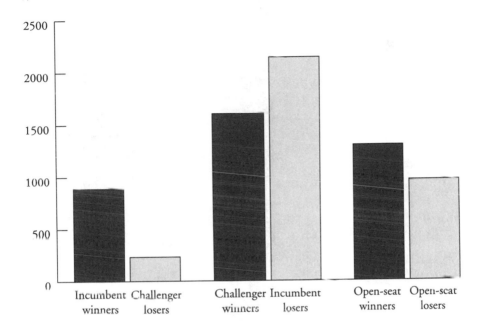

Source: Compiled from Federal Election Commission data.

Note: Figures are for major-party candidates in contested general elections; $N = 694$.

attributes of the candidate and to factors that were largely under their campaign's control. They believe that the candidate's image was the most important determinant of their election. Successful incumbents credit their record in office next. They also acknowledge the advantages they derived from incumbency.

The winners of House races rank issues as having been moderately to very influential in producing the outcomes of their elections. Many Democratic winners in 2002 believed that they benefited from focusing on jobs and the economy, Social Security, Medicare and health care generally, education, the environment, or some other traditional Democratic issue. Many successful Republican candidates believed they helped themselves by concentrating on tax cuts, moral values, national defense, and other issues that have traditionally formed the core of the GOP's communications efforts. Many victorious Republican House candidates also believed that they gained from focusing on the war on terrorism and the potential outbreak of hostilities in Iraq. Even so,

FIGURE 9-2

Average Campaign Expenditures of Senate Winners and Losers in 2002

$, thousands

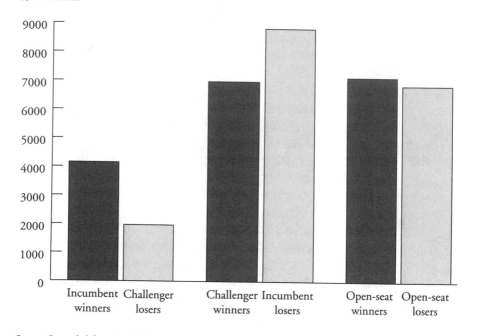

Source: Compiled from Federal Election Commission data.

Note: Figures are for major-party candidates in contested general elections; $N = 60$.

relatively few winners from either party believed that the election was nation-alized. Indeed, local concerns were roughly as important as national domestic issues and more important than ones related to foreign affairs or defense. Winning candidates rate the partisan loyalties of voters in their districts as moderately important.

Finally, winners generally believe that newspaper endorsements, the influ-ence of U.S. Senate, state, or local elections, negative campaigning, debates, and political scandal were much less important to the outcomes of their con-tests. The winners' opinions reflect a tendency to attribute their victories to their own efforts and the wisdom of voters.[41] These beliefs stand in stark con-trast to political science theories that suggest that congressional election out-comes are primarily a function of national conditions and events.[42]

Defeated House candidates have very different views about what caused their candidacies to conclude as they did. First and foremost, losing challengers point to the incumbent's perquisites of office, which they believe to have been very to extremely important. Next, unsuccessful candidates point to money—specifically, the financial advantages of their opponent. They rank the partisanship of voters in their district third. Candidate images came in fourth, followed by national domestic issues, foreign affairs and defense-related issues, and party and interest group spending. Unsuccessful candidates typically believe that local issues and debates are less important than these other factors. They place more emphasis on the influence of Senate, state, and local elections than do winners. Defeated candidates prefer to rationalize their defeats by blaming them on factors over which neither they nor their campaigns had any control.[43] The losers' views bear similarities to political science theories that downplay the importance of individual candidates and campaigns.[44]

Senate candidates have a somewhat different view of the causes of their election outcomes than do House contestants. Both the winners and losers in Senate contests emphasize factors that are largely under their control. Contestants generally believe that the images they projected to the voters were the number one determinant of the outcome of their elections. Winners typically maintain that candidate imagery was extremely important, whereas losers believe it was moderately important. Winners are more likely to emphasize the importance of issues, ranking them second only to imagery. Losing challengers, in contrast, believe that the advantages of office holding are substantially more important. Winning and losing incumbents are equally likely to view incumbency as a two-edged sword, agreeing that the anger that many voters direct at Washington reduces their vote margins.

Senate incumbents place greater emphasis on the importance of their voting records than do Senate challengers, but both acknowledge that job performance was at least a moderately important determinant of the outcome of Senate elections. Both winners and losers also place moderate importance on the partisan loyalties of state voters. Senate candidates attribute less influence to such factors as debates, negative campaigning, local issues, and state and local elections than do House contestants.

SUMMARY

The efforts that candidates make to communicate with voters can have an impact on congressional elections, but they are especially important for House challengers and open-seat contestants. Challengers who carefully target their campaign resources, run on issues that draw distinctions between themselves and the House members they seek to unseat, spend significant sums on campaign advertising and voter mobilization, and attract local media endorsements can significantly increase the number of votes they receive. House challengers who must defeat an opponent to secure their party's nomination, who run in districts that have many members of their party, who oppose vulnerable incumbents, and who attract significant outside campaigning by their party and supportive interest groups also increase their share of the vote. House incumbents can do little to substantially increase their standing in the polls. The efforts they make to serve their constituents and deter a strong challenger from emerging result in most incumbents' beginning and ending their campaigns with commanding leads. Indeed, most House incumbent campaigns, like most incumbent fundraising, are driven by the threat that an opponent poses and are directed at shoring up the candidate's support. Campaigns for House open seats are usually very competitive. Voter targeting, issue selection, and candidate communications can be decisive in these races, even in districts that are inundated by outside campaign advertisements aired by parties and interest groups. Senate elections bear many similarities to House contests, but they are usually both more expensive and more competitive. Moreover, although contested primaries hurt Senate incumbents and incumbents' spending has a positive impact on their vote shares, these factors do not have the same effects on the votes that House incumbents garner.

Congressional campaigners have divergent views about the causes of their election outcomes. Successful campaigners credit their candidates' abilities and their organizations' strategic and tactical efforts for their wins. House losers focus on money, incumbents' perks of office, voter partisanship, and other factors outside of their control. Senate losers are somewhat more likely to acknowledge that candidate characteristics and some aspects of their campaigns contributed to their loss.

CHAPTER TEN

Elections and Governance

"The election is over, and now the fun begins." [1] Those were the words of one new House member shortly after being elected to Congress. Others had more sober, if not more realistic, visions of what lay ahead. Although getting elected to Congress is difficult, especially for those who have to topple an incumbent, staying there also requires great effort. The high reelection rates enjoyed by members of Congress are not a guarantee of reelection; they are the result of hard work, the strategic deployment of the resources that Congress makes available to its members, and the campaign dynamics discussed in previous chapters.

This chapter examines the efforts that members of Congress make in order to stay in office and analyzes the resources and strategies they use to shore up their electoral coalitions. Also reviewed is the impact of elections on Congress as a policy-making institution. First, I discuss the goals and activities of members of Congress and their congressional staffs. I then discuss the committees, issue caucuses, party organizations, and other groups that influence congressional activity. Finally, I comment on the policy-making process.

THE PERMANENT CAMPAIGN

As locally elected officials who make national policy, members of Congress almost lead double lives. The main focus of their existence in Washington, D.C., is framing and enacting legislation, overseeing the executive branch, and carrying out other activities of national importance. Attending local functions, ascertaining the needs and preferences of constituents, and explaining their Washington activities are what legislators do at home. Home is where members of Congress acquire their legitimacy to participate in the legislative process. The central elements of legislators' lives both at home and in Washington are representing the voters who elected them, winning federally funded projects for their state or district, and resolving difficulties that constituents encounter when dealing with the federal government. The two aspects of members' professional lives are unified by the fact that much of what representatives do in Washington is concerned with getting reelected, and a good deal of what they do at home directly affects the kinds of policies and interests they seek to advance.[2] In a great many respects, the job of legislator resembles a permanent reelection campaign.

Members of Congress develop home styles that help them to maintain or expand their bases of electoral support. One common element of these home styles concerns how legislators present themselves to voters. Members build bonds of trust between themselves and voters by demonstrating that they are capable of handling the job, care about their constituents, and are living up to their campaign promises.[3]

A second component of home style is concerned with discussing the Washington side of the job. Members describe, interpret, and justify what they do in the nation's capital to convey the message that they are working relentlessly on their constituents' behalf.[4] Many respond to the low opinion that people have of Congress by trying to separate themselves from the institution in the minds of voters. Members frequently portray themselves as protectors of the national interest locked in combat with powerful lobbyists and feckless colleagues.

Members of Congress and their staffs spend immense amounts of time, energy, and resources advertising the legislator's name among constituents, claiming credit for favorable governmental actions, and taking strong but often symbolic issue positions to please constituents.[5] Their offices provide them with abundant resources for these purposes. House members are annually entitled to roughly $1 million for personnel and office expenses, including $662,700 for staff, a travel budget of up to $67,200, a suite of offices in the Capitol complex, one or more district offices, and virtually unlimited long-distance telephone privileges. Members who are assigned to certain committees, occupy committee chairs, or hold party leadership positions receive extra staff, office space, and operating funds. Senators are allowed even greater budgets, reflecting their larger constituencies and the greater responsibilities associated with representing an entire state. Senators' staffs, office space, and budget allocations are determined by their state's population and by their committee assignments. The annual administrative and clerical allowance for a senator from one of the smallest states is $1.4 million, compared with $2.4 million for a senator from California.[6] Although few legislators consume all the resources they are allocated, many come close. The average House member hires approximately fourteen full-time aides; the average senator hires about thirty-four.[7] Among these aides are administrative assistants, legislative assistants, legislative correspondents, computer operators, schedulers, office managers, caseworkers, press secretaries, receptionists, staff assistants, and interns. Each performs a different set of functions, but nearly all are somehow related to building political support among constituents. Legislative correspondents, legislative assistants, and computer operators are highly conscious of the electoral connection when they send franked mail to constituents or set up their boss's web site.[8] Caseworkers help constituents resolve problems with the federal bureaucracy, knowing that their performance can directly affect the reelection prospects of the legislator for whom they work. Receptionists, staff assistants, and schedulers are well aware that the tours they arrange for visitors to Washington contribute to the support their member maintains in the district. Those who forget that constituents come first are quickly reminded of this by the member's administrative assistant, who is responsible for making sure that the office runs smoothly and frequently serves as the member's chief political adviser.

The most reelection-oriented staffers tend to be congressional press secretaries. Most members of Congress have at least one press secretary, and some have two or three deputy press assistants.[9] The press secretary is the chief public relations officer in a congressional office. Press secretaries write newsletters and press releases and are heavily involved in crafting the targeted mass mailings that most legislators send to constituents. They also produce copy for radio and television spots, which they arrange to have aired on local stations. Press secretaries help to organize town meetings, arrange interviews with the local correspondents, and disseminate to the news media transcripts and videotapes of their boss's floor and committee speeches. A good press secretary is often able to arrange for local media outlets to print or air a legislator's remarks verbatim or with minimal editing.[10]

Many factors led to the emergence of the press secretary as a key congressional aide, including the election of highly media-conscious members since the mid-1970s, increased television coverage of politics, the opening of Congress to greater media scrutiny, the growth in the size of the congressional press corps, and the availability of new communications technologies. These changes created both pressures and opportunities to increase the public relations side of congressional offices.[11] Members of Congress, who work in a resource-rich institution, responded by allowing themselves to hire specialized staff who could help them advance their political careers.

Congress also has allowed its members to exploit new computer technologies to firm up their relations with voters. Legislative aides use computerized databases to target large volumes of mail to specific audiences. Information on constituents who write or telephone their legislator about an issue is routinely entered into a computerized list that includes the constituent's name, address, and reason for the contact. They are then sent periodic communications that update them on what their legislator is doing in this area of concern. Constituents who contact members' offices via e-mail or by accessing their Internet web site often receive e-mails in return.

Subsidized House and Senate recording studios and party-owned recording facilities also help legislators reach out to voters. Many members use the studios to record radio shows and television briefings or to edit floor speeches that they deliver to local media outlets. Some make use of satellite technology to hold live "town meetings" with constituents located on the other side of the country.

A DECENTRALIZED CONGRESS

The candidate-centered nature of congressional elections provides the foundation for a highly individualized, fragmented style of legislative politics. Members are largely self-recruited, are nominated and elected principally as a result of their own efforts, and know they bear the principal responsibility for ensuring they get reelected. Local party organizations, Washington-based party committees, political action committees, and other groups and individuals may have helped them raise money and win votes, but politicians arrive in Congress with the belief that they owe their tenure to their own efforts.

Reelection Constituencies

Legislators' first loyalties are to their constituents, and most members staff their offices, decide which committee assignments to pursue, and choose areas of policy expertise with an eye toward maintaining voter support. Campaign contributors, including those who live outside a legislator's district or state, form another important constituency. Local elites and interest groups that provide campaign support or political advice routinely receive access to members of Congress, further encouraging legislators to respond to forces outside of the institution rather than within.[12] Other personal goals, including advancing specific policies, accruing more power in the legislature, or positioning themselves to run for higher office, also have a decentralizing effect on the legislative process.[13] Much of the work done to advance these goals—conducting policy research; disseminating press releases; drafting bills; attending committee meetings; overseeing the bureaucracy; and meeting with constituents, campaign contributors, and lobbyists—is borne by staffers who owe their jobs and their loyalties to individual legislators more than to the institution.[14] This, in turn, makes their bosses less dependent on congressional leaders and encourages members to march to their own beat.

Congressional Committees

The dispersal of legislative authority among nineteen standing committees and eighty-eight subcommittees in the House, sixteen standing committees and sixty-eight subcommittees in the Senate, four joint committees, and a small number of select committees in each chamber adds to the centrifugal tendencies that originate from candidate-centered elections. Each committee and subcommittee is authorized to act within a defined jurisdiction. A chair and a ranking member, who are among the majority and minority parties' senior policy experts, head each committee and subcommittee. Each also has its own professional staff, office, and budget to help it carry out its business.

The committee system was designed to enable Congress to function more efficiently. It allows Congress to investigate simultaneously a multitude of issues and to oversee a range of executive branch agencies. Although committees and subcommittees are Congress's main bodies for making national policy, much of what they do revolves around local issues, the distribution of federal grants and programs, and the reelection of individual legislators. Most legislators serve on at least one committee or subcommittee with jurisdiction over policies of importance to their constituents. Members use their committee assignments to develop expertise in policy areas, to actively promote their constituents' interests, to build reputations as champions of popular issues, and to attract political support.

Congressional committees can be categorized according to the objectives they enable members to pursue: reelection, prestige, and policy.[15] "Reelection committees," such as the House Transportation and Infrastructure Committee and the Senate Environment and Public Works Committee, enable their members to work directly on the policy areas that are most important to constituents. Reelection committees usually rank high among the assignments sought by new members of Congress. More than half of all first-term House members seek appointment to one or more of them.[16]

"Prestige committees" give their members influence over legislative activities that are of extraordinary importance to their congressional colleagues. The House and Senate Appropriations Committees are the ultimate prestige, or power, committees. They are responsible for funding federal agencies and programs and have the ability to initiate, expand, contract, or discontinue the flow of federal money to projects located across the country. This gives their members the power to affect the lives of the beneficiaries of these programs and the ability to influence the reelection prospects of legislators who represent them. The House Ways and Means and Senate Finance Committees' jurisdiction over tax-related matters, and particularly their ability to give tax breaks to various interests, give members of these panels sway with their colleagues. Members of prestige committees can help their constituents by acting directly or, by wielding their clout with other legislators, indirectly. Membership on one of the appropriating or tax-writing committees is particularly helpful when it comes to raising campaign funds from individuals and PACs associated with a wide array of economic interests.

In contrast to reelection and prestige committees, "policy committees," such as those that deal with criminal justice, education, or labor issues, are sought by legislators who have a strong interest in a particular policy area. These committees are among the most divisive because they are responsible for some highly charged issues, such as education, health insurance, and welfare reform, and many members use them to stake out conservative or liberal stands. Ambitious legislators who seek a career beyond Congress often use policy committees as platforms for developing a national reputation on salient issues.

Thus the committee system gives expression to the differing goals and viewpoints of representatives, senators, and their constituents. By so doing, it decentralizes Congress.

Congressional Caucuses

Congressional caucuses—informal groups of members who share legislative interests—have a similar but less powerful effect on Congress. Even though caucuses have been prohibited from having their own congressional staffs and office space since the 104th Congress, they continue to function as competing policy centers, alternative suppliers of information, and additional sources of legislative decision-making cues.[17] Groups such as the Congressional Black Caucus and the Congressional Women's Caucus are recognized as advocates for specific segments of the population. The Northeast-Midwest Senate Coalition, Western States Senate Coalition, and other geographically based groups seek to increase the clout of legislators from particular regions. The Steel, Auto, and Textile Caucuses have ties to outside industries and work to promote their interests in Congress. Although they do not hold any formal legislative powers, caucuses further add to the fragmentation of Congress by advancing disparate goals.

Interest Groups

Privately funded interest groups, which form an important part of the political environment with which Congress interacts, also have decentralizing effects on the legislative process. Like caucuses, interest groups are sources of influence that compete with congressional leaders for the loyalty of legislators on
certain issues. Roughly eighty thousand people work for trade associations,
legal firms, and consulting agencies in the Washington area.[18] Not all these
people are lobbyists, but in one way or another they work to advance the political interests of some group, and Congress is their number-one target.[19]

Interest groups work to influence the legislative process in many ways. Some
groups advertise on television, on radio, in newspapers, or through the mail to
influence the political agenda or stimulate grassroots support for or opposition
to specific pieces of legislation. Their efforts often resemble election campaigns. The debate over legislation designed to make it profitable for regional
Bell telephone companies—the "Baby Bells"—to invest in high-speed Internet connections exemplifies such efforts. The so-called "Tauzin-Dingell Bill,"
named after sponsors Reps. W. J. "Billy" Tauzin, R-La., and John Dingell,
D-Mich., pitted the Baby Bells, who supported the measure against "Voices
for Change," an interest group coalition comprising telecommunications giant
AT&T, Sprint, WorldComm, Internet providers, and some local telephone
companies. In addition to spending millions of dollars lobbying Congress directly, and contributing hundreds of millions of dollars to candidates and parties, both sides spent tens of millions of dollars on televised issue advocacy ads
intended to mobilize grassroots support for or against the bill. Although the
bill was ultimately passed in the House, whether the lobbying or the issue ads
were more important in producing the outcome remains an open question, as
do its prospects in the Senate.[20]

Most interest groups also advocate their positions in less visible ways, designed to play to the legislative and electoral needs of individual members of
Congress. Representatives of interest groups testify at committee hearings and
meet with legislators at their offices and informally at social events. Lobbyists
use a variety of forums to provide members and their staffs with technical information, impact statements of how congressional activity (or inactivity) can
affect their constituents, and insights into where other legislators stand on the
issues. Sometimes they go so far as to draft a bill or help design a strategy to
promote its enactment.[21]

Many groups supplement these "insider" techniques with approaches that
focus more directly on the electoral connection. Trade and business groups ask
local association members to contact their legislators. Unions, churches, and

other groups with large memberships frequently organize telephone and letter-writing campaigns. These communications show members of Congress that important blocs of voters and their advocates are watching how they vote on specific pieces of legislation.[22] The recent increase in interest group–sponsored issue advocacy advertising in connection with the legislative process and elections has resulted in some groups contributing to the permanent campaigns that consume a significant portion of the professional lives of most members of Congress.

Interest groups, congressional subcommittee members, and executive branch officials form collegial decision-making groups, which are frequently referred to as "iron triangles," "issue networks," or "policy subgovernments." [23] These issue experts often focus on the minutiae of arcane, highly specialized areas of public policy. Because they form small governments within a government, they further contribute to the decentralization of Congress.

POLITICAL PARTIES AS CENTRALIZING AGENTS

Unlike the structural, organizational, and political factors that work to decentralize Congress, political parties act as a glue—albeit sometimes a weak one—to bond together members. They socialize new members to Congress's norms and folkways, distribute committee assignments, set the legislative agenda, disseminate information, and carry out other tasks that are essential to Congress's lawmaking, oversight, and representative functions. Although they are not the central actors in elections, party committees do help individual candidates develop their campaign messages. Party campaign efforts on behalf of individual candidates and election agenda-setting efforts encourage legislators to vote for bills that are at the core of their party's agenda when Congress is in session.[24] Party issue advocacy that takes place outside of the campaign season is meant to increase or reduce support for specific bills or damage the reputations of members who voted against them. Issue advocacy ads, such as those the Democratic National Committee and the Democratic Congressional Campaign Committee aired in May 2001 blasting Bush and congressional Republicans living in California, New Jersey, and other areas experiencing power problems for driving up the costs of fuel, have given party organizations in the nation's capital a greater role in the permanent campaign.

The congressional parties' leadership organizations are structured similarly to those of legislative parties in other countries. The Democrats and Republicans are each headed by one leader in each chamber—the Speaker and minority leader in the House and the majority and minority leaders in the Senate.

Each party has several other officers and an extensive whip system to facilitate communications between congressional party leaders and rank-and-file legislators. Legislative parties convene caucuses and task forces to help formulate policy positions and legislative strategy. Providing campaign assistance, giving out committee assignments and other perks, setting the congressional agenda, structuring debate, and persuading legislators that specific bills are in the best interests of their constituents and the nation are tools that congressional leaders use to build coalitions.[25]

Nevertheless, party leaders have less control over the policy-making process than do their counterparts in other democracies.[26] The persuasive powers of party leaders are usually insufficient to sway members' votes when party policy positions clash with those of legislators' constituents and campaign supporters. Recognizing the primacy of the electoral connection, party leaders generally tell legislators to respond to constituents rather than "toe the party line" when the latter could endanger their chances of reelection. The efforts of congressional party leaders are probably less of a factor in explaining how party members cast their roll-call votes than are commonalities in political outlook or similarities among legislators' constituents.[27] The election of more ideologically oriented members and the drawing of safe, strongly partisan House districts prior to the 2002 elections have increased both.

Party leaders are most able to overcome the forces that fragment Congress when they seek to enact policies that have widespread bipartisan support or when the majority party possesses many more seats than the opposition and proposes popular legislation that advances its core principles. As the historic 104th Congress showed, a change in party control can also act as a catalyst for party unity. Members of the new House and Senate majorities were aware that their accomplishments as a party would directly influence their individual reelection campaigns and their party's ability to maintain control of Congress. Republican members of ensuing congresses also demonstrated an understanding of the importance of party unity and a record of performance in keeping control of a closely divided legislature. Democrats, on the other hand, unified in opposition to the Republicans and sought to portray them as presiding over "do-nothing" congresses.

RESPONSIVENESS, RESPONSIBILITY, AND PUBLIC POLICY

In representative democracies, elections are the principal means of ensuring that governments respond to the will of the people and promote their interests. Voters, through elections, hold public officials accountable for their actions and for the state of the nation as a whole. Elections are a blunt but powerful instrument of control that enables people to inform their individual representatives, or the government as a collectivity, of how political action or inaction has affected the quality of their lives. Elections are the primary means that democracies use to empower or remove political leaders at all levels of government. Campaigns help to establish standards by which officeholders are judged. Other paths of influence, such as contacting members of Congress and giving campaign contributions, are usually used to advance narrower goals, are more demanding, and are in practice less democratic.

Despite the extensive resources for building and maintaining relationships with constituents that Congress and the rest of the Washington establishment put at the disposal of representatives and senators, members cannot fully insulate themselves or Congress as an institution from the impact of electoral forces. Voters can, and occasionally do, expel large numbers of incumbents, leading to changes in the membership, leadership, operations, and output of Congress. The 1994 elections resulted in a new Republican majority taking control of Congress for the first time in forty years and led to the selection of Newt Gingrich—a relative newcomer to his party's leadership—as House Speaker. The elections also empowered the Republicans to claim a mandate to change some of the ways in which Congress operates and to overturn Democratic programs that originated more than sixty years earlier during the New Deal.

The 1998 midterm elections brought the Gingrich regime to an end and took much of the steam out of the Republicans' program to remake the federal government. The GOP's historic loss of five House seats cost Gingrich the confidence of his Republican House colleagues and led him to resign both the speakership and his House seat. After Republican Speaker–designate Robert Livingston of Louisiana acknowledged an extramarital affair and resigned from the House, Dennis Hastert, a consensus-building Republican from Illinois, rose from relative obscurity to become the new Speaker. In contrast to Gingrich's first session as the House's leader, Hastert's first session was characterized by few legislative accomplishments.

The 2002 midterm elections also brought about significant change. The Republicans increased their hold on the House by six seats and won a fifty-one-seat majority in the Senate, giving the GOP control of both the White House and the 108th Congress. Nevertheless, the transition to Republican control in the Senate was anything but smooth. As anticipated, Democrats and Republicans fought over the distribution of committee assignments and staff. What was unexpected was Mississippi Republican Trent Lott's forced resignation as Senate majority leader–designate after he made racially insensitive remarks at a retirement party for Sen. Strom Thurman. Replacing Lott as majority leader was Tennessee senator Bill Frist, who was first elected in 1994 and had served as National Republican Senatorial Committee chairman during the 2002 election cycle. The congressional elections held over the past two decades show that voters can shake up the status quo in Washington, inspire change in the direction of government, and set standards for what is considered acceptable behavior by public officials.

Individuals whose public service is contingent on getting reelected often straddle the fuzzy line that demarcates responsiveness and responsibility in government. On some occasions, legislators are highly responsive, functioning as delegates who advance their constituents' views. On others, they take the role of trustee, relying on their own judgment to protect the welfare of their constituents or the nation.[28] Responsible legislators must occasionally vote against their constituents' wishes in order to best serve the interests of the nation.

Election Systems and Public Policy

The type of political system in which elected officials function influences to whom they answer. The U.S. candidate-centered system is unique, and it results in a style of governance that contrasts sharply with that of parliamentary systems, which are used to govern the vast majority of democracies. Parliamentary systems feature party-focused elections that tend to hold elected officials accountable to national political majorities.[29] Members of the British Parliament, for example, perform casework and are attentive to their constituents, but they are inclined to vote for legislation fashioned to please national rather than local constituencies. They support party initiatives because they know that their prospects for reelection are tied closely to their party's ability to enact its legislative program. The candidate-centered nature of the U.S. system, in contrast, encourages elected officials to be responsive to the desires of constituents and organized groups that support their campaigns, sometimes in opposition to their party's leadership.

The separation of powers reinforces legislators' predispositions to support district voters first and their campaign's financial supporters second when making public policy. Even when one party controls the White House and both chambers of Congress, it may find it difficult to unify legislators because they can disagree with one another without fear of losing control of the government.

Members of the majority party in Congress cast roll-call votes secure in the knowledge that they will remain in office for their full two- or six-year terms even if their party suffers a major legislative defeat. In parliamentary systems, majority party members understand that a major policy defeat may be interpreted as a vote of no confidence in their party and force an election that could turn them out of office in less than a month. The separation of powers also affects the behavior of legislators who are in the minority party. They have little incentive to vote against legislation that could benefit their constituents just because it was sponsored by the majority party, since even a smashing legislative defeat would not force a snap election.

The defeat of President Bush's tax cut proposal in the Senate in March 2003 demonstrates the difficulties that parties face when they try to overcome the centrifugal forces influencing members of Congress. Bush, who campaigned aggressively for congressional Republicans and has emerged as one of the United States's most partisan recent presidents, was unable to get his tax cuts enacted despite Republican majorities in the House and Senate. The budget package passed by a largely party-line vote in the House, and prospects for passage in the Republican-controlled Senate initially appeared promising. However, following a presidential request for a supplemental budget of $74.7 million to fund the first six months of the war with Iraq, many senators of both parties became concerned about the implications the cuts would have on the national debt. As a result, a coalition of moderate Republican and Democratic senators voted to reduce the tax cuts by more than half, despite the president's pleas that the cuts were necessary to curb domestic spending and promote economic growth. The Republican senators who opposed the budget were Olympia Snowe of Maine, Lincoln Chafee of Rhode Island, George Voinovich of Ohio, and John McCain of Arizona. These legislators put their own views and those of their constituents above those of President Bush. In denying the head of their party the opportunity to write a budget during a time of war, they committed what some would decry an act of partisan treason. Indeed, the president denounced Voinovich's position at a rally held in the senator's own state, and the pro-Republican Club for Growth ran TV ads in both Ohio and Maine arguing that these "Franco-Republicans [Voinovich and Snowe] are as dependable as France was in taking down Iraqi dictator Saddam Hussein." [30]

Most acts of Congress are not as monumental as the defeat of a president's wartime budget. The separation of powers, bicameralism, federalism, and a fixed-date system of elections make it difficult for legislators to enact longer-term, more nationally focused policies. Members of Congress who believe that their individual images, policy positions, and public records were decisive in their election are less likely than legislators in party-centered democracies to sacrifice the interests of constituents or to compromise on salient issues to enact policies advocated by party leaders. House members, who must run for reelection every two years, respond strongly to parochial concerns.

The effects of parochialism are most apparent in distributive politics, which provide tangible benefits to private individuals or groups. Building coalitions in support of spending on roads, bridges, universities, museums, and other projects is relatively simple in a decentralized legislature such as the U.S. Congress. Bill sponsors can add new programs and projects in order to win enough legislative supporters to pass their plan.[31] A farm advocate who is hoping to subsidize northern sugar beets, for example, might build support for this cause by expanding the number of subsidized crops in a bill to include sugar cane, rice, corn, wheat, and even tobacco, thereby expanding support that began with representatives from Minnesota to include colleagues from Hawaii, Massachusetts, virtually every southern state, and the states of the Midwest.[32] Subsidies for ostrich farmers can be left out because they will not draw many legislative votes, but food stamps can be added to attract the support of legislators from poor urban districts.[33] Trading subsidies for votes is a simple example of logrolling. Other deals are cut over tax breaks, budget votes, and even appointments to the federal judiciary.

Logrolling and other forms of compromise usually do not allow individual legislators to get all the federal "pork" they would like for their constituents. Nevertheless, these compromises enable most legislators to insert enough pork into a bill to claim credit for doing something to help their constituents. A broadly supported distributive bill is an easy candidate for congressional enactment because, like a Christmas tree decorated by a group of friends, everyone can see his or her handiwork in it and find something to admire in the finished product.

Distributive politics are problematic because they are practiced with both eyes focused on short-term gains and little attention to long-range consequences. Broadening programs that were originally intended to provide benefits to one group to include others usually causes the programs to become ineffectively targeted, watered down, and overly expensive. When large sums are spent to benefit many groups, overall spending is increased, and fewer funds remain available to help the group originally targeted for assistance. This does little to promote the original goals of a bill and leads to deficit spending.[34] Pork-barrel spending and logrolling, which are at the heart of distributive politics, contribute heavily to the United States's national debt. Distributive politics are a prime example of what happens when independently elected officials seek to promote the interests of their constituents and campaign supporters without giving much thought to the effect of their collective actions on the nation. Recent congresses, especially those elected between 1994 and 2000, have taken steps to reduce government spending, generating budget surpluses in 1998 and 1999. However, constant wrangling over tax cuts, military spending, and other federal programs has hindered their attempts at debt reduction. The war on terrorism and the wars in Afghanistan and Iraq caused the deficit to balloon following the September 11, 2001, terrorist attacks.

Policy Gridlock and Political Cycles

Parochialism also leads to a reactive style of government and incremental policy making. Congress is better at making short-term fixes than at developing long-term initiatives. Congressional leaders often find it difficult to develop a vision for the future. During the 1980s House Democrats took steps to outline, publicize, and act on a partisan agenda. Parts of this effort were successful, but much of it was not. Differences in legislators' political philosophies, the diversity of their constituencies, and the limited resources available to party leaders made it difficult to develop and implement a Democratic game plan for the nation's future.[35] House Republicans also tried on several occasions in the 1980s to develop a partisan agenda, but prior to the Contract with America, they, too, enjoyed only limited success.[36]

Under most circumstances, election outcomes, constituent demands, interest group pressures, and White House initiatives support the continuation of the status quo or suggest only small changes in public policies. When pressure for change exists, Congress generally initiates limited reform, but only after a period of some delay. On some occasions, however, the federal government enacts comprehensive programs that significantly affect people's lives.

Major policy change is most likely to occur during periods of crisis and is frequently associated with partisan realignments. Realignments traditionally occur when a critical event polarizes voters on a major issue, the two major parties take clear and opposing stands on that issue, and one party succeeds in capturing the White House and large majorities in both the House and Senate. The ascendant party then has an electoral mandate to enact major policy change.[37]

The events leading up to and continuing through Franklin Roosevelt's presidency exemplify federal policy making during a period of crisis. The seeds of Roosevelt's New Deal programs were sown in the Great Depression of the 1930s. Republicans controlled the White House, the House of Representatives, and the Senate when the stock market crashed in 1929. The Democrats made a major campaign issue out of the Republicans' failure to initiate economic reforms to reverse the Depression. After winning the White House and both chambers of Congress, the Democrats used their mandate to replace laissez-faire economics with Keynesian policies, which relied on government intervention to revive the economy. Other partisan and policy realignments took place during the late 1820s, the Civil War era, and the 1890s.

Some major policy changes have been instituted in the absence of partisan realignments, but most of these were less sweeping than were those that followed critical elections. The civil rights and Great Society programs of the

1960s and the U.S. withdrawal from Vietnam are examples of major policy changes that occurred in the absence of a partisan realignment. Historical perspective is needed before scholars can conclude that the 1994 congressional elections constituted a full-scale realignment in favor of the Republicans, but Democratic hegemony over Congress has clearly ended.[38] Regardless of whether a realignment was constituted in 1994, the GOP was able to use its stunning electoral success to institute major changes in public policy and shift the national policy debate. Under Gingrich's leadership, the GOP-controlled Congress passed legislation reducing federal mandates on the states, cutting federal regulations, and changing the welfare system from a federally mandated program to one run by each state independently with a block grant from the federal government.[39] The Republicans also shifted the policy debate from how to improve the efficiency and performance of the federal government to how to decrease its scope. For the first time since the New Deal, the subject of reducing entitlement benefits dominated public debate. Politicians, commentators, and policy analysts discussed whether reducing current or future per-capita outlays for Social Security, Medicare, Medicaid, and other entitlement programs was an acceptable way to cut the size and cost of government, reduce the federal deficit, and pay for tax cuts.

Republican House leaders also restructured some major aspects of how the House did business. The GOP cut the number of House committees, subcommittees, and committee staffs; enacted term limits for committee chairs and the Speaker, and made other formal changes aimed at strengthening the hands of the majority party leadership. The Republicans eliminated legislative study organizations, which had formerly enhanced the representation of specific—mostly Democratic—constituencies. Republican leaders also bypassed the normal committee process in writing several important pieces of legislation, relying instead on task forces, which facilitate coalition building within the majority party but greatly reduce minority party input.[40]

After they claimed control of both chambers of Congress in 2003, the Republicans were once again poised to have a major impact on federal policy making. At the procedural level, the rules that House Republicans enacted for the 108th Congress grant more power to the majority at the expense of the minority. The new rules also weakened some of the ethics reforms passed in 1995.

Republican control of the Senate also led to some personnel changes that enhanced GOP prospects for introducing lasting change in the federal judiciary. The replacement of Sen. Patrick Leahy, D-Vt., by Orrin Hatch, R-Utah, as Senate Judiciary Committee chairman, should allow Bush's judicial appointments to enjoy smoother sailing in the confirmation process. Recognizing this, President Bush renominated all thirty appeals and district court judges whose appointments were stalled under the Democratic-controlled Senate in the 107th Congress, including Miguel Estrada, Priscilla Owen, and Charles W. Pickering, whose nominations the Judiciary Committee quashed previously. Moreover, Republican control of Congress subjected the Bush administration to less rigorous congressional oversight than would have been the case had the Democrats controlled at least one chamber.

The GOP also positioned itself to enact significant policy change. As the party in control of the White House and Congress, the GOP had the ability to dominate the political agenda. Partly as repayment for the extraordinary campaign efforts the president made on behalf of GOP congressional candidates, Republican members of Congress were strongly inclined to back the administration's policy initiatives. This improves GOP prospects for passing more tax cuts, including cutting dividend taxes and other taxes paid predominantly by the wealthy, arguably as a means for stimulating the economy. The Republicans also strongly positioned themselves to push for other parts of their political agenda, including limits on awards resulting from medical malpractice and asbestos lawsuits and other types of tort reform. Additional Republican-led efforts involving easing pollution restrictions for factories and power plants, promoting private sector models of prescription drug– and health care–related reforms, and outlawing certain abortion procedures are likely to receive more preferential treatment than they have had under Democratic-controlled and divided governments.

Some Republican policy initiatives also are likely to benefit from personnel changes at the committee level. Oklahoma Republican senator James Inhofe's replacement of James Jeffords, I-Vt., as chairman of the Senate Environmental and Public Works Committee has resulted in that committee becoming noticeably more receptive to the industry viewpoint that environmental protections often stand in the way of fuller utilization of natural resources and increased profits. Similarly, Massachusetts Democratic senator Ted Kennedy's handing over the reins of the Health, Education, Labor and Pensions Committee to Judd Gregg, R-N.H., creates a less favorable climate for the expansion of social safety net programs and will likely result in more oversight of federal programs concerned with health care and education.[41]

Turnover among legislators below the leadership level has contributed to substantial policy change, particularly in recent congresses. This is largely the result of the polarization of party activists. The nomination of candidates by partisans whose views are more ideologically extreme than those of the public has led to the election of Republicans who are more conservative, Democrats who are more liberal, and fewer moderates of either party during the past decade. As a result, Congress has become more polarized. More ideologically charged members of the majority party, particularly in the House, have enhanced the power of congressional party leaders in order to help their caucus achieve its electoral and policy-oriented goals. When strong party leaders, such as Gingrich, exploited these powers they were able to structure the congressional debate and control political outcomes. The result was that parties in Congress acted more programmatically.[42] The unity of its members has led the majority party, particularly the House Republicans, to achieve some stunning victories. Nevertheless, as the case of Bush's wartime tax cut demonstrates, this unity can be fleeting at critical times.

Elections that result in a shift in partisan control and the swearing in of many new members can be catalysts for Congress to overcome its normal state of decentralization, especially when a widespread consensus for change exists among the American people. When such partisan turnover occurs, congressional parties in the United States resemble both parliamentary parties in other countries and an idealized system of responsible party government.[43] However, once public support for sweeping change erodes, the centrifugal forces that customarily dominate Congress reassert themselves, and the legislature returns to its normal, incremental mode of policy making. The natural parochialism of members of Congress, bicameralism, the internal decentralization of the House and Senate, and other centrifugal forces promote political cycles marked by long periods of incremental policy making followed by short periods of centralized power and major policy change.

SUMMARY

The candidate-centered congressional election system has a major impact on how Congress functions. The electoral connection encourages members of Congress to develop home styles that result in their building bonds of trust with local voters. Congress, as an institution, provides its members with resources to help them accomplish this objective. The candidate-centered system also finds expression in the highly individualistic legislative behavior exhibited by most representatives and senators and in Congress's decentralized style of operation. Although political parties occasionally overcome the legislature's naturally fragmented state, the centrifugal forces exerted on Congress by constituents, campaign contributors, interest groups, committees, and other organizations within Congress itself cause the institution to return to its normal decentralized operations after short periods of centralization. The result is that national policy making in the United States is characterized by prolonged periods of gradual policy modification followed by brief episodes of sweeping political change.

CHAPTER ELEVEN

Campaign Reform

Congress has come under assault in recent years for its inability to solve some of the nation's most pressing problems, its perceived shortcomings in representing the general public, and its failure to keep its own house in order. Gridlock, deficit spending, scandal, the foibles of its members, and the operations of Congress itself have led many to champion congressional reform.[1] Reformers have called for a variety of changes, ranging from internal reforms consolidating the authorizing committees that create federal programs with the appropriations committees that fund them to term limits, which would restructure the political careers of members and would-be members. Campaign reform falls somewhere between these measures: it requires the passage of new legislation but does not require a constitutional amendment. In this chapter I focus primarily on the Bipartisan Campaign Reform Act of 2002, including an overview of the case for reform, a discussion of the politics preceding the bill's passage, some of the challenges the BCRA faced after its enactment, and its likely impact on congressional elections. I also discuss some additional reforms and reform proposals and their prospects for passage.

THE CASE FOR REFORM

Numerous arguments are routinely made for reforming congressional elections. Some proposals are quite sweeping, revolving around the question, Is this any way to elect a member of Congress? When this question was put to major-party candidates and campaign aides competing in the 2002 general elections for Congress, 35 percent responded that the campaign process prepares candidates "poorly" or "not at all" for holding office. The defeated candidates were more critical than the winners, but 24 percent of the winners also shared this view. Similarly, 58 percent of the campaigners agreed with the statement "there are only a few important connections between being a good candidate and being a good public official" and 21 percent maintained "there is little or no connection" between these two roles. Only one out of five candidates felt that "the best candidates are usually the best public officials." Although losers perceived fewer links between campaigning and governing, only 28 percent of the winners took the position that the best congressional candidates make the best members of Congress.[2]

These individuals also voiced skepticism about the substantive policy links between campaigning and governing. Ten percent agreed that "issues raised in political campaigns are almost never the most important for future governing," and another 60 percent held that campaign issues are "occasionally" the most important. Only 30 percent felt they were "usually" the most important. Moreover, the winners were no more likely than the losers to maintain that issues raised in campaigns were usually the most important for governing.[3]

Congressional contestants' dissatisfaction with the limited connections between campaigning and governing are important, but they are too amorphous to provide a basis for reform. How does one begin to write a law to ensure that the issues candidates discuss on the campaign trail are the same issues they act on when in office? Elections are the means voters use to hold government officeholders accountable. The disenchantment that politicians feel about the campaign process may be important, but most political reformers are consumed with more concrete shortcomings. Many reformers point out that the campaign system stacks the cards so much against challengers that incumbents almost always win, sometimes calling attention to congressional perks and the politics of redistricting. Even more reformers zero-in on money and politics, taking issue with the large sums routinely spent in congressional elections and bemoaning the fact that most of it comes from wealthy individuals and interest groups. That most incumbents raise and spend so much money, making it impossible for their opponents to compete, is another frequently issued complaint.

As enterprising politicians, party leaders, interest group executives, and political consultants found ways to work around the Federal Election Campaign Act, and the law became increasingly weakened by courtroom decisions and administrative rulings, reform groups became more vociferous in their objections to the campaign finance system. Public disapproval of the system grew. More than eight out of ten members of the public agreed with the statement that the campaign finance system "is broken and needs to be replaced" or that "it has problems and needs to be changed"; less than two out of ten maintained that "it has some problems but is basically sound" or "it is all right just the way it is and should not be changed" (see Table 11-1). Individuals who were active in the campaign finance system—those who contributed $200 or more to at least one congressional candidate—were as critical of the system, if not more so, than was the public. Among the criticisms that congressional contributors routinely levied were that "donors regularly pressure officeholders for favors," "officeholders regularly pressure donors for money," and "money has too big an impact on the outcomes of elections." Finally, congressional candidates were the most disparaging of the financing of elections prior to the enactment of the BCRA. Of course voters, donors, and candidates associated with different political parties were critical of different aspects of the system. The same was true of incumbents, challengers, and candidates for open seats.[4]

THE BIPARTISAN CAMPAIGN REFORM ACT

Enacting legislation is never easy, but it is particularly challenging when a bill promises to affect the political careers and livelihoods of those whose support is required to pass it. The members of Congress whose votes were required to pass the BCRA are the same individuals who had succeeded under the old campaign finance system. Moreover, the old system not only got them into Congress but also would keep them there because it generally favored incumbents. But the votes of current members will be needed to pass additional reforms. All of these legislators draw from a set of personal experiences and view themselves as experts on electoral politics. Each possesses a keen understanding of the provisions of the election system that work to his or her individual advantage or disadvantage. Party and interest group leaders know which aspects of the system benefit their organizations. Each member, candidate, and organizational leader also is able to speculate on how different reform packages, including the BCRA, would affect their ability to participate in elections and influence the policy-making process.

Not surprisingly, campaign reform is a highly charged issue. Members of Congress, congressional candidates, and party leaders often portray themselves as reformers while advocating changes that reflect their own self-interest. Incumbents are preoccupied with protecting elements of the system that benefit them. Challengers are just as vocal about doing away with those advantages, at least until they become incumbents. Republicans favor high contribution limits or no limits at all, which would enable them to take advantage of their superior fundraising prowess and larger donor base. Democrats are more favorably disposed toward public funding for campaigns and free media time and postage, which would reduce the impact of the Republicans' financial

TABLE 11–1

Assessments of the Campaign Finance System by Congressional Candidates,
Significant Donors, and the General Public

	Congressional candidates	Significant donors	General public
It is broken and needs to be replaced.	40%	32%	12%
It has problems and needs to be changed.	39	46	70
It has some problems but is basically sound.	21	21	14
It is all right just the way it is and should not be changed.	1	2	4
(*N*)	(326)	(1,027)	(807)

Sources: The Congressional Donors Survey; Paul S. Herrnson, The Campaign Assessment and Candidate Outreach Project 2000; *Washington Post* poll, January 14–19, 1997.

Notes: Congressional candidates include 2000 major-party primary and general election candidates. Significant donors are individuals who contributed $200 or more to a congressional candidate. Some columns do not add up to 100 percent because of rounding.

advantages. Democrats also are more inclined toward eliminating outside money and party and interest group issue advocacy ads than are Republicans.[5]

Interchamber differences also exist, reflecting differences between running in a House district and in a statewide Senate campaign. Additional differences of opinion derive from the demands that campaigning makes on different types of candidates. Women, African Americans, ethnic minorities, and members of other traditionally underrepresented groups, who depend on national donor networks, have preferences that differ from those of most white male candidates. Candidates' opinions about campaign reform also vary according to the characteristics of their constituencies. Candidates from wealthy urban seats tend to have fundraising opportunities, spending needs, and views on reform that are different from those from poor rural states or districts. Of course, not all differences are grounded in personal or partisan advantage. Philosophical differences also divide politicians and parties: the Republicans tend to favor marketplace approaches with few limits on campaign contributions; Democrats generally prefer regulatory measures, such as limits on contributions, accompanied by public subsidies.

The diversity of views and the complexity of the issue make it difficult for legislators to find the common ground needed to pass meaningful campaign reform. The sometimes questionable recommendations and inflammatory public relations campaigns of reform groups often widen, rather than close, gaps between members of Congress. Not surprisingly, legislators often find it challenging to move beyond public posturing and engage in serious reform efforts. Since the late 1970s House members and senators of both parties introduced comprehensive packages that they knew would never be adopted by their respective chambers, survive a conference committee, and be signed into law by the president. Their efforts were largely geared toward providing political cover for themselves rather than enacting campaign finance reform.

Passage of the Act

Nevertheless, there was a confluence of public pressure arising from political scandal and the growing amounts of soft money spent in politics, skillful bipartisan coalition building and the use of unorthodox approaches to lawmaking, resourceful insider lobbying and outside grassroots mobilization by reform groups, and a sympathetic portrayal of the struggle for reform by the mass media. All these factors enabled policy entrepreneurs Reps. Christopher Shays, R-Conn., and Martin Meehan, D-Mass., to pass the precursor to the BCRA over the opposition of the Republican House leadership during both the 105th and 106th congresses.[6] The bill's Senate sponsors, John McCain, R-Ariz., and Russell Feingold, D-Wisc., were not as successful, as the bill twice fell victim to a filibuster in the upper chamber.

The dynamics of the 107th Congress were different in some important respects from the two that preceded it. First, although the Republicans maintained procedural control over the House and won the White House, the Democrats gained control over the Senate when Sen. Jim Jeffords of Vermont quit the Republican Party to become an independent. Second, the turnover associated with the 2000 elections led to a small but important increase in the number of members of Congress who supported reform. Third, McCain's unexpected success in raising the profile of campaign finance reform in the Republican presidential nominating contest emboldened reformers. Fourth, the Enron scandal helped raise questions about the influence of corporate contributions on government regulatory decisions, leading some members to conclude that a vote for the BCRA was a good vehicle for showing their willingness to take action against corporate abuse.[7]

The sequencing of events was one of the most important differences between reform efforts in the 107th and preceding congresses. In both the 105th and 106th congresses the House passed a reform package first, with a significant number of signatories to the bill anticipating the Senate would later scuttle it. In the 107th Congress the order was reversed. Once the Senate had passed the BCRA it was up to the House to determine the bill's future because President Bush had previously announced that if given the opportunity to do so he would sign a campaign finance reform bill into law. This left representatives who had previously voted for reform, but did not actually want the BCRA to become law, in an awkward position. They could cast their votes consistently in support of the bill and live with the consequences of the new law, or they could reverse their positions on previous votes, deny the bill's passage, and look like hypocrites. Partisan pressure was high. The House Republican leadership opposed the legislation and would not have brought it up for a vote, but the bill's supporters garnered sufficient backing for a discharge petition to force the bill to the floor over the leadership's opposition, so the leadership relented. House Democrats and their leaders generally supported reform, although some among their ranks, including some prominent members of the Congressional Black Caucus, publicly opposed it.

The pro-reform camp argued the bill would go a long way in restoring the legitimacy of the federal government. Meehan addressed this issue, arguing that "Ending the soft money system will go a long way towards restoring public confidence in the decisions our government makes. Just as importantly, it will cut the ties between million dollar contributions and the legislators who write the laws that govern our nation." [8] Shays agreed, contending, "Our legislation bans soft money, insists that sham 'issue ads' are covered under campaign law, and gives the FEC the teeth necessary to enforce that law." [9]

Many who opposed the BCRA argued that the bill threatened to trample on free speech rights. In the words of then–House Majority Whip DeLay, "Americans must understand that if this bill becomes law, it will compromise their freedoms and entrench incumbent politicians. . . . Critics make a hollow argument by suggesting that political contributions corrupt elected officials. The central issues in this debate are the preservation of a vibrant freedom of speech and full political participation. I am fighting. . .to defend these core constitutional freedoms." [10] In attempting to rally his caucus, House Speaker Hastert declared the clash over the BCRA "Armageddon." [11]

Ultimately, Republican House leaders lost the battle over the BCRA. The House voted to pass a slightly different version of the bill than had been passed by the Senate. Senate sponsors McCain and Feingold successfully pressed their colleagues to accept the House version of the bill as a substitute for the version the Senate had previously adopted. On March 27, 2002, President Bush signed the BCRA into law.

Major Provisions

The BCRA is not intended to restructure the campaign finance system but rather to close some of the loopholes in the FECA that began to be exploited in the late 1980s. The BCRA seeks to prevent political parties and interest groups from circumventing federal contribution and expenditure limits and avoiding federal disclosure requirements. It also aims to reduce corruption and the appearance of corruption associated with federal candidates raising huge unregulated donations from wealthy interests for political parties.

The law has three major components: a ban on soft money, increased contribution limits, and restrictions on issue advocacy advertising.[12] The provisions for soft money prohibit national party organizations, including the Democratic National Committee, the Republican National Committee, the four Hill committees, or any entity they establish or control from raising, spending, or transferring funds that are not subject to federal regulation. The provisions also prohibit federal officeholders or candidates, or their agents, from raising, spending, or transferring nonfederal funds in connection with a federal election. In most instances, national party committees, state and local party committees, federal officeholders, and candidates for federal office also are prohibited from raising nonfederal funds for organizations, such as the 527 committees discussed in Chapters 1, 4, and 5. The law requires state and local parties to use only federal funds for all communications that feature a federal candidate. It also requires that all voter registration drives conducted during the last 120 days of a federal election that mention a federal candidate be financed with federal funds. State and local party voter registration drives that do not mention a federal candidate can be financed using a mix of hard and soft money.

The law's increased hard money contribution limits are designed to partially compensate political parties for the loss of soft money as a potential source of revenue and expenditures. The law raises from $25,000 to $95,000 the ceiling for aggregate annual contributions to federal candidates, party committees, and political action committees. Individuals are further limited to a maximum contribution of $37,500 to all federal candidates, $37,500 to all party committees, and a combined total of $57,500 to party committees and PACs over the course of a two-year period. Additional provisions specify annual contribution limits of $25,000 for a national party committee and $10,000 for a state party committee. The combined ceiling for national and senatorial campaign committee contributions to a Senate candidate was raised from $17,500 to $35,000. Finally, individual contributions to candidates were raised from $1,000 to $2,000 for each phase of the election (primary, general, and runoff). All but the limits for individual contributions to state party committees are indexed to inflation at least partially to accommodate increases in the costs of campaigning. The contribution limits for PACs did not increase.

The BCRA's provisions for issue advocacy advertising are designed to bring under federal regulation broadcast communications intended to affect the outcomes of congressional or presidential elections. Broadcast, cable, or satellite television or radio broadcasts that feature a federal candidate, are aired thirty days before a primary or sixty days before the general election, and are targeted at a candidate's constituency must be made with federal funds. Broadcasts made prior to this federal spending period can still be made using unregulated outside money.

Additional parts of the law allow party committees to make either limited coordinated expenditures on behalf of federal candidates or unlimited independent expenditures, but not both. The so-called "millionaire's provision" of the law uses a complicated formula to raise the limits for individual contributions and for party coordinated expenditures when a self-funded House candidate contributes more than $350,000 to his or her own campaign or a self-funded Senate candidate contributes $150,000 plus an amount equal to four cents times the state's eligible voting population. Once a self-financing House or Senate candidate exceeds the appropriate threshold, the limits for individual contributions and party coordinated expenditures gradually increase in response to the amount the self-financing candidate contributes to his or her own campaign.

Post–BCRA Challenges

Challenges to the BCRA were mounted before the ink from the president's signature on the law had even dried. In fact, the BCRA's opponents were lining up to contest the constitutionality of the law even before it was officially enacted. Leading the charge was Sen. Mitch McConnell, R-Ky., who while still filibustering against reform, stated, "Should the bill become law, I will be the lead plaintiff." [13] Among the dozens of others that joined the cause to overturn the law were the RNC, House Speaker Hastert, the California Democratic and Republican Parties, the Cato Institute, the American Civil Liberties Union (ACLU), the AFL-CIO, the National Rifle Association, and eight state attorneys general. These plaintiffs maintain the law's ban on issue advocacy advertising and restrictions on party financial activity are unconstitutional violations of free speech rights. The National Voting Rights Institute, the U.S. Public Interest Research Group (associated with consumer advocate Ralph Nader), and some other voter groups joined the suit for a different reason, claiming its increased contribution limits were unconstitutional because they favor the wealthy. Writing in defense of the law were the Committee on Economic Development (comprising many of the nation's business leaders), almost every living former member of the ACLU leadership, and twenty-one state attorneys general. [14]

In addition to legal wrangling that was destined to find its way to the U.S. Supreme Court, the BCRA encountered another set of challenges when the Federal Election Commission began drafting the regulations for administering the law. The BCRA was not warmly received by some members of the FEC. This was not surprising given that two commissioners—Bradley Smith and Chairman David Mason—made speeches and released statements challenging the bill during the congressional debate.[15] Moreover, numerous party committees, interest groups, and others—including supporters and opponents of the law—worked to influence the rule-making process. The ensuing rules weakened provisions of the law designed to prevent soft money from influencing federal campaigns. Among these were rules exempting Internet communications from the law's soft money prohibitions, and allowing federal candidates to be involved in state party soft money fundraising events. McCain, Feingold, Shays, and Meehan responded by issuing a statement that the commission adopted many regulations that "simply ignore the law," filing a legal challenge to the FEC's regulations, and drafting a congressional resolution to overturn the regulations under the Congressional Review Act.[16] The suits against the BCRA and the FEC's regulations and the congressional resolution could have a major impact on the law and the financing of congressional elections for years to come.

On May 2, 2003, a special three-judge panel of the U.S. District Court for the District of Columbia handed down a 1,638-page verdict in *McConnell v. FEC.*[17] The judges were sharply divided on many issues. Their verdict upheld most of the BCRA's main provisions but altered some aspects of the law concerning soft money and issue advocacy. It upheld the ban on federal officeholders and candidates soliciting nonfederal funds for federal party committees but allows these individuals to solicit such funds for state and local parties and candidates. It upheld the law's prohibitions against parties spending soft money for candidate-focused issue advocacy ads. It also extended beyond the thirty-day and sixty-day federal spending periods the ban on such advertisements, whether financed by parties or interest groups, thereby seemingly outlawing the financing of these ads with soft money altogether. Moreover, the ruling invalidated the ban on federal party committees raising or spending soft money on voter registration and get-out-the-vote drives and other generic party-focused activities.

Almost as soon as the three-judge panel handed down its decision, numerous parties, including most of those supporting or opposing the BCRA, filed appeals to the Supreme Court. Given the diversity of the judges' opinions, their ruling could have little bearing on the decision ultimately issued by the high court. Perhaps in recognition of this fact, the lower court judges issued a stay of their ruling. This decision restored the provisions of the law that the court had struck down or modified, leaving the original BCRA, as enacted by Congress and signed into law by the president, as the law governing the financing of federal elections, pending review by the Supreme Court.

THE BCRA'S LIKELY IMPACT

Predicting the impact of any new law is not easy, regardless of whether it is being challenged in the Supreme Court. The BCRA will have some unanticipated consequences even after the high court makes its ruling. The BCRA, like the FECA and early campaign legislation, most certainly will evolve according to the normal cycle of regulatory reform. The law's short-term effects should be greater than its medium-range influence because of the time it takes groups and individuals to adapt to the new regulatory regime. Of course, both the short-term and medium-range effects will differ from the long range effects that inevitably occur after politicians, party leaders, interest group executives, and other donors discover loopholes that weaken the law and after FEC commissioners and federal judges make rulings in response to the actions of these individuals and groups. Nevertheless, it is worthwhile to speculate about the impact that the BCRA will have on political parties, interest groups, candidates, and the public.

Political Parties

Numerous party leaders have complained that the BCRA would virtually eliminate the national parties' roles in congressional elections. Much of this response is hyperbole. Party organizations undoubtedly will adapt to whichever portions of the BCRA survive *McConnell v. FEC*, just as they adapted to the FECA, technological advancements, and larger systemic changes that have taken place in their environment. The law may even encourage the development of stronger parties. Should the provisions concerned with party fundraising and spending remain intact, the national parties' inability to spend large sums of hard and soft money in a small number of federal elections would encourage them to distribute their funds in a larger number of contests, thereby resulting in more races becoming competitive. The parties also might respond by investing more money in their own organizational development. There are some signs that the parties already have entered a new phase of party building similar to that which began in the 1970s. The national party organizations have begun efforts to expand their small and medium donor bases; to advise candidates about how to participate in the new campaign finance system; and to instruct state and local party leaders how to further develop their organizations' institutional capacities, fundraising, and campaign service programs without violating the law. These developments parallel those that took place shortly after passage of the FECA.[18]

Should they pass constitutional muster, the law's prohibitions against party soft money probably would result in the national party organizations losing some clout in their relationships with state and local party committees because national parties will be in a position to transfer fewer funds to state and local parties and candidates. The increased decentralization of campaign fundraising would naturally lead to an increased decentralization of strategic decision making and spending. State parties would have more autonomy in terms of how they spend their campaign funds because they would have raised more of their resources by themselves instead of receiving them through national party transfers.

The Hill committees can be expected to continue to have significant roles in congressional elections. They probably will remain important sources of campaign contributions, coordinated expenditures, and assistance with campaign management, fundraising, and the other aspects of campaigning discussed in Chapter 4. They also will continue to have a hand in coordinating the contributions and campaign efforts of wealthy interest groups and individuals. Further, congressional leaders and members of Congress from safe seats should be poised to increase their role in the financing of congressional elections. The increased ceilings for individual contributions will enable these legislators to raise more money from individuals and to redistribute it to needy candidates and party committees. Parties, particularly those at the state and local levels, will continue to be involved in grassroots campaign activities.

The prohibitions against party soft money and issue advocacy advertising will result in parties having less significant roles in campaign communications in close elections, should those provisions of the law remain intact. The provisions allowing parties to make either coordinated expenditures or independent expenditures would force the parties to choose between one means of communication and the other. Parties are likely to make coordinated expenditures in races that are moderately competitive and in which they do not plan to spend a tremendous amount of funds because such expenditures can be made in concert with a candidate's campaign efforts. Parties would probably spend funds in the form of independent expenditures in very close contests, where they feel the need to invest more than the maximum allowable coordinated expenditures.

Under the BCRA, as originally configured, parties will almost certainly provide less support to candidates in extremely tight congressional elections than they did in 2002, but they may help a larger number of competitive candidates because the ban on soft money eliminates the national parties' strategy of conserving hard money for the purpose of combining it with soft money in order to broadcast issue advocacy ads in a small number of close races. The broader distribution of party campaign resources could encourage more candidates with political experience to run for Congress, thereby improving electoral competition.

If the Supreme Court allows the BCRA's ban on unlimited soft money contributions to stand, the law should reduce somewhat the influence that wealthy interest groups have on political parties. Party committees will still cultivate interest group leaders to raise federally regulated contributions, but the levels of courtship would probably not go to the same extremes as they did when the parties sought million-dollar soft money donations from wealthy corporations, unions, and individuals. Instead, parties can be expected to devote more time to developing donor networks comprising individuals who give relatively modest contributions. Individuals who can bundle large numbers of modest contributions will probably become the new fat cats of campaign finance, replacing those who could simply write a check for hundreds of thousands or even millions of dollars. Parties can be expected to use the standard means to cultivate those individuals, including memberships in party clubs; invitations to briefings, receptions, and vacations with party leaders; and other special perks. Under the BCRA, party leaders also probably would devote more time to creating allied interest group organizations and helping them raise money and spend their money in ways that help their party's candidates.

If not drastically altered by the court, the law's prohibitions against soft money should further reinforce the candidate-centered nature of congressional elections. Recognizing they will be unable to rely on party committees to mount issue advocacy campaigns on their behalf, candidates would undoubtedly focus on raising federal funds for their own campaign treasuries rather than on raising nonfederal funds for party organizations or joint fundraising committees. The ban on issue advocacy ads would reduce the roles of parties in campaign advertising, restore more control of the substance of congressional campaigns to the candidates themselves, and probably reduce the negativity of congressional races.

Finally, the law most likely will favor the Republican Party, despite the fact that more Democratic members of Congress voted for the law than did Republicans. The GOP enjoys a number of advantages over the Democrats in terms of raising the relatively small and moderate individual contributions allowed under the BCRA. During the 2002 elections Republican candidates, party committees, and leadership PACs collected almost 303,900 contributions of at least $200, whereas the Democrats collected nearly 211,500 such contributions.[19]

Interest Groups

Should the BCRA survive its constitutional challenge, it can be expected to have several effects on interest groups. First, the elimination of soft money contributions to political parties would both deprive groups of a major means for gaining access to public officials and free them from the perceived necessity of making such contributions. Second, it would encourage groups that wish to participate in congressional elections to devote greater effort to strengthening their organizational capacities. The prohibitions against contributing soft money and making issue advocacy ads during the latter—and most important—part of the campaign season would free up resources and create incentives for interest groups to set up or strengthen PACs. One would expect these organizations to expand their PACs' small and moderate donor bases and abilities to bundle campaign contributions.[20]

Third, the prohibition against using outside money to air issue advocacy ads during the federal spending periods would have a major impact on groups' campaign activities. Some groups may exit the issue advocacy arena. Others can be expected to use nonfederal funds for internal communications with their members and to try to set the campaign agenda in individual races during the early nonfederal spending periods. They also would probably use PACs to give donations to parties and candidates and to make independent expenditures during the federal spending period.[21]

Fourth, the law almost certainly will encourage some interests to form entirely new groups or graft new organizational entities onto existing groups. As described in Chapter 5, interest groups, such as the League of Conservation Voters, create complex organizational structures to help them accomplish their goals. The enactment of the BCRA already has led to the formation of new groups, often with the assistance of party leaders. Former representative and National Republican Congressional Committee chair William Paxon and Susan Hirschmann, a former aide to then House majority whip DeLay, created the Leadership Forum, a 527 committee, to help drug companies, the chemical industry, and foreign banking interests, among others, use nonfederal dollars to influence congressional elections. The group received initial backing of $1 million in soft money from the NRCC but returned the funds after several campaign finance watchdog organizations filed a complaint with the FEC.[22]

Another recently formed organization, the National Committee for a Responsible Senate (NCRS), has strong connections to the NRSC and prominent

Republican lawyers and is incorporated as a 501(c)(6) organization, the tax designation used by most trade associations. This designation enables the NCRS to accept unlimited donations without disclosing its donors and to run very aggressive issue advocacy campaigns. The same lawyers that founded the NCRS also created Americans for Responsible Government, a 501(c)(4) group that will promote tax cuts, economic growth, and strengthening families.[23] A third organization, the Democratic Senate Majority Political Action Committee, is headed by Monica Dixon, a former aide to Al Gore and former executive director of the House Democratic Caucus. This group has a federal PAC to make contributions to congressional candidates and it uses soft money from a separate account to finance issue advocacy advertisements.[24] These groups seem poised to succeed. Given the backgrounds of their organizers, these groups should be able to provide donors with opportunities to achieve their goals, including gaining access to federal lawmakers; supporting candidates who share their views; and socializing with political leaders, celebrities, and other elites. Their organizers also possess sufficient know-how and connections to make the groups influential in campaign and legislative politics.

The creation of new interest group entities, the augmentation of existing organizations, and the implementation of new group fundraising strategies are bound to have some unanticipated effects on the roles of groups in congressional elections. However, should the law's outright prohibitions against national party soft money and party issue advocacy remain in place, interest groups would probably end up having more influence vis-à-vis party committees in congressional elections.

Finally, barring radical restructuring by the Supreme Court, the law probably will have an impact on the balance of power in the interest group community. Because business PACs, including those sponsored by corporations, trade associations, and cooperatives, raise substantially more money than labor PACs—$350.8 million as opposed to almost $191.7 million in 2002—business interests will probably continue to hold a significant edge in the contributions they make to congressional candidates. Moreover, business interests are undoubtedly in a better position than is organized labor to increase its influence through bundling. For one thing, business PACs possess significant advantages organizationally. In 2002 they outnumbered labor PACs by 2,856 to 1,741. Also, business PAC contributions are collected through personal solicitations, direct mail, and many other approaches that rely on deliberate decisions on the part of donors, whereas labor PAC contributions are collected using automatic payroll deductions from which members must deliberately take steps to withdraw their contributions. Additionally, business PACs have wealthier donors who are used to supporting a variety of organizations and groups. These contrasts suggest that business PACs would be in a better position to ask their donors to write checks to specific candidates than would labor PACs. Nevertheless, the impact of the law on 527 committees suggests that should these organizations continue to raise and spend soft money at their current pace, labor unions will continue to outspend business groups. Another area in which organized labor can expect to continue to outpace business interests is the provision of campaign volunteers.

Candidates

The BCRA's impact on candidates is likely to vary by chamber, incumbency, and party. As discussed in Chapter 6, Senate candidates depend on individual contributions for a greater portion of their campaign receipts than do their House counterparts. Given their larger numbers of individual donors, candidates for the upper chamber are more likely to capitalize on the law's higher individual contribution limits, under the possibility that the Supreme Court allows these limits to continue to stand. Incumbents, particularly congressional leaders, who have in the past raised large sums of hard and soft money from established donor networks, should be in a position to raise more $2,000 contributions than challengers and candidates for open seats. Nevertheless, the higher limits for individual contributions might help nonincumbents, especially those in close races, to raise more funds. Given that challengers have the greatest need to raise and spend money, an increase in the sums they raise as a result of the higher limits could have a notable impact on the conduct of their campaigns, whereas a comparable increase in receipts would have only a marginal effect on incumbents' campaigns.

The law probably will give Republican candidates a fundraising advantage over Democrats, particularly as long as the GOP continues to control Congress. When it comes to raising individual contributions, Republican congressional candidates enjoy advantages over their Democratic opponents that parallel those enjoyed by Republican Party committees. Perhaps the Republicans' most important advantage is a broader base of individuals who more routinely make small and moderate contributions. When individuals who contributed at least $200 to one congressional candidate were asked how they would respond to increased contribution limits, 15 percent said they would contribute more, 80 percent reported they would not change their levels of contributions, and 5 percent maintained they would give less money. One-quarter of all strong Republicans said that they would give more, compared with only 12 percent of strong Democrats. Weak Republicans also were more likely than weak Democrats to maintain that they would give more. Although donors respond to a variety of stimuli, including the quality of the candidates, local and national political conditions, and who is soliciting the contribution, the responses of significant congressional donors suggest that Republican candidates will be the primary beneficiaries of the BCRA's higher ceilings for individual contributions.[25]

The Public

Few members of the public reach for their wallets when politicians arrive on the scene, reflecting most Americans' hesitation to actively engage in politics. Roughly 7 percent of all voters claim to have made a contribution to any candidate for public office, and only 0.3 percent donated $200 or more to a candidate for Congress.[26] The average individual contribution is less than $75, and the top 1 percent of all individual donors account for roughly 10 percent of all individual donations.[27] The BCRA may broaden the base of congressional donors slightly, but if allowed to stand the law's increased contribution limits probably would result in fewer donors accounting for a larger share of all individual donations.

It is also unlikely that the law would do much to restore trust in the campaign finance system or overcome suspicions about the role of money in politics more generally. Most voters do not understand the differences between hard and soft money or independent expenditures, coordinated expenditures, and issue advocacy ads. They are unlikely to notice the law's impact on campaign finance or the broader conduct of congressional elections. Rather, most voters will continue to adhere to their preconceived notions about the role of money in politics. News stories about campaign spending, lavish fundraising events, and the power of high-priced lobbyists will continue to feed those negative preconceptions. Public opinion is difficult to change, and Americans traditionally have had a healthy skepticism about politics.

The growing disconnection between the campaign for votes and the campaign for resources contributes to voters' skepticism. During the golden age of parties, when local party activists were among the most important campaign resources, an intimate connection existed between the two campaigns. Elections were neighborhood affairs, and campaigns involved personal contact between candidates, party activists, other volunteers, and voters. Personal contact between voters and campaigners existed before, during, and after the election season. Parties provided ordinary voters and campaigners with ongoing relationships with members of Congress and others involved in the political system. Often these relationships revolved around jobs, contracts, social clubs, and opportunities to improve oneself or one's neighborhood. Such relationships humanized government for voters and built bonds of trust between people and political institutions.[28]

Contemporary campaigns encourage fewer meaningful ties to develop between voters and candidates. Despite efforts of political parties, interest groups, and candidate organizations, the campaign for votes is still relatively impersonal, consisting largely of television, radio, direct mail, mass telephone calls, and the free media they generate. Fleeting contacts occasionally take place among citizens, candidates, and party and campaign activists, but they rarely lead to enduring personal relationships. Moreover, campaigns for resources rarely focus on ordinary voters, turning instead toward national party organizations, PACs, and wealthy individuals in a position to provide the wherewithal needed to mount a contemporary campaign. Corporations, unions, and other organizations that finance independent, parallel, and coordinated campaigns also have become important targets in the campaign for resources.

Many voters believe that the elite special interests that spend large sums in elections, rather than individuals who vote in them, possess the strongest and most beneficial relationships with members of Congress and others in government.[29] Because members of Congress and the organizations that elect them have relatively little patronage, few preferments, and hardly any opportunities for social advancement to distribute to their constituents, many voters have come to believe that these "goodies" are being distributed instead to wealthy campaign contributors in Washington and the nation's other financial centers. Transformations in the way that campaigns are conducted at home and in Washington have contributed to the public's belief that the operation of the federal government has changed in ways that favor special interests in Washington over the folks back home.

BEYOND THE BCRA

Although the enactment of the BCRA has been hailed as a major victory by the reform community, most members of that community consider it a short step on a long road to a system of model elections. Indeed, the BCRA that was enacted is a mere shadow of the first campaign reform bill introduced by McCain and Feingold. That bill proposed to ban PACs, prohibit bundling, require candidates to raise 60 percent of their funds from within their state, and offer candidates free television time and reduced postage in exchange for voluntary spending limits. Previous bills included provisions for public funding.

Other measures entertained by a variety of reform groups include term limits, the creation of multimember districts for House candidates, and public funding for candidates and parties. Among the reforms that have received more serious consideration are improved disclosure of campaign expenditures intended to influence federal elections; free or subsidized campaign communications for candidates and political parties; tax credits for individual contributors; restructuring of the FEC; revamping of state redistricting processes; initiatives to increase voter turnout; and, most recently, measures to improve voting machines, ballots, and election administration.

Regardless of their goals, reformers should base their proposals on an understanding that elections are fought primarily between candidates and that party committees, PACs, and other organizations have important supplemental roles in them. Reformers need to appreciate the different goals and resources that individuals and groups bring to elections and to consider how their proposals will affect these groups.

Campaign reform should be predicated on the assumption that highly participatory, competitive elections are desirable because they are the best way to hold elected officials accountable to voters, enhance representation, and build trust in government. Reform should make congressional elections more competitive by encouraging additional talented candidates to run and by improving the ability of candidates, particularly nonincumbents, to communicate with voters. Campaign reform should also seek to increase the number of people who vote and give campaign contributions. It should attempt to minimize the amount of unregulated money spent to influence federal elections. The recommendations that follow are not a comprehensive reform package but a series of proposals that would make congressional elections more participatory and more competitive and perhaps eventually instill greater public confidence in the political system.

Disclosure

One of the most important and broadly supported provisions of the original FECA and its amendments concerns the full disclosure of receipts and expenditures made in federal elections. Disclosure enables the public to track the money flow in election campaigns. Timely publication of a campaign's financial transactions allows voters to hold candidates accountable for where they raise their funds and how they spend them, making it possible for campaign financing to become an issue in an election. Moreover, combined with information about legislators' roll-call votes, candidates' campaign finances provide citizens with information they can use to gauge whether an incumbent appears to be held captive by one or more specific interests. Similarly, publication of a party committee's or PAC's receipts, contributions, and other expenditures enables interested voters to develop a sense of whom these organizations depend on for their resources and how they seek to influence elections, legislators, and policy making in general.

For much of its history, the FECA was largely successful in enabling voters to follow the money trail in federal elections. Watchdog groups, particularly the Center for Responsive Politics and Political Money Line, improved on the FEC's disclosure efforts by making it possible for individuals and reporters to easily visit a web site that provides detailed information about candidates' reliance on various interests and organizations for their campaign finances.[30] As a result, news reports on campaign finance have become at least as prevalent as stories about substantive campaign issues.

However, the emergence of soft money and outside spending by interest groups on issue advocacy ads weakened the financial disclosure of funds spent in connection with federal elections. Although the FECA required national party committees to disclose their soft money receipts, and the BCRA prohibits national parties from collecting such funds, disclosure requirements for state and local parties vary by state and usually are not as rigorous. Moreover and as noted earlier, some interest group entities that participate in congressional and presidential elections are not subject to the same rigorous disclosure requirements as are federal candidates, party committees, and PACs, despite legislation that attempts to correct for the problem. As a result, the sources, amounts, and exact expenditures some interest groups undertake to influence congressional elections are largely hidden from public purview. As explained in Chapter 5, this becomes especially problematic when interests, such as the pharmaceutical industry, hide their identity by forming shadow groups with innocuous sounding names for the purposes of disseminating issue advertisements and then proceed to spend as much as, if not more than, the candidates. The fact that most members of the public are unable to discern these ads from candidate ads further exacerbates the problem by blurring accountability. The BCRA partially addresses undisclosed or partially disclosed expenditures by shadow groups by outlawing issue advocacy ads during the federal spending periods preceding primaries and general elections. However, the law could be improved by subjecting to strict disclosure laws any organization that spends money at any time to influence federal elections, regardless of that group's designation under the federal election law or the federal tax code.

Free or Subsidized Communications

Free or subsidized campaign communications—whether in the form of postage, television or radio time, or communications vouchers—would give candidates, particularly challengers, the opportunity to present their messages to the public. The promise of free or heavily discounted communications resources would probably encourage better candidates to run for Congress because it would guarantee access to some of the resources needed to campaign.[31] By encouraging the entry of better candidates and providing them with communications resources, this reform should lead to more competitive congressional elections.

The availability of communications resources also might indirectly encourage greater electoral competition. Congressional challengers and open-seat candidates who use these resources effectively would be in a position to attract the attention of local journalists, thereby helping the candidates communicate more effectively with voters and helping voters cast their ballots on the basis of more information. Because campaign communications help stimulate public interest in elections, reforms that ensure both candidates have adequate communications resources also probably would increase voter turnout.[32] A perception of greater competitiveness also might encourage some PACs and wealthy individuals to contribute to challengers, although most would likely continue to employ access or mixed strategies, which dictate contributing primarily to incumbents.

Free or subsidized mailings would give candidates opportunities to present targeted, detailed information about their qualifications, issue positions, and political objectives. Giving congressional candidates free postage for three or four first-class mailings—including postage for one or two newsletters of six to ten pages—is a simple reform that would improve the quality of the information that voters receive and increase voter turnout and electoral competitiveness.

Parties also could be offered free postage to mobilize current supporters and attract new ones. Minor parties and their candidates, as well as candidates who run as independents, could be given free postage if they persuaded a threshold number of voters to register under their label prior to the current election, if the candidates had received a minimum number of votes in the previous contest, or if they met some other threshold requirement. Minor parties and their candidates and independent candidates also could be reimbursed retroactively for postage if they reached some threshold level of votes in the current election. Extending free postage to candidates and parties is justified by the fact that it would contribute to the education of citizens—the same argument used to justify congressionally franked mail and reduced postage for party committees and nonprofit educational groups.

Giving candidates access to radio and television broadcast time would be more complicated because of disparities in rate charges and because congressional districts and media markets often do not match one another.[33] One solution is to require local broadcasters to provide Senate candidates with free television time and to require local radio stations to give free radio time to both House and Senate candidates. Broadcasters could be required to issue back-to-back, prime-time segments to opposing candidates. Candidates could be issued five-minute blocks of time early in the campaign season, which they could use to air "infomercials." These time slots would be lengthy enough for candidates to communicate some information about their personal backgrounds, political qualifications, issue positions, and major campaign themes. Later in the campaign season, two- or one-minute time slots could be distributed so that candidates could reinforce the images and campaign themes they introduced earlier. Thirty- or fifteen-second time slots could be made available during the summation phase of the election for candidates to pull together their campaign messages and rally their supporters.

This system of structured, free media time would give candidates the opportunity to communicate positive, substantive messages. It also would encourage voters to compare those messages. The differences in requirements for each chamber reflect the fact that television is an efficient and heavily used medium in virtually all Senate elections but is less practical and less frequently used in House contests, especially those held in major metropolitan areas.

The Democratic and Republican national, congressional, and senatorial campaign committees also should be given free blocks of television and radio time so that each could have the opportunity to remind voters of their party's accomplishments, philosophies, and objectives. Giving parties resources they can use to influence the political agenda during and after an election could introduce more collective responsibility into the political system.[34] Minor parties and candidates should be given free broadcast time on terms similar to those for free postage.

Requiring local broadcasters to provide free political advertisements is justifiable because the airwaves are public property and one of the conditions of using them is that broadcasters "serve the public interest, convenience, and necessity."[35] The United States is the only major industrialized democracy that does not require broadcasters to contribute air time to candidates for public office—a distinction that should be eliminated.[36] Cable and satellite television operators also should be required to distribute advertising time to House and Senate candidates and parties with the justification that much of what is viewed on cable television passes through the public airwaves or over publicly maintained utility lines.

An alternative to providing candidates and parties with communications resources is government distribution of communications vouchers. This practice would allow campaigners to exercise more freedom in designing their communications strategies. Campaigns that felt the need to allocate more resources to setting the agenda could use their vouchers to purchase mass media ads. Campaigns that wished to focus on mobilizing specific population groups could devote a greater portion of their vouchers to targeted direct mail or telephone calls.

The Political Campaign Broadcast Activity Improvements Act that senators McCain, Feingold, and Richard Durbin, D-Ill., introduced during the 107th Congress includes some of these ideas.[37] It provides House candidates who raise at least $25,000 in individual contributions in amounts of $250 or less and do not spend more than $125,000 in personal funds (including funds from immediate family members) with $3 in broadcast vouchers for every $1 the candidate raises in individual contributions in amounts not exceeding $250. It provides Senate candidates who raise at least $25,000 in individual contributions in amounts of $250 or less and do not spend more than $500,000 in personal funds with $3 in broadcast vouchers for every $1 they raise in individual contributions in amounts not exceeding $250. The ceiling for vouchers for House candidates is $375,000, and the ceiling for vouchers for Senate candidates is $375,000 times the number of House members who represent the state. Candidates who receive vouchers but do not wish to use them can exchange them with their party for an equivalent amount of cash, which they could then spend on other campaign activities.

The proposal sets aside an aggregate total of up to $100 million in broadcast vouchers to be divided among the political parties. Major political parties (defined as those that have received 25 percent or more of the popular vote in the preceding presidential election) automatically qualify for vouchers. Minor parties qualify once they have fielded candidates who qualify for vouchers in twenty-two House races or five Senate races. A minor party would receive vouchers proportionate to the number of qualified candidates it fields. A minor party that fields candidates who qualify for vouchers in at least 218 House elections or 17 Senate elections is eligible for the same number of vouchers as a major party.

The bill also has some public affairs programming requirements. It requires all radio and television broadcast stations to devote a minimum of two hours per week to candidate-centered or issue-focused programming for a total of six weeks before a primary or general election. This programming must be aired during popular time slots: one-half must be between 5 P.M. and 11:35 P.M.; none may be broadcast between midnight and 6 A.M. The bill requires that during the 45 days before a primary and the 60 days before the general election, candidates and parties be given the lowest unit rate charge that the station has charged any other advertiser during the 120 days preceding a candidate's or party's request. Finally, the bill prohibits stations from preempting air time purchased by candidates or parties on behalf of a candidate in favor of other customers.

Tax Incentives

Tax incentives should be used to broaden the base of campaign contributors and to offset the impact of funds collected from wealthy and well-organized segments of society. Prior to the tax reforms introduced in 1986, individuals were able to claim a tax credit of $50 if they contributed $100 or more to federal candidates. (Couples who contributed $200 could claim a tax credit of $100.) Although a significant number of taxpayers took advantage of these credits, the credits themselves were not sufficient to encourage many citizens to give campaign contributions.[38]

A system of graduated tax credits similar to those used in some other western democracies might accomplish this goal.[39] Individuals who are eligible to claim a 100 percent tax credit for up to $100 in campaign contributions would be more likely to make them. Credits of 75 percent for the next $100 and 50 percent for the following $100 would encourage further contributions. Tax credits would encourage candidates and parties to pursue small and moderate contributions more aggressively. Because being asked is one of the most important determinants of who actually makes a contribution, tax credits for individual donations are likely to have a positive impact on the number of taxpayers who make them.[40] Using taxpayer dollars to increase the number of individuals who give money to federal candidates is an expensive proposition, but it would probably be the most effective way to increase the number of people who participate in the financing of congressional elections. Increasing the base of small contributors is the best way to offset the influence of individuals and groups that make large contributions while maintaining a tie between a candidate's level of popular and financial support.

The Federal Election Commission

The FEC should be strengthened. The commission is currently unable to investigate many of the complaints brought before it, has a backlog of cases that is several years old, and has been criticized for its failure to dispense quickly with frivolous cases and pursue more important ones. Some of these shortcomings are the result of the committee often being micromanaged by its oversight committees in Congress and by its severe underfunding. Other shortcomings are due to the FEC's structure—it has three Democratic and three Republican commissioners, which lends itself to indecision and stalemate.

It is essential that the FEC be restructured so that it operates in a more decisive fashion. Only strong enforcement by the FEC, with backup from the Justice Department and a specially appointed independent counsel on appropriate cases, can discourage unscrupulous politicians from violating the law. Recent failures by the FEC to enforce the law adequately have encouraged members of Congress to spend tens of millions of dollars on partisan investigations. Such investigations, which may be useful for embarrassing political opponents, are an inadequate substitute for impartial administration of the law.

Redistricting

As a result of redistricting, 2002 set a contemporary record for the number of uncompetitive House elections. Deals cut between Democratic and Republican House members resulted in an absence of competition in most incumbent-challenger races. In only a few states, most notably Iowa, were there a significant number of competitive House races. The contrast between Iowa and most other states suggests that competition would be increased if states passed reforms emulating Iowa's redistricting commission, which does not take into account partisanship or incumbency when drawing congressional seats.

Another reform related to redistricting is to prohibit state legislatures from redrawing House seats following the initial redistricting that takes place after reapportionment. Republicans in Colorado and Texas sought to do precisely that after their party won control of both the legislature and the governorship of these states following the 2002 elections. The GOP succeeded in redrawing the congressional seats in Colorado, although their actions have been challenged in the Colorado state Supreme Court.[41] The Republicans failed in Texas because more than fifty Democratic state lawmakers fled to neighboring Oklahoma to deny the GOP the quorum needed to enact the plan or conduct any other official business.[42] If allowed to stand, the efforts of the GOP state lawmakers could set a precedent that would encourage politicians to seek to create new district boundaries every time party control of a state's government changes hands rather than wait until the decennial census, reapportionment, and redistricting cycle runs its normal course. Such "repeat redistricting" can only inject more discord into an already conflict-ridden process and increase the number of lawsuits that accompany the drawing of congressional seats.

Voter Turnout Initiatives

Campaign reform should address low voter turnout in elections. In 2002 only 39 percent of all eligible voters turned up at the polls—a figure in line with recent midterm elections. Citizen apathy and disenchantment with the political system are probably responsible for some voter abstention, but voter registration laws are believed to depress turnout by about 9 percent.[43] The motor-voter law, enacted in 1993, has eased some barriers to voter registration. Requiring all states to include a check-off box on their income tax forms to enable citizens to register to vote when they file their tax returns could further reduce the barriers to voting.

Measures that make it easier for voters to exercise the franchise also should be considered. Making election day a national holiday is one possibility. Making wider use of mail-in ballots, such as those used in Oregon, is another. "Early," "countywide," and "mobile" voting procedures also should be considered. Such procedures currently allow voters in Texas to cast their ballots over a seventeen-day period commencing twenty days before an election at any of the numerous locations in the county in which they are registered to vote. These locations include mobile units that are dispatched to parks and other popular locations on weekends. It also might be possible to allow people to vote by telephone or via the Internet. Measures that make it easier to register to vote or cast a ballot will not cause a groundswell in voter turnout, but they should increase it, especially when combined with increased competition and greater efforts by candidates and parties to mobilize voters.[44]

Improving the Way Americans Vote

The 2000 presidential election was a wake-up call for voters, election administrators, and candidates for public office. It showed that something was amiss with how Americans vote. Between 4 million and 6 million presidential votes and as many as 3.5 million senatorial and gubernatorial votes were lost in the balloting process. Approximately 7.4 percent of the forty million registered voters who did not vote stated that they did not cast a ballot because of problems with their registration. An additional 2.8 percent of all registered voters who did not vote attributed their failure to turn up at the polls to long lines, inopportune hours, or inconveniently located polling places.[45]

Discussions of "butterfly ballots," "chads," "undervotes," "overvotes," and partisan decision-making by election officials and the courts also left many people unsettled. Reports that substantial numbers of the poor and members of minority groups were turned away at the polls and evidence the votes cast by members of these groups were less likely to be counted than votes cast by wealthy or middle-class white voters raised concerns about adherence to the principal of one person, one vote. Learning about the absence of clearly delineated procedures for vote recounts in many states and localities also was cause for some anxiety. The fact that 1960s technology was still being widely used in twenty-first-century elections was another cause of voter dissatisfaction.[46]

Congress responded to public pressure for reform by passing the Help America Vote Act of 2002 (HAVA), which the president signed into law on October 29, 2002. HAVA provides $3.9 billion in federal funds for distribution to the states over the course of three years for the purposes of replacing outdated voting machines, improving voter education, and training poll workers. The states must ensure that voting machines have minimal error rates and allow voters to review, and if necessary correct, their ballots before casting them. Moreover, each polling place is required to have at least one voting machine that is accessible to individuals with disabilities. HAVA also requires states to have a computerized voter registration system in place by 2004 and to provide provisional ballots to individuals whose names do not appear on the voter rolls and to count their ballots once their registration is verified. It also requires first-time voters who registered by mail to provide identification the first time they show up to cast their ballots.[47]

HAVA depends on state governments, and ultimately the county governments that administer elections in most states, for implementation. Thus, its success depends largely on the capabilities and resources of those governments. Complicating the picture is the fact that these governments depend on private manufacturers and vendors for voting equipment, poll-worker training, and much of the software needed to run the new voting machines and manage voter rolls. Of the voting machines currently available, those employing optically scanned paper ballots have the best track record, but even they could be improved.[48] Moreover, many states are purchasing the more impressive-looking "digital recording electronic" or "ATM-style"—voting machines. Tests of this equipment indicate that there is substantial room for improvement.[49] HAVA is an important step in improving how Americans vote, but actions must be taken by many governmental and private institutions for it to be effective. As the 2000 elections demonstrated, voting technology, ballot designs, and election administration are important, especially when elections are competitive.

CONCLUSION

The rules and norms that govern congressional elections resemble those that structure any activity: they favor some individuals and groups at the expense of others. In recent years the number of Americans who believe that the electoral process is out of balance and provides too many advantages to incumbents, interest groups, wealthy individuals, and other "insiders" has grown tremendously. Their views are reflected in the growing distrust that citizens have of government, the sense of powerlessness expressed by many voters, and the public's willingness to follow the leads of insurgent candidates and reformers without scrutinizing their qualifications or objectives. These are signs that the prestige and power of Congress are in danger. They also are signs that meaningful campaign reform is in order.

Campaign reform should make congressional elections more competitive and increase the number of citizens who participate in them, both as voters and as financial contributors. Campaign reform should enable candidates to spend less time campaigning for resources and more time campaigning for votes. Reform also should seek to enhance representation, accountability, and trust in government. If not overturned in the Supreme Court, the BCRA will accomplish some but not all of these goals.

Without major campaign reform, incumbency will remain the defining element of most congressional elections. Challengers, particularly those who run for the House, will continue to struggle to raise campaign funds and attract the attention of the media and voters. The dialogues in House incumbent-challenger contests will remain largely one-sided, whereas those in open-seat contests and Senate races will continue to be somewhat more even. Interest groups will continue to spend outside money on issue ads designed to influence the campaign agenda prior to the federal spending periods preceding primaries and the general election. Party and interest group independent expenditures and interest group issue advocacy may continue to overshadow the election activities of candidates in very close races. Congress, elections, and other institutions of government will remain targets for attack both by those who have a sincere wish to improve the political process and by those seeking short-term partisan gain.

Elections are the most important avenues of political influence that are afforded to the citizens of a representative democracy. They give voters the opportunity to hold public officials accountable and to reject politicians with whom they disagree. Respect for human rights and political processes that allow for citizen input are what make democratic systems of government superior to others. Yet all systems of government have their imperfections, and some of these are embodied in their electoral processes. Sometimes these imperfections are significant enough to warrant major change. Such change should bring the electoral process closer in line with broadly supported notions of liberty, equality, and democracy as well as with the other values that bind the nation. Despite the enactment of the BCRA and the HAVA, the current state of congressional elections demonstrates that change is warranted in the way in which Americans elect those who serve in Congress.

Notes

INTRODUCTION

1. Abraham Lincoln, Gettysburg Address.

2. Once the Supreme Court determines the status of the BCRA, information about the law and how it will affect congressional elections will be posted on the web site for this book (http://herrnson.cqpress.com).

1. THE STRATEGIC CONTEXT

1. Thomas A. Kazee, "The Emergence of Congressional Candidates," in *Who Runs for Congress? Ambition, Context, and Candidate Emergence*, ed. Thomas A. Kazee (Washington, D.C.: Congressional Quarterly, 1994), 1–14; L. Sandy Maisel, Linda L. Fowler, Ruth S. Jones, and Walter J. Stone, "Nomination Politics: The Roles of Institutional, Contextual, and Personal Variables," in *The Parties Respond: Changes in the American Party System*, 2d ed., ed. L. Sandy Maisel (Boulder, Colo.: Westview Press, 1994), 145–168.

2. Leon D. Epstein, *Political Parties in Western Democracies* (New York: Praeger, 1967), chap. 8.

3. Kenneth Martis, *The Historical Atlas of U.S. Congressional Districts, 1789–1983* (New York: Free Press, 1982), 5–6.

4. See, for example, Frank J. Sorauf, "Political Parties and Political Action Committees: Two Life Cycles," *Arizona Law Review* 22 (1980): 445–464.

5. Jerrold B. Rusk, "The Effect of the Australian Ballot Reform on Split Ticket Voting: 1876–1908," *American Political Science Review* 64 (1970): 1220–1283.

6. See, for example, V. O. Key, *Politics, Parties, and Pressure Groups* (New York: Thomas Y. Crowell, 1964), 371.

7. Ibid., 389–391.

8. Committee on Political Parties, American Political Science Association, "Toward a More Responsible Two-Party System," *American Political Science Association*, supp. 44 (1950): 21.

9. The FECA's predecessor, enacted in 1971, had little effect on congressional elections. For an overview of the FECA and the campaign finance system that existed prior to it, see Herbert E. Alexander, *Financing Politics: Money, Elections, and Political Reform* (Washington, D.C.: CQ Press, 1992), esp. chaps. 2 and 3. For more recent coverage of the law, see Anthony Corrado, Thomas E. Mann,

Daniel R. Ortiz, Trevor Potter, and Frank J. Sorauf, eds., *Campaign Finance Reform: A Sourcebook* (Washington, D.C.: Brookings Institution, 1997).

10. The only subsidy the FECA gives to the parties is a grant to pay for their presidential nominating conventions. As nonprofit organizations, the parties also receive a discount for bulk postage.

11. Karl-Heinz Nassmacher, "Comparing Party and Campaign Finance in Western Democracies," in *Campaign and Party Finance in North America and Western Europe,* ed. Arthur B. Gunlicks (Boulder, Colo.: Westview Press, 1993), 233–263.

12. Arthur B. Gunlicks, "Introduction," in *Campaign and Party Finance,* 6.

13. Sorauf, "Political Parties and Political Action Committees," 445–464.

14. Paul S. Herrnson, *Party Campaigning in the 1980s* (Cambridge, Mass.: Harvard University Press, 1988), 82.

15. The term *soft money* was coined by Elizabeth Drew in *Politics and Money: The New Road to Corruption* (New York: Macmillan, 1983), esp. 15. See also Herbert E. Alexander and Anthony Corrado, *Financing the 1994 Election* (Armonk, N.Y.: M. E. Sharpe, 1995), chap. 6.; Robert Biersack, "The Nationalization of Party Finance," in *The State of the Parties,* 108–124.

16. Federal Election Commission, "Party Committees Raise More than $1 Billion," press release, March 20, 2003.

17. Kenneth Goldstein and Joel Rivlin, "Advertising in the 2002 Elections," upublished manuscript.

18. Anthony Corrado, *Campaign Finance Reform: Beyond the Basics* (New York: The Century Foundation Press, 2000), 93.

19. *FEC v. Massachusetts Citizens for Life, Inc.,* 479 U.S. 248 (1986); *Colorado Republican Federal Campaign Committee v. FEC,* 116 S.Ct. 2309 (1996).

20. As is explained in Chapter 4, the FEC has ruled that a portion of the party money that is spent on issue advocacy must be hard money.

21. Paul S. Herrnson and Diana Dwyre, "Party Issue Advocacy in Congressional Elections," in *The State of the Parties,* 3d ed., ed. John C. Green and Daniel M. Shea (Lanham, Md.: University Press of America, 1999), 86–104.

22. Louis Hartz, *The Liberal Tradition in America* (New York: Harcourt, Brace, 1955).

23. See, for example, Robert A. Dahl, *Democracy in the United States: Promise and Performance* (Chicago: Rand McNally, 1967), 252; Herbert McClosky and John Zaller, *The American Ethos: Public Attitudes toward Democracy* (Cambridge: Harvard University Press, 1984), 62–100.

24. See Rusk, "The Effect of the Australian Ballot."

25. Key, *Politics, Parties, and Pressure Groups,* 342, 386; Nelson W. Polsby, *The Consequences of Party Reform* (Oxford: Oxford University Press, 1983), 72–74; William J. Crotty, *American Parties in Decline* (Boston: Little, Brown, 1984), 277–278.

26. Lee Ann Elliot, "Political Action Committees—Precincts of the '80s," *Arizona Law Review* 22 (1980): 539–554; Kay Lehman Schlozman and John T. Tierney, *Organized Interests and American Democracy* (New York: Harper and Row, 1986), 75–78.

27. John R. Petrocik, *Party Coalitions: Realignments and the Decline of the New Deal Party System* (Chicago: University of Chicago Press, 1981), chaps. 8 and 9; Paul Allen Beck, "A Socialization Theory of Partisan Realignment," in *Controversies in American Voting Behavior,* ed. Richard G. Niemi and Herbert F. Weisberg (Washington, D.C.: CQ Press, 1984), 396–411; Martin P. Wattenberg, *The Decline of American Political Parties, 1952–1988* (Cambridge: Harvard University Press, 1990), chap. 4.

28. Austin Ranney, *Channels of Power: The Impact of Television on American Politics* (New York: Basic Books, 1983), 110; Doris Graber, *Mass Media and American Politics,* 4th ed. (Washington, D.C.: CQ Press, 1993), 250–252.

29. Jack Dennis, "Support for the Party System by the Mass Public," *American Political Science Review* 60 (1966): 605.

30. CBS News/*New York Times* poll, October 1986, cited in Bruce E. Keith, David B. Magleby, Candice J. Nelson, Elizabeth Orr, Mark C. Westlye, and Raymond E. Wolfinger, *The Myth of the Independent Voter* (Berkeley: University of California Press, 1992), 8.

31. This group includes independents who "lean" toward one of the parties. Figures for party identification and voting behavior are compiled from Nancy Burns, Donald R. Kinder, and National Election Studies, *American National Election Study, 2002: Post-Election Survey* (Ann Arbor: University of Michigan, Center for Political Studies, 2003).

32. Sorauf, "Political Parties and Political Action Committees," 447.

33. Robert Agranoff, "Introduction/The New Style of Campaigning," in *The New Style in Election Campaigns,* ed. Robert Agranoff (Boston: Holbrook Press, 1972), 3–50; Larry J. Sabato, *The Rise of the Political Consultants: New Ways of Winning Elections* (New York: Basic Books, 1981).

34. See Ranney, *Channels of Power,* 110; and Graber, *Mass Media,* 250.

35. Agranoff, "Introduction/The New Style of Campaigning."

36. Sorauf, "Political Parties and Political Action Committees."

37. Cornelius P. Cotter and John F. Bibby, "Institutional Development and the Thesis of Party Decline," *Political Science Quarterly* 95 (1980): 1–27; David Adamany, "Political Parties in the 1980s," in *Money and Politics in the United States: Financing Elections in the 1980s,* ed. Michael J. Malbin (Washington, D.C.: American Enterprise Institute, 1984), 70–121; Herrnson, *Party Campaigning,* chaps. 3 and 4; Stephen E. Frantzich, *Political Parties in the Technological Age* (New York: Longman, 1989), 81–90, 182–186.

38. Another four House Democrats lost in primaries in 1994.

39. See, for example, Key, *Politics, Parties, and Pressure Groups,* 421.

40. David R. Butler and Bruce Cain, *Congressional Redistricting: Comparative and Theoretical Perspectives* (New York: Macmillan, 1992), 10, 87; Michael Lyons and Peter F. Galderisi, "Incumbency, Reapportionment, and U.S. House Redistricting," *Political Review Quarterly* 49 (1995): 857–873. For another view, see Richard Niemi and Alan I. Abramowitz, "Partisan Redistricting and the 1992 Elections," *Journal of Politics* 56 (1994): 811–817.

41. David R. Mayhew, *Congress: The Electoral Connection* (New Haven, Conn.: Yale University Press, 1974); Morris P. Fiorina, *Congress: Keystone of the Washington Establishment* (New Haven, Conn.: Yale University Press, 1978), 19–21, 41–49, 56–62; Diane E. Yiannakis, "The Grateful Electorate: Casework and Congressional Elections," *American Journal of Political Science* 25 (1981): 568–580; Bruce Cain, John Ferejohn, and Morris Fiorina, *The Personal Vote* (Cambridge: Harvard University Press, 1987), 103–106; Gary C. Jacobson, *The Politics of Congressional Elections,* 4th ed. (New York: Longman, 1997), 28–33; George Serra and Albert Cover, "The Electoral Consequences of Perquisite Use: The Casework Case," *Legislative Studies Quarterly* 17 (1992): 233–246.

42. Harrison W. Fox and Susan Webb Hammond, *Congressional Staffs: The Invisible Force in American Lawmaking* (New York: Free Press, 1977), 88–99, 154–155.

43. Herrnson, *Party Campaigning,* chap. 4; Frank J. Sorauf, *Inside Campaign Finance* (New Haven, Conn.: Yale University Press, 1992), 80–84.

44. Donald Ostdiek, "Congressional Redistricting and District Typologies," *Journal of Politics* 57 (1995): 533–543.

45. Bruce I. Oppenheimer, James A. Stimson, and Richard W. Waterman, "Interpreting U.S. Congressional Elections: The Exposure Thesis," *Legislative Studies Quarterly* 11 (1986): 227–247; James E. Campbell, "The Presidential Surge and Its Midterm Decline in Congressional Elections, 1868–1988," *Journal of Politics* 53 (1991): 478–487; J. W. Koch, "Candidate Status, Presidential Approval, and Voting for U.S. Senator," *Electoral Studies* 19 (2000): 479–492.

46. Michael S. Lewis-Beck and Tom W. Rice, *Forecasting Elections* (Washington, D.C.: CQ Press, 1992), chaps. 4–6.

47. Jerome M. Clubb, William H. Flanigan, and Nancy H. Zingale, *Partisan Realignment: Voters, Parties, and Government in American History* (Beverly Hills, Calif.: Sage Publications, 1980), 258–260.

48. On coattail effects, see Barry C. Burden and David C. Kimball, *Why Americans Split Their Tickets* (Ann Arbor: University of Michigan Press, 2002), esp. 78–96, 134–138; Randall L. Calvert and John A. Ferejohn, "Coattail Voting in Recent Presidential Elections," *American Political Science Review* 77 (1983): 407–419; Richard Born, "Reassessing the Decline of Presidential Coattails: U.S. House Elections, 1952–1980," *Journal of Politics* 46 (1980): 60–79; James E. Campbell, "Predicting Seat Gains from Presidential Coattails," *American Journal of Political Science* 30 (1986): 397–418; Gary C. Jacobson, *Electoral Origins of Divided Government, 1946–1988* (Boulder, Colo.: Westview Press, 1990), 80–81.

49. Edward R. Tufte, "Determinants of the Outcomes of Midterm Congressional Elections," *American Political Science Review* 69 (1975): 812–826; Lewis-Beck and Rice, *Forecasting Elections*, 60–75.

50. Morris P. Fiorina, *Retrospective Voting in American National Elections* (New Haven, Conn.: Yale University Press, 1981), 165; Eric M. Uslaner and M. Margaret Conway, "The Responsible Electorate: Watergate, the Economy, and Vote Choice in 1974," *American Political Science Review* 79 (1985): 788–803.

51. The Republicans picked up an additional five House and two Senate seats as a result of Democratic incumbents who switched parties following the 1994 election. The Democrats picked up another House seat in 1999, when Michael Forbes of New York switched parties.

52. Gerald Kramer, "Short-Term Fluctuations in U.S. Voting Behavior," *American Political Science Review* 65 (1971): 131–143; Gary C. Jacobson and Samuel Kernell, *Strategy and Choice in Congressional Elections* (New Haven, Conn.: Yale University Press, 1983), chap. 6; Gary C. Jacobson, "Does the Economy Matter in Midterm Elections?" *American Journal of Political Science* 34 (1990): 400–404. For alternative interpretations, see Robert S. Erikson, "Economic Conditions and the Vote: A Review of the Macro Level Evidence," *American Journal of Political Science* 34 (1990): 373–399; Patrick G. Lynch, "Midterm Elections and Economic Fluctuations," *Legislative Studies Quarterly* 227 (2002): 265–294.

53. Norman Nie and Kristi Andersen, "Mass Belief Systems Revisited: Political Change and Attitude Structure," *Journal of Politics* 36 (1974): 540–591; Crotty, *American Parties in Decline*, 49–50.

54. Richard A. Brody and Benjamin I. Page, "The Assessment of Policy Voting," *American Political Science Review* 66 (1972): 450–458; Norman H. Nie, Sidney Verba, John R. Petrocik, *The Changing American Voter* (New York: Twentieth Century Fund, 1979), esp. chap. 18.

55. *Thornburg v. Gingles,* 478 U.S. 30 (1986).

56. Redistricting Task Force for the National Conference of State Legislatures, "Action on Redistricting Plans: 2001–02," February 12, 2003, http://www.senate.leg.state.mn.us/departments/scr/redist/redsum2000/action01-02.htm, May 14, 2003.

57. Richard F. Fenno Jr., *Home Style: House Members in Their Districts* (Boston: Little, Brown, 1978), 164–168.

58. David B. Magleby, Kelly D. Patterson, and Stephen H. Wirls, "Fear and Loathing of the Modern Congress: The Public Manifestation of Constitutional Design" (paper presented at the annual meeting of the Midwest Political Science Association, Chicago, April 1994), 14–16; see also Gary C. Jacobson, "The 1994 House Elections in Perspective," in *Midterm: The Elections of 1994 in Context,* ed. Philip A. Klinkner (Boulder, Colo.: Westview Press, 1996); and John R. Hibbing and Elizabeth Theiss-Morse, *Congress as Public Enemy: Public Attitudes toward American Political Institutions* (Cambridge: Cambridge University Press, 1995), 31–33, 69–71, 96–100.

59. On the 1994 elections, see the essays in Klinkner, *Midterm.*

60. James G. Gimpel, *Fulfilling the Contract: The First 100 Days* (Boston: Allyn and Bacon, 1996).

61. Richard F. Fenno Jr., "If, as Ralph Nader Says, Congress Is 'the Broken Branch,' How Come We Love Our Congressmen So Much?" in *Congress in Change: Evolution and Reform,* ed. Norman J. Ornstein (New York: Praeger, 1975).

62. On public approval of Congress, see, for example, Siena Research Institute, "Bush Approval Drops, But Still Above Pre-9/11 Rating. Congress Back to Pre-9/11 Standing," press release, November 12, 2002.

63. Richard Morin and Claudia Deane, "Poll: Strong Backing for Bush, War," *Washington Post,* March 11, 2002.

64. Rep. Jay Kim, R-Calif., the sole incumbent who was defeated in the 1998 primaries, had pled guilty to violating campaign finance laws prior to this defeat.

65. The three incumbents who were defeated in the 2000 primaries lost as a result of some unusual circumstances. Merrill Cook, R-Utah, had exhibited strange behavior that led many politicians and the media to publicly question the soundness of his judgment. Forbes, of New York, who was first elected to Congress in 1994 as a Republican, switched to the Democratic Party in 1999 and was attacked by Republican Party committees as well as activists of both parties. The defeat of Matthew Martinez, D-Calif., was largely the result of his casting congressional votes at odds with constituents' views on labor issues, abortion rights, and gun control.

66. Twenty percent is an appropriate victory margin given the heightened level of uncertainty in contemporary congressional elections. A narrower margin, such as 15 percent, would have eliminated campaigns that were competitive for part of the election season but were ultimately decided by more than 15 percent of the vote. Slightly changing the boundaries for the competitiveness measure does not significantly change the results. Moreover, the twenty-point classification produces results similar to the forecasts of political journalists who handicap Democratic elections. When the categories for seats the *Rothenberg Political Report* rates as "leaning" or "tilting" toward one party are combined with "toss-up" races into one category, its May 8, 2002, forecast classifies 88 percent of the races the same as the twenty-point classification used here. Similarly, collapsing the *Cook Political Report's* May 28, 2002, "lean," "likely," and "toss-up" races into one category also results in an 88 percent overlap with the races categorized as competitive using the twenty-point classification. The *Rothenberg Political Report's* July 29, 2002, and *CQ Weekly's* June 4, 2002, forecasts overlap 87 percent and 85 percent, respectively, with the twenty-point classification. For a more complete discussion of the classification scheme, see the appendix to the first edition of this book.

67. Alexander P. Lamis, "The Two-Party South" in *Southern Politics in the 1990s,* ed. Alexander P. Lamis (Baton Rouge: Louisiana State University Press, 1999), 1–49; Gary C. Jacobson, *The Politics of Congressional Elections,* 23–24.

68. L. Sandy Maisel, Walter J. Stone, and Cherie Maestas, "Quality Challengers to Congressional Incumbents: Can Better Candidates Be Found?" in *Playing Hardball: Campaigning for the U.S. Congress,* ed. Paul S. Herrnson (Upper Saddle River, N.J.: Prentice Hall, 2001), 12–40.

69. Quoted in Brian Nutting and H. Amy Stern, eds., *CQ's Politics in America 2002: The 107th Congress* (Washington, D.C.: Congressional Quarterly, 2001), 616.

70. This figure includes Lisa Murkowski, R-Alaska, who was selected by her father, Frank Murkowski, to complete his term after he was elected Alaska's governor.

71. Figures exclude Rep. Ed Case, D-Hawaii, who was elected on November 30 to finish out the last days of Patsy Mink's tenure before winning a special election on January 4.

2. CANDIDATES AND NOMINATIONS

1. E. E. Schattschneider, *Party Government* (New York: Holt, Rinehart, and Winston, 1942), 99–106.

2. Thomas A. Kazee, "The Emergence of Congressional Candidates," in *Who Runs for Congress? Ambition, Context, and Candidate Emergence,* ed. Thomas A. Kazee (Washington, D.C.: Congressional Quarterly, 1994), 1–14; L. Sandy Maisel, Walter J. Stone, and Cherie Maestas,

"Quality Challengers to Congressional Incumbents: Can Better Candidates Be Found?" in *Playing Hardball: Campaigning for the U.S. Congress,* ed. Paul S. Herrnson (Upper Saddle River, N.J.: Prentice Hall, 2001), 12–40.

3. Joseph A. Schlesinger, *Ambition and Politics: Political Careers in the United States* (Chicago: Rand McNally, 1966), 11–12, 16–19, 198–199; Gary C. Jacobson and Samuel Kernell, *Strategy and Choice in Congressional Elections* (New Haven, Conn.: Yale University Press, 1983), chap. 3; William T. Bianco, "Strategic Decisions on Candidacy in U.S. Congressional Districts," *Legislative Studies Quarterly* 9 (1984): 360–362; Kazee, "The Emergence of Congressional Candidates"; David T. Canon, *Actors, Athletes, and Astronauts: Political Amateurs in the United States Congress* (Chicago: University of Chicago Press, 1990), 76–79.

4. L. Sandy Maisel, Linda L. Fowler, Ruth S. Jones, and Walter J. Stone, "The Naming of Candidates: Recruitment or Emergence?" in *The Parties Respond: Changes in the American Party System,* ed. L. Sandy Maisel (Boulder, Colo.: Westview Press, 1990); Linda L. Fowler and Robert D. McClure, *Political Ambition: Who Decides to Run for Congress* (New Haven, Conn.: Yale University Press, 1990), 231.

5. Gary C. Jacobson and Samuel Kernell, "National Forces in the 1986 U.S. House Elections," *Legislative Studies Quarterly* 15 (1990): 65–87; Canon, *Actors, Athletes, and Astronauts,* 106–108.

6. See, for example, John Alford, Holly Teeters, Daniel S. Ward, and Rick Wilson, "Overdraft: The Political Cost of Congressional Malfeasance," *Journal of Politics* 56 (1994): 788–801.

7. Timothy Groseclose and Keith Krehbiel, "Golden Parachutes, Rubber Checks, and Strategic Retirements from the 102nd House," *American Journal of Political Science* 38 (1994): 75–99; Gary C. Jacobson and Michael Dimock, "Checking Out: The Effects of Bank Overdrafts on the 1992 House Election," *American Journal of Political Science* 38 (1994): 601–624.

8. See n. 3.

9. David R. Mayhew, *Congress: The Electoral Connection* (New Haven, Conn.: Yale University Press, 1974); Morris P. Fiorina, *Congress: Keystone of the Washington Establishment* (New Haven, Conn.: Yale University Press, 1978), 19–21, 41–49, 56–62. Members of the House receive an official personnel and office allowance of approximately $1 million per year plus stationery, office space, furnishings, and equipment in Washington and in their districts. See Roger H. Davidson and Walter J. Oleszek, *Congress and Its Members,* 8th ed. (Washington, D.C.: CQ Press, 2002), 149.

10. Richard F. Fenno Jr., *Home Style: House Members in Their Districts* (Boston: Little, Brown, 1978), 164–168.

11. Peverill Squire, "Preemptive Fundraising and Challenger Profile in Senate Elections," *Journal of Politics* 53 (1991): 1150–1164; Janet M. Box-Steffensmeier, "A Dynamic Analysis of the Role of War Chests in Campaign Strategy," *American Journal of Political Science* 40 (1996): 352–371. For other viewpoints, see Jonathan S. Krasno and Donald Philip Green, "Preempting Quality Challengers in House Elections," *Journal of Politics* 50 (1988): 920–936; Jay Goodliffe, "The Effect of War Chests on Challenger Entry in U.S. House Elections," *American Journal of Political Science* 45 (2001): 830–844.

12. Sara Fritz and Dwight Morris, *Gold-Plated Politics: Running for Congress in the 1990s* (Washington, D.C.: Congressional Quarterly, 1992), esp. chap. 2.

13. On redistricting, see Richard G. Niemi and Laura R. Winsky, "The Persistence of Partisan Redistricting Effects in Congressional Elections, *Journal of Politics* 54 (1992): 565–571.

14. Stephen E. Frantzich, "De-Recruitment: The Other Side of the Congressional Equation," *Western Political Quarterly* 31 (1978): 105–126; Michael K. Moore and John R. Hibbing, "Is Serving in Congress Fun Again? Voluntary Retirements from the House Since the 1970s," *American Journal of Political Science* 36 (1992): 824–828; Eric M. Uslaner, *The Decline of Comity in Congress* (Ann Arbor: University of Michigan Press, 1993), esp. chap. 2.

15. Frantzich, "De-Recruitment," 105–126; Joseph Cooper and William West, "The Congressional Career in the 1970s," in *Congress Reconsidered,* ed. Lawrence Dodd and Bruce

Oppenheimer (Washington, D.C.: CQ Press, 1981); John R. Hibbing, "Voluntary Retirement from the U.S. House: The Costs of Legislative Service," *Legislative Studies Quarterly* 8 (1982): 57–74.

16. Jonathan Poet, "Pennsylvania Congressman Bud Shuster Retiring Effective Jan. 31," Associate Press, January 4, 2001.

17. Brian Nutting and H. Amy Stern, eds., *CQ's Politics in America 2002: The 107th Congress* (Washington, D.C.: Congressional Quarterly, 2001), 868.

18. Steven G. Livingston and Sally Friedman, "Reexamining Theories of Congressional Retirement: Evidence from the 1980s," *Legislative Studies Quarterly* 18 (1993): 231–254; John B. Gilmour and Paul Rothstein, "Early Republican Retirement: A Cause of Democratic Dominance in the House of Representatives," *Legislative Studies Quarterly* 18 (1993): 345–365; D. Roderick Kiewiet and Langche Zeng, "An Analysis of Congressional Career Decisions, 1947–1986," *American Political Science Review* (1993): 928–941; Richard L. Hall and Robert P. Van Houweling, "Avarice and Ambition in Congress: Representatives' Decisions to Run or Retire from the U.S. House," *American Political Science Review* 89 (1995): 121–136.

19. Jim VandeHei, "Rumors Revisit Oklahoma Republicans," *Washington Post*, June 21, 2002.

20. John Williams. "Election 2002; Bell, Carter Get Clear Cut Wins." *Houston Chronicle*, April 10, 2002. On dynasties more generally, see John Orman and Darrell M. West, *Celebrity Politics* (Upper Saddle River, N.J.: Prentice Hall, 2003).

21. For a comprehensive assessment of these conditions, see Canon, *Actors, Athletes, and Astronauts*, 103–110.

22. Some of the data used in Figures 2-2 through 2-6 and Tables 2-1 through 2-4 come from various editions of *Who's Who in American Politics* (New Providence, N.J.: Marquis Who's Who); *Who's Who among African Americans* (Detroit, Mich.: Gale Research); "Election '96: Republican National Convention," *AsianWeek*, August 9–15, 1996; "Election '96: Democratic National Convention," *AsianWeek*, August 23–29, 1996; the Joint Center for Political and Economic Studies; and the National Association of Latino Elected and Appointed Officials.

23. On the impact of term limits, see Richard J. Powell, "The Impact of Term Limits on the Candidacy Decisions of State Legislators in U.S. House Elections," *Legislative Studies Quarterly* 25 (2000): 645–661. On the number of states with term limits, see U.S. Term Limits, "State Legislative Term Limits," http://www.termlimits.org, January 27, 2003.

24. On ambitious, policy, and experience seeking or hopeless amateurs, see Canon, *Actors, Athletes, and Astronauts*, xv, 26–32; and David T. Canon, "Sacrificial Lambs or Strategic Politicians? Political Amateurs in U.S. House Elections," *American Journal of Political Science* 37 (1993): 1119–1141.

25. Throughout this chapter, seats are categorized according to their status (open or incumbent-occupied) at the beginning of the election cycle. Seats that began the election cycle as incumbent-occupied but featured two nonincumbents in the general election are classified as open from chap. 3 forward.

26. See, for example, E. J. Dionne, Jr., *Why Americans Hate Politics* (New York: Simon and Schuster, 1991).

27. On the decision making of quality challengers, see Gary W. Cox and Jonathan N. Katz, "Why Did the Incumbency Advantage in U.S. House Elections Grow?" *American Journal of Political Science* 40 (1996): 478–497.

28. An exception to this rule occurs in Texas, where an individual can appear on the ballot for two offices simultaneously.

29. Harold D. Lasswell, *Power and Personality* (Boston: W. W. Norton, 1948), 39–41.

30. The generalizations that follow are drawn from responses to question 18 of the 1992 Congressional Campaign Study; see the appendix to the first edition of this book and the book's web site (http://herrnson.cqpress.com). See also L. Sandy Maisel, *From Obscurity to Oblivion: Running in the Congressional Primary* (Knoxville: University of Tennessee Press, 1982), 31–32; Paul S. Herrnson,

Party Campaigning in the 1980s (Cambridge, Mass.: Harvard University Press, 1988), 86; and Kazee, "The Emergence of Congressional Candidates."

31. Thomas A. Kazee and Mary C. Thornberry, "Where's the Party? Congressional Candidate Recruitment and American Party Organizations," *Western Political Quarterly* 43 (1990): 61–80; Steven H. Haeberle, "Closed Primaries and Party Support in Congress," *American Politics Quarterly* 13 (1985): 341–352.

32. Herrnson, *Party Campaigning*, 51–56.

33. Jenny Backus, communications director, DCCC, interview, November 14, 2002.

34. See, for example, Fowler and McClure, *Political Ambition*, 205–207.

35. On WISH List, see Craig A. Rimmerman, "New Kids on the Block: WISH List and the Gay and Lesbian Victory Fund," in *Risky Business? PAC Decisionmaking in Congressional Elections*, ed. Robert Biersack, Paul S. Herrnson, and Clyde Wilcox (Armonk, N.Y.: M. E. Sharpe, 1994), 214–223; Mark J. Rozell, "WISH List: Pro-Choice Women in the Republican Congress," in *After the Revolution: PACs and Lobbies in the New Republican Congress*, ed. Robert Biersack, Paul S. Herrnson, and Clyde Wilcox (Boston: Allyn and Bacon, 1991), 184–191.

36. Brian Nutting and H. Amy Stern, eds., *CQ's Politics in America 2002: The 107th Congress* (Washington, D.C.: Congressional Quarterly, 2001), 992–993.

37. Ibid.

38. Web site of Rep. Larry Combest, "Combest Biography," http://www.house.gov/combest/bio. htm, May 22, 2003.

39. Fenno, *Home Style*, 176–189.

40. See Paul S. Herrnson, "National Party Organizations and the Postreform Congress," in *The Postreform Congress*, ed. Roger H. Davidson (New York: St. Martin's Press, 1992), 48–70.

41. Rhodes Cook, "Close Races for House Seats Scarce," *Newsday*, October 11, 2002.

42. Figures exclude incumbents running against other incumbents.

43. See, for example, Schlesinger, *Ambition and Politics*, 99; and Canon, *Actors, Athletes, and Astronauts*, 50–53, 56–58; L. Sandy Maisel, Elizabeth J. Irvy, Benjamin D. Ling, and Stephanie G. Pennix, "Re-exploring the Weak-Challenger Hypothesis: The 1994 Candidate Pools," in *Midterm: The Elections of 1994 in Context*, ed. Philip A. Klinkner (Boulder, Colo.: Westview Press, 1996); L. Sandy Maisel, Walter J. Stone, and Cherie Maestas, "Reassessing the Definition of Quality Candidates" (paper presented at the annual meeting of the Midwest Political Science Association, Chicago, April 1999).

44. "Condit to Blame for His Political Self-Destruction," *Modesto Bee*, March 6, 2002.

45. Ibid.

46. Ibid.

47. Chris Cillizza, "A Changing Landscape?" *Roll Call*, May 20, 2002.

48. Julia C. Marinez, "Feeley, Beauprez for 7th," *Denver Post*, August 14, 2002.

49. *Rocky Mountain News*, August 1, 2002.

50. Frank Bell, "Eight Candidates Running for New Seat," *Aurora Sentinel*, April 10, 2002.

51. Ibid.

52. Congressional candidates can get on Colorado's ballot in two ways: by collecting 1,000 petition signatures or via the state's caucus system. In the first step of the caucus system, party members elect delegates to congressional district assemblies. In the second step, delegates cast ballots and the candidate with the most votes gets "top line" designation on the primary ballot. Other candidates who receive 30 percent or more of the delegate votes also win a place on the ballot and are listed in the order in which they placed. Candidates who petition to get on the ballot, such as Rogers and Zakhem, are listed on the ballot below those who got on it using the caucus system. John Straayer, Colorado State University, personal communication, January 31, 2003.

53. Julie C. Martinez, "GOP Picks Hopefuls for 7th District," *Denver Post*, May 31, 2002.

54. LeRoy Standish, "New District Brings Challengers to Forefront," *Jefferson County Sentinel*, January 31, 2002.

55. Gregory L. Geroux, "No Clear Favorite in Race for Colorado Seat," *Washington Post,* August 2, 2002.

56. Hagedorn fell short of the necessary 1,000 signatures after having 414 signatures rejected by the State Board of Elections.

57. Martinez, "GOP Picks Hopefuls."

58. Bell, "Eight Candidates Running for New Seat."

59. Ibid.

60. Donald R. Matthews, "Legislative Recruitment and Legislative Careers," *Legislative Studies Quarterly* 9 (1984): 551.

61. Amy Keller, "The *Roll Call* Fifty Richest," *Roll Call,* September 9, 2002.

62. Figure excludes Rep. Patsy Mink, D-Hawaii, who was reelected posthumously and replaced by Ed Case in a special election.

63. R. Darcy, Susan Welch, and Janet Clark, *Women, Elections, and Representation* (New York: Longman, 1987), 93–108.

64. Ibid., 138–140; Robert A. Bernstein, "Why Are There So Few Women in the House?" *Western Political Quarterly* 29 (1986): 155–164; Linda L. Fowler, *Candidates, Congress, and the American Democracy* (Ann Arbor: University of Michigan Press, 1993), 127–136.

65. Barbara Burrell, "Women Candidates in Open-Seat Primaries for the U.S. House: 1968–1990," *Legislative Studies Quarterly* 17 (1992): 493–508.

66. On the impact of religious participation on the development of political and civic skills, see Sidney Verba, Kay Lehman Schlozman, and Henry E. Brady, *Voice and Equality: Civic Voluntarism in American Politics* (Cambridge: Harvard University Press, 1995), 333.

67. On the effect of race on candidate selection, see Fowler, *Candidates, Congress, and the American Democracy,* 136–142.

68. Kevin A. Hill, "Does the Creation of Majority Black Districts Aid Republicans? An Analysis of the 1992 Congressional Elections in Eight Southern States," *Journal of Politics* 57 (1995): 384–401; Charles Cameron, David Epstein, and Sharyn O'Halloran, "Do Majority-Minority Districts Maximize Substantive Black Representation in Congress?" *American Political Science Review* 90 (1996): 794–812.

69. David T. Cannon, *Race, Redistricting, and Representation: The Unintended Consequences of Black Majority Districts* (Chicago: University of Chicago Press, 1999).

70. Keller, "The *Roll Call* Fifty Richest."

71. See, for example, Richard L. Fox, Jennifer L. Lawless, and Courtney Feeley, "Gender and the Decision to Run for Office," *Legislative Studies Quarterly* 26 (2001): 411–435.

72. Alan Ehrenhalt, *The United States of Ambition: Politicians, Power, and the Pursuit of Office* (New York: Random House, 1991), 225–226.

73. Compiled from various editions of *CQ's Politics in America.*

74. Beginning with the U.S. House, and proceeding in the order listed, only the highest office is included. Compiled from various editions of *CQ's Politics in America.*

75. Chris LaCivita, political director, NRSC, interview, February 3, 2003.

76. This generalization is drawn from responses to question 18 of the 1992 Congressional Campaign Study; see the appendix to the first edition of this book and the book's web site (http://herrnson. cqpress.com).

3. THE ANATOMY OF A CAMPAIGN

1. See, for example, Edie N. Goldenberg and Michael W. Traugott, *Campaigning for Congress* (Washington, D.C.: CQ Press, 1984), 19–24.

2. Committee on Political Parties, American Political Science Association, "Toward a More Responsible Two-Party System," *American Political Science Association,* supp. 44 (1950): 21; Robert Agranoff, "Introduction/The New Style of Campaigning," in *The New Style in Election Campaigns,* ed. Robert Agranoff (Boston: Holbrook Press, 1972), 3–50; Larry J. Sabato, *The Rise of the Political Consultants: New Ways of Winning Elections* (New York: Basic Books, 1981).

3. James A. Thurber, Candice J. Nelson, David A. Dulio, "Political Consulting: A Portrait of the Industry" (paper presented at the annual meeting of the American Political Science Association, Boston, 1998); Bill Hamilton and Dave Beattie, "The Big Metamorphosis: How Campaigns Change Candidates," *Campaigns & Elections,* August 1999, 34–36.

4. The figure includes office furniture, supplies, rent, salaries, taxes, bank fees, lawyers, accountants, telephone, automobile, computers, other office equipment, and fundraising expenses. Compiled from data provided by Political Money Line.

5. Ibid.

6. There have been important exceptions to this generalization in recent years. See David T. Canon, *Actors, Athletes, and Astronauts: Political Amateurs in the United States Congress* (Chicago: University of Chicago Press, 1990), 3, 36.

7. Paul S. Herrnson, *Party Campaigning in the 1980s* (Cambridge, Mass.: Harvard University Press, 1988), 61–63, 92–94.

8. Interview with an anonymous political consultant, April 5, 2002.

9. Michael Margolis, David Resnick, and Chin-chang Tu, "Campaigning on the Internet," *Harvard International Journal of Press/Politics* 2 (1997), 59–78; David A. Dulio, Donald L. Groff, and James A. Thurber, "Untangled Web: Internet Use During the 1998 Election," *PS: Political Science and Politics* 32 (1999), 53–58.

10. This finding supports Fenno's observation that the explanatory power of challenger quality and political experience is largely the result of the quality of the candidates' campaign organizations. See Richard F. Fenno Jr., *Senators on the Campaign Trail: The Politics of Representation* (Norman: University of Oklahoma Press, 1996), 100.

11. Steve Rice, consultant to the Ose campaign, interview, February 28, 2003.

12. Howard Beeman, candidate for Congress, interview, February 27, 2003.

13. Brian Nutting and H. Amy Stern, eds., *CQ's Politics in America 2002: The 107th Congress* (Washington, D.C.: Congressional Quarterly, 2001), 468–469.

14. Walter Lee Dozier, "Will Lierman Get Another Chance?," *Montgomery County Gazette,* November 10, 2000.

15. Brandon DeFrehn, field coordinator, Morella for Congress, interview, November 21, 2002.

16. DeFrehn, interview, November 21, 2002; Steven T. Dennis, "District 8 Rivals Intensify Ground War," *The Gazette,* December 8, 2002, http://www.gazette.net/200242/weekend/a_section/126900-1.html.

17. Van Hollen for Congress web site (http://www.vanhollen2002.com/biography.htm).

18. Andrew Smith, "A Congressional Race That Breaks the Mold: Maryland's 8th District in 2002," unpublished paper, University of Maryland, College Park, December 9, 2002; Rebecca Chanales, "Maryland's Eighth District: Part I," unpublished paper, University of Pennsylvania, October 15, 2002.

19. Daniel A. Smith, "Strings Attached: Outside Money in Colorado's Seventh Congressional District," in *The Last Hurrah? Soft Money and Issue Advocacy in the 2002 Congressional Elections,* ed. David B. Magleby and J. Quinn Monson (Provo, Utah: Center for the Study of Elections and Democracy, 2003), 194.

20. Ibid.

21. This figure is slightly lower than the 6 percent spent in 1992 and the 7 percent spent in 1996, probably because many House candidates were able to develop targeting strategies using the

geodemographic research conducted by party committees and other groups. Following reapportionment, such organizations invest significant sums on geodemographic research for redistricting purposes and later make this information available to many candidates.

22. Figures compiled from Political Money Line (http://www.tray.com).

4. THE PARTIES CAMPAIGN

1. Frank J. Sorauf, "Political Parties and Political Action Committees: Two Life Cycles," *Arizona Law Review* 22 (1980): 447.

2. See, for example, Robert Agranoff, "Introduction/The New Style of Campaigning," in *The New Style in Election Campaigns,* ed. Robert Agranoff (Boston: Holbrook Press, 1972), 3–50.

3. Joseph A. Schlesinger, "The New American Political Party," *American Political Science Review* 79 (1985): 1151–1169; Paul S. Herrnson, *Party Campaigning in the 1980s* (Cambridge, Mass.: Harvard University Press, 1988), chaps. 2–3.

4. Herrnson, *Party Campaigning,* chap. 2.

5. For more on the concept of party issue ownership, see John R. Petrocik, "Issue Ownership in Presidential Elections, with a 1980 Case Study," *American Journal of Political Science* 40 (1996): 825–850; and George Rabinowitz and Stuart McDonald, "A Directional Theory of Voting," *American Political Science Review* 65 (1989): 93–122.

6. Paul S. Herrnson, Kelly D. Patterson, and John J. Pitney Jr., "From Ward Heelers to Public Relations Experts: The Parties' Response to Mass Politics," in *Broken Contract? Changing Relationships between Citizens and Government in the United States,* ed. Stephen C. Craig (Boulder, Colo.: Westview Press, 1996), 251–267.

7. Richard K. Armey, Jennifer Dunn, and Christopher Shays, *It's Long Enough: The Decline of Popular Government under Forty Years of Single Party Control of the U.S. House of Representatives* (Washington, D.C.: Republican Conference, U.S. House of Representatives, 1994); Richard K. Armey, *Under the Clinton Big Top: Policy, Politics, and Public Relations in the President's First Year* (Washington, D.C.: Republican Conference, U.S. House of Representatives, 1993); James G. Gimpel, *Fulfilling the Contract: The First 100 Days* (Boston: Allyn and Bacon, 1996); Robin Kolodny, "The Contract with America in the 104th Congress," in *The State of the Parties,* ed. John C. Green and Daniel M. Shea (Lanham, Md.: Rowman and Littlefield, 1996), 314–327.

8. John E. Mueller, "Presidential Popularity from Truman to Johnson," in *The Presidency in Contemporary Context,* ed. Norman C. Thomas (New York: Dodd, Mead, and Company, 1975), 83–106.

9. Even though the reports that candidates filed with the FEC indicate that some received large national committee contributions and coordinated expenditures, this spending is almost always directed by a congressional or senatorial campaign committee's election strategy.

10. The term *Hill committees* probably originates from the fact that the congressional and senatorial campaign committees were originally located in congressional office space on Capitol Hill.

11. These figures include hard dollars, which can be spent directly on individual federal campaigns, and soft money, which can be spent on issue advocacy advertisements, party building, and voter mobilization activities. See Federal Election Commission, "Party Committees Raise More Than $1 Billion in 2001–2002," press release, March 19, 2003.

12. Lynton Weeks, "Red, White and Greenbacks at GOP Fundraiser," *Washington Post,* June 24, 2002; Mike Allen, "Bush Enlists Government in GOP Campaign," *Washington Post,* October 24, 2002; Brian Faler, "Bush Is Back on the Money Trail," *Washington Post,* November 24, 2002.

13. Andrew Grossman, political director, DSCC, interview, February 27, 2003.

14. Figures are compiled from data provided by the Center for Responsive Politics.

15. Herrnson, *Party Campaigning,* 46; Robin Kolodny, "Electoral Partnerships: Political Consultants and Political Parties," in *Campaign Warriors,* ed. James A. Thurber and Candice J. Nelson (Washington, D.C.: Brookings Institution Press, 2000), 121; David B. Magleby, Kelly D. Patterson, and James A. Thurber, "Campaign Consultants and Responsible Party Government," in *Responsible Partisanship?,* ed. John C. Green and Paul S. Herrnson (Lawrence: University Press of Kansas, 2003), 101–119.

16. Gary C. Jacobson, "Party Organization and Campaign Resources in 1982," *Political Science Quarterly* 100 (1985–1986): 604–625.

17. On the use of congressional and senatorial campaign committee chairmanships as vehicles for advancing in the congressional leadership, see Paul S. Herrnson, "Political Leadership and Organizational Change at the National Committees," in *Politics, Professionalism, and Power,* ed. John Green (Lanham, Md.: University Press of America, 1993), 186–202; Brooks Jackson, *Honest Graft: Big Money and the American Political Process* (New York: Alfred A. Knopf, 1988), 286–290; Robin Kolodny, *Pursuing Majorities: Congressional Campaign Committees in American Politics* (Norman: University of Oklahoma Press, 1998), 175–195.

18. Gary C. Jacobson and Samuel Kernell, *Strategy and Choice in Congressional Elections* (New Haven, Conn.: Yale University Press, 1983), 39–43, 76–84.

19. The information on committee strategy, decision making, and targeting is from numerous interviews conducted before, during, and after the 1992, 1994, 1996, and 1998 election cycles with several high-ranking officials of the congressional and senatorial campaign committees.

20. On the 1990 election, see Les Frances, "Commentary," in *Machine Politics, Sound Bites, and Nostalgia,* ed. Michael Margolis and John Green (Lanham, Md.: University Press of America), 58; on the 1994 election, see Paul S. Herrnson, "Money and Motives: Spending in House Elections," in *Congress Reconsidered,* 6th ed., ed. Lawrence C. Dodd and Bruce I. Oppenheimer (Washington, D.C.: CQ Press, 1996), 106–107; on the 1992 and 1996 elections, see previous editions of this book.

21. The forecasts of specialized journalists who handicap congressional elections parallel those of party leaders. See chap. 1, n. 66, for information on those forecasts.

22. Robert Biersack and Paul S. Herrnson, "Political Parties and the Year of the Woman," in *The Year of the Woman? Myths and Realities,* ed. Elizabeth Adell Cook, Sue Thomas, and Clyde Wilcox (Boulder, Colo.: Westview Press, 1994), 173–174.

23. Rep. Tom Davis, chairman, NRCC, interview, February 27, 2003.

24. As noted in the Introduction, the financing of congressional elections held after 2002 will be regulated by the Bipartisan Campaign Reform Act of 2002.

25. These are considered separate elections under the FECA. Party committees usually give contributions only to general election candidates.

26. The coordinated expenditure limit for states with only one House member was originally set at $20,000 and reached $71,820 in 2002.

27. Herrnson, *Party Campaigning,* 43–44.

28. Diana Dwyre, "Spinning Straw into Gold: Soft Money and U.S. House Elections," *Legislative Studies Quarterly* 21 (1996): 409–424.

29. Most of the contributions and coordinated expenditures made by state and local parties in connection with Senate races are the result of money swaps.

30. For data on prior elections see the previous editions of this book, and Paul S. Herrnson and Kelly D. Patterson, "Financing the 2000 Congressional Elections," in *Financing the 2000 Election,* ed. David B. Magleby (Washington, D.C.: Brookings Institution, 2002), 106–132. Herrnson, "Money and Motives"; Paul S. Herrnson, "National Party Decision Making, Strategies, and Resource Distribution in Congressional Elections," *Western Political Quarterly* 42 (1998): 301–323; Jacobson, "Party Organization and Campaign Resources in 1982," 604–625.

31. Davis, interview.

32. Ross K. Baker, *The New Fat Cats: Members of Congress as Political Benefactor* (New York: Twentieth Century Fund, 1989), 31.

33. Figures are from the Center for Responsive Politics (http://www.opensecrets.org).

34. The coverage of these topics draws heavily from Herrnson, *Party Campaigning,* chaps. 4 and 5.

35. Grossman, interview.

36. In some cases the congressional campaign committees require candidates to use the services of one of their preferred consultants as a precondition for committee support. Although these cases are rare, they can arouse the ire of both candidates and political consultants. See Herrnson, *Party Campaigning,* 56–57; Stephen E. Frantzich, *Political Parties in the Technological Age* (New York: Longman, 1989), 82, 87–88; and Barbara G. Salmore and Stephen A. Salmore, *Candidates, Parties, and Campaigns: Electoral Politics in America,* 2nd ed. (Washington, D.C.: CQ Press, 1989), 240–241.

37. Jenny Backus, communications director, DCCC, interview, November 14, 2002.

38. Davis, interview.

39. Grossman, interview.

40. The allocable costs of the polls vary by their type and size and by when they are released to candidates. FEC regulations specify that candidates must pay 100 percent of the costs if they receive the poll results within 15 days of when the poll was completed, 50 percent if they receive them between 16 and 60 days, and 5 percent if the results are received between 61 and 180 days. After 180 days, a poll can be given to a candidate free of charge. See General Services Administration, *Title 11–Federal Elections,* sec. 2 U.S.C. 106.4, 11–78. An added advantage to this arrangement is that because the party claims that it used the poll for planning purposes, the poll's cost does not count against the party's contribution or coordinated expenditure limits.

41. Davis, interview.

42. Chris LaCivita, political director, NRSC, interview, February 3, 2003.

43. Figures provided by DSCC staff.

44. Paul S. Herrnson, "The National Committee for an Effective Congress: Ideology, Partisanship, and Electoral Innovation," in *Risky Business? PAC Decisionmaking in Congressional Elections,* ed. Robert Biersack, Paul S. Herrnson, and Clyde Wilcox (Armonk, N.Y.: M. E. Sharpe, 1994), 39–55.

45. Steve Schmidt and Carl Forti, "Words Matter in the Social Security Debate," NRCC memo, August 26, 2002.

46. Davis, interview; Steve Schmidt, communications director, and Brad Moore, intern, NRCC, interview, November 14, 2002.

47. DSCC staff; Grossman, interview.

48. LaCivita, interview.

49. PAC kits typically include information about the candidate's personal background, political experience, campaign staff, support in the district, endorsements, issue positions, and campaign strategy.

50. David Maraniss and Michael Weisskopf, "Speaker and His Directors Make the Cash Flow Right," *Washington Post,* November 27, 1995.

51. Herrnson, *Party Campaigning,* 75.

52. See, for example, Larry J. Sabato, *PAC Power: Inside the World of Political Action Committees* (New York: W. W. Norton, 1984), 144–149.

53. These generalizations are drawn from responses to questions VI.1 through VI.7 of the 2002 Congressional Campaign Study.

54. Cornelius P. Cotter, James L. Gibson, John F. Bibby, and Robert J. Huckshorn, *Party Organizations in American Politics* (Pittsburgh, Pa.: University of Pittsburgh Press, 1989), 20–25.

55. Ibid.; Herrnson, *Party Campaigning,* 102–106; Robert Huckfeldt and John Sprague, "Political Parties and Electoral Mobilization: Political Structure, Social Structure, and the Party Canvass," *American Political Science Review* 86 (1992): 70–86; Gregory A. Caldeira, Samuel C. Patterson, and Gregory A. Markko, "The Mobilization of Voters in Congressional Elections," *Journal of Politics* 47

(1985): 490–509; Michael A. Krassa, "Context and the Canvass: The Mechanisms of Interactions," *Political Behavior* 10 (1988): 233–246; Peter W. Wielhower and Brad Lockerbie, "Party Contacting and Political Participation, 1952–90," *American Journal of Political Science* 38 (1994): 211–229.

56. 116 S. Ct. 2309 (1966).

57. James A. Thurber and R. Sam Garrett, "Campaign Consultants, BCRA, and Coordination" (paper presented at the annual meeting of the Midwest Political Science Association, Chicago, April 2003).

58. Paul S. Herrnson and Diana Dwyre, "Party Issue Advocacy in Congressional Elections," in *The State of the Parties,* 3rd ed., ed. John C. Green and Daniel M. Shea (Lanham, Md.: University Press of America, 1999), 86–104.

59. Backus, interview.

60. Davis, interview; Schmidt, interview; Carl Forti, deputy communications director, NRCC, e-mail correspondence, March 18, 2003.

61. Figures provided by DSCC staff.

62. LaCivita, interview.

63. Dan Balz and David S. Broder, "Close Election Turns on Voter Turnout," *Washington Post,* November 1, 2002.

64. LaCivita, interview.

65. Quote from Curt Anderson, RNC, in Balz and Broder, "Close Election Turns on Voter Turnout."

66. LaCivita, interview.

67. Balz and Broder, "Close Election Turns on Voter Turnout."

68. Ibid.

69. Figures include only expenditures by joint fundraising committees or other soft money committees directly affiliated with current or former members of Congress. They exclude hard money. The figures are conservative because they are compiled from a list that includes only the 200 wealthiest 527 organizations, and they exclude other organizations that may have participated in the 2002 elections. Figures are compiled from data provided by Public Citizen.

70. Quoted in Daniel A. Smith, "Strings Attached: Outside Money in Colorado's Seventh Congressional District," in *The Last Hurrah? Soft Money and Issue Advocacy in the 2002 Congressional Elections,* ed. David B. Magleby and J. Quin Monson (Provo, Utah: Center for the Study of Elections and Democracy, 2003), 194.

71. Jason Embry, "Edwards Using Farley's Radio Comments Against Him—Again," *Waco Herald Tribune,* July 23, 2002; Chris Cillizza, "After Flubbing First Shot at Rep. Edwards GOP Goes Back on the Air for the Challenger," *Roll Call,* July 25, 2002.

72. See n. 53. To some degree the assessments also reflect the propensity of campaign managers and candidates in the candidate-centered system to view themselves as the nucleus of all campaign activity and to understate the contributions others make to the campaign.

73. On individual donor networks, see Peter L. Francia, John C. Green, Paul S. Herrnson, Lynda W. Powell, and Clyde Wilcox, *The Financiers of Congressional Elections: Investors, Ideologues, and Intimates* (New York: Columbia University Press, 2003).

74. Some of the DNC funds were used in Colorado's Senate race.

75. Smith, "Strings Attached."

76. Ibid.

77. Some of the RNC funds were used in Colorado's Senate race.

78. Smith, "Strings Attached."

79. Ibid.

80. See n. 53. Some of the information for Senate elections is drawn from responses to the 1992 Congressional Campaign Study. See also, Herrnson, *Party Campaigning,* chap. 4.

81. Most of these funds were transferred by the NRSC and RNC. NRCC transfers accounted for only $145,001.

82. The NRCC spent an additional $465,000 solely to help Janklow.

83. James Meader and John Bart, "South Dakota At-Large and Senate Race 2002," in Magleby and Monson, *The Last Hurrah?*, 156–176.

84. Most of these funds were transferred by the DSCC. DNC and DSCC transfers accounted for only $994,859 and $548,590, respectively.

85. Meader and Bart, "South Dakota At-Large and Senate Race 2002."

86. Ibid.

5. THE INTERESTS CAMPAIGN

1. See, for example, Herbert E. Alexander, *Financing Politics: Money, Elections, and Political Reform* (Washington, D.C.: CQ Press, 1992), 10–17.

2. Although it was referred to as a political action committee from its inception, COPE operated somewhat differently from modern (post-1974) PACs until the enactment of the FECA. See Clyde Wilcox, "Coping with Increasing Business Influence. The AFL-CIO's Committee on Political Education," in *Risky Business? PAC Decisionmaking in Congressional Elections*, ed. Robert Biersack, Paul S. Herrnson, and Clyde Wilcox (Armonk, N.Y.: M. E. Sharpe, 1994), 214–223.

3. PACs that do not meet these requirements are subject to the same $1,000 contribution limit as are individuals.

4. FEC Advisory Opinion 1975-23 (December 3, 1975).

5. *Buckley v. Valeo*, 424 U.S. 1 (1976).

6. The number of nonconnected PACs excludes leadership PACs.

7. Removing the 663 defunct PACs from the calculation reduces the number of inactive PACs to 22 percent of the total, but it does not affect the generalization that a small portion of the PAC community accounts for the overwhelming majority of all PAC expenditures.

8. Anthony Corrado, *Campaign Finance Reform: Beyond the Basics* (New York: The Century Foundation Press, 2000), 93.

9. Philip A. Mundo, "League of Conservation Voters," in *After the Revolution: PACs, Lobbies, and the Republican Congress*, ed. Robert Biersack, Paul S. Herrnson, and Clyde Wilcox (Boston: Allyn and Bacon, 1991), 118–133.

10. See, for example, Theodore J. Eismeier and Philip H. Pollock III, *Business, Money, and the Rise of Corporate PACs in American Elections* (New York: Quorum Books, 1988), 27–30; J. David Gopoian, "What Makes PACs Tick? An Analysis of the Allocation Patterns of Economic Interest Groups," *American Journal of Political Science* 28 (May 1984): 259–281; Craig Humphries, "Corporations, PACs, and the Strategic Link between Contributions and Lobbying Activities," *Western Political Quarterly* 44 (1991): 353–372; Frank J. Sorauf, *Inside Campaign Finance* (New Haven, Conn.: Yale University Press, 1992), 64–65, 74–75; case studies in *Risky Business?*

11. Laura Langbein, "Money and Access: Some Empirical Evidence," *Journal of Politics* 48 (1986): 1052–1062; Richard Hall and Frank Wayman, "Buying Time: Moneyed Interests and the Mobilization of Bias in Congressional Committees," *American Political Science Review* 84 (1990): 797–820.

12. John Frendreis and Richard Waterman, "PAC Contributions and Legislative Behavior: Senate Voting on Trucking Deregulation," *Social Science Quarterly* 66 (1985): 401–412; Janet M. Grenzke, "PACs and the Congressional Supermarket: The Currency Is Complex," *American Journal of Political Science* 33 (February 1989): 1–24; John Wright, "Contributions, Lobbying, and Committee Voting in the U.S. House of Representatives," *American Political Science Review* 84 (1990): 417–438; Kevin B. Grier and Michael C. Munger, "Comparing Interest Group PAC Contributions to House and

Senate Incumbents, 1980–1986," *Journal of Politics* 55 (August 1993): 615–643; Thomas Romer and James M. Snyder Jr., "An Empirical Investigation of the Dynamics of PAC Contributions," *American Journal of Political Science* 38 (1994): 745–769.

13. David B. Magleby and J. Quin Monson, "Campaign 2002: 'The Perfect Storm' " (Provo, Utah: Center for the Study of Elections and Democracy, 2003).

14. Gary C. Jacobson and Samuel Kernell, *Strategy and Choice in Congressional Elections* (New Haven, Conn.: Yale University Press, 1983), esp. chap. 4.

15. Theodore J. Eismeier and Philip H. Pollock III, "The Tale of Two Elections: PAC Money in 1980 and 1984," *Corruption and Reform* 1 (1986): 189–207; Sorauf, *Inside Campaign Finance,* 67–77; Brooks Jackson, *Honest Graft: Big Money and the American Political Process* (New York: Alfred A. Knopf, 1988), 69–70, 77–81, 90–93.

16. Paul S. Herrnson, "Money and Motives: Spending in House Elections," in *Congress Reconsidered,* 6th ed., ed. Lawrence C. Dodd and Bruce I. Oppenheimer (Washington, D.C.: CQ Press, 1996), 122–124; Thomas J. Rudolph, "Corporate and Labor PAC Contributions in House Elections: Measuring the Effects of Majority Party Status," *Journal of Politics* 61 (1999): 195–206; Gary W. Cox and Eric Mager, "How Much Is Majority Status in the U.S. Congress Worth?" *American Journal of Political Science* 93 (1999): 299–309.

17. Sorauf, *Inside Campaign Finance,* 61–71.

18. See the case studies in *Risky Business?* and *After the Revolution.*

19. Clyde Wilcox, "Organizational Variables and the Contribution Behavior of Large PACs: A Longitudinal Analysis," *Political Behavior* 11 (1989): 157–173.

20. John Wright, "PACs, Contributions, and Roll Calls: An Organizational Perspective," *American Political Science Review* 79 (1985): 400–414.

21. Larry J. Sabato, *PAC Power: Inside the World of Political Action Committees* (New York: W. W. Norton, 1984), 44–49; Robert Biersack, "Introduction," in *Risky Business?*

22. The information on the Realtors PAC is from Anne H. Bedlington, "The Realtors Political Action Committee: Covering All Contingencies," in *After the Revolution,* 170–183.

23. On AT&T's PAC, see Robert E. Mutch, "AT&T PAC: A Pragmatic Giant," in *Risky Business?*; and Robert Mutch, "AT&T PAC: The Perils of Pragmatism," in *After the Revolution.* On AMPAC, see Michael K. Gusmano, "The AMA in the 1990s: Surviving in a Crowded Policy Network," in *After the Revolution.*

24. The information on WASHPAC is from Barbara Levick-Segnatelli, "WASHPAC: One Man Can Make a Difference," in *Risky Business?*

25. Brett Kappel, legal counsel, Powell, Goldstein, Frazer, and Murphy PAC, interview, August 17, 1999.

26. Ibid.

27. On lead PACs, see the introduction to part I in *Risky Business?,* 17–18. On the NCEC, see Paul S. Herrnson, "The National Committee for an Effective Congress: Ideology, Partisanship, and Electoral Innovation," in *Risky Business?* On COPE, see Clyde Wilcox, "Coping with Increasing Business Influence," in *Risky Business?*; and Robin Gerber, "Building to Win, Building to Last: The AFL-CIO COPE Takes on the Republican Congress," in *After the Revolution,* 77–93. On BIPAC, see Candice J. Nelson, "The Business-Industry PAC: Trying to Lead in an Uncertain Climate," in *Risky Business?*; and Candice J. Nelson and Robert Biersack, "BIPAC: Working to Keep a Pro-Business Congress," in *After the Revolution,* 36–46.

28. On the flow of PAC money in the 1996 elections, see the previous edition of this book; for information on the 1994 elections, see Herrnson, "Money and Motives," 110–113; and Paul S. Herrnson, "Interest Groups, PACs, and Campaigns," in *The Interest Group Connection: Electioneering, Lobbying, and Policymaking in Washington,* ed. Paul S. Herrnson, Clyde Wilcox, and Ronald G. Shaiko (Chatham, N.J.: Chatham House, 1997).

29. Theodore J. Eismeier and Philip H. Pollock III, "Political Action Committees: Varieties of Organization and Strategy," in *Money and Politics in the United States: Financing Elections in the 1980s*, ed. Michael J. Malbin (Washington, D.C.: American Enterprise Institute, 1984), 122–141; Margaret Ann Latus, "Assessing Ideological PACs: From Outrage to Understanding," in *Money and Politics in the United States*, 150–160; Sabato, *PAC Power*, 93–95.

30. On abortion rights PACs, see, for example, Sue Thomas, "NARAL PAC: Reproductive Choice in the Spotlight," in *Risky Business?*

31. Linda L. Fowler and Robert D. McClure, *Political Ambition: Who Decides to Run for Congress* (New Haven, Conn.: Yale University Press, 1989), 205–207.

32. Ronald G. Shaiko and Marc A. Wallace, "From Wall Street to Main Street: The National Federation of Independent Business and the Republican Majority," in *After the Revolution*; James G. Gimpel, "Peddling Influence in the Field: The Direct Campaign Involvement of the Free Congress PAC," in *Risky Business?*

33. Herrnson, "The National Committee for an Effective Congress."

34. See, for example, Sabato, *PAC Power*, 44–49.

35. Peter L. Francia, "Early Fundraising by Nonincumbent Female Congressional Candidates," *Women & Politics* 23 (2001): 7–20.

36. Peter L. Francia, John C. Green, Paul S. Herrnson, Lynda W. Powell, and Clyde Wilcox, *The Financiers of Congressional Elections: Investors, Ideologues, and Intimates* (New York: Columbia University Press, 2003).

37. Janet Harris, communications director, EMILY's List, interview, April 11, 2003.

38. Club for Growth web site (http://www.clubforgrowth.org/index1.php).

39. Francia et al., *The Financiers of Congressional Elections*.

40. The figures for candidate contributions include all federal candidates, and a small portion of these funds may have been given to the accounts of presidential candidates. Figures are from the Center for Responsive Politics (http://www.opensecrets.org).

41. Federal Election Commission, "PAC Activity Increases for 2002 Election," press release, March 27, 2003.

42. The figures include only nonfederal expenditures by interest group 527 committees and exclude the party-connected 527 committees and joint fundraising committees discussed in Chapter 4. The figures are conservative because they are compiled from a list that includes only the 200 wealthiest 527 organizations, and they exclude other organizations that may have participated in the 2002 elections. Figures are compiled from data provided by Public Citizen.

43. Kenneth Goldstein and Joel Rivlin, "Advertising in the 2002 Elections," unpublished manuscript.

44. For spending estimates in a subset of competitive House and Senate races, see *The Last Hurrah? Soft Money and Issue Advocacy in the 2002 Congressional Elections*, ed. David B. Magleby and J. Quin Monson (Provo, Utah: Center for the Study of Elections and Democracy, 2003), 41, 45–47.

45. Mass media advertising is the one campaign activity where Democratic and Republican House campaigns report receiving equal amounts of help from interest groups. These generalizations are drawn from questions VI.1 through VI.7 of the 2002 Congressional Campaign Study.

46. All individual contributions referred to in this section were made in amounts of $200 or more. Figures are from the Center for Responsive Politics (http://www.opensecrets.org).

47. Daniel A. Smith, "Strings Attached: Outside Money in Colorado's Seventh Congressional District," in *The Last Hurrah?*, 205–206.

48. Figure includes contributions from corporations without stock.

49. Center for Responsive Politics (http://www.opensecrets.org).

50. Smith, "Strings Attached," 205–206.

51. See n. 48.

52. Center for Responsive Politics (http://www.opensecrets.org).

53. James Meader and John Bart, "South Dakota At-Large and Senate Race 2002," in Magleby and Monson, *The Last Hurrah?,* 173–174.

54. The 70 percent figure includes contributions from PACs sponsored by corporations, corporations without stock, trade associations, and cooperatives.

55. Meader and Bart, "South Dakota At-Large and Senate Race 2002," 169.

6. THE CAMPAIGN FOR RESOURCES

1. Quoted in David Adamany and George E. Agree, *Political Money: A Strategy for Campaign Finance in America* (Baltimore, Md.: Johns Hopkins University Press, 1975), 8.

2. George Thayer, *Who Shakes the Money Tree? American Campaign Finance Practices from 1789 to the Present* (New York: Simon and Schuster, 1973), 25.

3. These figures exclude Torricelli and Wellstone, whose names were not on the ballot on election day.

4. The figures for House and Senate campaign contributions and coordinated expenditures include spending by all candidates involved in major-party contested general elections, excluding those in incumbent-versus-incumbent House races.

5. The denominator used to calculate the percentages is the candidates' total receipts plus any coordinated spending the parties made on the candidates' behalf. Coordinated expenditures are included because candidates have some control over the activities on which they are spent.

6. Frank J. Sorauf, *Inside Campaign Finance* (New Haven, Conn.: Yale University Press, 1992), 47.

7. This figure includes only out-of-state contributions of $200 or more because the FEC does not require candidates to report information about individuals who contribute less than $200 to their campaigns.

8. Figures are compiled from Paul S. Herrnson, *The Campaign Assessment and Candidate Outreach Project, 2000 Survey* (College Park, Md.: Center for American Politics and Citizenship, University of Maryland, 2000).

9. On direct-mail fundraising, see Kenneth R. Godwin, *One Billion Dollars of Influence: The Direct Marketing of Politics* (Chatham, N.J.: Chatham House, 1988).

10. Center for Responsive Politics (http://www.opensecrets.org).

11. Figures are from question IV.2 of the 2002 Congressional Campaign Study.

12. Peter L. Francia, John C. Green, Paul S. Herrnson, Lynda W. Powell, and Clyde Wilcox, *The Financiers of Congressional Elections: Investors, Ideologues, and Intimates* (New York: Columbia University Press, 2003), esp. chap. 3.

13. Ibid., chaps. 3 and 5.

14. See, for example, Sorauf, *Inside Campaign Finance,* 124–127.

15. The figure for PACs excludes contributions by leadership PACs. The members were Roy Blunt, R-Mo. (chief deputy whip and a member of the Energy and Commerce Committee), Shelley Moore Capito, R-W.Va. (vice chairwoman of the Congressional Caucus for Women's Issues), John Dingell, D-Mich. (ranking member of the Energy and Commerce Committee), Richard Gephardt, D-Mo. (House minority leader), Dennis Hastert, R-Ill. (Speaker of the House), Nancy Johnson, R-Conn. (chair of the Health Subcommittee of the Ways and Means Committee), Earl Pomeroy, R-N.D. (a member of the Ways and Means Committee), and Karen Thurmon, D-Fla. (a member of the Ways and Means Committee).

16. Francia et al., *The Financiers of Congressional Elections,* esp. chap. 4.

17. Center for Responsive Politics (http://www.opensecrets.org).

18. Ibid.

19. Some argue that preemptive fundraising by incumbents may not discourage quality challengers from running. See Jonathan S. Krasno and Donald Philip Green, "Preempting Quality Challengers in House Elections," *Journal of Politics* 50 (1988): 920–936; Peverill Squire, "Preemptive Fundraising and Challenger Profile in Senate Elections," *Journal of Politics* 53 (1991): 1150–1164.

20. Gary C. Jacobson, *Money in Congressional Elections* (New Haven, Conn.: Yale University Press, 1980), 113–123; Jonathan S. Krasno, Donald Philip Green, and Jonathan A. Cowden, "The Dynamics of Fundraising in House Elections," *Journal of Politics* 56 (1994): 459–474.

21. Sorauf, *Inside Campaign Finance*, 75.

22. Center for Responsive Politics (http://www.opensecrets.org).

23. The remainder came from interest on investments and miscellaneous funds.

24. Forty-eight percent of all challengers spent one-fourth of their personal campaign schedule fundraising. See n. 8.

25. Robert Biersack, Paul S. Herrnson, and Clyde Wilcox, "Seeds for Success: Early Money in Congressional Elections," *Legislative Studies Quarterly* 18 (1993): 535–553; Krasno, Green, and Cowden, "The Dynamics of Fundraising in House Elections."

26. Paul S. Herrnson, *Party Campaigning in the 1980s* (Cambridge, Mass.: Harvard University Press, 1988), 75.

27. Figure for the Bush fundraising event was provided by Mark Knoller, CBS News.

28. Paul S. Herrnson, "Campaign Professionalism and Fundraising in Congressional Elections," *Journal of Politics* 54 (1992): 859–870.

29. Clyde Wilcox, "Coping with Increasing Business Influence: The AFL-CIO's Committee on Political Education," in *Risky Business? PAC Decisionmaking in Congressional Elections*, ed. Robert Biersack, Paul S. Herrnson, and Clyde Wilcox (Armonk, N.Y.: M. E. Sharpe, 1994), 214–223; Robin Gerber, "Building to Win, Building to Last: The AFL-CIO COPE Takes on the Republican Congress," in *After the Revolution*, ed. Robert Biersack, Paul S. Herrnson, and Clyde Wilcox (Boston: Allyn and Bacon, 1991), 77–93; Denise L. Baer and Martha Bailey, "The Nationalization of Education Politics: The National Education Association PAC and the 1992 Elections," in *Risky Business?*, 65–78.

30. The WISH List's name is an acronym for "Women in the Senate and House." See Craig A. Rimmerman, "New Kids on the Block. WISH List and the Gay and Lesbian Victory Fund," in *Risky Business?*; Rimmerman, "The Gay and Lesbian Victory Fund Comes of Age: Reflections on the 1996 Elections," in *After the Revolution;* and Mark J. Rozell, "WISH List: Pro-Choice Women in the Republican Congress," in *After the Revolution.*

31. Howard Beeman, candidate for Congress, interview, February 27, 2003.

32. Center for Responsive Politics (http://www.opensecrets.org.)

33. See n. 8.

34. See n. 5.

35. Feeley received no contributions from corporations without stock.

36. The figure for nonconnected PAC contributions excludes contributions from leadership PACs.

37. The figures exclude contributions by leadership PACs.

38. Figures for out-of-state money are from the Center for Responsive Politics (http://www.opensecrets.org).

39. Figures from the Center for Responsive Politics (http://www.opensecrets.org).

40. Total resources include party-coordinated expenditures and receipts. See n. 5.

41. The corresponding figure for all House candidates is 49 percent. See n. 8. The figure for Senate candidates also draws from Paul S. Herrnson, *The Campaign Assessment and Candidate Outreach Project, 1998 Survey* (College Park, Md.: Center for American Politics and Citizenship, University of Maryland, 1998).

42. Center for Responsive Politics (http://www.opensecrets.org).

7. CAMPAIGN STRATEGY

1. Angus Campbell, Philip E. Converse, Warren E. Miller, and Donald E. Stokes, *The American Voter* (New York: John Wiley and Sons, 1960), 541–548; and Donald R. Kinder and David O. Sears, "Public Opinion and Political Action," in *Handbook of Social Psychology*, 3rd ed., ed. Gardner Lindzey and Elliot Aronson (New York: Random House, 1985), 659–741.

2. Figures compiled from Virginia Sapiro, Stephen J. Rosenstone, and National Election Studies, *American National Election Study, 1998: Post-Election Survey* (Ann Arbor: University of Michigan, 1999).

3. On Senate elections, see Alan I. Abramowitz and Jeffrey A. Segal, *Senate Elections* (Ann Arbor: University of Michigan Press, 1992), 39; Peverill Squire, "Challenger Quality and Voting Behavior," *Legislative Studies Quarterly* 17 (1992): 247–263.

4. Figures compiled from Nancy Burns, Donald R. Kinder, and National Election Studies, *American National Election Study, 2002: Post-Election Survey* (Ann Arbor: University of Michigan, Center for Political Studies, 2003).

5. For the importance of information in democratic politics in general and American politics in specific, see, for example, Michael X. Delli Carpini and Scott Ketter, *What Americans Know about Politics and Why It Matters* (New Haven, Conn.: Yale University Press, 1996), 1–16, 22–61.

6. Alan I. Abramowitz, "A Comparison of Voting for U.S. Senator and Representative in 1978," *American Political Science Review* 74 (1980): 633–640; Gerald C. Wright and Michael B. Berkman, "Candidates and Policy in United States Senate Elections," *American Political Science Review* 80 (1986): 567–588; Mark C. Westlye, *Senate Elections and Campaign Intensity* (Baltimore, Md.: Johns Hopkins University Press, 1992), 122–151.

7. Robert D. Brown and James A. Woods, "Toward a Model of Congressional Elections," *Journal of Politics* 53 (1991): 454–473; John R. Zaller, *The Nature and Origins of Mass Opinion* (Cambridge: Cambridge University Press, 1992), chap. 10.

8. See n. 4.

9. See n. 4.

10. Wright and Berkman, "Candidates and Policy in United States Senate Elections," 567–588; and Westlye, *Senate Elections and Campaign Intensity*, chap. 6.

11. See, for example, Raymond E. Wolfinger and Steven J. Rosenstone, *Who Votes?* (New Haven, Conn.: Yale University Press, 1980), 34–36, 58–60, 102–114.

12. Zaller, *The Nature and Origins of Mass Opinion*, chap. 10; Westlye, *Senate Elections and Campaign Intensity*, esp. chap. 5; Milton Lodge, Marco R. Steenbergen, and Shawn Brau, "The Responsive Voter: Campaign Information and the Dynamics of Candidate Evaluation," *American Political Science Review* 89 (1995): 309–326; Jon K. Dalager, "Voters, Issues, and Elections: Are the Candidates' Messages Getting Through?" *Journal of Politics* 58 (1996): 496–515.

13. See Morris P. Fiorina, *Retrospective Voting in American National Elections* (New Haven, Conn.: Yale University Press, 1981); Edward R. Tufte, "Determinants of the Outcomes of Midterm Congressional Elections," *American Political Science Review* 69 (1975): 812–826; James E. Campbell, "Explaining Presidential Losses in Midterm Congressional Elections," *Journal of Politics* 47 (1985): 1140–1157; Samuel C. Popkin, *The Reasoning Voter: Communication and Persuasion in Presidential Campaigns* (Chicago: University of Chicago Press, 1991), esp. chaps. 3 and 4.

14. Alan I. Abramowitz, Albert D. Cover, and Helmut Norpoth, "The President's Party in Midterm Elections: Going from Bad to Worse," *American Journal of Political Science* 30 (1986): 562–576; Henry W. Chappell Jr. and Motoshi Susuki, "Aggregate Vote Functions for the U.S. Presidency, Senate, and House," *Journal of Politics* 55 (1993): 207–217; Gary C. Jacobson, "Reversal of Fortune: The Transformation of U.S. House Elections in the 1990s" (paper presented at the annual meeting of the Midwest Political Science Association, Chicago, April 10–12, 1997). See also the studies cited in n. 13.

15. Morris P. Fiorina, *Divided Government* (Boston: Allyn and Bacon, 1996), 109–110; Stephen P. Nicholson and Gary M. Segura, "Midterm Elections and Divided Government: An Information-Driven Theory of Electoral Volatility" (paper presented at the annual meeting of the Midwest Political Science Association, Chicago, April 10–12, 1997).

16. Alan I. Abramowitz and Kyle L. Saunders, "Ideological Realignment in the U.S. Electorate," *Journal of Politics* 61 (1998): 634–652.

17. Raymond E. Wolfinger, "Candidates and Parties in Congressional Elections," *American Political Science Review* 74 (1980): 622–629; Barbara Hinckley, "House Re-Elections and Senate Defeats: The Role of the Challenger," *British Journal of Political Science* 10 (1980): 441–460; and Gary C. Jacobson, *The Politics of Congressional Elections*, 4th ed. (New York: Longman, 1997), 106–108.

18. David R. Mayhew, *Congress: The Electoral Connection* (New Haven, Conn.: Yale University Press, 1974); Stephen Ansolabehere, James M. Snyder, Jr., and Charles Stewart III, "Old Voters, New Voters, and the Personal Vote," *American Journal of Political Science* 44 (2000): 17–34.

19. Richard F. Fenno Jr., *Home Style: House Members in Their Districts* (Boston: Little, Brown, 1978), esp. chaps. 3 and 4.

20. Steve Rice, political consultant, McNally Temple Associates, interview, February 26, 2003.

21. On polls, see Barbara G. Salmore and Stephen A. Salmore, *Candidates, Parties, and Campaigns: Electoral Politics in America*, 2nd ed. (Washington, D.C.: CQ Press, 1989), 116–119.

22. Bryce Bassett, director of marketing support, the Wirthlin Worldwide, presentation to the Taft Institute Honors Seminar in American Government, June 15, 1993.

23. See, for example, Robert Axelrod, "Where the Votes Come From: An Analysis of Presidential Election Coalitions, 1952–1968," *American Political Science Review* 66 (1972): 11–20.

24. Manuel Perez-Rivas, "Opponent Tries to Make Party Label Stick to Morella," *Washington Post*, March 7, 1996.

25. These generalizations are drawn from responses to question III.3 of the 2002 Congressional Campaign Study.

26. Axelrod, "Where the Votes Come From," 11–20; Henry C. Kenski and Lee Sigelman, "Where the Vote Comes From: Group Components of the 1988 Vote," *Legislative Studies Quarterly* 18 (1993): 367–390.

27. This generalization is from question III.3 of the 2002 Congressional Campaign Study.

28. Brandon DelRehn, field coordinator, Morella campaign, interview, November 21, 2002.

29. Howard Beeman, candidate for Congress, interview, February 27, 2003.

30. Rice, interview.

31. See n. 27.

32. See, for example, Patrick J. Sellers, "Strategy and Background in Congressional Campaigns," *American Journal of Political Science* 92 (1998): 159–171.

33. Joel C. Bradshaw, "Who Will Vote for You and Why: Designing Campaign Strategy and Theme" (paper presented at the Conference on Campaign Management, American University, Washington, D.C., December 10–11, 1992).

34. The logic behind the battle for the middle ground is presented in Anthony Downs, *An Economic Theory of Democracy* (New York: Harper and Row, 1957), chap. 8.

35. Fred Hartwig, vice president, Peter Hart and Associates, presentation to the Taft Institute Honors Seminar in American Government, June 15, 1993.

36. Ladonna Y. Lee, "Strategy," in *Ousting the Ins: Lessons for Congressional Challengers*, ed. Stuart Rothenberg (Washington, D.C.: Free Congress Research and Education Foundation, 1985), 18–19.

37. Kathleen Hall Jamieson, *Dirty Politics: Perception, Distraction, and Democracy* (New York: Oxford University Press, 1992), esp. chap. 2.

38. Interview with an anonymous political consultant, December 1992.

39. Fenno, *Home Style*, chaps. 3 and 4.

40. See Peter Clarke and Susan H. Evans, *Covering Campaigns: Journalism and Congressional Elections* (Stanford, Calif.: Stanford University Press, 1983), 38–45.

41. On the differences between valence issues and positional issues, see Donald E. Stokes, "Spatial Models of Party Competition," in *Elections and the Political Order*, ed. Angus Campbell, Philip E. Converse, Warren E. Miller, and Donald E. Stokes (New York: John Wiley and Sons, 1966), 161–169.

42. See, for example, Gary C. Jacobson and Samuel Kernell, "National Forces in the 1986 U.S. House Elections," *Legislative Studies Quarterly* 15 (1990): 65–87.

43. Jacobson, *The Politics of Congressional Elections*, 112–116.

44. On the role of candidate's backgrounds on campaign strategy, see Sellers, "Strategy and Background in Congressional Campaigns."

45. James Meader and John Bart, "South Dakota At-Large and Senate Race 2002," in *The Last Hurrah? Soft Money and Issue Advocacy in the 2002 Congressional Elections*, ed. David B. Magleby and J. Quin Monson (Provo, Utah: Center for the Study of Elections and Democracy, 2003), 156–176; quotation taken from p. 167.

46. See Philip Paolino, "Group Salient Issues and Group Representation: Support for Women Candidates in the 1992 Senate Elections," *American Journal of Political Science* 39 (1995): 294–313; Kirsten la Cour Dabelko and Paul S. Herrnson, "Women's and Men's Campaigns for the U.S. House of Representatives," *Political Research Quarterly* 50 (1997): 121–135; Paul S. Herrnson, J. Celeste Lay, and Atiya Kai Stokes, "Women Running 'as Women': Candidate, Gender, Campaign Issues, and Voter-Targeting Strategies," *Journal of Politics* 64 (2003): 244–255.

47. James G. Gimpel, *Fulfilling the Contract: The First 100 Days* (Boston: Allyn and Bacon, 1996); Robin Kolodny, "The Contract with America in the 104th Congress," *The State of the Parties*, ed. John C. Green and Daniel M. Shea (Lanham, Md.: Rowman and Littlefield, 1996), 314–327.

48. Interview with an anonymous 1992 House candidate, December 1992.

49. Richard F. Fenno, "If, as Ralph Nader Says, Congress Is 'The Broken Branch,' How Come We Love Our Congressmen So Much?" in *Congress in Change: Evolution and Reform*, ed. Norman J. Ornstein (New York: Praeger, 1975).

50. For a discussion of partisan divergence on the issues, see Constantine J. Spilliotes and Lynn Vavreck, "Campaign Advertising: Partisan Convergence or Divergence?" *Journal of Politics* 64 (2002): 249–261.

51. The generalization is based on responses to question I.2 of the 2002 Congressional Campaign Study.

52. Hartwig presentation.

53. Phil Duncan, ed., *Politics in America, 1992: The 102nd Congress* (Washington, D.C.: Congressional Quarterly, 1991), 1133.

54. See, for example, James Innocenzi, "Political Advertising," in *Ousting the Ins*, 53–61; Salmore and Salmore, *Candidates, Parties, and Campaigns*, 159.

55. On the demobilization thesis, see Stephen Ansolabehere, Shanto Iyengar, Adam Simon, and Nicholas Valentino, "Does Attack Advertising Demobilize the Electorate?" *American Political Science Review* 88 (1994): 829–838; and Stephen Ansolabehere and Shanto Iyengar, *Going Negative: How Attack Ads Shrink and Polarize the Electorate* (New York: Free Press, 1995), esp. chap. 5. On the mobilization thesis, see Steven Finkel and John G. Geer, "Spot Check: Casting Doubt on the Demobilizing Effect of Attack Advertising," *American Journal of Political Science* 42 (1998): 573–595; Richard R. Lau and Gerald M. Pomper, "Effects of Negative Campaigning on Turnout in U.S. Senate Elections, 1988–1998," *Journal of Politics* 63 (2001): 804–819; Ken Goldstein and Paul Freedman, "Campaign Advertising and Voter Turnout," *Journal of Politics* 64 (2002): 721–740; and Martin P. Wattenberg and Craig Leonard Birans, "Negative Campaign Advertising" *American Political Science Review* 93 (1999): 891–900. Also see Richard P. Lau, Lee Sigelman, Caroline Heldman, and Paul

Babbitt, "The Effects of Negative Political Advertisements," *American Political Science Review* 93 (1999): 851–875; and Kim Fridkin Kahn and Patrick J. Kenney, "Do Negative Campaigns Mobilize or Suppress Turnout?" *American Political Science Review* 93 (1999): 877–889.

56. These generalizations are drawn from responses to question 11 of the 1998 Congressional Campaign Study and question 28 of the 1992 Congressional Campaign Study. See also Ken Goldstein and Paul Freedman, "Lessons Learned: Campaign Advertising in the 2000 Elections," *Political Communication* 19 (2002): 5–28.

57. Richard R. Lau, "Negativity in Political Perception," *Political Behavior* 4 (1982): 353–377; Richard R. Lau, "Two Explanations for Negativity Effects in Political Behavior," *American Journal of Political Science* 29 (1985): 110–138; Jamieson, *Dirty Politics,* 41.

58. On differences in the effects of negative campaigning on incumbents and challengers, see Richard R. Lau and Gerald M. Pomper, "Effectiveness of Negative Campaigning in U.S. Senate Elections," *American Journal of Political Science* 46 (2002): 47–66.

59. Lee, "Strategy," 22.

60. Jamieson, *Dirty Politics,* 103.

61. Collen O'Brien, "Exception to the Rule: Defeating a Republican Incumbent in the 2002 Congressional Elections," University of Maryland, unpublished paper, December 9, 2002.

62. Lawrence Levy, "A Dem's Heart Bleeds as He Seeks an Upset," *Newsday,* October 11, 2002.

63. See, for example, Dale Russakoff, "Torricelli Beats Opposition to TV Spots," *Washington Post,* April 3, 2002.

64. Interview with an anonymous campaign manager for a 1992 House candidate, December 1992.

8. CAMPAIGN COMMUNICATIONS

1. Matthew Katz, "Living Without TV: More Time to Get a Life," *Washington Times,* September 17, 1998.

2. Pew Research Center, "Election Pleases Voters Despite Mudslinging," November 1998, http://www.people-press.org/nov98que.htm.

3. David B. Magleby and J. Quin Monson, "Campaign 2002: 'The Perfect Storm'" (Provo, Utah: Center for the Study of Elections and Democracy, 2003).

4. Darrell M. West, *Air Wars: Television Advertising in Election Campaigns, 1952–1992* (Washington, D.C.: Congressional Quarterly, 1993), esp. chap. 6.

5. Quoted in Frank I. Luntz, *Candidates, Consultants, and Campaigns* (Oxford: Basil Blackwell, 1988), 77.

6. Darrell M. West, "Political Advertising and News Coverage in the 1992 California U.S. Senate Campaigns," *Journal of Politics* 56 (1994): 1053–1075.

7. This generalization is drawn from responses to question IV.1 of the 2002 Congressional Campaign Study. For Senate campaigns, which are few in number in a given election year, additional information is drawn from the 1992 Congressional Campaign Study and Paul S. Herrnson, The Campaign Assessment and Candidate Outreach Project, 1999 and 2001, Center for American Politics and Citizenship, University of Maryland, College Park, Maryland.

8. John R. Alford and Keith Henry, "TV Markets and Congressional Elections," *Legislative Studies Quarterly* 9 (1984): 665–675.

9. Luntz, *Candidates, Consultants, and Campaigns,* 76.

10. Mark H. Rodeffer, "Van Hollen Highlights Newspaper Articles," *Nationaljournal.com,* http://nationaljournal.com/members/adspotlight.

11. Mark H. Rodeffer, "Morella's Bio Debute Touts Independence," *Nationaljournal.com,* http://nationaljournal.com/members/adspotlight.

12. James Meader and John Bart, "South Dakota At-Large and Senate Race 2002," in *The Last Hurrah? Soft Money and Issue Advocacy in the 2002 Congressional Elections,* ed. David B. Magleby and J. Quin Monson (Provo, Utah: Center for the Study of Elections and Democracy, 2003), 156–176.

13. As discussed in chapter 7, whereas valence issues, such as a strong economy, have only one side and are universally viewed by voters in a favorable light, positional (or wedge) issues, which would include either position in the abortion rights debate, divide voters because they have two or more sides.

14. Kim F. Kahn, Patrick J. Kenney, and Tom W. Rice, "Ideological Learning in U.S. Senate Elections" (paper presented at the annual meeting of the American Political Science Association, Washington, D.C., September 2–5, 1993). See also Jay Bryant, "Paid Advertising in Political Campaigns" (paper presented at the Conference on Campaign Management, American University, Washington, D.C., December 10–11, 1992).

15. See n. 7.

16. Figure provided by J. Quin Monson, Department of Political Science, Brigham Young University, April 16, 2003.

17. Luntz, *Candidates, Consultants, and Campaigns,* 108.

18. Frank Luther Mott, *American Journalism: A History of 250 Years, 1690 to 1940* (New York: Macmillan, 1947), 411–430.

19. See n. 7.

20. Luntz, *Candidates, Consultants, and Campaigns,* 109–110.

21. See n. 7.

22. Magleby and Monson, "Campaign 2002: 'The Perfect Storm.'"

23. Kenneth R. Godwin, *One Billion Dollars of Influence: The Direct Marketing of Politics* (Chatham, N.J.: Chatham House, 1988), chaps. 1–3; Jonathan Robbin, "Geodemographics: The New Magic," in *Campaigns and Elections,* ed. Larry J. Sabato (Glenview, Ill.: Scott Foresman, 1989), 105–124; Sabato, "How Direct Mail Works," in *Campaigns and Elections,* 88–89.

24. Barbara G. Salmore and Stephen A. Salmore, *Candidates, Parties, and Campaigns: Electoral Politics in America,* 2nd ed. (Washington, D.C.: CQ Press, 1989), 86–87.

25. Mass mailings consist of five hundred or more pieces of the same letter.

26. Owen G. Abbe, "The 2002 Maryland Eight District Race," in *The Last Hurrah?,* 245.

27. Daniel A. Smith, "Strings Attached: Outside Money in Colorado's Seventh Congressional District," in *The Last Hurrah?,* 205.

28. Meader and Bart, "South Dakota At-Large and Senate Race 2002," 173–174.

29. See n. 7.

30. Abbe, "The 2002 Maryland Eight District Race."

31. See n. 16.

32. Peter Clarke and Susan Evans, *Covering Campaigns: Journalism in Congressional Elections* (Stanford, Calif.: Stanford University Press, 1983), chap. 6.

33. Xandra Kayden, *Campaign Organization* (Lexington, Mass.: D. C. Heath, 1978), 125.

34. Clarke and Evans, *Covering Campaigns,* 60–62; Doris A. Graber, *Mass Media and American Politics,* 4th ed. (Washington, D.C.: CQ Press, 1993), 262, 268–270.

35. Richard Born, "Assessing the Impact of Institutional and Election Forces on Evaluations of Congressional Incumbents," *Journal of Politics* 53 (1991): 764–799.

36. Kayden, *Campaign Organization,* 126.

37. Clarke and Evans, *Covering Campaigns,* 60–62; Edie N. Goldenberg and Michael W. Traugott, *Campaigning for Congress* (Washington, D.C.: CQ Press, 1984), 127.

38. Anita Dunn, "The Best Campaign Wins: Coverage of Down Ballot Races by Local Press" (paper presented at the Conference on Campaign Management, American University, Washington, D.C., December 10–11, 1992).

39. Manuel Perez-Rivas and Deirdre M. Childress, "Lots of Foes, Little Hope," *Washington Post,* February 29, 1996.

40. Karl Vick, "Always Up to the Challenge," *Washington Post,* October 27, 1996.

41. These generalizations are drawn from the following four sources, which together demonstrate that political experience, campaign professionalism, and campaign receipts are positively related to the free media coverage that campaigns receive: (1) candidates' campaign receipts, (2) the political experience measure developed in Chapter 2, (3) the measure of campaign professionalism developed in Chapter 3 (total number of campaign activities performed by paid staff or consultants), and (4) responses to question I.6 of the 2002 Congressional Campaign Study and to question 25 of the 1992 Congressional Campaign Study.

42. The quotations are from Laura Manserus, "First Debate for Torricelli and Forrester," *New York Times,* September 6, 2002.

43. Matthew Cooper, "Fallout from a Memorial," *Time Online edition,* November 9, 2002.

44. See Ronald A. Faucheux, ed. *The Debate Book* (Washington, D.C.: Campaigns & Elections, 2003).

45. See n. 7.

46. See also Clarke and Evans, *Covering Campaigns,* chap. 4.

47. This generalization is drawn from responses to question I.8 of the 2002 Congressional Campaign Study. See also Kim Fridkin Kahn and Patrick J. Kenney, "The Slant of the News: How Editorial Endorsements Influence Campaign Coverage and Citizens' Views of Candidates," *American Political Science Review* 96 (2002): 381–394.

48. On media bias see Herbert J. Gans, "Are U.S. Journalists Dangerously Liberal?" *Columbia Journalism Review* 24 (1985): 29–33. On politicians and the press, see also Lance W. Bennett, *News: The Politics of Illusion* (New York: Longman, 1983), 76–78; Austin Ranney, *Channels of Power: The Impact of Television on American Politics* (New York: Basic Books, 1983), 54–55.

49. Magleby and Monson, "Campaign 2002: 'The Perfect Storm.'"

50. Paul S. Herrnson, "National Party Organizations and the Postreform Congress," in *The Postreform Congress,* ed. Roger H. Davidson (New York: St. Martin's Press, 1992), 65–66.

51. These generalizations are drawn from responses to questions V.15 and V.16 of the 2002 Congressional Campaign Study.

52. On the effectiveness of personal campaigning see Alan S. Gerber and Donald P. Green, "The Effects of Personal Canvassing, Telephone Calls, and Direct Mail on Voter Turnout," *American Political Science Review* 94 (2000): 653–664.

53. See Table 8-3 in the previous edition of this book.

54. Using a narrower victory margin to measure competitiveness did not substantively alter the findings.

9. CANDIDATES, CAMPAIGNS, AND ELECTORAL SUCCESS

1. Larry M. Bartels, "Partisanship and Voting Behavior, 1952–1996," *American Journal of Political Science* 44 (2000): 42–43.

2. Morris P. Fiorina, *Congress: Keystone of the Washington Establishment* (New Haven, Conn.: Yale University Press, 1978); John A. Ferejohn, "On the Decline of Competition in Congressional Elections," *American Political Science Review* 71 (1997): 166–177.

3. See Michael Krashinsky and William J. Milne, "Incumbency in U.S. Congressional Elections, 1950–1988," *Legislative Studies Quarterly* 18 (1993); also see the sources cited in chap. 1, nn. 41–43.

4. William C. Miller Jr., Representative Morella's campaign manager and chief of staff of her congressional office, interview, March 14, 1997.

5. Brandon DeFrehn, field coordinator, Morella campaign, interview, November 21, 2002.

6. On the effect of candidate gender on voting behavior see Monika L. McDermott, "Voting Cues in Low-Information Elections: Candidate Gender as a Social Information Variable in Contemporary United States Elections," *American Journal of Political Science* 41 (1997): 270–283; Paul S. Herrnson, Celeste Lay, and Atiya Stokes, "Women Running 'as Women': Candidate Gender, Campaign Issues and Voter Targeting Strategies," *Journal of Politics* 65 (2003): 244–255.

7. The figures for candidate spending on campaign communications equal the sum of candidate expenditures on direct mail, television, radio, campaign literature, newspapers, mass telephone calls, the Internet, voter registration and get-out-the-vote drives, and other campaign communications. These funds exclude money spent on overhead and research and on contributions made to other candidates, party committees, and other political groups, which sometimes constitute considerable sums.

8. Tables 9-1, 9-2, and 9-3 were created using ordinary least squares regressions to analyze data from major-party contested House general elections conducted in 2002. The full regression for Table 9-1 is as follows: Percent of vote = $57.28 - 1.96/(1.32)$ district is completely different or completely new + $.15/(.03)$ partisan bias + $.92/(.67)$ ideological strength − $3.71/(2.62)$ incumbent implicated in scandal − $.84/(.21)$ opponent spending on campaign communications (per \$100,000) + $.13/(.20)$ incumbent spending on campaign communications (per \$100,000) + $5.22/(2.31)$ incumbent received most media endorsements from local media + $2.02/(1.25)$ Republican national partisan tide; $F = 12.18, p < .0001$, Adj. R-square = $.48$, $N = 97$. The equations are the product of an extensive model-building process that tested the impact of numerous variables using a variety of statistical techniques. Because the hypotheses that were tested were pre-specified, one-tailed tests of significance were used. A .10 level was used to determine statistical significance because of the small sample sizes. Numerous regressions were tested prior to selecting the final equations. The final models were selected for reasons of statistical fit, parsimony, and ease of interpretation. They are statistically robust. The models replicated to the extent possible similar analyses for the 1992, 1994, 1996, and 1998 elections to verify that the basic relationships that are presented held across elections. More information about the equations and an overview of the survey and statistical methods used to conduct the study are presented at this book's web site (http://herrnson.cqpress.com).

9. Partisan bias was measured using the respondents' answers to question III.2 of the 2002 Congressional Campaign Study.

10. John H. Aldrich and David W. Rohde, "The Logic of Conditional Party Government: Revisiting the Electoral Connection," in *Congress Reconsidered,* 7th ed., ed. Lawrence C. Dodd and Bruce I. Oppenheimer (Washington, D.C.: CQ Press, 2001), 269–292; Steven S. Smith and Gerald Gramm, "The Dynamics of Party Government in Congress," in *Congress Reconsidered,* 245–268.

11. A moderate incumbent would win 0 percent extra votes (0 multiplied by 0.92), and an extremely liberal or conservative incumbent would win 2.76 percent extra votes (3 multiplied by 0.92).

12. These generalizations are similar to those reported in Edie N. Goldenberg and Michael W. Traugott, *Campaigning for Congress* (Washington, D.C.: CQ Press, 1984), chap. 3.

13. Other studies of the impact of campaign spending on congressional elections use all candidate disbursements (including overhead, research, and contributions to candidates and other political organizations). See Gary C. Jacobson, *Money in Congressional Elections* (New Haven, Conn.: Yale University Press, 1980); Gary C. Jacobson, "The Effects of Campaign Spending in House Elections: New Evidence for Old Arguments," *American Journal of Political Science* 34 (1990): 334–362; Jonathan S. Krasno and Donald Philip Green, "Salvation for the Spendthrift Incumbent," *American Journal of Political Science* 32 (1988): 844–907; Donald Philip Green and Jonathan S. Krasno, "Rebuttal to Jacobson's 'New Evidence for Old Arguments,'" *American Journal of Political Science* 34 (1990): 363–372.

14. Jacobson, *Money in Congressional Elections,* 113–123; Jonathan S. Krasno, Donald Philip Green, and Jonathan A. Cowden, "The Dynamics of Fundraising in House Elections," *Journal of*

Politics 56 (1994): 459–474; Christopher Kenney and Michael McBurdett, "A Dynamic Model of Congressional Spending on Vote Choice," *American Journal of Political Science* 36 (1992): 923–937.

15. Jacobson, *Money in Congressional Elections*, 38–45; Jacobson, "The Effects of Campaign Spending"; and Krasno and Green, "Salvation for the Spendthrift Incumbent."

16. Local media endorsements are measured using respondents' answers to question I.8 of the 2002 Congressional Campaign Study.

17. This generalization is drawn from question I.5 of the 2002 Congressional Campaign Study.

18. The partisan bias of these districts averaged 15.30, as opposed to 7.36 for elections where parties and groups did not try to set the agenda. This generalization is drawn from question III.1 of the 2002 Congressional Campaign Study.

19. The ideological strength measure of these incumbents was 1.42, as opposed to 1.14 for incumbents in elections where parties and groups did not try to set the agenda. This generalization is drawn from question I.4 of the 2002 Congressional Campaign Study.

20. The regression equation for incumbents in races in which parties and groups sought to set the campaign agenda is as follows: Percent of vote = 59.89 − 4.95/(2.29) district is completely different or completely new + .10/(.05) partisan bias + 1.93/(1.27) ideological strength − 9.03/(4.88) incumbent implicated in scandal − 1.02/(.33) opponent spending on campaign communications (per $100,000) + .13/(.26) incumbent spending on campaign communications (per $100,000) + 4.38/(3.33) incumbent received most media endorsements from local media + 1.43/(2.25) Republican national partisan tide; $F = 6.82$, $p < .0001$, Adj. R-square = .54, $N = 41$.

21. Owen G. Abbe, "The 2002 Maryland Eighth Congressional District Race," in Magleby and Monson, *The Last Hurrah?*, 245–246.

22. The full regression equation for Table 9-2 is as follows: Percent of vote = 25.29 + .13/(.03) partisan bias + 2.46/(1.03) contested primary + 2.50/(1.05) targeted own party members, independents, or both + 1.84/(1.09) advertising focused on challenger or incumbent's issue positions + .31/(.15) challenger spending on campaign communications (per $100,000) + .56/(.18) opponent spending on campaign communications (per $100,000) + 5.50/(2.12) challenger received most endorsements from local media + 2.50/(1.17) Republican national partisan tide; $F = 19.94$, $p < .0001$, Adj. R-square = .52, $N = 138$.

23. See, for example, Richard F. Fenno Jr., *Senators on the Campaign Trail: The Politics of Representation* (Norman: University of Oklahoma Press, 1996), 100.

24. The figures for each form of campaign communication expenditure (for radio, direct mail, and so on) are regression coefficients that were generated using separate equations. The equations used the same variables as those that appear in Table 2, except that they substituted the spending on the specific form of expenditure for overall spending on campaign communications. See the Appendix (http://herrnson.cqpress.com) for more details.

25. The regression equation for challengers in races in which parties and groups sought to set the campaign agenda is as follows: Percent of vote = 29.71 + .24/(.05) partisan bias + 2.54/(1.51) contested primary + .47/(1.94) targeted own party members, independents, or both + 1.75/(1.72) advertising focused on challenger or incumbent's issue positions + .50/(.001) challenger spending on campaign communications (per $100,000) + .20/(.001) opponent spending on campaign communications (per $100,000) + 6.62/(2.84) challenger received most endorsements from local media + 2.22/(1.53) Republican national partisan tide; $F = 13.86$, $p < .0001$, Adj. R-square = .61, $N = 66$.

26. The full regression equation for Table 9-3 is as follows: Percent of vote = 24.15 + .17/(.06) partisan bias + 4.68/(3.15) targeted own party members, independents, or both + 7.42/(3.84) Republican ran on Republican issues + 4.18/(3.48) Democrat ran on Democratic issues + 3.81/(.83) natural log of open-seat candidate spending on campaign communications − 3.06/(.69) natural log of opponent spending on campaign communications + 6.70/(2.23) candidate received most

endorsements from local media + 8.52/(3.46) Republican national partisan tide; $F = 14.69$, $p <$ .0001, Adj. R-square = .69, $N = 50$.

27. The Pearson correlations between the candidates' percent of the vote and the communications techniques are: campaign literature, $r = .27$ ($p<.01$); direct mail, $r = .26$ ($p<.01$); television = .05 ($p = .31$); radio, $r = .29$ ($p<.01$); campaign literature, $r = .27$ ($p<.01$); direct mail, $r = .26$ ($p < .01$); television $r = .05$ ($p = .31$).

28. David B. Magleby and J. Quin Monson, "Campaign 2002: 'The Perfect Storm,' " Provo, Utah: Center for Elections and Democracy, Brigham Young University, November 13, 2002.

29. The regression equation for open-seat candidates in races in which parties and groups sought to set the campaign agenda is as follows: Percent of vote = 21.15 − .18/(.08) partisan bias + 7.39/(4.48) targeted own party members, independents, or both + 11.21/(5.80) Republican ran on Republican issues + 1.81/(3.88) Democrat ran on Democratic issues + 4.35/(1.10) natural log of open-seat candidate spending on campaign communications − 3.40/(1.02) natural log of opponent spending on campaign communications + 3.65/(2.97) candidate received most endorsements from local media + 6.39/(4.21) Republican national partisan tide; $F = 9.60$, $p<.0001$, Adj. R-square = .67, $N = 35$.

30. Jonathan S. Krasno, *Challengers, Competition, and Reelection: Comparing Senate and House Elections* (New Haven, Conn.: Yale University Press, 1994), esp. chaps. 4–7; Peverill Squire and Eric R. A. N. Smith, "A Further Examination of Challenger Quality in Senate Elections," *Legislative Studies Quarterly* 21 (1996): 231–248.

31. Alan I. Abramowitz and Jeffrey A. Segal, *Senate Elections* (Ann Arbor: University of Michigan Press, 1992), 109–114; Kim Fridkin Kahn and Patrick J. Kenney, *The Spectacle of U.S. Senate Campaigns* (Princeton, N.J.: Princeton University Press, 1999), 216–223.

32. John R. Hibbing and John R. Alford, "Constituency Population and Representativeness in the United States Senate," *Legislative Studies Quarterly* 15 (1990): 581–598.

33. Kahn and Kenney, *The Spectacle of U.S. Senate Campaigns*, 12. See also Michael A. Bailey, "So Close and Yet So Far: Two Unpopular Incumbents Meet with Different Fates in California and New York," in *Campaigns and Elections: Contemporary Case Studies*, 43–44.

34. See Mark C. Westlye, *Senate Elections and Campaign Intensity* (Baltimore, Md.: Johns Hopkins University Press, 1992), chaps. 7 and 8; Abramowitz and Segal, *Senate Elections*, 109–115.

35. The coverage of the Johnson-Thune contest draws heavily from James Meader and John Bart, "South Dakota At-Large and Senate Race 2002," in *The Last Hurrah? Soft Money and Issue Advocacy in the 2002 Congressional Elections*, ed. David B. Magleby and J. Quin Monson (Provo, Utah: Center for the Study of Elections and Democracy, 2003), 156–176.

36. Evans's campaign receipts were below the $5,000 threshold required for candidates to file their financial transactions with the FEC.

37. Werner's campaign receipts were below the $5,000 threshold required for candidates to file their financial transactions with the FEC.

38. Meader and Bart, "South Dakota At-Large and Senate Race 2002," 172–174.

39. Meader and Bart, "South Dakota At-Large and Senate Race 2002," 160.

40. The first four items in Table 9-4, and items seven, eight, nine, and sixteen are from the 2002 Congressional Campaign Study (N for winners = 137; N for losers = 171); the rest are from the 1998 Congressional Campaign Study (N for winners = 154; N for losers = 159).

41. See John W. Kingdon, *Candidates for Office: Beliefs and Strategies* (New York: Random House, 1968), chap. 2.

42. See the sources listed in nn. 45–50 and 52 of chap. 1.

43. See Kingdon, *Candidates for Office,* chap. 2.

44. See the sources listed in nn. 45–50 and 52 of chap.1.

10. ELECTIONS AND GOVERNANCE

1. Interview with a member-elect of the U.S. House of Representatives, November 14, 1992.

2. See Roger H. Davidson and Walter J. Oleszek, *Congress and Its Members*, 8th ed. (Washington, D.C.: CQ Press, 2002), esp. chap. 1.

3. Richard F. Fenno Jr., *Home Style: House Members in Their Districts* (Boston: Little, Brown, 1978), 54–61.

4. Ibid., 153.

5. David R. Mayhew, *Congress: The Electoral Connection* (New Haven, Conn.: Yale University Press, 1974), 49–68.

6. The figures are from Davidson and Oleszek, *Congress and Its Members*, 149, 150.

7. Ibid., 150.

8. Scott Adler, Chariti E. Gent, and Cary B. Overmeyer, "The Home Style Home Page: Legislative Use of the World Wide Web for Constituent Contact," *Legislative Studies Quarterly* 23 (1998): 585–596.

9. Timothy E. Cook, *Making Laws and Making News: Media Strategies in the U.S. House of Representatives* (Washington, D.C.: Brookings Institution, 1989), 71.

10. See, for example, Ben H. Bagdikian, "Congress and the Media: Partners in Propaganda," *Columbia Journalism Review* 12 (1974): 5.

11. Ibid., 2, 3, 37, 90.

12. Laura Langbein, "Money and Access: Some Empirical Evidence," *Journal of Politics* 48 (1986): 1052–1062; John Wright, "Contributions, Lobbying, and Committee Voting in the U.S. House of Representatives," *American Political Science Review* 84 (1990): 417–438.

13. Richard F. Fenno Jr., *Congressmen in Committees* (Boston: Little, Brown, 1973), 13.

14. Harrison W. Fox and Susan Webb Hammond, *Congressional Staffs* (New York: The Free Press, 1977), 121–124.

15. Fenno, *Congressmen in Committees*, 1–14.

16. Kenneth J. Cooper, "The House Freshmen's First Choice," *Washington Post*, January 5, 1993.

17. Davidson and Oleszek, *Congress and Its Members*, 355–357; Susan Webb Hammond, "Congressional Caucuses in the 104th Congress," in *Congress Reconsidered*, 6th ed., ed. Lawrence C. Dodd and Bruce I. Oppenheimer, 274–292.

18. "80,000 Lobbyists? Probably Not, but Maybe," *New York Times*, May 12, 1993.

19. Kay Lehman Schlozman and John T. Tierney, *Organized Interests and American Democracy* (New York: Harper and Row, 1986), 272.

20. Juliet Eilperin, "A Contest of Connections," *Washington Post*, February 7, 2002; Juliet Eilperin and Yuki Noguchi, "The House Passes Internet Access Legislation," *Washington Post*, February 28, 2002.

21. Schlozman and Tierney, *Organized Interests and American Democracy*, 289–310.

22. Linda L. Fowler and Ronald D. Shaiko, "The Grass Roots Connection: Environmental Activists and Senate Roll Calls," *American Journal of Political Science* 31 (1987): 484–510; James G. Gimpel, "Grassroots Organizations and Equilibrium Cycles in Group Mobilization and Access," in *The Interest Group Connection: Electioneering, Lobbying, and Policymaking in Washington*, ed. Paul S. Herrnson, Clyde Wilcox, and Ronald G. Shaiko (Chatham, N.J.: Chatham House, 1997).

23. See Gordon Adams, *The Iron Triangle* (New York: Council on Economic Priorities, 1981), 175–180; Hugh Heclo, "Issue Networks and the Executive Establishment," in *The New American Political System*, ed. Anthony King (Washington, D.C.: American Enterprise Institute, 1978), 87–124.

24. Paul S. Herrnson and Kelly D. Patterson, "Toward a More Programmatic Democratic Party? Agenda Setting and Coalition Building in the House," *Polity* 27 (1995): 607–628; Paul S. Herrnson and David M. Cantor, "Party Campaign Activity and Party Unity in the U.S. House of Representatives," *Legislative Studies Quarterly* 22 (1997): 393–415.

25. Kelly D. Patterson, *Political Parties and the Maintenance of Liberal Democracy* (New York: Columbia University Press, 1996), chap. 4.

26. See Leon D. Epstein, *Political Parties in Western Democracies* (New York: Praeger, 1967), 340–348.

27. See, for example, Herbert F. Weisberg, "Evaluating Theories of Congressional Roll Call Voting," *American Journal of Political Science* (1978): 554–577.

28. Hannah Pitkin, *The Concept of Representation* (Berkeley: University of California Press, 1967).

29. Bruce Cain, John Ferejohn, and Morris Fiorina, *The Personal Vote* (Cambridge: Harvard University Press, 1987).

30. Quoted in Dana Milbank, "In Ohio, It's George vs. George: Tax-Cutting Bush Faces Off Against Voinovich, Backer of Spending Cuts," *Washington Post,* April 24, 2003.

31. R. Douglas Arnold, "The Local Roots of Democracy," in *The New Congress,* ed. Thomas E. Mann and Norman J. Ornstein (Washington, D.C.: American Enterprise Institute, 1981), 250–287.

32. Davidson and Oleszek, *Congress and Its Members,* 278–279.

33. John Ferejohn, "Logrolling in an Institutional Context: A Case Study of Food Stamp Legislation," in *Congress and Policy and Change,* ed. Gerald C. Wright Jr., Leroy N. Rieselbach, and Lawrence C. Dodd (New York: Agathon Press, 1986), 223–253.

34. In recent Congresses, legislation was supposed to stay within a set of overall budgetary limits in order to limit growth of the federal deficit. This zero-sum process has frequently required legislators to cut spending in some areas if they wish to increase it in others.

35. Herrnson and Patterson, "Toward a More Programmatic Democratic Party?"; Herrnson and Cantor, "Party Campaign Activity and Party Unity."

36. Paul S. Herrnson, Kelly D. Patterson, and John J. Pitney Jr., "From Ward Heelers to Public Relations Experts: The Parties' Response to Mass Politics," in *Broken Contract? Changing Relationships between Citizens and Government in the United States,* ed. Stephen C. Craig (Boulder, Colo.: Westview Press, 1996), 251–267.

37. V. O. Key Jr., "A Theory of Critical Elections," *Journal of Politics* 17 (1955): 3–18; Walter Dean Burnham, *Critical Elections and the Mainsprings of American Politics* (New York: W.W. Norton, 1970); Everett Carll Ladd Jr. with Charles D. Hadley, *Transformations of the American Party System* (New York: W.W. Norton, 1978).

38. Alan I. Abramowitz, "The End of the Democratic Era? 1994 and the Future of Congressional Election Research," *Political Research Quarterly* 48 (1995): 873–889; Gary C. Jacobson, *The Politics of Congressional Elections,* 4th ed. (New York: Longman, 1997), 219–224.

39. James G. Gimpel, *Fulfilling the Contract: The First 100 Days* (Boston: Allyn and Bacon, 1996).

40. On the evolution of and most recent changes in the legislative process, see Barbara Sinclair, *Unorthodox Lawmaking* (Washington, D.C.: CQ Press, 1997), esp. chaps. 1 and 6.

41. See, for example, Samuel Goldreich, "Environmentalists Put on Defensive," *CQ Weekly,* November 9, 2002; Mary Agnes Carey and Bill Swindell, "Closer Scrutiny Expected on Health," *CQ Weekly,* November 9, 2002.

42. John H. Aldrich and David W. Rohde, "The Logic of Conditional Party Government: Revisiting the Electoral Connection," in *Congress Reconsidered,* 7th ed., ed. Lawrence D. Dodd and Bruce I. Oppenheimer (Washington, D.C.: CQ Press, 2001), 269–292; Steven S. Smith and Gerald Gramm, "The Dynamics of Party Government in Congress," in *Congress Reconsidered,* 7th ed., 245–268.

43. Committee on Political Parties, American Political Science Association, "Toward a More Responsible Two-Party System," *American Political Science Association,* supp. 44 (1950): 21; Leon D. Epstein, *Political Parties in the American Mold* (Madison: University of Wisconsin Press, 1986), 30–38.

11. CAMPAIGN REFORM

1. See, for example, John R. Hibbing and Elizabeth Theiss-Morse, *Congress as Public Enemy: Public Attitudes toward American Institutions* (Cambridge: Cambridge University Press, 1995), 63–71.

2. These generalizations are drawn from responses to questions V.1 and V.2 of the 2002 Congressional Campaign Study.

3. The winners were somewhat more likely to state that campaign issues were occasionally important and somewhat less likely to state they were never important. These generalizations are drawn from responses to question V.3 of the 2002 Congressional Campaign Study.

4. Peter L. Francia, John C. Green, Paul S. Herrnson, Lynda W. Powell, and Clyde Wilcox, *The Financiers of Congressional Elections: Investors, Ideologues, and Intimates* (New York: Columbia University Press, 2003); Peter L. Francia and Paul S. Herrnson, "The Thrill and the Agony: Winners' and Losers' Perceptions of Campaigning," in *Campaign Battle Lines*, ed. Ronald A. Faucheux and Paul S. Herrnson (Washington: D.C.: *Campaigns & Elections*, 2002), 284–290; Kevin E. Greene and Paul S. Herrnson, "Running Against a Stacked Deck," in *Campaign Battle Lines*, 278–283.

5. These generalizations are drawn from responses to question VIII.3 of the 2002 Congressional Campaign Study.

6. On the passage of the Bipartisan Reform Act in the House, see Diana Dwyre and Victoria A. Farrar-Myers, *Legislative Labyrinth: Congress and Campaign Finance Reform* (Washington, D.C.: CQ Press, 2001); on unorthodox lawmaking, see Barbara Sinclair, *Unorthodox Lawmaking: New Legislative Processes in the U.S. Congress* (Washington, D.C.: CQ Press, 1997).

7. Anthony Corrado, "Money and Politics," in *The New Campaign Finance Sourcebook*, ed., Anthony Corrado, Thomas Mann, Daniel Ortiz, and Trevor Potter (Washington, D.C.: Brookings Institution, 2003).

8. Rep. Martin Meehan, "Time to Kick the Soft Money Habit," February 28, 2002, http://www.house.gov/apps/list/press/ma05_meehan/NRCFROpEd022802.html.

9. Rep. Christopher Shays, "Shays' Statement on the Successful Discharge Petition for the Bipartisan Campaign Reform Act," press release, January 24, 2002, http://www.house.gov/shays/news/2002/january/jan24.htm.

10. Majority Whip Tom DeLay, "Bill Jeopardizes Freedom," Tuesday, April 3, 2001, http://www.majoritywhip.gov/News.asp?FormMode=SingleOpEds.

11. Dana Milbank, "Tactics and Theatrics Color Decision Day," *Washington Post*, February 14, 2002.

12. For a more detailed review of the BCRA, see Corrado et al., *The New Campaign Finance Sourcebook*.

13. Adam Clymer, "Foes of Campaign Finance Bill Plot Legal Attack," *New York Times*, February 17, 2002.

14. Helen Dewar, "Lawsuits Challenge New Campaign Law," *Washington Post*, May 8, 2003.

15. Amy Keller, "Debate Rocks FEC," *Roll Call*, March 4, 2002; Helen Dewar, "FEC Rules on 'Soft Money' Challenged," *Washington Post*, October 9, 2002.

16. Dewar, "FEC Rules"; quotation is from Thomas B. Edsall, "FEC to Allow 'Soft Money' Exceptions," *Washington Post*, June 21, 2002.

17. For some useful commentaries on the ruling, see Thomas E. Mann, "A District Court Panel Rules on Campaign Finance," May 5, 2003; Roger Witten, Seth Waxman, Randolph Moss, and Fred Wertheimer, "Summary of *McConnell v. FEC* Decision"; and the other summaries available at http://www.campaignlegalcenter.org.

18. See, for example, Herrnson, *Party Campaigning*.

19. Center for Responsive Politics(http://www.opensecrets.org).

20. If the lower district court's ruling prohibiting candidate-focused issue advocacy ads stands, this would increase the impetus of interest groups to focus more of their resources on influencing elections through other means.

21. Ibid.

22. Thomas B. Edsall, "Campaign Money Finds New Conduits as Law Takes Effect," *Washington Post,* November 5, 2002; John Bresnahan, "Leadership Forum Returns $1 Million," *Roll Call,* January 8, 2003.

23. Paul Kane, "NRSC or NCRS," *Roll Call,* November 25, 2002.

24. Ibid.

25. Francia et al., *The Financiers of Congressional Elections.*

26. The 7-percent figure is from the figures compiled from Burns et al., *American National Election Study, 2002;* the other figure is from Center for Responsive Politics (http://www.opensecrets.org).

27. Francia et al., *The Financiers of Congressional Elections.*

28. The parties of the golden age, especially the political machines, also had shortcomings, including corruption, secrecy, and formal and informal barriers to the participation of women and various racial, ethnic, and religious groups. For some lively accounts, see William Riordan, *Plunkitt of Tammany Hall* (New York: E. P. Dutton, 1905) and Mike Royko, *Boss: Richard J. Daley* (New York: E. P. Dutton, 1971).

29. See Hibbing and Theiss-Morse, *Congress as Public Enemy,* esp. chap. 5.

30. Center for Responsive Politics (http://www.opensecrets.org).

31. L. Sandy Maisel, "Competition in Congressional Elections: Why More Qualified Candidates Do Not Seek Office," in *Rethinking Political Reform,* ed. Ruy A. Teixeira, L. Sandy Maisel, and John J. Pitney Jr. (Washington, D.C.: Progressive Foundation, 1994), 29.

32. Gary W. Cox and Michael C. Munger, "Closeness, Expenditures, and Turnout in the 1982 U.S. House Elections," *American Political Science Review* 83 (1989): 217–231.

33. Free television and radio time is an idea that has been around for many years. See, for example, Twentieth Century Fund Commission on Campaign Costs, *Voters' Time* (New York: Twentieth Century Fund, 1969); and Campaign Study Group, "Increasing Access to Television for Political Candidates" (Cambridge: Institute of Politics, Harvard University, 1978).

34. Herrnson, *Party Campaigning,* 127.

35. Doris A. Graber, *Mass Media and American Politics,* 4th ed. (Washington, D.C.: CQ Press, 1993), 53–55.

36. Larry J. Sabato, *Paying for Elections: The Campaign Finance Thicket* (New York: Twentieth Century Fund, 1989), 31.

37. For more information on this bill, see "Summary of S. 3124, the Free Air Time Bill Introduced by Senators McCain, Feingold and Durbin," *The Political Standard,* Washington, D.C.: Alliance for Better Campaigns, October 2002.

38. See Ruth S. Jones and Warren E. Miller, "Financing Campaigns: Macro Level Innovation and Micro Level Response," *Western Political Quarterly* 38 (1985): 190, 192.

39. For countries and American states that offer citizens the opportunity to obtain tax credits for political contributions, see the case studies in Arthur B. Gunlicks, ed., *Campaign and Party Finance in North America and Western Europe* (Boulder, Colo.: Westview Press, 1993).

40. Francia et al., *The Financiers of Congressional Elections.*

41. John J. Sanko, *Rocky Mountain News,* June 4, 2003.

42. Les Hockstader, "GOP Plan Prompts a Texas Exodus," *Washington Post,* May 13, 2003.

43. Raymond E. Wolfinger and Stephen J. Rosenstone, *Who Votes?* (New Haven, Conn.: Yale University Press, 1980), 61–88.

44. J. Eric Oliver, "The Effects of Eligibility Restrictions and Party Activity on Absentee Voting and Voter Turnout," *American Journal of Political Science* 40 (1996): 498–513; Peter L. Francia and Paul S. Herrnson, "The Effects of Campaign Effort and Election Reform on Voter Participation in State Legislative Elections," *State Politics and Policy Quarterly,* forthcoming.

45. CalTech/MIT Voting Technology Report, "What Is; What Could Be," July 2002, 8–9, 21, 32, http://www.vote.caltech.edu.

46. Paul S. Herrnson, "Improving Election Technology and Administration: Toward a Larger Federal Role in Elections?," *Stanford Law and Policy Review* 13 (2002): 147–159.

47. "Bush Signs Help America Vote Act," U.S. Department of State, October 29, 2002, http://usinfo.state.gov/usa.

48. CalTech/MIT Voting Technology Report, 17–25.

49. See, for example, Benjamin B. Bederson, Bongshin Lee, Robert M. Sherman, Paul S. Herrnson, and Richard G. Niemi, "Electronic Voting System Usability Issues," ACM Conference on Human Factors in Computing Systems, *CHI Letters* 5 (2003), forthcoming.

Index

Tables and figures are indicated by *t* and *f* respectively.

Notes Name Index